D0841952

Rebuilding Buddhism

Rebuilding Buddhism

THE THERAVADA MOVEMENT IN TWENTIETH-CENTURY NEPAL

SARAH LEVINE

DAVID N. GELLNER

HARVARD UNIVERSITY PRESS
Cambridge, Massachusetts, and London, England

Copyright © 2005 by the President and Fellows of Harvard College
All rights reserved
Printed in the United States of America

First Harvard University Press paperback edition, 2007

Library of Congress Cataloging-in-Publication Data

LeVine, Sarah, 1940–
Rebuilding Buddhism: the Theravada movement in twentieth-century Nepal / Sarah LeVine and David N. Gellner.
p. cm.
Includes bibliographical references and index.
ISBN-13 978-0-674-01908-9 (cloth: alk. paper)
ISBN-10 0-674-01908-3 (cloth: alk. paper)
ISBN-13 978-0-674-02554-7 (pbk.)
ISBN-10 0-674-02554-7 (pbk.)
1. Theravåda Buddhism—Nepal—History—20th century. I. Gellner, David N. II. Title.

BQ394.L48 2005
294.3'91'095496—dc22 2005046208

To all our Nepali friends and colleagues who cooperated so willingly and have waited so patiently

Contents

important additional source of information was provided by LeVine's travels to Bodh Gaya, Burma, Thailand, Taiwan, and Hong Kong, all places where Nepali Theravadins are to be found and from which, as discussed below, many of the important influences on Buddhist revivalism in the Kathmandu Valley have come. Adams (1996: 125) has stressed the transnational nature of Sherpa Buddhism, and the same applies, though with less Western input, to Theravada Buddhism among the Newars.

It would be have been impossible to disguise the more prominent figures in the Buddhist revival movement. However, in order to protect their privacy to some degree, most of our informants have been given pseudonyms. We discussed this course with them and they nearly all agreed to the procedure, even though it arose from our concerns, not theirs.

In Chapter 10, we compare the revival of monasticism in the Kathmandu Valley that we describe with the introduction of celibate monasteries among the Sherpas, which has been described in detail by Sherry Ortner (1989a). Our motivations for carrying out the present study were not totally dissimilar to Ortner's for examining social and religious change. In order to establish herself as an anthropologist, Ortner, as she herself has related, began by studying the Sherpas in the 1970s in as "male" and as "traditionally anthropological" a way as she could, focusing on Sherpa religion, ritual, and social interaction and leaving out of focus, as mere background material, consideration of historical trends, of the wider politico-economic context, of gender, and of childhood. She also studiedly ignored, in her first fieldwork, the Sherpas' involvement in mountain climbing and even in tourism, faults which she has attempted to overcome in later work. We too have sought to make up for the lacunae or biases of previous work, to produce a historically informed account of Buddhism among the Newars as it is being made and remade, one that does justice to the viewpoints of those involved, whether "big" people or "small" people, male or female, monastic or lay. There is one obvious difference between us and Ortner, however: Ortner set out to compose a work that would both argue the case for "practice theory" and simultaneously exemplify it, whereas, at least in this monograph, we have no such theoretical ambitions. We hope that our ethnography does indeed exemplify what are supposed to be the virtues of "practice theory"—the ability to combine in one analysis both impersonal "objective" forces and the cultural forms, ideas, and subjectivities of the people written about, without reducing either side to the other. Ortner includes only as much ethnography and history as is compatible with still making her theoretical case, whereas we seek to provide as rich and as many-sided an ethnography and ethnographic history of this local form of Buddhism modernism as possible, in the belief that contributing to the ethnographic record is a good in itself, and because others may later wish to use our material and ask questions of it that we did not think to ask ourselves.

There is one fairly unusual feature of this ethnography, namely, that is produced by two people, one female, one male, who spent most of their time working apart. At the same time, we have of course frequently worked together on both sides of the Atlantic as well as in Nepal. Teamwork in anthropology usually leads to a division of labor, so that the written products are different parts of a book or entirely different books. In our case, two different ethnographers, with different skills and different ways of relating to people, have produced a genuinely shared effort. We think that this has resulted in a more rounded and richer ethnography than either of us could have achieved on our own, and we are surprised that this has not been attempted more often—though given the very personal nature of ethnographic fieldwork and ethnographic writing, as well as the highly individualistic character of most anthropologists, perhaps we should not be surprised. In any case, this book is, we believe, better for our collaboration; and we are still talking to each other.

Some of the more common technical terms used throughout the book, such as "nirvana," "dharma," and "vihara," appear in roman type without diacritics and in general we have kept diacritics in the main text to a minimum. Fuller explanations and full diacritics are given in the glossary. Our usage of the terms "Nepalese" and "Nepali" is a compromise between English euphony and emerging Nepali usage. The language and the people are referred to as "Nepali," but in more abstract contexts, "Nepalese" is used as the appropriate adjective.

In the writing of this book we have both accumulated many debts. The first is to the people it is about. They will know how long it has taken, and some may have given up waiting for it altogether. They have all cooperated and helped us well beyond the call of politeness or friendship. We cannot mention everyone by name, but we must record our grateful thanks to Vinaya Dhakhwa, Suman Kamal Tuladhar, Nirmal Man Tuladhar, the late Gyan Jyoti Kansakar, Bhikshu Gyanapurnika, Dhammawati Guruma, Chameli Guruma, Chini Guruma,

Punam Rana, Mallika Shakya, Father John Locke S. J., Father Gregory Sharkey S. J., Ratna Man Shakya, Sachit and Deepa Pokharel, Ramendra and Mridula Sharma, Sudhindra Sharma, Subarna Man Tuladhar, Karma Lekshe Tsomo, Charles Hallisey, Jim Benson, and Will Tuladhar-Douglas (who introduced us in Oxford in October 1996). Many others involved in Buddhism in Nepal have given us their time and searched for, or provided, written materials for us (for the latter we thank the Ven. Bodhigyan, Sharad Kasa, Mrigendra Karki, Kesar Lall, Chiara Letizia, Mallika Shakya, Dharma Man Newa, and Subarna Man Tuladhar). We would both like to thank our families who have put up with our absences, in Nepal while doing the research and in the study while writing it up.

Research trips to Kathmandu were funded for Gellner by the British Academy and the International Centre for Ethnic Studies, Colombo, and for LeVine by the W. T. Grant Foundation and the Spencer Foundation of Chicago. Gellner would also like to record his deep gratitude to the Leverhulme Trust: but for the award of a Leverhulme Major Research Fellowship from October 2002 it is likely that the process of drafting the book would have been put off for many years more. Final corrections and revisions to the manuscript were done while he was a visiting professor at, and enjoying the magnificent facilities of, the Research Institute for the Study of the Languages and Cultures of Asia and Africa, Tokyo University of Foreign Studies, Japan (2003–2004).

Many people have read through part or all of the manuscript and helped to save us from errors, ambiguities, and convoluted sentences: Bhikshu Sugandha (Anil Sakya), Bhikshu Vipassi, Bhikshu Sujan, Steven Collins, Lance Cousins, Richard Gombrich, Todd Lewis, Kitsiri Malalgoda, K. P. Malla, Min Bahadur Shakya, Subarna Man Tuladhar, D. P. Martinez, Kim Gutschow, Peter Skilling, and Leonard van der Kuijp as well as two anonymous reviewers. For errors that remain, as well as for the emphases and interpretations offered, we take full responsibility. We would be grateful to have any factual errors brought to our attention. We have written about personal matters which could well be controversial, and so we have tried to protect some of those we write about with pseudonyms. It is, therefore, no mere formality if we insist that none of those who helped us, or read our manuscript, should be held responsible for the biases of our interests or our observations.

When we first conceived this study in 1997, the Maoists' "People's War" had only just been launched and was confined to a few hill areas in Nepal, mostly far from Kathmandu. For some years it remained small in scale and limited in its impact. By the time we were preparing the manuscript for publication in 2004, the Maoist insurgency had grown to become overwhelmingly the most serious problem affecting the country with an impact—often tragic—on the lives of all Nepalis. The civil war and the mass disruption that have resulted do not play a large part in the account that follows, but they must be understood as the background to the years since 2001. There is a burgeoning literature on the Maoist issue; for an introduction, see Thapa and Sijapati (2004). We thank the following people for alerting us to errors that were corrected in the paperback edition: Bhikshu Vipassi, K. P. Malla, Rajendra Pradhan, Subarna Man Tuladhar, Nirmal Man Tuladhar, Sumon Tuladhar, and John Whelpton.

Sarah LeVine
David N. Gellner
Oxford, September 2004

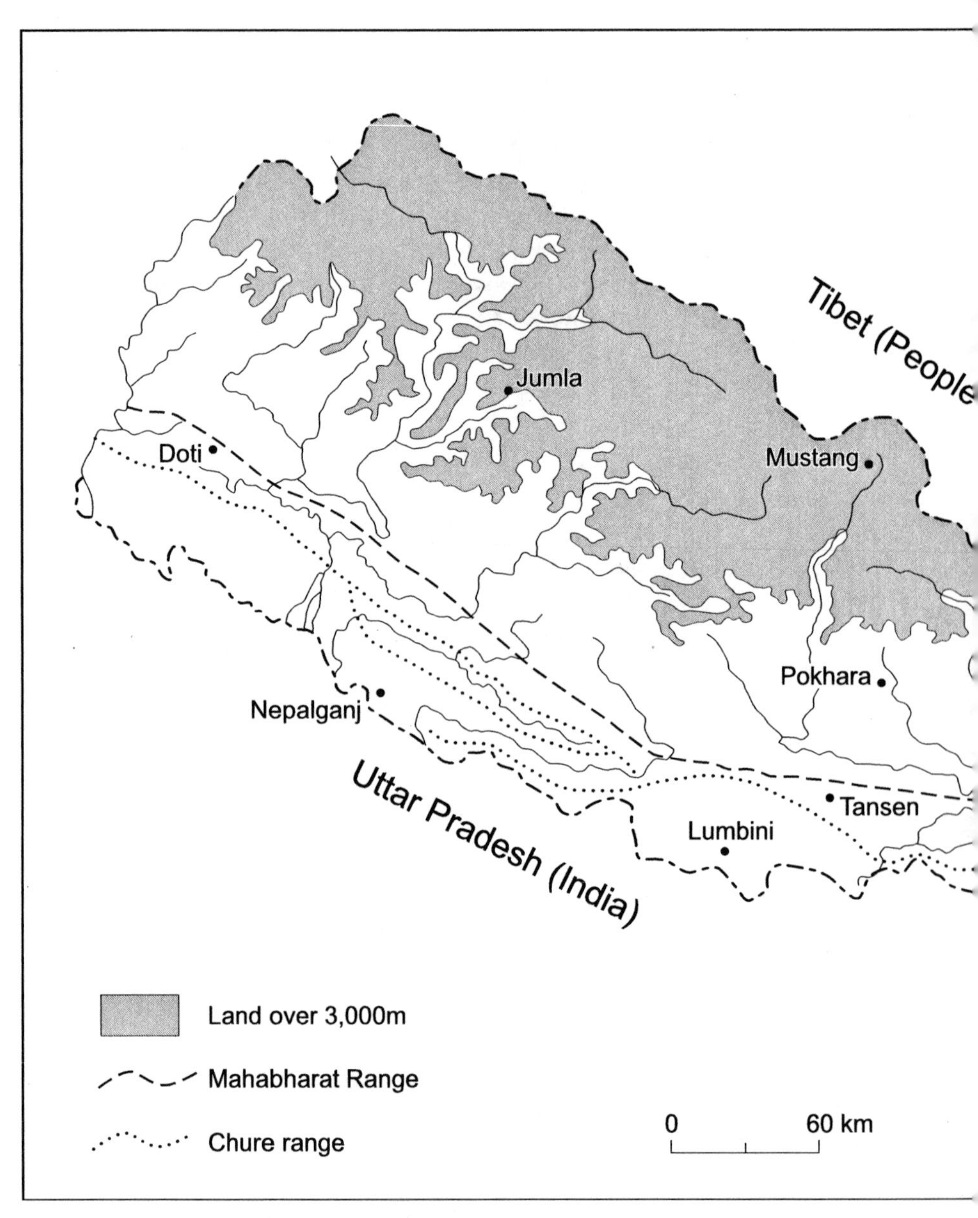

Nepal and the Kathmandu Valley

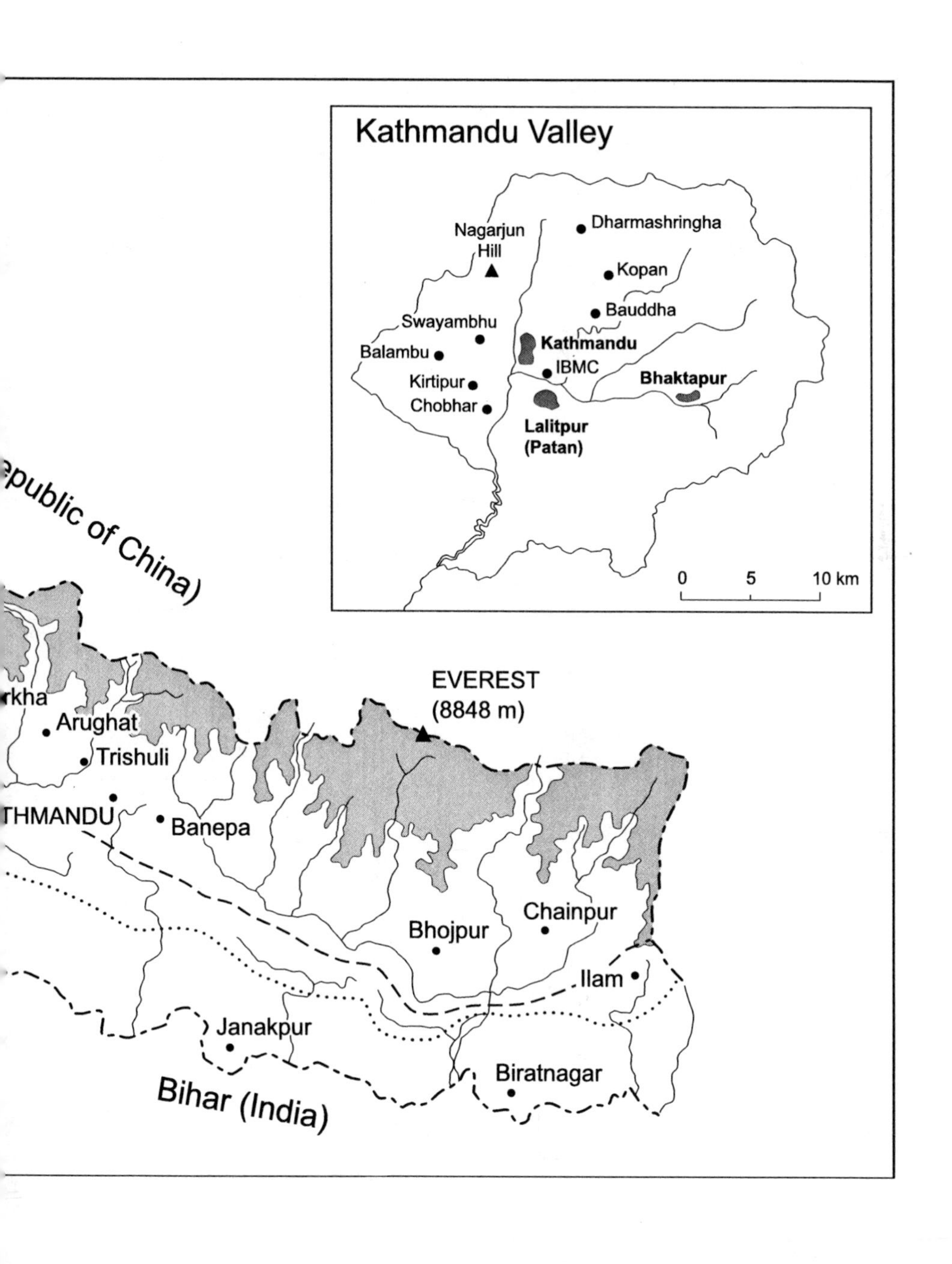

Kathmandu Valley
Nagarjun Hill
Dharmashringha
Kopan
Bauddha
Swayambhu
Balambu
Kathmandu
IBMC
Kirtipur
Chobhar
Bhaktapur
Lalitpur (Patan)
0
5
10 km
epublic of China)
EVEREST (8848 m)
rkha
Arughat
Trishuli
THMANDU
Banepa
Chainpur
Bhojpur
Ilam
Janakpur
Biratnagar
Bihar (India)

CHAPTER ONE

Introduction: The Origins of Modernist Buddhism

Buddhism is one of the earliest, if not the earliest, example of a world religion. Nowadays, it might be called a transnational religious movement. The Buddha sent his followers off in all directions to preach his doctrine "for the good of the world." The Emperor Asoka, who reigned over most of South Asia in the mid third century BCE, was evidently a convinced Buddhist even though he protected all religions within his diverse and multilingual realm. He sent or encouraged missionaries to spread Buddhism well beyond his own kingdom. Later, in order to transmit their voluminous scriptures across major cultural boundaries, Buddhist monks were involved in two gigantic and heroic efforts of translation from Sanskrit and Prakrit, first into Chinese (between the second and eleventh centuries of the common era) and later into Tibetan (between the seventh and fourteenth centuries); in both cases they had to evolve whole new vocabularies in order to do so. Ideas and practices were carried enormous distances in this way so that even today, despite the fact that until the modern period there had been almost no direct contact between the countries involved, the mantras used in Tantric Buddhism in Japan are recognizably similar to those still in use in Tibet and Nepal, and the script in which they are inscribed on Japanese funerary markers and sacred sites is easily recognizable as a variant of scripts still found in Nepal. Furthermore—a fact of great significance for the story in this book—there are still monks and nuns in China and Japan who observe an ancient monastic code that closely resembles the codes followed in the Theravada Buddhist countries of

Southeast Asia, even though the two traditions diverged from each other and have had little contact for over a thousand years.

Once these different forms of Buddhism were transmitted to the different countries of Asia, the monks and priests who carried them embarked on a process of adaptation to their local cultural environments. New waves of proselytization and revitalization occurred, but principally within, rather than between, different cultural and linguistic regions.[1] All this was to change with the advent of the modern world, which brought with it the rise of Western scholarship on Buddhism, rising levels of Western-style education in Asia, and easier, and intensified, contact between Buddhists from different Asian countries. In 1893, there occurred a key event in this process—one that made the West aware of Asian religions as never before and simultaneously helped to launch the process of the modernization of Asian religions, which was a precondition for Hindus or Buddhists to become organized internationally. A "World Parliament of Religions" was held in Chicago, as one of twenty congresses—on subjects as diverse as agriculture, women's progress, engineering, and music—held to celebrate four hundred years since the arrival of Columbus in the Americas (Seager 1995).

The World Parliament of Religions has been interpreted as marking the culmination of a century in which the West gradually came to replace condemnation and ignorance with sympathetic understanding in relation to Asian religions (Jackson 1981). At the same time, the Parliament was a key event in the transformation of those very Asian religions, because it launched the careers of two of the most important modernizers, Swami Vivekananda and Anagarika Dharmapala. Vivekananda was instrumental in the creation of a modernized Hinduism in Bengal. Dharmapala (1864–1933), who was born as Don David Hewawitarana into a newly wealthy Sinhalese Buddhist family and educated at Christian mission schools, was arguably even more important in influencing the development of Buddhism in Sri Lanka and elsewhere.[2]

When Dharmapala addressed the Chicago Parliament, the *St. Louis Observer* reported that,

> with his black curly locks thrown back from his broad brow, his keen, clear eyes fixed upon the audience, his long brown fingers emphasizing the utterances in his vibrant voice, he looked the very image of a propagandist, and one trembled to know that such a figure stood at the head of the movement to consolidate all the disciples of Buddha and to spread 'the light of Asia' throughout the civilized world.[3]

Dharmapala argued that the Buddha had been twenty-five hundred years ahead of his time. The "fundamental principles of evolution and monism," which were, he claimed, coming to be accepted "by the most thoughtful men of the day," were anticipated by the Buddha himself:

> Twenty-five centuries ago India witnessed an intellectual and religious revolution which culminated in the overthrow of monotheism, priestly selfishness, and the establishment of a synthetic religion, a system of life and thought which was appropriately called Dhamma—Philosophical Religion. All that was good was collected from every source and embodied therein, and all that was bad discarded . . . Speculation in the domain of false philosophy and theology ceased, and active altruism reigned supreme. (Dharmapala 1893: 863)

Dharmapala stressed that Buddhism was a religion of brotherhood and equality, and that it was scientific, in that nothing was to be accepted on faith (ibid.: 878).

Dharmapala and His Achievements

Sri Lanka, the land of Dharmapala's birth, is the Theravada Buddhist country with the longest history of colonialism. Beginning in the early sixteenth century, its coastal regions had been colonized first by the Portuguese, then by the Dutch, and lastly by the British. Colonization had brought Christian missionaries, initially Roman Catholics and later, with the Dutch and the British, Protestants. By the mid-nineteenth century not only was the Sinhala lowland elite thoroughly anglicized in language and education, but many had also converted to Christianity. Since the Choḷa invasions of the eleventh century, Buddhism in Sri Lanka had gone through many sequences of decline followed by renewal spearheaded by Thai, Mon, Arkanese, or Burmese monks whom Sinhalese kings, as protectors and purifiers of the Sangha, had periodically called in to reestablish higher ordination and raise standards of monastic conduct (Blackburn 2003). With the final defeat of the king of Kandy in 1815, however, Sinhala Buddhism lost its principal patron, protector, purifier, and mediator. Although the monarch's religious responsibilities shifted to the colonial government, in Sri Lanka, as in the direct-rule areas of India, the British accepted them reluctantly (Appadurai 1981). Before too long, the colonial government in Sri Lanka, under pressure from missionaries, began looking for a way to surrender its religious authority. It stopped enforcing the authority of monastery chiefs and could no longer be relied upon to expel from the Sangha monks who broke the rules. The roles of maintaining standards of conduct and practice and of defending the Buddhist community from the predations of Christian missionaries were assumed by the monks and the laity themselves. This meant there was no longer any authority able to enforce unity (or the privileges of the dominant Goyigama caste) in cases of disagreement.[4]

It was in these years that there began, among the lowland monastic fraternities (*nikayas*), the process of modernization that would lead to what H. L. Seneviratne (1989) has termed the Sinhala-Buddhist or "*Mahavamsa*-view" of history, namely that the mission of Sri Lanka, as the stronghold of Buddhism and Buddhist civilization, is to protect not only Sri Lankan but also world Buddhism. The first major innovation that the bhikkhus adopted was to acquire a printing press on which, in response to Christian publications, they began to produce tracts that the lay elite soon read and absorbed. Between 1865 and 1873, after decades of Christian missionary invitations and provocations, Buddhist monks agreed to engage with Christian missionaries in a series of written and oral debates on doctrinal issues. Heavily attended by laypeople and with written accounts published and republished in the aftermath, Buddhists saw these as triumphant victories for Buddhism, especially the Panadura debate of 1873.[5] They were a dramatic public demonstration of the process whereby the middle-class laity, whose traditional role had hitherto been restricted to giving material support to the Sangha, began to recognize the depth and significance of their own tradition, to disengage from Christian churches and organizations, and to involve themselves in Buddhist reform.[6]

At a time when many well-to-do Sinhala people had become Christians, Dharmapala's parents had resisted conversion and supported the Buddhist revival movement. Their eldest son, while a student in Christian missionary schools in Colombo, frequently attended lectures given by the celebrated orator monk Mahottivatte Gunananda Thera, the lead debater with the Christian missionaries. An account of the famous Panadura debate was read in New York by the American Civil War veteran Colonel Olcott (1832–1907) and by Madame Blavatsky (1831–1891), a Russian emigré aristocrat. In New York in 1875, they had together founded the Theosophical Society, the initial aim of which was to reform spiritualism and investigate its scientific claims (Viswanathan 1998: ch. 6). By 1877, the year in which Blavatsky's *Isis Unveiled* was published, they had recast their aims as introducing Oriental wisdom to the West, had recruited members in South Asia, and had begun corresponding with Dayananda Saraswati in India and the reformist monk Hikkaduve Sumangala in Sri Lanka about the possibility of translating their scriptures into English (Prothero 1996: 62–67). Despite clear indications from Saraswati that their beliefs were not the same, Olcott and Blavatsky formally merged their society with Saraswati's, accepted his leadership, and prepared to depart for Asia.

After a year lecturing and touring in India, in which it became obvious that Saraswati's Arya Samaj and their Theosophical Society would have to remain separate entities, Blavatsky and Olcott set sail for Colombo. On May 5, 1880, they publically went for refuge to the Three Jewels (Buddha, Dharma, and Sangha) and took the Five Precepts, "the first European-Americans to formally embrace Buddhism."[7] Olcott energetically set about helping Sinhala Buddhists to organize Buddhist Theosophical societies and schools, explicitly modeling his methods on those of the Christian missionaries. On a second tour of Sri Lanka in 1881, Olcott composed his *A Buddhist Catechism*, which was hugely influential and went through many reprints. It took for granted Olcott's own anticlerical and antiritualist Protestant background and specifically attacked "ceremonialism," "rites," and "priests" (Obeyesekere 1995b: 248), but it was accepted by Hikkaduve Sumangala as "in agreement with the Canon of the Southern Buddhist Church" (Prothero 1996: 101).

The young Don David Hewawitarana (Dharmapala) attended the first lecture that Colonel Olcott gave in Colombo in 1880 and from then on followed the Theosophists' activities closely. In 1884, he was initiated as a member of the Buddhist Theosophical Society, spent some time in Adyar with Madame Blavatsky, and then returned to Colombo to run the Theosophical Society's office there. He renounced householder life to become a *brahmacarin* (religious celibate), and took the name Dharmapala (Protector of the Dharma) and the title Anagarika (a Sanskrit word meaning "homeless one," but effectively a new Buddhist status halfway between monk and layman).[8] In 1889, he accompanied Olcott on a speaking tour of Japan, where Olcott laid out the plan, which he had conceived before his first visit to Burma in 1885, of uniting all Buddhists, whether Mahayana or Theravada, into a single world Buddhist church. In 1891, Dharmapala set out on a pilgrimage to the sacred Buddhist sites in north India. At Bodh Gaya, as he wrote in his diary on January 22, 1891, he was shocked to see "laying scattered here and there broken statues etc. of our blessed Lord. . . . As soon as I touched with my forehead the Vajrasana [diamond throne] a sudden impulse came to my mind. It prompted me to stop here and take care of this sacred spot—so sacred that nothing in the world is equal to this place where Prince Sakya Sinha gained enlightenment under the Bodhi Tree . . ."[9]

After the destruction of the north Indian Buddhist monasteries by Muslim invaders and the disappearance of Buddhism in India during the Middle Ages, the temple at Bodh Gaya had become an exclusively Hindu holy place connected to nearby Gaya, one of the most meritorious sites for performing Hindu funerals. Since the sixteenth century, the Bodh Gaya temple, together with extensive landholdings, had been in the hands of Shaivite Mahanta priests. By the time Dharmapala visited Bodh Gaya, the restoration of the temple—or stupa, as it is popularly called—had been accomplished by Burmese efforts, and Buddhist pilgrims were beginning to arrive from as far away as Mongolia. The temple, however, remained in the hands of the Hindu Mahant.[10] On his return to Colombo from Bodh Gaya, Dharmapala established the Maha Bodhi Society, whose objectives were as follows:

1. To work for the restoration of the Buddha Gaya Vihara to the Buddhists and to revive Buddhism in India.
2. To promote, foster and protect the spiritual, intellectual, and social welfare of the Buddhists of Ceylon [Sri Lanka] in particular and of the Buddhists of the world in general.
3. To establish and maintain schools, hospitals, dispensaries, orphanages, libraries, museums, reading rooms, scholarships, and other similar institutions.
4. To establish printing presses, publish and arrange for the publication of newspapers, books, periodicals and other literature dealing with the Buddhist religion, Buddhist education, and Buddhist culture.
5. To work for and assist in the propagation of the Buddhist religion and Buddhist culture and to train Dharmaduta[11] Bhikkhus and lay workers of both sexes.
6. To affiliate Societies and take over Trusts having similar objects.
7. To take all such steps as may be found incidental or conducive to the attainment of any one or more of the above objectives. (Ratnatunga 1991: 9)

In the following year, 1892, Dharmapala started a journal titled *The Maha-Bodhi and the United Buddhist World*. The front cover of each issue carried a picture of the Mahabodhi temple with an invitation to subscribers as follows: "to revive Buddhism in India, to disseminate Buddhist Literature, to publish Buddhist tracts in the Indian Vernaculars, to educate the illiterate millions of Indian people, to maintain Bhikkhus at Buddha Gaya, Benares, Kusinārā, Sāvatthi and Calcutta, to build Dharmasalas at these places, to send Buddhist missionaries abroad, the Maha-Bodhi Society asks every Buddhist to contribute 1/20 of his daily expenses to the Maha-Bodhi Fund."

By establishing the Maha Bodhi Society, Dharmapala signaled his determination to pursue his own goals separately from the Theosophists.[12] Within months of the society's founding he had dispatched four Sri Lankan "dharmaduta" missionaries to Bodh Gaya and organized the first international Buddhist conference in Colombo. In the belief that he would be better placed to carry on his campaign for the return of the Bodh Gaya temple from Hindu to Buddhist control in India, the following year, 1892, Dharmapala moved the society's headquarters to Calcutta.[13] By the time he received the invitation to Chicago to attend the World Parliament of Religions as the only representative of the "Southern Buddhist Church," he was already energetically working on the agenda that he had set for the society. Although his efforts with regard to Bodh Gaya would repeatedly meet with frustration, and would come to fruition only after his death, Dharmapala's missionary and institution-building activities in South and Southeast Asia, and ultimately in the West, would have remarkable success. Furthermore, he and his organization would have considerable influence on Bengali intellectuals and on religious developments in Nepal.

Dharmapala, influenced by Olcott and others, set most of the agenda for Buddhist modernism or what Richard Gombrich, G. Obeyesekere, and K. Malalgoda call "Protestant Buddhism," described in more detail below. He was also a key figure in the development of modern Sinhala nationalism, even though he spent most of his life in India and traveling the world. As T. Brekke (2002: 114) points out, his "long struggle to gain control over Bodh Gaya was a struggle to define Buddhist identity for himself and for the Sinhalese nation in relation to their symbolic centre." But he was more than just a nationalist. In the words of the Ven. Sangharakshita, "Dharmapala was a leading figure in initiating two outstanding features of Buddhism in the twentieth century. He was a great pioneer in the revival of Buddhism in India after it had been virtually extinct there for several centuries. And he was the first Buddhist in modern times to preach the Dharma in three continents, in Asia, in America, and in Europe" (Sangharakshita 1996: 17). And as

Sangharakshita emphasizes, he was also a Buddhist practitioner, not just an activist: he meditated every day and he evolved the new role of anagarika, effectively blurring the monk-lay distinction that had hitherto been fundamental to Buddhism. More than this, he transformed radically the understanding that educated Buddhists had of their own religion by his insistence that all Buddhists should strive for nirvana in this very birth, regardless of whether they were monks, nuns, or laypeople.

In 1900, Dharmapala went on a fundraising visit to Burma and, while there, he persuaded the prominent monk U Chandrima to send one of his disciples to India as a missionary: this was the Ven. Chandramani (1876–1972). Since the time of King Mindon (1853–1878), the Burmese had considered providing a Buddhist presence at each of the major north Indian sacred sites, but to date they had built only a resthouse, which opened in 1885 in the temple grounds at Bodh Gaya. Recruited by Dharmapala to represent the Maha Bodhi Society as well as the Burmese Sangha, the young Chandramani, accompanied by an Indian monk named Mahavir Swami who had ordained in Sri Lanka, set out for Kushinagara, the place in Uttar Pradesh where the Buddha died. In 1902, the two monks established a vihara there and, with Burmese funds, began restoring the two ruined stupas and the temple that housed a thirty-foot-long image of the recumbant Buddha in parinirvana (i.e., on his deathbed) (Sangharakshita 1997: 396). In addition to his restoration work, Chandramani, who would spend most of the rest of his very long life in Kushinagara and die there aged ninety-six, provided shelter to generations of pilgrims and taught the fundamentals of Buddhism to those who wished to learn, including, from the 1920s onward, many Nepali men and women (Singh 1996: 70–72). The English monk Sangharakshita, founder of the Western Buddhist Order, who received *pabbajja* ordination from Chandramani in 1949, described him as "an impressive figure. . . . Though he was well over seventy, and looked his age, his frame was sturdy and robust. His deeply furrowed face . . . expressed both strength and determination. 'So you want to be ordained, do you,' he said with a chuckle, apparently by no means displeased at the idea. . . . For the next hour, we were subjected to an interrogatory which, though kindly, was extremely searching" (Sangharakshita 1997: 394).

Dharmapala would also profoundly influence the first Nepali Buddhist modernist, Dharma Aditya Dharmacharyya (1902–63), who was born Jagat Man Vaidya, a Shakya by caste, from Chikã Bahi in Lalitpur. The story of how, as a student in Calcutta, he became a devotee of Dharmapala and formulated a new vision for Nepalese Buddhism, is told in Chapter 2.

Buddhism as "Not Hinduism"

A key part of Buddhist modernism is the attempt to mark Buddhism off as clearly distinct from Hinduism; indeed it is sometimes aggressively anti-Hindu. This feature was certainly Dharmapala's contribution, which owed nothing to his teacher Olcott. All tendencies within Buddhism of which the Buddhist modernist disapproves are labeled as Hindu (or Mahayana) influences. A paradigmatic exponent of this form of Buddhism was Bhimrao ("Babasaheb") Ambedkar (1891–1956), leader of India's Untouchables, who announced in 1935 that he would not die a Hindu. In 1956, shortly before his death, he publicly became a Buddhist and led half a million of his followers into Buddhism. He was strongly influenced by Buddhist modernism of Dharmapala's sort and wished to use Buddhism as a tool of social liberation. He gave many indications throughout his later life that he intended to convert to Buddhism, but held off, no doubt so as to extract the maximum political concessions on behalf of the Untouchables, or Dalits as they are called today (Viswanathan 1998: ch. 7). He was surely also aware of the symbolism of converting in 1956, the two thousand five hundredth anniversary of the Buddha's enlightenment.[14]

Ambedkar must have been influenced by a small Buddhist conversion movement among Tamil Untouchables, the Dravidian Buddhist Society (DBS), led by Pandit K. Ayothi Doss (1865–1914) and a teacher called P. Krishnaswami.[15] Olcott addressed their inaugural meeting in 1898 in Madras as follows:

> [Buddhism] will make every man, woman and child among you *free* of all the oppression of caste; *free* to work; *free* to look your fellowmen bravely in the face; *free* to rise to any position within the reach of your talents, your intelligence and your perseverence; *free* to meet men, whether Asiatics, Europeans or Americans on terms of friendly equality and competition . . . ; *free* to follow out the religious path traced to the Lord Buddha without any priest having the right to block your way; *free to become teachers and models of character to mankind.*[16]

The DBS leaders subsequently left for Colombo, where they took, i.e vowed to keep, the Five Precepts at a huge public meeting and thus became Buddhists, just as Olcott and Blavatsky had done eight years earlier. In fact, it seems that the program of the DBS was largely drawn up by Colonel Olcott. When he began to withdraw from specifically Buddhist activism, under pressure from Blavatsky, and devoted himself to the Theosophical Society, the DBS failed to develop. Dharmapala was alienated by what he saw as the Theosophists' tilt toward Hinduism, and eventually Olcott and Dharmapala began to publish attacks on each other in 1899. When Dharmapala attempted a reconciliation in 1905, hostilities flared to a new height, with Olcott arguing in print that the Buddha's tooth relic in Kandy was a fabricated deer's horn and Dharmapala severing his connections with the Theosophists forever. After Olcott's death in 1907, Dharmapala wrote: "Although he became a Buddhist he does not seem to have grasped the fundamentals of Buddhism. To say that all religions have a common foundation only shows the ignorance of the speaker. . . . Dharma alone is supreme to the Buddhist."[17]

In Olcott's hands the movement for Buddhist unity was anti-Christian in inspiration, but never anti-Hindu. For Dharmapala and even more for Ambedkar, opposition to Hinduism became central. In Sri Lanka, the anti-Hindu agenda had nationalist implications, whereas for Indian Untouchables it was a way of avoiding Gandhian condescension while still following an Indian religion. Ambedkar added twenty-two vows to the traditional Five Precepts, the recitation of which makes one a Buddhist layperson. Of the twenty-two, seven were explicitly anti-Hindu and/or anti-Brahmin. For example, the first was "I will not regard Brahma, Vishnu and Mahesh as Gods nor will I worship them," the sixth was "I will never perform any Sharaadha nor will I offer any Pinda" (i.e., any kind of Hindu ancestor worship is excluded), and the eighth was "I will never get any SAMSKAAR [life-cycle ritual] performed by Brahmins." The fifth of Ambedkar's new vows was addressed explicitly to the neo-Hindu attempt to include Buddhism as a minor, incomplete path within Hinduism: "I do not believe that Lord Buddha was the Incarnation of Vishnu. I believe this propaganda as mischievous and false."[18]

Buddhist modernism—of which Dharmapala and Ambedkar were exemplary exponents—was and is a form of religious revivalism. It is important to note, however, that not all revivalism is modernist in nature. Revivalism in some form or other is found in most religions, even in some nonliterate ones: it consists in prophetic or other kinds of leaders calling people (back) to their religious duty, however defined.

There have always been such movements within Buddhism, in which men go off to the forest to try and establish a purer monasticism and to avoid the entanglements in worldly affairs of ordinary monks.[19] Such movements have also taken the form, in all Buddhist countries, of the establishment or reestablishment of monasticism as the highest way of practicing Buddhism where it is absent:[20] this happened in Sri Lanka in 1753 when the monastic ordination tradition was reintroduced from Thailand. It happened in many places in the Tibetan cultural world after the rise of the Gelukpa, though by no means always in a Gelukpa idiom (Samuel 1993). Even the non-Buddhist Bonpo sect established a monastic wing. A good example of this entirely traditional form of Buddhist revivalism, consisting of the expansion of monastic institutions and the replacement of married specialists, is the introduction of monasteries to the Sherpa territory in Nepal in the early twentieth century, a theme that has been well explored by Sherry Ortner (1989a).

Buddhist modernists mark a radical departure from traditional Buddhist revivalists, because they seek to monasticize the laity as well, that is, to bring the laity up to a level of Buddhist virtue that had previously been thought possible and appropriate only for monks. Modernist revivalism is frequently combined with social reform, and usually consists in viewing the religion in question as scientific or at least as compatible with modern science. It is also often, as was certainly the case with Dharmapala, combined with ethno-nationalism. When attempting to analyse a specific situation, it may be difficult to decide which kind of revivalism is taking place, and the difference may not be of any concern to the actors themselves. Indeed, some influential participants may have a more traditional revivalist outlook, others a more modernist one. Some religious activists combine elements of both modernist and traditionalist outlooks simultaneously: Dharmapala himself advocated pilgrimage, temple-building, and traditional rituals, and, as previously noted, he revered the Buddha's tooth relic, indignantly rejecting Olcott's Protestant deprecation of it. Before proceeding further, however, it is necessary to backtrack and introduce some basic Buddhist history and terminology.

"Traditional" Buddhism: Theravada, Mahayana, Vajrayana

Buddhism today is divided into two major forms—Theravada and Mahayana—and nowhere are they juxtaposed so strikingly as in contemporary Nepal. Trevor Ling (1993) has rightly protested about the ways in which simplistic stereotypes of these two forms of Buddhism have impeded study of the considerable differences *within* the two traditions, both between different countries and within them. All the same, in Nepal today, the stereotypical contrast between Theravada and Mahayana can be justified as a first and approximate description of "things on the ground." By tradition, the Newars of the Kathmandu Valley follow the ornate and ritualistic Tantric form of Mahayana Buddhism, but since the 1930s they have taken enthusiastically to Theravada Buddhism as well, so the contrast between Theravada and Mahayana appears in modern Nepal as a choice between two radically opposed views both of Buddhism and of the human condition.[21] As a preliminary and doubtless highly simplified summary, the Theravada appears to offer an austere, simple, and predominantly rationalist and historical understanding of the Buddhist approach to life, whereas the Mahayana offers great scope for ritual, mysticism, and worldly involvement. Having said that, it is essential to bear in mind that for many Nepali Buddhists the two types of Buddhism should not be seen as radically opposed, or even as opposed at all: for them, the differences between different Buddhist traditions are trivial in comparison to what they share.

Theravada Buddhism is the dominant religion today in Burma, Thailand, Laos, Cambodia, and Sri Lanka, and it has spread from there to Indonesia and the West in modern times. Mahayana Buddhism is found in Nepal, Tibet, China, Korea, Japan, and Vietnam. It has spread around the globe with the Chinese and Tibetan diasporas. Tibetan Buddhism, as many will have noticed, has found a sympathetic reception throughout the Western world, including Hollywood (Prebish 1999).

In Nepal, two different forms of Mahayana Buddhism have traditionally been practiced: (1) Tibetan Buddhism, predominantly of the Nyingma tradition, which is found in the ethnically Tibetan enclaves strung out along the north of the country and among the Gurungs, Thakalis, and Tamangs; (2) "Newar" Buddhism of the Newar people of the Kathmandu Valley.[22] Theravada Buddhism has in recent years begun to spread beyond its foothold among the Newars, but it was among the Newars that it was first practiced and they are still overwhelmingly dominant in its ranks. This book is principally concerned with the way in which a small number of Newars who wished to reform Newar Buddhism created a movement that has gone on to become a permanent, vital, and established part of the religious scene in Nepal. From a handful of monks and nuns in the 1930s and 1940s, the movement grew to around 44 monks and 37 nuns in the mid-1970s, to 59 monks, 72 novices, and 70 nuns by the end of the 1980s, and to 78 monks, 94 novices, and 118 nuns in 2001.[23] The proportion of Newars has been falling, from 95 percent or more to just over 75 percent of the novices; as discussed in Chapter 6, it could fall still further in future. There were no Theravada monasteries in Nepal in 1930; today there are 98, including 17 nunneries; most are in the Kathmandu Valley, but there are many in outlying towns of Nepal as well (see Appendix 2).

Both Theravada and Mahayana Buddhism focus on an elite of celibate monks: "celibate" both in the sense of unmarried and in the popular sense of "chaste" or "sexually inactive." However, Mahayana Buddhism has, at least in some countries, given a legitimate place to married religious practitioners as well. In Theravada countries, although "married monks" have existed in some periods (e.g., Sri Lanka in the eighteenth century), they have always lacked legitimacy. Furthermore, within Mahayana Buddhism there is an esoteric ritual path known as the Vajrayana, which is central to Nepali and Tibetan Buddhism. The Vajrayana used to exist in China and is still represented in Japan by the Tendai and Shingon sects. Vajrayana gives a prominent place to sexual symbolism, and, in this type of Buddhism, the married religious specialist is frequently held to be superior to the monk.

In both Theravada and Mahayana Buddhism there is also a celibate path for women, but female religious specialists lack the prominence or importance that they have in Jainism, for example. According to the Vinaya, all nuns are supposed to consider themselves as junior to even the most junior monk, and the rules for nuns are far more numerous and stringent than the rules for monks. In Theravada Buddhism, the full ordination of women as nuns died out in the eleventh century, so celibate women in Theravada Buddhism are technically only "anagarika," or "homeless ones," who have to obey ten or eight rules (see below), and not "bhikkhuni," or "nuns," who have to follow 311 or 348 precepts (depending on the ordination tradition). (Theravada monks have to keep 227 rules according to their Vinaya.) The rules cover everything from how to eat, how to walk, how to behave with members of the opposite sex, and how to go to the toilet. Traditionally, it was held that anagarika could never become bhikkhuni because the higher female religious status had been lost irrevocably. But, encouraged by Western feminist Buddhists, who pointed out that bhikkhuni ordination had been preserved among Chinese Mahayana Buddhists, in 1988 three Nepali Theravada anagarikas went to Los Angeles to receive full ordination as nuns according to Chinese rites from the Fo Guang Shan sect of Taiwan. This move was opposed by most of the leading Nepali Theravada monks, just as it was and is by most leading monks in Burma, Thailand, and Sri Lanka. Another anagarika was subsequently ordained in Taiwan. In 1997, five Nepali nuns received full ordination in China, and in February 1998, twelve more did so in Bodh Gaya, together with fifty-three Theravadins drawn from several South and Southeast Asian countries. The controversy surrounding these ordinations is described in Chapter 7.

The historical relationship between Theravada and Mahayana is complex. Theravada Buddhism was just one of the many—traditionally eighteen—ordination traditions in early Buddhism. It was by no means the most numerous or most important of them, but it so happens that it was the tradition that predominated in the south and east of India. Those traditions that existed elsewhere in India died out when Indian Buddhism itself died out; their texts survived as part of Mahayana Buddhism—in Tibet and China, for example. (These texts included the Dharmaguptaka Vinaya, according to whose prescriptions the Fo Guang Shan ordained the Nepali anagarikas as bhikkhunis.) Thus, Theravada Buddhism is the only form of ancient Buddhism that survives into the present day without being part of a larger Mahayanist system—which is not to say, of course, that it survives unchanged.

Mahayana Buddhism arose around the turn of the common era, and represented an innovation in three connected ways. First, it introduced a whole new set of scriptures (supposedly taught by the Buddha himself, but preserved until such time as people were ready to receive them). Second, it introduced a new and elaborate pantheon. This inevitably reduced the overwhelming importance of the cult of the historical Buddha. The new pantheon included a host of savior figures known as bodhisattvas, particularly Avalokiteshvara (bodhisattva of compassion) and Manjushri (bodhisattva of wisdom). Third, the aim of serious practitioners was no longer simply to attain nirvana, but to become a Buddha: this means taking a vow to be a bodhisattva, someone devoted to being a Buddha.

This enlargement of the aim of serious practitioners meant that followers of the Mahayana saw themselves as more altruistic and more large-hearted than those who did not accept the new scriptures and the new pantheon of celestial bodhisattvas and other Buddhas. Thus they called all non-Mahayanists the "Hinayana" or "Lesser Way," with the implication that its followers were selfish and superficial. "Hinayana" is still sometimes heard; however, there were far more than just the Theravadins included in this category, so it is both inaccurate and derogatory to use this term to refer to Theravada Buddhism.

Once someone has had the idea of introducing new scriptures, it is a hard process to stop. There was another wave that came anywhere between five hundred and one thousand years after the first appearance of the Mahayana; it is known generically as the Vajrayana or Diamond Way, because it is symbolized by the *vajra* or thunderbolt. Vajra also means "diamond," the sense being that the absolute in Vajrayana Buddhism is thought to be as unchanging as a diamond. It is also sometimes known as Mantrayana or the Way of Mantras. Vajrayana Buddhism is an esoteric, ritualistic, and elaborate path within Mahayana Buddhism. Sociologically, it helped to legitimate the development of hereditary priesthoods in Tibet, Nepal, and Japan (though in Japan these occurred in non-Tantric traditions also).[24]

An important point about these three forms of Buddhism is that they were cumulative. Mahayana Buddhism did not reject the iconography, the pantheon, the scriptures, or the values of early Buddhism; it simply added more of everything on top. The same goes for the relationship of Vajrayana Buddhism to Mahayana Buddhism. Thus, whereas Theravada Buddhists do not accept the scriptures and pantheon of Mahayana Buddhism or Vajrayana Buddhism, the reverse is not true. For traditionalist Mahayana Buddhists, all their scriptures are the word of the Buddha: all record teachings given by him, so there is no question of "earlier" or "later" Buddhisms, though they do accept that some classes of scripture came to light later than others.

The Buddhism of the Newars is of the Vajrayana and Mahayana type. This means that the ascetic values of early Buddhism are preserved, but largely in restricted contexts or as a temporary measure. There are no permanently celibate monks, but rather a caste made up of priests (Vajracharyas) and householders who are part-time monks. Clearly, Newar Buddhism has come a long way from the Buddhism of the Buddha's time, at least in its outward form. This is perhaps ironic because the modern state of Nepal boasts the birthplace of the Buddha—although an Indian official claimed in 2001 (to understandable Nepali outrage) that it was Siddhartha Gautama who was born in Nepal, whereas the Buddha was born in India, at Bodh Gaya, where he attained enlightenment.[25] Be that as it may, traditional Newar Buddhism has traveled a long way historically and conceptually, even if geographically it remains close to Buddhism's point of origin. And this contrast between the inherited tradition of Newar Buddhism and Buddhism "as it was originally supposed to be" is one of the keys to the changes described in this book.

The gods and the rituals of Tantric or Vajrayana Buddhism certainly appear very anomalous to those familiar with Theravada Buddhism. Richard Gombrich, one of the foremost scholars of Theravada and early Buddhism, writes that

> for about a thousand years Buddhism in India was a religion which could be characterised as antithetical to tantra, or at least to Saiva/Sākta tantra. . . . [A]round the time of [the Chinese pilgrim] Hiuen Tsang . . . Buddhism was massively invaded by tantra, and the Vajrayāna tradition was born. Both in depending on the practitioner's identification with gods/demons, a sophisticated ideologisation of possession, and in drawing power from impurity, Buddhist tantra is paradoxical Buddhism and has turned the tradition on its head in a way which deserves the label of syncretism. But it has been recolonised by Buddhist ethics: its purposes are never immoral. . . . [W]hat makes the Vajrayāna Buddhist is its ethics. (Gombrich 1996: 163–164)

Mahayanists and Vajrayanists may object to Gombrich's way of phrasing the matter, but one way to sum up the story we are trying to tell in this book is that it attempts to describe how many Nepali Buddhists have come to learn and internalize this view of traditional Newar Buddhism, with its complex pantheon of divinities, its baroque rituals, and its ornate shrines, as "paradoxical Buddhism." This has involved a fairly radical shift of perspective. Despite the small numbers of monastics involved, Theravada Buddhists have succeeded in defining the terms and the discourse in which most educated Buddhists in Nepal define themselves today.

Quite apart from views of what is original or authentic Buddhism, and what is not, when they are confronted by actually existing Buddhism, Westerners have tended, not surprisingly, to approach it with Christian-influenced presuppositions about the nature of religion in mind. Thus, underlying many representations of Buddhism, including many of the more ethnographic accounts written by colonial administrators and missionaries with firsthand experience of it, was a Protestant-Catholic model. In this model, Theravada Buddhism was interpreted as typical of Protestantism, and Mahayana and Vajrayana were seen as similar to Catholicism.[26] It is true that Theravada has much simpler rituals than Mahayana, and a much simpler pantheon, but it is ultimately a misleading comparison. Anyone who wandered into, say, Shri Kirti Vihara in Kirtipur, a large and impressively ornate Theravada monastery in the Thai style that dominates the view of Kirtipur hill as one approaches from Kathmandu, would hardly be reminded of a Protestant church. The visitor is confronted by ubiquitous baroque goldleaf decoration, brightly painted statues of the gods and of the Buddha in dioramas illustrating his life story, ornate reliquaries, the use of incense, and a life-size statue of the dead monk and leader of the Nepalese Theravadin Order, Pragyananda. Unlike Protestantism, traditional Theravada Buddhism gives an important place to the worship of relics. It preserves its scriptures in a sacred language not understood by the laity. Traditionally, it did not emphasize literacy for laypeople, and even monks rarely meditated before the modern period. It was not a protest against the abuses of the established church, but, on the contrary, saw itself as the established church, against which Mahayana Buddhism innovated illegitimately.

"Protestant" Buddhism

Although there *is* a form of Buddhism that bears a close resemblance to Protestantism—the revivalist Buddhism advocated by Olcott and Dharmapala—it arose only in the modern period, under the impact of colonialism and Christian missionary activity.[27] Heinz Bechert has called it "Buddhist modernism"; Gombrich and Malalgoda follow Obeyesekere, who first called it "Protestant Buddhism."[28] It is "Protestant" because

(1) it was a double protest both against the colonial authorities and against Christian missionaries;

(2) it undercut the hierarchical nature of traditional Buddhism, with its division between monastic personnel and laypeople, by making social activism (including charity work) and meditation the duty of every Buddhist equally; it was therefore distinctly anticlerical;

(3) its adherents emphasized the importance of literacy, education, preaching, and printing books and magazines, and it created a network of Buddhist Sunday schools and produced the primers that were used in them;

(4) it polemicized against other religions, especially Christianity and Hinduism;

(5) it tended to be fundamentalist in its attitude toward Buddhism, believing—against traditionalists—that nirvana was possible now for all Buddhists, just as in the Buddha's time;

(6) it saw Buddhism as a philosophy (and therefore as scientific) rather than as a religion, and was hostile to ritual;

(7) it depended on English-language concepts (e.g., superstition, corruption, priestcraft, mysticism, even "religion") and it had a distinct affinity with middle-class values.[29]

To justify their program, "Protestant" Buddhists harked back to the mythic simplicity of early Buddhism. At the same time, by downplaying ritual in favor of belief and a rational epistemology, they claimed to be modern, even scientific. Gombrich and Obeyesekere have written that the essence of the Protestant Buddhist orientation

> lies in the individual's seeking his or her ultimate goal without intermediaries . . . [which] means denying that only through the Sangha can one seek or find salvation, *nirvāṇa*. The most important corollaries of this rejection are spiritual egalitarianism . . . and an emphasis on individual responsibility that must lead to self-scrutiny. Religion is privatized and internalized: the truly significant is not what takes place in a public celebration or in ritual, but what happens inside one's own mind or soul. At the same time religion is universalized: its injunctions apply to everyone at all times and in all contexts. . . .
>
> The hallmark of Protestant Buddhism . . . is its view that the layman should permeate his life with his religion; that he should strive to make Buddhism permeate his whole society; and that he can and should try to reach *nirvāṇa*. (Gombrich and Obeyesekere 1988: 215–216)

The effects of Protestant Buddhism, which emerged first in Sri Lanka, were to reach Nepal eventually, in large part through the influence of Anagarika Dharmapala and his Maha Bodhi Society. All the seven features listed above as characteristic of Protestant Buddhism in Sri Lanka were eventually to become, to a greater or lesser extent, characteristic of modernist Buddhism in Nepal as well. The fourth feature, the tendency to polemicize, needs qualification: polemicizing against Christianity hardly arose in Nepal, because Christians were so few; polemicizing against Hinduism had to be kept in check for political and pragmatic reasons, depending on the historical period; the polemical tendency was and is usually exercised by Buddhist modernists in Nepal against their own ancestral religion, Vajrayana Buddhism. Because Nepal lacks Sri Lanka's long history of colonialism and missionary activity, it does not seem appropriate to talk of Protestant Buddhism in the Nepalese context, and therefore "Buddhist modernism" will be used; both terms may serve as alternative labels for the same general phenomenon.

Female Renouncers in South and Southeast Asia in Early Modern Times

As noted above, the Sri Lankan Bhikkhu Sangha (Order of Monks) suffered frequent and extended periods of decline but, through repeated Burmese interventions, it was revived. The Bhikkhuni Sangha, by contrast, did not survive. Its disappearance from India in the tenth century and from Sri Lanka in the eleventh did not mean, however, that the Buddhist female renunciant tradition was extinguished entirely. Here and there renunciate women, not defined as "bhikkhunis," survived. Because the evolution of the Nepali nuns' Order, which grew out of this tradition, is a central focus of this book, a general introduction to female renunciation in Theravada Buddhism is necessary here.

Although occasional glimpses of female mendicants are evident in Thailand and elsewhere, given that the bhikkhuni ordination lineage died out before Theravada Buddhism became firmly established in Southeast Asia, these were "pious laywomen" not fully ordained nuns.[30] They appear to have been elderly women, many of them widows, who sought solace in the temple where their function was to cook for the monks and wash their clothes, to clean the temple, and to chant at ceremonies. Few performed rituals themselves, and, instead of going on the alms round, they were given a share of the alms food that the monks received. In the nineteenth century, the Thai Sangha underwent one of its periodic processes of purification and renewal. Because this included a renewed emphasis on scholastic training, it only served to marginalize the nuns further, as most were illiterate and from poor rural backgrounds.[31]

While Burmese sources indicate that "female monasteries" existed in Burma many centuries ago, little is known about them. The first Western report on Burmese nuns dates from 1834 when Lieutenant William Foley, a British naval officer, encountered women whom he identified as *Bhi Kuni* on the Island of Rambree off the coast of Arakan.[32] They were not in fact bhikkhuni but "eight-precept laywomen" or *thilashin* (one who owns virtue), a term derived from the Burmese *thilathay*, meaning "one who bears the burden of virtue," which, in the eighteenth century, was used to refer to both men and women who lived temporarily in temple compounds in order to meditate (Jordt 1988). Until the end of the nineteenth century, *thilashin*, like *maechi* in Thailand, lived in temples where their focus was on making merit through performing services for the monks and teaching the dharma, mostly to laywomen. Although *thilashin* did go out for alms, unlike monks who received cooked food from the laity on a daily basis, they went out only twice a month and received husked rice, which they cooked in the temple, and money, with which they purchased other foods and necessities. Kawanami (1990) reports that, as Foley had claimed (see note 32), some were spinster daughters whom their families, concerned about sexual scandal should they remain in the community, had encouraged to ordain; however, most were widows and formerly married women who retired to the temple seeking tranquility and relief from family responsibilities and the opportunity to meditate and earn merit.

In 1885, Upper Burma was annexed by the British and absorbed into the Indian Empire. When the last Burmese king, who, as in other Buddhist countries, had been the primary benefactor, protector, and purifier of the Sangha, was deposed, the unifying, state-imposed monastic structure collapsed.[33] New Buddhist organizations slowly emerged to fill the vacuum, notably the Young Men's Buddhist Association (founded by Dharmapala in 1906) and, when that faded in the 1930s, the lay meditation movement with its hundreds of meditation centers (see Chapter 8).

Around 1900, there occurred a second movement, which might be termed the "female monastery movement." Its roots lay in the spread of secular education in the colonial period and the admission of girls, or at least girls from elite backgrounds, to newly established government schools. The status of Burmese nuns started to rise as young educated women from well-to-do families began to renounce lay life (almost always over the strong opposition of their parents), to establish separate living quarters and, insisting on access to Buddhist learning, to find scholar monks willing to teach them. Although the young virgins (*ngebyu*), as these learned nuns came to be called only took eight precepts, whereas monks vowed to abide by the 227 Patimokka rules, in reality every nunnery imposed a detailed code of behavior on its residents.[34] The *ngebyu*, as a compromise between the old white *thilashin* dress and the reddish-brown robe of the *bhikkhu*, changed their dress to pink worn over an orange underskirt. They gradually succeeded, by virtue of their comportment, disciplined manner, and their success in national Sangha examinations, in convincing the laity that they were worthy of their respect and financial support (Kawanami 2000). *Ngebyu* did not officiate at public rituals; nor did they preach in public but only in private homes and in their own nunneries. Nor were they included in the ranks of leading meditation teachers. Nevertheless, they did include celebrated scholar nuns whom some of the most distinguished monks regularly consulted on doctrinal issues. It was with the *ngebyu* that, between the 1930s and the 1980s—when they started to diverge from them over the issue of full ordination—, the Nepali nuns would form their closest foreign ties.

Female renouncers could also be found in Sri Lanka. Bishop Copleston, writing about the history of Buddhism in the island, noted the presence of pious laywomen (*upasika*) "dressed in white, especially in Kandy, or on the way to Adam's Peak" (1892: 391). Although Gombrich and Obeyesekere (1988: 275) suggest that they may have taken the Ten Precepts on a permanent basis, there is no indication that these elderly white-robed women had any connection with any organization or movement but rather "wandered" from one pilgrimage place to another or else continued to live in their own homes, often in garden huts.

Dharmapala's Initial Impact on Female Renunciation

As a Western-educated layman in monk's dress, Dharmapala personally bridged the monastic-lay division to become the movement's ideal leader. Whereas for centuries attainment of nirvana had most often been presented as the goal of monks alone, and in many epochs was considered impossible, Dharmapala preached a gospel of liberation for all humanity: nirvana was possible now for the laywoman as well as the layman. He wrote in his diary in 1897 that reviving the Bhikkhuni Order in Sri Lanka was one of his priorities (Bartholomeusz 1994: 47). In the heady revivalist atmosphere in Sri Lanka around the turn of the twentieth century, a few men and women, with Dharmapala's encouragement, forsook lay life, and "went into homelessness." The men drew on the *ganninanse* tradition of the Kandyan period when, in response to a decline in monastic piety, laymen in white and ochre robes had launched their own reform movement. Rather than becoming recluses, however, Dharmapala's followers chose to remain in the world in order to engage with and be helpful to their supporters (Bartholomeusz 1994: 40).

In 1893, Catherine de Alwis, the daughter of socially prominent Sinhalese parents who had become involved in the Buddhist Theosophy movement, left for Burma where she studied near Sagain with the celebrated meditation master Thaton Mingun Zetawun Sayadaw.[35] Twelve years later, she returned to Sri Lanka after taking the Ten Precepts from her teacher and the ordination name Sudharmachari. Elizabeth Nissan (1984) suggests that in going to Burma to become a nun, Sudharmachari may have been following the model provided by early nineteenth-century Sri Lankan male renouncers who had brought back new lines of ordination to their homeland from Burma. In any event, her intention was to establish an order of female renunciants in Sri Lanka. She appears to have had no interest in reestablishing the Bhikkhuni Sangha, however; in her view, the role of the pious laywoman who retained a foothold in the world—following Dharmapala's model—was more valuable than that of the fully ordained nun who withdrew into the cloister. She founded an organization that she called the Sudharma Society, and two years later, with the enthusiastic support of the governor's wife, Lady Blake, established an *upasikaramaya* in Kandy. There, *dasa sil mata* ("ten precept mothers"), as she called her devotees, followed a routine of social service, teaching indigent girls, scriptural study, and meditation. The Sudharma Society attracted considerable attention and support from the Sinhala elite and initially seemed to thrive.

Although over the next decade a few more such "aramayas" were founded, each was, so to say, a tub on its own bottom, and whether it floated or sank depended on the impression residents made on the surrounding lay community. Despite being generally disciplined, composed, and friendly, *dasa sil matas* received far fewer donations than the monks. Responding to pressure from the Sinhala elite, they modeled themselves on Roman Catholic nuns whose focus was social service—teaching, nursing, and running orphanages (Bartholomeusz 1994: 91–98). Most Sinhala monks appear to have shared this view, believing that nuns, excluded from higher studies and the fulfillment of public roles through lack of full ordination, should provide what amounted to support services, it was with this same idea that some of the first Nepali monks to be trained in Sri Lanka returned to Nepal in the 1930s. Meanwhile, as few Sri Lankan women, regardless of age or social status, found these support roles appealing, the *dasa sil mata* movement attracted few recruits until the reintroduction of vipassana meditation from Burma in the 1950s (Bloss 1984). How Nepali women came to be attracted to this movement, their pursuit of religious education in Burma, and subsequently in Sri Lanka, Thailand, Taiwan, and elsewhere; and how they came to embrace the ambition to become full bhikkhunis is examined in Chapters 4–8.

CHAPTER TWO

Theravada Missionaries in an Autocratic State

Nineteenth-century Nepal was run as a patrimonial state, which is to say that the Rana aristocracy treated the country as their own private fiefdom: its resources and people existed, as far as they were concerned, to satisfy their own personal needs. The kings of Nepal were kept under a kind of permanent house arrest and all real power lay with the hereditary Rana Prime Ministers. In foreign affairs, the Ranas followed a policy of isolating the country. In the nineteenth century this was mostly an attempt to minimize British influence and to forestall any attempt to incorporate Nepal within British India (Nepal was forbidden, by the terms of the Sagauli Treaty of 1816, to forge relations with other powers). Toward the end of the nineteenth century, it became clear that the British had no designs on Nepal provided that the regime remained friendly; at the same time, British rule in India started to be challenged by the Indians who had graduated from the education system that the British themselves had introduced. As circumstances in India changed, the Ranas' isolationism gradually shifted from being a defence against British aggrandizement into a deliberate policy of preventing their own subjects from being affected by the pernicious democratic and nationalist ideas circulating in India. A further motivation, which dated from the foundation of the Nepalese state by Prithvi Narayan Shah in 1769 and continued unchanged, was to forestall possible conversion by Christian missionaries, who had attempted to establish themselves in Nepal in the eighteenth century and had been active in nearby Bengal throughout the nineteenth century.

For half a century or more, the Rana strategy of repression and isolation was largely effective in dealing with all opposition, except that coming from within the ranks of the elite itself (Joshi and Rose 1966; Sever 1993). The malaria-infested and heavily forested border region of the Tarai confined movement into and out of the country to the cold season, which meant that it could be more easily regulated. Only a handful of Westerners were permitted to enter Nepal. Nepalis from the Kathmandu Valley who wished to travel to India could do so only with government permission and were checked at Thankot on their way in and out. Those who served in the Gurkhas or went to Tibet had to undergo ritual purification, which included sleeping and eating separately from their families for several days, on their return. The ethnic backbone of Rana rule was formed by the Chetri (Kshatriya) caste, the largest single caste in the country, whose members frequently took wives from "tribal" (Janajati) groups, their offspring eventually being absorbed into their father's caste. The Ranas themselves, though Chetris by origin, raised their own status to that of Thakuri, the royal subcaste (Whelpton 1991). Key support for the Ranas came from the Bahuns (or Brahmans) who provided the priests, astrologers, scribes, and bureaucrats of their realm.

The Ranas' determination to seal off the country and block the infiltration of foreign influence was ultimately doomed to failure. Nepalis were going abroad in increasing numbers, as soldiers, traders, or students. Gurkha soldiers, including both Chetris and Janajatis (chiefly Magars, Gurungs, Rais, and Limbus—known in those days as "tribes"), were recruited by the British into the Indian army in ever greater numbers.[1] They were followed to their posts in India and in Burma, which became a British colony in 1885, by Newar goldsmiths. Though a few settled permanently in Burma, most traveled back and forth, carrying with them a growing familiarity with Burmese Buddhism.

Another factor that undermined the Ranas' isolationism was their own craving for foreign goods (Prithvi Narayan Shah had presciently warned against this over a hundred years before).[2] Obtaining Western luxuries required the development of trading networks in India. The majority of these traders were Udays, Newar merchants from Kathmandu, many of whom also had business in Tibet[3]. In the years following 1860, the India-Tibet trade was rerouted from Patna-Kathmandu-Kyirong/Kodari-Shigatse-Lhasa to Calcutta-Kalimpong-Gyantse-Lhasa, and some Newar merchants opened permanent establishments (*kothi*) in Calcutta. There they met and were impressed by Maha Bodhi Society missionaries led by their founder, the Sri Lankan Anagarika Dharmapala. The Society had its headquarters in Dharmarajika Vihara in College Square and its members were campaigning for Bodh Gaya to be returned to Buddhist control. Throughout Buddhist history, merchants have been among the first to hear the dharma from missionary monks and to provide for their support along the trade routes of Asia. The support of Buddhist merchants in the early years of the Nepalese Buddhist revival was to be crucial.

Nepali students were yet another conduit for "pernicious" ideas. At the end of the nineteenth century, the Ranas finally acknowledged their need for Western-educated bureaucrats. Since Jang Bahadur's time, there had been a palace school in which Indian, and sometimes British, teachers were employed to instruct the Ranas' sons and the sons of their counselors and courtiers.[4] Until 1918, when Tri Chandra College was established, no institution of higher learning existed in Kath-

The Nepalese Chamber of Commerce in Lhasa, Tibet, in 1947. In the center is the President, Triratna Man Sahu, to his left a young Gyan Jyoti. (Courtesy of Gyan Jyoti)

mandu. Thus the government was obliged to finance the education of some young men in India where they were exposed not only to the incendiary ideas of the Free India movement but also—from a Newar Buddhist perspective—to the equally radical ideas of the Maha Bodhi Society.

Dharmaditya Dharmacharyya

The first Newar to embrace the new Buddhism was a young Shakya from Chikã Bahi in Lalitpur named Jagat Man Vaidya. His father was the Ayurvedic physician to Prime Minister Juddha Shamsher. He had five sons, two of whom became teachers and two doctors. Jagat Man was the youngest: at the age of eighteen he went for two months to Calcutta in 1921 to take his matriculation exam. Jagat Man's father had managed to obtain a scholarship from Juddha Shamsher for his son to study commerce in Calcutta, a subject not offered at Tri Chandra College. In fact, Jagat Man was to devote most of his time and energy to Buddhist and Newar revivalism. On his first stay in Calcutta, he met Anagarika Dharmapala, an experience so compelling for Jagat Man, according to V. P. Lacoul (1985: 45–6), that it was like meeting Shakyamuni Buddha himself. Dharmapala, on his side, saw Jagat Man as a messenger sent from heaven to propagate Theravada Buddhism in Nepal, the land of the Buddha's birth. Over the next few years Jagat Man changed his name to Dharmaditya Dharmacharyya, donned yellow monastic-type clothing, referred to himself as "the Venerable Dh. Dharmacharyya," and dedicated himself to learning Pali and reviving Newar Buddhism.[5] Briefly back home in Kathmandu in 1923, he attempted to establish a "Nepal Buddhopasak Sangha" or Nepalese Buddhist Laymen's Association at a meeting in Dhama Sahu's shrine room. Dharma Man Tuladhar (1861–1937), or Dhama Sahu as he was popularly known, was a rich Newar merchant who had spent much time in Tibet and whose financial contributions to and sponsorship for all forms of Buddhism in the 1920s were very important. For example, he had organized the renovation of the Swayambhu *stupa* in 1918, a task requiring the extensive mobilization of both Tibetan and Nepali money and resources. This renovation gave rise to a widely repeated ditty: "The Tibetans gave the money, Dhama Sahu got the fame . . . ," which was in fact very unfair as Dhama Sahu had contributed significant amounts from his own pocket as well.[6]

In Calcutta, Darjeeling, and Kalimpong, Dharmacharyya's principal strategies for reviving Nepalese Buddhism included publishing journals in Hindi, Bengali, Nepali, Nepal Bhasha, and English, which appeared sporadically, and translating extracts of Sanskrit and Pali Buddhist texts into Nepal Bhasha.[7] His journal, *Buddha Dharma*, the first issue of which was published in 1925 for Baisakh Purnima (the full moon of the month of Baisakh), was the first ever magazine or newspaper in Nepal Bhasha. Its message was that the Newars' traditional texts contained the fundamentals of Buddhism as understood in Theravada countries and, in particular, that these texts emphasized the central importance of celibate monasticism. In other words, Newar Buddhists might have failed to grasp the essentials of their own religion but reform was still possible.

The 1920s were not just a time of religious revivalism: the British were introducing compulsory examination papers in the vernacular to Indian universities. The Newars studying in India were suddenly made politically conscious of their mother tongue for the very first time (Lacoul 2001: 15). Dharmacharyya was persuaded to turn *Buddha Dharma* into a joint Buddhist and literary magazine, *Buddha Dharma wa Nepal Bhasha*, a model that later served for the monthly journal *Dharmodaya* in the late 1940s and 1950s. Dharmacharyya began a futile campaign for Nepal Bhasha to be recognized in Indian universities as Nepali, rather than the Parbatiyas' language, which was already generally known by that name, at least outside Nepal.[8]

In 1926, back in Kathmandu on the occasion of Baisakh Purnima, Dharmacharyya organized a celebration of the Buddha's birth, enlightenment, and passing away—the first celebration of Buddha Jayanti, as it is now called, in Nepal. In 1928, he organized an all-India Buddhist conference in Calcutta, which focused on the status of Buddhism in Nepal. Even though he himself was never ordained, Dharmacharyya campaigned for the reëstablishment of a monastic order.[9] The British government of India was aware of Dharmacharyya's activities, but did not take them very seriously. The chief secretary of the government of Bengal referred to him in a secret letter to the government of India as follows: "[T]he All-India Buddhist movement [is] led by a Nepali Buddhist, Dr. Dharmacharyya, a learned man and a religious and social reformer, who, however, owing to his unorthodoxy, has not many followers."[10]

As a result of the time taken up by his reformist and cultural activities, Dharmacharyya failed his commerce exams and his scholarship was terminated. Nonetheless, when he returned to Nepal, he was recruited to the new government Industry Department by Gunja Man Singh, who had also studied in Calcutta.

Like his guru Dharmapala, Dharmacharyya had occupied a status in between that of monastic and lay; unlike Dharmapala, however, he married two months after his permanent return to Nepal in 1936 and had four daughters and two sons (Darshandhari 1998: 14). He spent the rest of his working life as a government official, as a private tutor, and as an occasional employee of Bhaju Ratna Kansakar, a wealthy Uday merchant, and father of Maniharsha and Gyan Jyoti (on whom, see Chapter 5). Bhaju Ratna had become a devotee of Dharmapala in Calcutta and was for many years a generous financial backer of the Theravadins. Dharmacharyya continued to be involved in the propagation of the Theravada message; among his other contributions, he founded a laywoman's organization and helped establish a nunnery, Tana Vihara, in Lalitpur. His activities in Nepal were on a much smaller scale than his accomplishments in Calcutta in the 1920s and early 1930s. As part of a general clampdown on what were perceived as oppositional activities he was imprisoned for three months in 1940 in Singha Darbar, along with other Nepal Bhasha writers, after which he had to keep a low profile until 1951 (Darshandhari 1998: 16). Toward the close of the Rana period, he and an old friend tried to start a factory together, which failed, causing considerable hardship to his family. Kesar Lall (1986: 14) concludes: "Upon his return to Nepal . . . his talent and learning were wasted and his great learning withered in a hostile environment."

Traditional Newar Society

The Newar society from which Dharmacharyya came was, and to a great extent still is, a caste society.[11] In order to understand the dynamics of change in the Kathmandu Valley, and in particular to understand how Buddhism has changed, it is essential to know something of the "traditional" Newar caste order. According to the census of 2001, there are 1.27 million Newars (5.5 percent of the total population of Nepal), approximately half of whom live in their heartland, the Kathmandu Valley. Just over a third of Newars (most outside the Valley) report Nepali, not Nepal Bhasha (Newari), as their mother tongue. The proportion of Newars speaking Nepali only, and having

BUDDHIST LITERARY CONFERENCE

either a passive understanding or no knowledge of Nepal Bhasha, is probably an absolute majority outside the Valley, and it is increasing rapidly among the younger generation within the Kathmandu Valley.

Internally, the Newars are divided into a complex caste hierarchy of around twenty different castes, which fall into six broad categories or blocs as shown in Table 2.1. Some of these castes are large and are found wherever there are Newars (for instance, the Shrestha trading and land-owning caste, and—within the Kathmandu Valley—the Maharjan-Jyapu agriculturalist caste). Others are highly localized (e.g., the Uday/Uray found principally in Kathmandu). Yet others are small and specialized, found in small numbers wherever Newars can support them (e.g., the Napit barber caste, or the Rajopadhyaya Brahman caste).

The Buddhist priestly caste is made up of two ranked sections: the Vajracharyas, who are priests for others (much as Brahmans are priests for Hindus), and the Shakyas (about two-thirds of the total), who tend to be artisans by profession. In the western half of the Kathmandu Valley, dominated by the cities of Kathmandu and Lalitpur, most Newars—all Uday, some Shresthas, all agriculturalists, and the majority of the artisan/ritual specialist bloc—have Vajracharya rather than Brahman domestic priests, so that, at least by the criterion of priest, they count as Buddhists.[12] This means that they must invite their household's traditional Vajracharya priest to perform all life-cycle rituals for their family, though they may invite any priest they choose (even a Brahman) for optional ritual services. In the east of the Valley, centered on the city of Bhaktapur, Hinduism is relatively stronger and there are fewer Newar castes who make use of Vajracharya priests. There has also been a trend for upward mobility, the exact extent and geography of which is controversial, expressed by means of adopting a Shrestha

The All-India Buddhist Literary Conference organized at the Maha Bodhi Society's Dharmarajika Vihara, Calcutta in 1928 (December 27–29th) by Dharmaditya Dharmacharyya, who is the young garlanded figure at the center of the row seated on chairs. Two spaces to his left is Annie Besant, and in between them probably Dharmaditya's friend Benimadhab Barua. Nara Shamsher Rana identified himself as the young man standing in the lighter suit in the middle of the back row (photo courtesy of Dharma Man Newa, Dharmaditya's son)

Table 2.1 Simplified model of the Newar caste hierarchy (For further details see Gellner and Quigley 1995.)

(1) Priests:	(1a) Brahmans (Rājopadhyāya, Dyahbhāju)–Hindu (1b) Vajrāchāryas (Gubhāju) and Shākyas–Buddhist
(2) Patrons/Landholders:	(2a) Shresthas–mostly Hindu (2b) Udāy (Tulādhars and others)–Buddhist
(3) Agriculturalists:	Maharjan, Dangol, Suwāl (Jyāpu)
(4) Artisans and Ritual Specialists numerous small castes, e.g. (occupational castes):	Barbers (Nāpit), Oil-Pressers (Mānandhar), Painters (Chitrakār)
(5) Milksellers/Butchers (water-unacceptable but not untouchable):	Khadgi, Shāhi (Np. Kasāi)
(6) Sweepers (untouchable):	Dyahlā (Np. Pode)

identity and/or replacing the traditional Vajracharya domestic priest with a Brahman priest.[13] In all Newar settlements, many laypeople think of themselves as Hindu, despite having a Buddhist priest. Public self-identification as Hindu was encouraged by the state under the Panchayat regime (1960–90) and before: Buddhism was seen then, and many people still regard it, as a sub-sect or offshoot of Hinduism, so they see no contradiction in being both a Buddhist and a Hindu and no problem with practicing or combining both Hindu and Buddhist forms of worship. Many other inhabitants of Kathmandu and Lalitpur, however, even if they were returned as Hindus in the censuses before 1990, still had a personal commitment to Buddhism, which they understood as superior to Hinduism. Many Maharjans have started to support Buddhism openly since 1990 as an aspect of identity politics.[14]

Unlike Vajracharyas, Shakya men may not be priests for others, but together with Vajracharya men they are the members of the traditional Newar Buddhist monasteries, known honorifically as vihāra and colloquially as *bāhā* or *bahi*. In so far as Shakya and Vajracharya men filled their roles in the monastery, they were monks. In effect, they were married, part-time monks.[15] Because they are all householders, it is only sons of Vajracharya and Shakya men by Vajracharya or Shakya mothers who may in boyhood be initiated as a monk in their father's monastery. This four-day ritual makes them a member of the monastic community (sangha) of that monastery, which means they must share the duty of daily worship with other members in turn. It also gives them the right to become an elder of the monastery, a position that is usually reached by seniority.[16] Thus, both Shakyas and Vajracharyas are unequivocally Buddhist in their religious affiliations, but it is primarily the Vajracharyas who are closely associated with the Vajrayana (Tantric) form of Buddhism as its preservers, teachers, and leaders. The Shakyas, by contrast, had the identity of "sons of the Buddha": they took the surname either "Buddhist monk" (Shakyabhikshu, more common in Kathmandu) or "of the Buddha's lineage" (Shakyavamsha, more common in Lalitpur).[17] Either way, they shared the origin myth that they were descendants of the Buddha's ethnic group, who had fled thousands of years ago to the Kathmandu Valley after they were attacked by the Kosalans.[18] Shakyas have, therefore, a very strong attachment to Buddhism, but not necessarily to Vajrayana Buddhism. This has meant that Shakyas were and are much more open than Vajracharyas to alternative forms of Buddhism, whether Tibetan or Theravadin (and the same goes for Uday). It was to combat and reform the Newars' Vajrayana form of Buddhism, and in particular to replace the tradition that its leaders can embody the role of monks on a part-time basis while simultaneously continuing the life of a householder, that the Nepalese Theravada movement was established.

The Vajracharya-Shakya caste is neither, like Shresthas, found in large numbers everywhere nor, like the Napits (Barbers) and other artisan or specialist castes of a similar status, found as a small minority everywhere. Rather, its distribution is lumpy: in some places it is large and significant, in others, small and insignificant. Its greatest concentration is in the city of Lalitpur (Patan), which explains the strongly Buddhist character of that city. The next biggest concentration is in Kathmandu. Elsewhere they are in a minority, and they look to Kathmandu and Lalitpur for leadership.

The fact that traditional Buddhism is concentrated in or near Kathmandu and Lalitpur means that the greatest support for Theravada and the most important Theravada monasteries are also to be found there. There are many Newar bazaars in the hills of Nepal, e.g. Tansen in the west, where Shakyas and Vajracharyas are present as goldsmiths or makers of brass pots. These hill bazaar towns have also been important outposts of Buddhist activity and have contributed significantly to the

The façade of Uku Baha, Lalitpur, a typical traditional Newar Buddhist "monastery," the only modern feature being the addition of tiles. The main shrine is flanked by statues of the Buddha's closest disciples, Maudgalyayana and Shariputra. In front of it is a whitewashed Licchavi-period chaitya protected by a much later canopy supported by holy serpents. In front of it is a *dharmadhatu*, a cult object dedicated to the bodhisattva Manjushri. (Sarah LeVine)

Theravada Buddhist revival movement.[19] As strongly Buddhist castes who are yet denied full priestly authority within Vajrayana, it is no coincidence that Shakyas (many of them marginalized by their ancestors' migration to the bazaar towns of the hills) and Udays (all from Kathmandu, often wealthy and educated) should have provided the bulk of the recruits in the early stages of the Theravada movement.[20]

Traditional Nepalese Buddhism

It was suggested in Chapter 1 that it is a mistake to identify Theravada Buddhism with Protestantism and Mahayana Buddhism with Catholicism. Nonetheless, if the Protestant-Catholic contrast is reinterpreted as a broad and gradual spectrum rather than as a simple either-or opposition, traditional Newar Buddhism is nearer to the Catholic, and Theravada Buddhism nearer to the Protestant, end of the spectrum. Traditional Newar Buddhism is characterized by

(1) numerous rituals, both simple and elaborate, for both social and instrumental purposes;
(2) frequent feasting, including the religiously sanctioned use of meat and alcohol;
(3) spiritual and social hierarchy;
(4) the restriction of literacy and religious study to males of the highest castes (and even among them few study the scriptures, as opposed to reciting them);
(5) the restriction of the highest salvific practice—Tantric Initiation (*diksa*)—to the elite (i.e., high castes);
(6) an elaborate and baroque pantheon with forms of worship for almost every human eventuality;
(7) use of the hereditary principle both for recruitment to specialist roles and for ties to specialists.

It is fair to say that this form of Buddhism is in decline and that in the 1980s it appeared to be facing a severe and possibly terminal crisis. Until the 1950s, virtually all Vajracharya men, even those without hereditary patrons (*jajmān, jaymā*) of their own, learned the rituals and took Tantric Initiation (Gellner 1992: 262–263, 270). It was a matter of pride in their priestly caste status. But for many decades now, even practicing priests do not wish their sons to continue as priests, but prefer them to become doctors or engineers. The same is true of those Vajracharyas who practice as Ayurvedic doctors (Durkin-Longley 1982: 193). There have been some attempts to revive traditional Newar Buddhism, including conferences organized by the Lotus Research Institute, classes run by Badri Ratna Vajracharya at the Sanskrit University, and other classes sponsored by Shishinkai of Japan at Aksheshwar Mahavihara in Lalitpur. But such efforts appeared to be powerless to prevent the vicious circle by which only boys who are unable to forge any other career enter the priesthood. Such recruits are hardly likely to inspire respect, either by their ascetic spirituality or by their learning. Therefore, the laity respect Vajracharya priests less and less, which ensures that only those who have no alternative enter the priesthood.

In recent years, however, there have been some slight signs that, at least among a minority, there may be the will to preserve the Newar Vajrayana tradition. Some young Vajracharya men do seem to have a genuine spiritual vocation and a genuine desire to preserve their tradition (as illustrated by the cases of Kiran in Chapter 8 and Bir Bajra in Chapter 9). Commitment is often expressed in terms of academic study of the Tibetan tradition, learning Newar Buddhist Tantric songs and dances, putting on exhibitions and plays, attending and organizing conferences, and exploring other Buddhist traditions. Most young Vajracharyas, however, unless they come from active priestly families, appear to be unwilling to learn how to perform rituals. Young Vajracharya men who do not themselves have patrons, and who are not therefore obliged to do so, do not learn the rituals.

In stark contrast to the practices of traditional Newar Buddhism, Theravada Buddhism, even in the traditionalist forms found in Southeast Asia and Sri Lanka, is nearer the Protestant end of the spectrum. It is characterized by:

(1) few and simple rituals that are supposed to be commemorative and not instrumental;

(2) worship mainly of Shakyamuni Buddha himself, other gods being defined as under the protection of Buddhism and acknowledging its hegemony;

(3) access to the highest salvific role, monasticism, being open to all males, even if, as in Sri Lanka, different castes tend to be associated with different ordination traditions;

(4) a general hostility to possession states as well as to magical interpretations of its rituals.

Thus, despite the caveats made above about viewing Theravada Buddhism as equivalent to Protestantism in its social effects or ethos, one can still say, speaking in a loose Weberian idiom, that there is an "elective affinity" between Theravada Buddhism and Protestantism, and between both of these and the egalitarian, individualist, and rationalist values of the modern era. Furthermore, the "elective affinity" was still stronger and more obvious in the case of the revivalist, modernizing form of Theravada pushed by Dharmapala's Maha Bodhi Society. Modernist Theravada Buddhism did indeed become a movement that was in stark contrast and opposition to the traditional practices of Newar Buddhists.

Today traditional Newar Buddhism is unquestionably in retreat before Theravada Buddhism. How that happened is the story that we wish to tell in this book. *That* it has happened can hardly be contested.[21] Nepalese Buddhist laypeople are willing to fund new monasteries and new initiatives and to donate land and other valuables to Theravada Buddhism and to Tibetan Buddhism. Similar levels of money and commitment do not go into Newar Buddhism. Where traditional Newar Buddhism is concerned, it is largely a question of preserving it, or some of it, as a form of cultural heritage. In questions of belief (where there is conflict) and in relation to deep personal as opposed to communal commitments, traditional Newar Buddhism has largely lost the battle. No reflective practicing Vajrayanist would deny that Newar Buddhism is in need of reform and revival.

One may well ask: Why did Tibetan Buddhism not have such an impact, since Newars were in continuous touch with Tibetan Buddhism for centuries and Tibetan Buddhism is closer to Newar Buddhism? The answer may lie partly in the relative accessibility of Theravada scriptures and teachings—in Hindi and in English. Tibetan is hard to learn well, whereas Hindi and Pali are relatively easy for Nepali-speakers. Furthermore, Theravada Buddhism was located in the relatively more developed and accessible south, and was thus identified with progress and development. In the long run, Theravada success may have been assisted by the greater role that laypeople are able to play in Theravada initiatives. Yet, at the origin of the Theravada movement in Nepal, and even today in order to provide symbolic leadership, monks were and are essential. Dharmacharyya, as a layman, could do very little if there were no monks.

Another part of the answer rephrases the question. The fact is that Tibetan Buddhism *did* have a radical impact on Newar Buddhists in the 1920s. The early founding monks and activists started out as Tibetan Mahayanists and only later became Theravada monks. They do not appear to have seen these two statuses as radically opposed, at least not initially. The switch from Tibetan to Theravada Buddhism may be considered a "conversion," but it was emphatically not a conversion of the radical Pauline sort. In other words, adopting Theravada Buddhism was understood to be a decision adopted on the basis of a series of relatively pragmatic considerations (e.g., the ease of learning Pali compared to Tibetan, the difficulty of surviving in Tibet, and so on). However, the decision to renounce lay life and become a monk was often, as the cases of Mahapragya and Pragyananda described below will show, a radical personal leap, apparently a form of compulsion, very much on the Pauline model.

The Impact of Kyangtse Lama

In the early years of the twentieth century, there were the beginnings of a Newar cultural renaissance. Pandit Nisthananda Vajracharya, having told the life story of the Buddha in numerous places in Kathmandu on the basis of the traditional Mahayanist account, the *Lalitavistara*, decided to bring out a published version. He did not simply translate from the scriptural Sanskrit into Nepal Bhasha, but reworked and supplemented the original with material from other scriptures, such as the *Bhadrakalpa Avadana*, the *Swayambhu Purana*, the *Gunakarandavyuha*, the *Astasahasrika Prajnaparamita*, and so on.[22] Nisthananda had to go to Calcutta and design and make the type (from wood), and oversee the whole printing process himself. His *Lalitavistara* came out in 1914, to considerable government disapproval, and was the second book ever printed in Nepal Bhasha (the first was a translation of the *Ekavimsati Stotra* that Nisthananda had published five years earlier). It had a major influence on many of the early figures in the revival.[23]

In 1925, shortly after Dharmaditya Dharmacharyya had begun his campaigns, which taught people that Nepal was the land of the Buddha's birth, a charismatic Tibetan teacher appeared in Kathmandu.[24] The Newars know him as Kyangtse (Kyangtsa) Lama (he was Kunsho Loseb in Tibetan). He came to the Kathmandu Valley on a pilgrimage, having taken four and a half years to prostrate all the way from central Tibet to Swayambhu. His teachings were translated into Nepal Bhasha for huge crowds. In the same year, a play version of the Buddha's life was put on by the Shakyas of Uku Baha, based on the *Lalitavistara*, which also made a deep impression on many people. The first monks were inspired by the sermons of Kyangtse Lama and by their reading of the Lalitavistara to become "real" monks. According to Satya Mohan Joshi (1990: 64), it was this "fortunate conjunction" of Nisthananda's mother-tongue version of the Buddha's life story, Dharmacharyya's revivalism, and the appearance of Kyangtse Lama that ensured that the "seed of dharma" Kyangtse Lama planted should bear such impressive and immediate fruit.

Kyangtse Lama arrived first at Namobuddha, a Buddhist pilgrimage site to the east of the Kathmandu Valley, believed to mark the spot where the Buddha, in his previous life as the Prince Mahasattva, fed his body to hungry tiger cubs, thereby demonstrating the virtues of charity, compassion, and forbearance.[25] Kyangtse Lama was met at Namobuddha by Newar Buddhists, who, impressed by his feat of prostrating all the way from Tibet, invited him to stay in Kathmandu. As they got to know him, the Newar laity were very impressed, despite his uncouth appearance (his hair was in matted locks and his clothes were ragged). He was persuaded to give teachings, which he did, based on Patrul Rinpoche's commentary on the *Longchen Nyingtig* of Jigme Lingpa. His Tibetan was translated into Nepal Bhasha by Bekha Ratna Tamrakar, and then rephrased in more religious language by *pandit* Buddhi Raj Vajracharya; some say this last step was necessitated by the fact that Bekha Ratna had a very soft voice. Large crowds came to hear his teachings, which stressed the importance of prostrations, reciting the Vajrasattva mantra, offering the ratna mandala, and practicing guruyoga-samadhi.[26] Several minor miracles were ascribed to Kyangtse Lama, as often happens with Tibetan Buddhist teachers: one dark evening he magically fetched his books, drum, and vajra, among other things, from Swayambhu to Kathmandu; on another occasion he pressed his hand into a marble stone leaving an imprint (Joshi 1990: 14–15).

Despite the fact that his teachings were very largely compatible with their own tradition, some of the Vajracharya priests of Kathmandu were not at all pleased by the popularity of this Tibetan competitor and decided to take action against their Uday patrons who were supporting him. They appealed to the government and charged the Udays with accepting *prasād*, that is, blessed food offerings, from Kyangtse Lama, a Tibetan, and therefore with losing caste. Some Udays asked for pardon from their Vajracharya priests and were granted absolution; others refused to do so, continuing to support Kyangtse Lama. Some marriages split over the issue, notably that of Moti Laxmi Upasika, sister of the poet Hridaya.

Subsequently, the Kathmandu Vajracharyas decided, as a body, to refuse to eat boiled rice in the homes of their patrons after performing rituals for them. Traditionally, and privately, Vajracharya priests had always done this in Uday households (though not in the homes of other, lower-caste patrons). Now, they decided, conditions had changed and the difference of caste rank between the Vajracharya priests and their Uday patrons needed to be enforced rigorously. They assumed that the Ranas' law courts would support them, in line with the regime's strict interpretation of Hinduism; this would enable them to assert their authority and leadership over the Uday. They encouraged the Rana regime to deal harshly with Kyangtse Lama and his followers, with subsequent followers of Tibetan Buddhism, and with the Theravada monks who came after.

In a long and detailed article based on the memories of many who lived through the dispute, Colin Rosser (1966) has described how this policy on the part of the leaders of traditional Newar Buddhism backfired disastrously. It angered many rich and influential Uday (many of whom were pious and supportive Vajrayanist Buddhists, in some cases as learned as many Vajracharyas). It led to a series of ultimately indecisive court cases, which served only to divide Newar Buddhists in Kathmandu against each other. Two Vajracharyas who sided with the Uday were sent to prison for between one and two years in 1932 for accusing the other Kathmandu Vajracharyas of falsifying a document presented in court (Rosser 1966: 110). Only two or three Uday households sided with the Vajracharyas and were boycotted by their caste fellows for years after.

This long-running dispute caused the majority of the Uday and many Shakyas to become disaffected from the Vajracharyas' form of Buddhism, or at the very least to be well disposed to supporting the alternatives—Tibetan Mahayana and Theravada imported from Burma via India—that were soon to be available. In any event, both Shakyas and Udays, given the involvement of these two communities in international trade, tended to be more familiar with the outside world—and more receptive to new ideas—than were other Buddhist castes.

The connection between the Uday-Vajracharya dispute and the rise of the Theravada is made particularly clear in the monk Dhammalok's autobiographical *A Pilgrimage in China* (Dharmaloka 1999). Dhammalok was born as Das Ratna Tuladhar in 1890. He was much affected by the death of his wife, which occurred while he was away trading in Lhasa. After returning home in 1925, he and his son began teaching Tibetan Buddhism in Kindo Baha, the same small Newar monastery near Swayambhu where Kyangtse Lama had also taught. His son later left for ordination in Sri Lanka, where he became the monk Aniruddha. (At the time of his death in 2003, Aniruddha was the Sangha Nayaka, the most senior member of the Nepalese Sangha.) Dhammalok visited Aniruddha in Sri Lanka, returning with a monk's robe, which he and his followers placed on an altar and treated as an object of reverence. He continued his teaching and was reported to the Rana authorities in

1931 by another Uday for propagating an unorthodox religion (*ādambar mat*).[27] Dhammalok, along with eleven other Udays, including Dhama Sahu, and the poets Jogbir Singh (Kansakar) and Chittadhar Hridaya (Tuladhar), were punished by the Ranas with fines and short periods of imprisonment. Following his release, Dhammalok went to Kushinagara and was ordained as a monk by Chandramani in 1933 (Dharmalok 1999: 13–15, 123).

Trailblazer: Mahapragya, Buddhist Monk

Central to the survival of the early Theravada mission were a handful of charismatic individuals who combined imagination, determination, and extraordinary energy with an unusual ability to communicate their convictions and beliefs. Dhammalok was one such figure. Another was a monk named Mahapragya. Born Prem Bahadur Shrestha, in his youth he was known to everyone as "Nani Kaji."[28] Mahapragya's parents had moved from Bhaktapur to Kathmandu after a family quarrel, and at the time he was born they were lodging in the house of a Vajracharya. When his father became the caretaker of a Hindu temple, the family moved there.[29] Although the young Nani Kaji learned tailoring, his passion was music, and from boyhood on he composed and participated in religious entertainments of many sorts. His adolescence seems to have been especially turbulent. He married early, but for reasons that are unclear, his parents sent his bride back to her home. Later on he fell in love with a lower-caste woman whom he brought to live with him; given commensality rules however, he could not eat the rice that she cooked and so he asked her to bring him a second wife (presumably his caste equal) to cook for him. Not surprisingly this led to quarrels. Meanwhile, he had begun to show a preference for the company of ascetics and adopted vegetarianism. His parents, despairing that he would never secure work or earn a living, suggested that he travel, whereupon he spent some time in the eastern part of the country. On his return, a friend lent him Nisthananda's Nepal Bhasha version of the *Lalitavistara*, the life of the Buddha, the idea being that he should draw on it for the composition of Buddhist hymns. After studying it intensively, he composed a number of hymns (in Hindi), which soon became popular. In 1925, he attended Kyangtse Lama's religious discourses in Kindo Baha and was so impressed that when Kyangtse Lama was about to leave for Tibet, Nani Kaji asked to accompany him.[30] But the Lama refused his request, saying that he could practice the dharma just as well in Nepal as a householder as in Tibet as a monk.

> Although the lama had gone [Mahapragya wrote, many years later] my mind did not leave off the idea of renunciation. My mind would not be quiet. Like a leaf on a tree it was constantly moving. Even if I was at home in body, my mind was not at home, but was wandering from hill to hill. My mind was filled to overflowing with the hymns of detachment. I sang those songs with my mouth as well. If I stayed at home the words of Grihalakshmi [i.e., his wife] were like being shot by an arrow. If I went to my parents' house, they too would be angry with me, because I had had no work and had nothing to eat. They would tremble with rage like a demoness about to devour me, and with angry tears their words would beat down on my head as hard as stones. If I went out to the neighborhood, the neighbors would tease me in all sorts of ways for my interest in dharma; they would use bad words and make fun of me by hitting tin boxes as if they were playing a musical instrument. . . . It was as if I was being confirmed in my desire to renounce the world. It was as if the world itself had grabbed me by the throat and thrown me out. . . . The more I read the *Lalitavistara* by Nisthananda Vajracharya the more agitated I became with mental renunciation. My feelings were such that it was like sinking myself in a pool of the *Lalitavistara* to cool the burning of renunciation. (Mahapragya 1983: 12–13)

Nani Kaji asked Kushyo Rinpoche, whom he had met at Dhama Sahu's house, to take him to Tibet, but he too refused the young man's request. Nani Kaji followed him nonetheless and soon caught up with him. On the path he ran into two other Newars, Harsha Dev Shakya of Uku Bahah, Lalitpur, and Kancha Shakya of Punche Galli, Kathmandu, who spoke Tibetan. All three Newars were ordained as Nyingmapa novices in Phakpa Gompa, Kyirong. Soon afterward, two of the three—Nani Kaji whose ordination name was Mahapragya and Kancha (now Mahachandra)—returned to the Kathmandu Valley. There they went to live on Nagarjun hill with a recently arrived Tibetan Nyingma lama named Tsering Norbu, originally from near Simla in India, who had studied in the monastery of the Shakyashri Lama. They were joined on Nagarjun Hill by three of Mahapragya's friends: Dalchini Manandhar (who had originally lent him the *Lalitavistara*), Bekha Raj Shakya from Lalitpur, and Gyan Shakya from Hyumata in Kathmandu. All three were ordained and given monastic names on the model of Mahapragya and Mahachandra: Mahavirya, Mahagyana, and Mahakshanti respectively. The five Newar monks were supported by lay Buddhists from Kathmandu, to whom they went on alms-begging expeditions, and they spent the rest of their time translating and propagating their guru's teachings. Writing over two decades later, the poet Hridaya recalled, "When the people of Nepal saw bhikshus wearing the forgotten ochre robe, for some, their eyes filled with tears, others praised them as real Buddhas" (Hridaya 1950: 235).

The Rana government objected to the novices going for alms, which they regarded as a violation of the commensality rules in the same way as accepting food from a Tibetan, and on several occasions ordered Tsering Norbu to stop the practice. In 1926, the Vajracharyas of Kathmandu who were attempting to assert their caste superiority to the Uday brought to the government's attention the fact that Mahapragya, a Shrestha and therefore presumed to be a Hindu by birth, had converted to Buddhism. The Ranas expelled all five novices as well as Tsering Norbu, who had initiated them, to India. Tsering Norbu took his disciples to Bodh Gaya and they were impressed by the Burmese monk whom they met there. In his autobiography, Mahapragya claims that not only he and his novice companions but also their guru Tsering Norbu took *pabbajja*, donned the ochre robe (*kasaya vastra*), and stayed two weeks in Bodh Gaya learning the precepts and the rules of Theravada novicehood. When they found fasting after noon hard, their Burmese preceptor gave them some medicine and sherbet with sugar (Mahapragya 1983: 41). From Bodh Gaya they traveled on to Calcutta, where they encountered the Maha Bodhi Society and Dharmaditya Dharmacharyya, who organized publicity to protest the monks' expulsion from Nepal.[31] Despite these influences, Mahapragya still considered himself Tsering Norbu's disciple and, when his teacher invited to him to Tibet to learn Buddhism so that he could preach in Nepal, he agreed to go (Mahapragya 1983: 48).

In Lhasa, Mahapragya ordained as a monk and, because the teachings he gave on the Lam Rim Path were considered so effective, he received authorization to ordain novices himself. But instead of remaining in Lhasa and pursuing further studies, he wandered about central Tibet as a mendicant. As a result of the altitude, the harsh climate, and a steady diet of tsampa, he became very sick and, returning to Lhasa, was treated by an Uday healer (*jharphuke baidya*) named Kul Man Singh Tuladhar, who restored him to health. Mahapragya convinced Kul Man Singh to renounce lay life and to leave his Tibetan wife and child.[32] Kul Man Singh took monastic vows and a new name, Karmasheel, and joined Mahapragya in his quest. After spending eleven months meditating in a cave near Shigatse, the two men, frustrated

The five expelled monks and their preceptor Tsering Norbu in a 1926 photograph that Dharmacharyya used to publish their plight and appeal to the Ranas to let them back in the country. This comes from the April 1927 issue of *Buddhist India*, opposite page 259, and the caption identifies them as "The six Buddhist Monks who were expelled from Nepal. From the left:—(1) Rev. Mahaviryya. (2) Mahachandra. (3) Rev. Tshering Nurbu (of Simla). (4) Rev. Mahapragya (Vaishya Convert). (5) Rev. Mahakhanti. (6) Rev. Mahagnana." (Courtesy British Library)

---

with their practice, abandoned it and set out on pilgrimage to India. For two years Mahapragya had been mulling over what he had learned about Theravada Buddhism in Bodh Gaya and Calcutta, and now he was eager to learn more. Arriving in Kushinagara, he and Karmasheel submitted themselves to Chandramani's tutelage and received ordination as Theravada novices. As noted in Chapter 1, the Ven. Chandramani was a Burmese monk who spent most of his life in Kushinagara where he ordained the majority of the early members of the Nepalese Sangha as novices.[33] He also ordained D.P.E. Lingwood in 1949 (Lingwood, who would later become well known as the monk Sangharakshita, eventually returned to the United Kingdom, where he founded the Western Buddhist Order in the 1960s) and Dr Ambedkar, the Indian Untouchable leader, in 1956.

Karmasheel/Pragyananda's biography describes his conversion to Theravada Buddhism as a combination of two factors: first, an overwhelming emotional experience in front of the recumbent statue of Lord Buddha in final and full nirvana and, second, the encounter with Chandramani. (When he took higher ordination in Burma, Karmasheel became Pragyananda.) Chandramani taught him a few words of Pali, which he found easy as he had studied some Sanskrit as a boy, and persuaded him that it would be easier for Nepalis to learn Buddhism in Pali, the Lord Buddha's own language, than in Tibetan (Bandya 1975: 60). By the time this story was retold after Pragyananda's death in 1993, it was the straightforward attraction of "the pure teaching of the Buddha (*suddha buddhasasana*)" as expounded by Chandramani that persuaded Karmasheel to give up being a Tibetan monk and take Theravadin ordination (Bandya 1995: 6).

In 1930, Karmasheel/Pragyananda returned to Nepal, leaving at the border Mahapragya, who, having once been expelled, would have been denied permission to enter. Pragyananda is therefore celebrated as the first ochre-robed "pure Buddhist monk" to walk the streets of Kathmandu since the time of Jaya Sthiti Malla in the late fourteenth century (Bandya 1995: 7).[34] Shortly afterward, Mahapragya, disguised as a woman, slipped through the police post at Thankot on the edge of the Kathmandu Valley and went on to Kathmandu (Mahapragya 1983: 80–83). These two were the first Theravada monastics to appear in Nepal; however, a year later they decided to take higher ordination and, because the ritual's required a quorum of ten monks would be difficult to assemble in India, in 1931 they set off for Burma, where they both received full ordination (*upasampada*).

The Nepali Nuns

In 1931, three Newar widows, all Uday, walked down from Kathmandu to Kushinagar where they asked Chandramani to ordain them as Buddhist nuns. They had been inspired to renounce the year before when they had participated in a performance in Kindo Baha of the *astami vrata*, the traditional Newar Buddhist fasting ritual, which incorporates the basic precepts of lay Buddhism. Dhammalok (who was still a householder at that time) organized the event and he had asked Pragyananda to administer the Eight Precepts (D. R. Shakya 1999: 83). Given that the Theravada nuns' ordination lineage had died out in the eleventh century, Chandramani was unable to administer the higher ordination rite of *bhikkhuni upasampada* or even *samanerika pabbajja*, the rite of novice ordination, to the three women. All he could give them was the Ten Precepts (*dasa sila*) of the ordained laywoman. He deemed the three *anāgārikā*, the female form of the Sanskrit word meaning "homeless one," a term he borrowed from Anagarika Dharmapala. They were the equivalent of Burmese *thilashin*, Sri Lankan *dasa sil mata*, and Thai *maechi*. They changed their saris for the pink and orange dress worn by Burmese ordained laywomen and were given the ordination names of Dhammapali, Sanghapali, and Ratnapali. Although there is inscriptional record of the existence of Buddhist nuns in the Kathmandu Valley from the fifth through the eleventh century, the likelihood is that they belonged either to the Mulasarvastivada or to the Mahasanghika schools.[35] There is no evidence that there had ever been Theravada nuns in the Kathmandu Valley before 1931.

Marginal as the monks' situation was, that of the nuns was even more so. As women, they were socially and legally inferior to men, and as nuns they were regarded as lesser "fields of merit" and were therefore less able than monks to attract donations (*dana*), the principal means by which the laity earned spiritual merit (*punya*) leading to a good rebirth. On their return to Kathmandu, the first three anagarikas (or *gurumas*, meaning "mother-teacher," as the wives of Vajracharyas were traditionally addressed), lacking any alternative, settled in Kindo Baha, which, at Dharmaditya Dharmacharyya's suggestion, Dhama Sahu had renovated as a center for Theravadins.[36] The monastery housed an eclectic collection of Tibetan lamas and Theravada monks, or *bhantes*, as the people called them, together with a Vajrayana Tantric named Dharma Guruju and his two *sakti* consorts. There they were joined by other women, widows and abandoned wives, who, like themselves, had taken refuge in the Order from the *duhkha* (suffering) of social marginality. Not only did the women suffer harassment from the government, but also persistent interference from the monks who, as elsewhere in South Asia, expected them to act as cooks and laundresses and tried to restrict their teaching activities in the lay community.

Dhammapali, Ratnapali, and Sanghapali belonged to a group of Uday women who had heard Kyangtse Lama preach at Kindo Baha and, on his departure for Tibet, had started meeting together in order to study Buddhist books under the tutelage of a widow named Laxmi Nani Tuladhar. Learning of their activities, Prime Minister Chandra Shamsher Rana summoned them to his palace and told them that their behavior ill-befitted females. According to Hindu tradition, religious texts were for male eyes only, he declared, and ordered them to return to their houses and take care of their families (M. B. Shakya n.d.). But they continued to study in secret.

The leader of the group, Laxmi Nani, had been married at age twelve in 1910, but, after the death of her husband and children, had turned, in her early twenties, to the Tibetan monks for solace. One of very few literate women of her generation, she read whatever Buddhist books in Nepal Bhasha, Nepali, and Hindi she could lay her hands on.[37] She began to teach her friends what she had learned and soon gathered a group of female students around her. When Mahapragya and Karmasheel appeared in Kathmandu in 1930, the women went to hear them preach; however, when three of them went down to India to take the precepts, Laxmi Nani held back. Only in the aftermath of the great earthquake of 1934, when she enraged her in-laws by distributing the contents of their shop to starving townspeople, did she resolve to leave lay life. Taking five friends with her, she made her way to Kushinagara only to be told by Chandramani that in his view they were not ready for ordination. He sent them on to a nunnery in Arakan, Burma, so that they could have firsthand experience of the renouncer's life before committing themselves to it. After some months all six were pronounced "ready," whereupon they took the precepts and new dharma names. Laxmi Nani became Dharmachari.

As ordained laywomen, not bhikkhunis, they were excluded from the Nepalese Sangha. Nevertheless, on their return to Kathmandu, having nowhere else to go, they joined the other three gurumas in Kindo Baha. Despite having to contend with government suspicion as well as the determination of the monks to keep the nuns subordinated, Dharmachari continued to study whatever Buddhist books she could find and to transmit what she gleaned to her companions. Meanwhile, she gave instruction to laypeople, and to women in particular, on core Buddhist beliefs and practices.

Exile and Return

By the 1940s serious opposition to the Ranas had mobilized, provoking a major crackdown on political "subversives." In 1941, four "martyrs" were hanged in public for organizing a political party, the Praja Parishad. It was a time of fear and underground opposition throughout Nepal, but especially in the Kathmandu Valley.[38] The Theravadins were the objects of suspicion as well. In 1944, after police had stopped Dhammalok from giving the precepts to a female recruit, on the grounds that a woman who renounced lay life was undermining the institution of the family, eight monks and novices in Kathmandu and Lalitpur were ordered to sign an undertaking that they would desist from teaching, performing ordination, or worship. When they refused to comply, Prime Minister Juddha Shamsher exiled them to India where they joined other Nepali emigrés at Sarnath.[39] Four months later, there was a move to expel the nuns as well, but the nuns organized a petition to the government and were allowed to stay. Four of them—Dharmachari, Virati, Arati, and Vimukha—decided it would be a good time to go to Trishuli, a market town a day's journey north and west of Kathmandu, and stay with Virati's maternal uncle. Situated on the path to Kyirong in Tibet, as well as on the main path westward to Pokhara and on to Muktinath, Trishuli had a prosperous Newar trading community. The nuns performed Buddha puja, received *dana*, and taught the dharma to those who came to them. When the Ranas heard about this they arrested them but released them two days later (D. R. Shakya 1999: 85). In the western part of the country, both Bhikshu Shakyananda (in Tansen) and Anagarika Dharmashila, a Tamrakar woman from a well-to-do family (in Pokhara), successfully evaded detection by the Rana authorities and continued their activities throughout this period; in fact, Anagarika Dharmashila's vihara in Pokhara became a meeting place for political opponents of the regime.[40]

In India, meanwhile, in November 1944 the exiled monks founded, the Dharmodaya Sabha, the Buddhist Society of Nepal. Chandramani was president (a position he held until his death at age 96 in 1972); Bhikshu Amritananda, a Shakya from Tansen in the middle hills, was secretary; and Maniharsha Jyoti, a wealthy trader who would later become the leading industrialist of Nepal, was treasurer.[41] The Burmese monks who were based in Varanasi as well as different branches of the Maha Bodhi Society wrote letters protesting the monks' exile to the Rana government; in its replies the government reiterated that

> Hinduism based on Sanatana Dharma is the religion of the country; Rules and laws that conversion from the established Hindu Sanatana Dharma to any other Dharma is not tolerated and is disallowed by the law of the country [sic]. To seduce minors and women and to convert them to the Buddha Dharma is a penal offence. The monks that you refer to were found guilty of this offence.[42]

Two years later, Amritananda persuaded the prominent Sinhalese monk, Narada Mahathera of Vajirarayama Vihara in Colombo, with

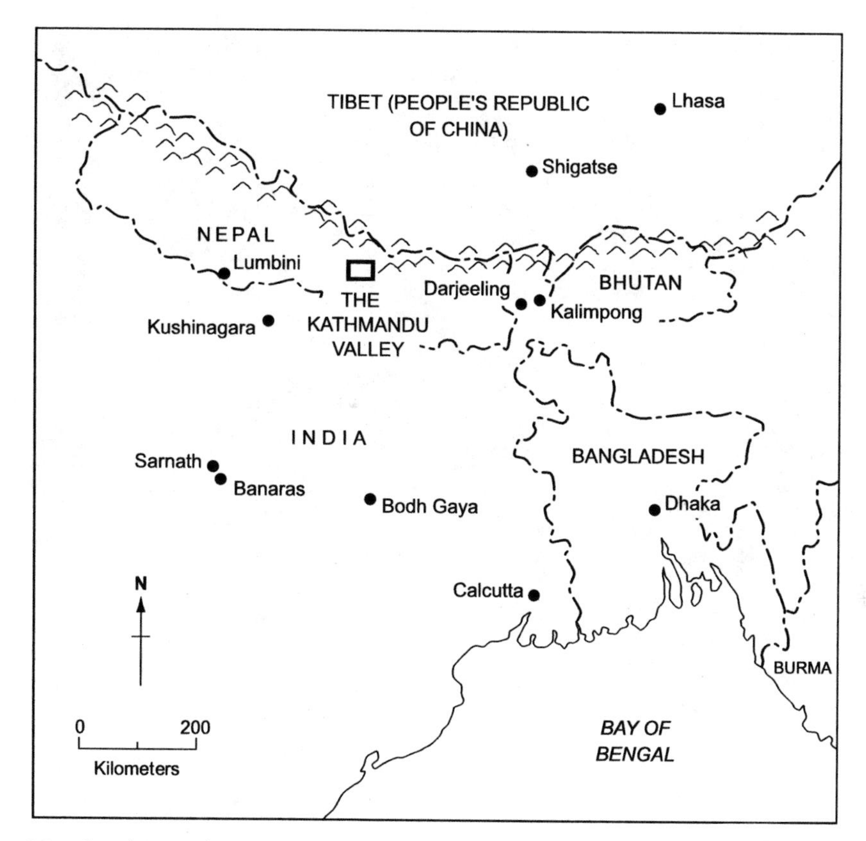

Nepal and its wider region

whom he had studied, to request permission to come to Nepal for pilgrimage and research. Once there, Narada assured the Rana government that the Theravadins' aims were purely religious. Padma Shamsher, the new prime minister, was (compared to other Ranas) a liberal. He was seeking allies in the changed political situation in South Asia following the end of World War II and imminent Indian independence, so he permitted the Theravada monks to return to Kathmandu.

New Directions

Exile proved a turning point for the monastics. Already in 1943, Pragyananda had shifted from Kindo Baha to Lalitpur, taking up residence

Buddhist monks in exile in Kalimpong in 1944 at the house of Bhaju Ratna. Bhaju Ratna is seated in a white cap at the front. Also seated, wearing glasses is Mahabir Kansakar, and behind him on a chair, Bhikshu Amritananda. The two monks standing at the center are Pragyananda and Mahapragya (Mahapragya in the darker robes). A young Gyan Jyoti is the figure on the left looking out of the window. (Courtesy of Gyan Jyoti)

in Sumangal Vihara, a traditional lineage *baha* and a branch of Uku Baha, whose owners had donated it to the monks. The exiled monks returned to their old quarters at Kindo Baha which, when new recruits began to trickle in, soon became cramped. They had their devotees expand a cottage known as Ananda Kuti in the woods on the northwestern slope of Swayambhu, which Dhammalok had constructed some years before as a rainy season retreat (Dharmalok 1999: 89–90). As soon as the new vihara was habitable in early 1947, the Kindo monks moved in. Within months Narada Mahathera visited from Sri Lanka bringing with him a Buddha relic to be enshrined in the new Lanka Chaitya and a seedling Mahabodhi tree from Anuradhapura.[43] With these symbols of "authentic" Buddhism and international recognition in place, Ananda Kuti was recognized as the new headquarters of the Theravada mission in Nepal and Amritananda as its head, a position he would hold for forty years.

Bhaju Ratna carrying a sapling of the Bodhi tree on his head to Ananda Kuti in April 1947. Amritananda is behind him to the right, and Dhammalok to the left. (Courtesy of Gyan Jyoti)

Group photo in Ananda Kuti after the establishment of the Lanka Chaitya, with its Buddha relic from Sri Lanka, and the planting of the Bodhi sapling. (Courtesy of Gyan Jyoti)

Narada returned to Nepal a year later in June 1948, and in his speech at Ananda Kuti, while tactfully expressing the hope that Buddhism and Hinduism would continue to exist in harmony in Nepal, he also articulated modernist Buddhists' hopes for the land of the Buddha's birth. In the words of an anonymous reporter for the *Maha-Bodhi:* "The audience was tense with hushed emotion when Narada Thera said, 'Let not Nepal be venerated merely as the land of the Buddha's birth but also as the repository of His Sublime Teachings in their pristine purity.' He also advised them to follow the rational and clear path of the historic Sakyamuni Buddha in preference to the mystical and complicated paths of mythological Buddhas" (Narada 1948: 266).

Meanwhile, the nuns, having had a taste of freedom in Trishuli, also decided that they had to have new quarters. They were tired of lay gossip—wild rumors circulated, for instance, that Dharmachari herself had given birth to a baby fathered by a monk!—as well as constant interference by the monks with their activities. With personal funds, Dharmachari purchased some land a short distance from Kindo Baha and with donations from her devotees built a nunnery, the first in Nepal. Because its puja hall housed a great statue of the Buddha at his *parinirvana*, a source of wonder throughout the Valley, the new nunnery was called Nirvana-murti Upasikarama. Colloquially, it came to be known as Kindol Vihara. A few years later she added a guest house for women from outside the city and soon Kindol, as a haven and a center of devotion and learning, was drawing Buddhist women from all over the Kathmandu Valley and beyond.

Exile proved a turning point for Mahapragya also. Between his ordination and the outbreak of war, he had traveled back and forth between Nepal and Burma, where he spent long stretches meditating in the jungle; World War II found him in Bhojpur and the Tarai and, latterly, in exile in north India. While waiting in Kalimpong to be readmitted to Nepal in 1945, he disrobed in order to marry the widow in whose house he was lodging and by whom he fathered two children. (In his autobiography, he claimed that she had put an enchanted substance in his food [Mahapragya 1983: 283].) For many years, he earned his living as a photographer but continued to teach Buddhism in the Newar community of Kalimpong and to publish articles on Buddhism in *Dharmodaya* under the name M. P. Pradhan. Regretting his "fall into householdership," he made several attempts to return to monastic life, only to be pursued and brought back to Kalimpong by his wife.

When he finally broke with her in 1962, he stayed first in Sumangal Vihara, Lalitpur, then at Gana Vihara, Kathmandu, before settling in a *kuti* (now known as Dharmachakra Vihara) that his devotees built for him in Bag Bazaar, Kathmandu, in the bustling new city center. There he was supported, among others, by Bhikshu Subodhanand who, in 1963, published a verse rendition of the Buddha's life that Mahapragya had composed (R. S. Shakya 1993: 42).

Mahapragya called himself a Buddhist sage (*bauddha rishi*) rather than *bhikkhu* and wore a long beard and maroon Tibetan monk's dress. As a "defeated one" (*pārājika*) he could not be readmitted to the Sangha, and so had to sit separately from the monks when he was invited with them for *bhojan*. Some monks disapproved of his use of magical powers (*riddhi*) generated in meditation for healing purposes, but others (notably Pragyananda) occasionally did the same themselves. Mahapragya was still a dynamic preacher, teacher, and composer of devotional songs and continued to attract many devotees. His seventieth birthday was celebrated in May 1970 as the official opening of Dharmachakra Ashram/Vihara, with speeches and plaudits from the luminaries of the Nepal Bhasha literary world (R. S. Shakya 1993: 43). He was paralyzed in 1971; two years later he moved to a new vihara in Anamnagar, which was registered in the name of his devotee, Chaitya Maya. He died in 1979.

Planning for the Future

Even after their return from exile in 1946, the Theravadins continued to be kept under close government surveillance. They found that outside the city they were undisturbed, however, and thus in the final years of Rana rule they focused their efforts on urban centers in the Tarai and in the western hills, wherever there was a sizeable Newar population. Pragyananda spent much time in the largely Maharjan village of Balambu, a few miles northwest of Kathmandu, which has ever after remained a bastion of Theravada Buddhism and the source of a surprisingly large number of recruits to the Order.

The English monk Sangharakshita, who shortly after he received *pabbajja* in Kushinagara in 1949 was sent by his preceptor Chandramani to teach in Nepal, reported in his memoirs that he and his companion, an Indian monk named Buddharakshita, were greeted with delight by the Newar Buddhist community in the Tarai town of Butwol. As the small rusty-roofed vihara had no resident monk, the local people were eager to take the Triple Refuge and Five Precepts from the foreigners. From Butwol, the two monks continued to the hill town of Tansen, which happily did have a resident monk, Bhikkhu Shakyananda, who had relocated from Pokhara to Tansen and, like themselves, had been ordained by Chandramani.[44] Shakyananda, who lived in Ananda Vihara in the lower part of the town, welcomed them warmly and later that same day sent them on to the upper part of the town where a second monastery, Maha Chaitya Vihara, was located. Like Ananda Vihara, Maha Chaitya Vihara consisted of only a narrow oblong building that contained an altar at one end and at the opposite end, two cupboards. It differed from Ananda Vihara however in one respect:

> Outside, in the middle courtyard, stood a chaitya or stupa, seven or eight feet in height. This whitewashed monument with the brass finial, after which the Vihara was named, was not the modern Theravadin type, as might have been expected, but a genuine product of traditional Nepalese Buddhism. From the image-table inside the Vihara, the Ceylon- and Burma-trained revivalists had banished all the Buddhas except the historical Shakyamuni, to say nothing of all the Bodhisattvas; but outside, from their niches in the four sides of the chaitya, the transcendental Buddhas, Amoghasiddhi or "Unobstructed Success," Ratnasambhava "the Jewel-Born One," Akshobya or "the Imperturbable," and Amitabha "the Infinite Light" still looked out upon the four quarters of space—Vairochana, the Buddha of the centre, being hidden within the body of the monument. (Sangharakshita 1997: 418–419)

Sangharakshita noted that because there was no resident monk in the upper vihara, it had been entrusted to Anagarika Sushila, "a tiny, intense woman," who, together with another nun, ran a girls' school. During the course of his visit, Sangharakshita got to know Sushila quite well and came to appreciate her humor and feistiness. When Sangharakshita's Indian monk companion, Buddharakshita, pointed out to her that, in speaking Hindi, she forgot to inflect her verbs so that she referred to herself as if she were a man, she retorted that since she was a nun, and was supposed to have discarded worldly conventions, she didn't think it mattered much whether she spoke like a man or a woman.[45]

On their return from exile in India, the senior members of the Sangha were also planning for a future which, as the regime's hold on the country gradually slackened, seemed near at hand. In the winter of 1950–51, they listed their objectives in the Dharmodaya Sabha journal which, due to government censorship, was still being published in Kalimpong. Most were adopted from the Maha Bodhi Society's program:

1. To open Buddhist schools all over Nepal;
2. To build a vihāra in every town or village where the majority of the people were Buddhist, and to have one or two monks live there to provide religious instruction and free medical services;
3. To publish translations of Canonical texts as well as other books on Buddhism in Nepali and Newari [Nepal Bhasha];
4. To educate Nepalese to propagate Buddhism;
5. To publish two journals, one in English and one in Nepali;
6. To persuade the Nepalese authorities to take the necessary steps to preserve the ancient Buddhist monuments (Lumbini, Kapilavastu);
7. To encourage Buddhists of other countries to visit Nepal and offer facilities to Buddhist scholars;
8. To guard against institutions active in converting people to other faiths (mainly meant against Christian missionaries). For the realization of this programme they asked the assistance of other Buddhist nations, especially in providing scholarships to Nepalese students and in giving moral and material support.[46]

How the monks and their supporters attempted to put this program into action in the new freer environment after 1951 is the subject of the next chapter.

 CHAPTER THREE

Creating a Tradition

As soon as they were permitted to work openly, the Theravadins established the All-Nepal Bhikshu Mahasangha with Amritananda as president and set about making their blueprint a reality. They faced many obstacles, not least their small number: in 1951, there were less than two dozen monks and novices and thirty nuns. Most of the Nepali monks had spent more time abroad, either in Maha Bodhi monasteries in India, or in Burma and Sri Lanka, where they received some religious training before taking full ordination, than they had in Nepal. Although they all followed the Theravada Vinaya, they belonged to different ordination lineages and traditions. Their ideas about dress, diet, and the alms round varied, and most, on returning to Nepal, were loath to depart from the practices in which they had been trained.

Amritananda tried, as president of the Bhikshu Mahasangha, to impose uniformity on the community, but he often failed, and mechanisms for resolving disputes were lacking. Some monks wished to be free of Amritananda's day-to-day control, and so, when offered abandoned and often dilapidated Vajrayana monasteries in Bhaktapur as well as Kathmandu and Lalitpur—sometimes these had been used as toilets by local people—they accepted them and organized their devotees to rebuild them. Whether renovated monasteries or new foundations, the new viharas were very simple to begin with, becoming more elaborate over time as funds permitted.[1] Ultimately they would consist of a dharma hall and Buddha shrine, sleeping quarters, and a kitchen arranged around a courtyard in the center of which there would often

Table 3.1 Some differences between monastic observances in Theravada countries

1. *Dress:* monastic robes are orange in Sri Lanka, brown in Burma (and ochre in Thailand—however, in the early period there was little Thai influence in Nepal).
2. *Diet:* according to the Vinaya, monastics should accept whatever they are given by the laity, including meat, on the grounds that since the animal has not been slaughtered on their orders they are not guilty of killing a sentient being. Vegetarianism is not normative for Sinhala Buddhists; however some do practice it while others eat most meat and fish but do not accept beef, the cheapest meat available. Newar Buddhists eat all meat except pork, chicken, and beef (the slaughter of cattle is prohibited by the Hindu state); buffalo meat is considered a special delicacy and the laity tend to offer it to the monks. (In Thailand, the laity offer all kinds of meat to the monks.)
3. *Alms round:* In Burma and Thailand all except the old and sick or the very busy go for alms daily. In Sri Lanka, a caste society, the laity bring food to the monastery and prepare it *in situ*.

be a traditional Vajrayanist *chaitya*. Only two Valley monasteries—Ananda Kuti, headed by Amritananda, and Sumangal Vihara in Lalitpur, initially headed by Pragyananda[2]—had *uposatha* halls for bimonthly recitations of the Patimokkha rules. In sharp contrast with traditional temples, the early viharas were noticeably bare of ornamentation, housing just an image of Shakyamuni Buddha and featuring a few colored illustrations of his main life events tacked up on the walls.[3]

Lack of state support was the Sangha's most pressing problem. In Thailand and Burma, Buddhism is the state religion. In Sri Lanka also Buddhism had been a kind of state religion, until it was disestablished by the British in the nineteenth century. Although it languished during the colonial period, in the early decades of the twentieth century, Buddhism, especially in its modernist form, received the endorsement of the Sri Lankan nationalist movement. The constitution that Sri Lanka adopted after independence in 1947 afforded Buddhism a privileged position. Initially, the Nepali Theravadins had reason to hope that they too might receive government backing.

Amritananda, who had spent most of his exile in Colombo where he had first gone as a novice to study in 1937, had initiated and participated in the negotiations between Narada Mahathera and the Rana government for the readmission of the Theravadin exiles to Nepal.

Confident that during the Rana period he had established a good relationship with King Tribhuvan, Amritananda lost no time after the reestablishment of the monarchy in approaching His Majesty, who appeared receptive to Buddhism as an alternative to the brahmanical orthodoxy of the Ranas, his erstwhile regent-jailers. Within months of the restoration, the king had attended Buddha Jayanti at Ananda Kuti, received a protective thread from the monks, and declared Budda Jayanti, the full moon of the month of Baisakh when Theravadins celebrate the birth, enlightenment, and full nirvana of the Buddha, a national holiday for all Nepalis.[4] Shortly afterward, the Nepalese Sangha borrowed relics of Shariputra and Maudgalyayana, two of the Buddha's closest disciples, from the Maha Bodhi Society headquarters in Calcutta where they were temporarily located.[5] During the fortnight that the relics were in Kathmandu they were presented to King Tribhuvan in the Narayan Hiti palace; in return, His Majesty, as a Buddhist upasaka, gave *dana* to the monks. In 1952, the king and Crown Prince Mahendra again attended Buddha Jayanti in Ananda Kuti Vihara. The following year, 1953, to mark his own birthday, King Tribhuvan invited Amritananda and a delegation of monks to his palace where they performed the nightlong protective ritual of *mahaparitrana* in which sutras were chanted by successive teams of monks.[6] At its conclusion, the king gave *dana* to the monks and provided them and their lay devotees with a feast. In 1954, the recitation was shifted to Ananda Kuti where it has been performed each year ever since on the birthday of the reigning king.

In 1956, the year marking the two thousand five hundredth year since the Buddha's *parinirvana* according to the most widely accepted chronology, Nepal hosted the Fourth World Fellowship of Buddhists Conference, the first international conference ever held in Nepal. King Tribhuvan had died the previous year. His son, King Mahendra, was less inclined toward Buddhism than his father had been; nonetheless he agreed to have animal sacrifice banned throughout the kingdom on the day of Buddha Jayanti, thus effectively giving Buddhism a place second only to Hinduism in Nepal.[7] King Mahendra opened the conference in Singha Darbar Hall in Kathmandu on November 14, 1956, with delegates from over forty countries. Ever since the fall of the Rana regime, which had been so strongly associated with Hinduism, Newar Buddhists had formed high hopes for the advancement of their religion. Recalling his visit to Nepal accompanying the relics of Maudgalyayana and Shariputra in 1951 five years earlier, the English Bhikshu San-

The visit of the relics of Shariputra and Maudgalyayana to Kathmandu in 1951. Bhaju Ratna accompanies them on an elephant through the city. (Courtesy of Gyan Jyoti)

gharakshita wrote: "More than once, as I sat listening to the numerous and lengthy speeches which were delivered at the various functions in honour of the Sacred Relics, I heard pronouncements which might have led one to suppose that a revival of Buddhism was, if not actually sweeping like fire from one end of Nepal to the other, at least about to do so at any moment."[8]

The millennial mood was revived by the 1956 celebrations, and it was reinforced by the modernists' strong belief that, of all Asian religions, Buddhism was uniquely suited to modern times. A contributing factor to these millennial expectations may have been the arrival at the conference of Bhimrao Ambedkar, just one month after he had led half a million of his Untouchable followers into Buddhism in Nagpur, India, with the Five Precepts being administered by the Ven. Chandramani (R. S. Shakya 1992a: 2). The whole world seemed poised at the threshold of a new era of democracy and modernization for which Buddhism, so Buddhists believed, was the ideal religion. Such millennial expectations were also shared by Buddhists in Sri Lanka.[9]

Buddhist activists' hopes for a rapid expansion of Buddhism, and for governmental support, were to be disappointed. King Mahendra, unlike his father, had no special relationship with Amritananda. The prospect of significant state backing for the Theravada movement began to fade away. In the era of "Panchayat democracy," which began in 1959 with the dismissal of the elected Prime Minister B. P. Koirala and the banning of political parties, the regime looked to Hinduism for its main legitimation. Buddhism was tolerated and encouraged only as a subordinate partner in an officially Hindu kingdom. The official position was that Buddhism was a "branch" of Hinduism. The fact that the Buddha was included as the ninth of the canonical list of Vishnu's ten incarnations on earth was much cited to support this interpretation—a view of the Buddha and Buddhism that incensed the more modernist and aggressive of Buddhist activists, and against which they campaigned in the 1970s and 1980s.

If strong support from the state was not forthcoming, what other sources of support were available? Thus far, only a small section of the Newar Buddhist community was willing to provide time and money to the new monks and nuns; but there remained many Newars with a commitment to Buddhism who could be mobilized, and beyond them there were many non-Newar Nepalis who might be open to Theravada Buddhism as an alternative to state-sponsored Hinduism or Tibetan Buddhism.

Building a Community

Nepalese law forbade religious conversion; thus the Theravadins were only authorized to preach to people who were Buddhist by birth.[10] Although, at a stretch, Tamangs and other Janajati peoples who followed the Tibetan tradition might also be approached, the missionaries, Newars themselves, frequently relied on relatives for support and focused their efforts in the early years almost exclusively on Newars, both inside the Kathmandu Valley and outside. They sought to engage them with a combination of new and familiar ideas and symbols. Central to the "new" Buddhism—as to the traditional—were the practices of generosity and living a moral life which, of the traditional list of "ten good deeds" of Theravada Buddhism, are the two most stressed for the laity.[11] Thus, from the outset, the missionaries impressed upon their devotees their economic responsibility for the Sangha on the one hand and the importance of observing the Five Precepts (not to kill, steal, have extramarital sexual relations, lie, or drink alcohol) on the other. Devotees were urged to take them formally for twenty-four-hour periods on full moon days and whenever possible to take three additional precepts (not to eat after noon, not to wear ornaments, and not to attend or participate in entertainments).[12]

The "new" lifestyle—and here it diverged sharply from the "old"—required receiving regular religious instruction. Given the focus of Vajrayana Buddhism on ritual and devotion to Buddhist divinities, many who came to hear the Theravadins preach had never heard of the Four Noble Truths or the Eightfold Path. One layman recalled his shock and repulsion on being taught, as a young man, that life was suffering (*duhkha*): as far as he was concerned, his life thus far had been quite enjoyable! In viharas and in private houses, basing their sermons on *Jataka* stories, the *Dhammapada*, the *Milinda Panha*, and the *Sigalovada Sutta* (known as the "householder's *Vinaya*"), the Theravada missionaries explained Buddhist beliefs and ethics in such a way that largely unschooled audiences could understand and absorb them. They set themselves to translating Burmese, Sinhala, Hindi, and Pali versions of canonical texts, as well as to publishing pamphlets they authored themselves on scores of religious topics. Although the *Dharmodaya* journal, which had appeared monthly from 1947, ceased publication in 1960, it was replaced from 1972 by the much more strictly Buddhist *Ananda Bhoomi*, a monthly magazine that included community news and articles for the edification of Buddhist readers in Nepal Bhasha and Nepali and occasionally in English.[13]

Amritananda was one of a few monks who wrote equally in Nepal Bhasha and Nepali. As he had been born and brought up in Tansen, for him, as for other Newars whose homes were outside the Valley, he had equal fluency in both languages.[14] Other monks wrote more often in Nepal Bhasha less because they saw their movement as being part of the Newar cultural and literary renaissance than because their Nepali was not so fluent. The importance of Buddhism, and specifically Theravada Buddhism, in the burgeoning Nepal Bhasha literary movement, can be seen from the fact that, of 819 books published in Nepal Bhasha up to 1979, 305 (37.25 percent) were on religious subjects; 285 of those were Buddhist, whereas only 20 were Hindu. Of the 285 Buddhist publications, 22 books were by nuns (14 by Dhammawati) and 159 by monks or novices (including 18 by Amritananda, 12 by Dhammalok, 14 by Pragyananda, 24 by Sudarshan, and 12 by Vivekananda).[15]

The production costs of all these publications were covered only to a limited degree by sales. In Nepal, as everywhere in the Buddhist world, religious books were and are venerated as sacred objects, though modern printed texts are treated with somewhat less reverence. In Nepal, unlike China and Tibet, the printing only began in the twentieth century; before then, scriptures and handbooks were always painstakingly copied by hand. Sponsorship of the copying of texts had always been regarded as an important merit-making activity. In a transformation of this tradition, it soon became normative for families to sponsor the publication of Theravadin texts in memory of deceased relatives or to celebrate an important occasion such as a patriarch's birthday.

The Domestication of Theravada Buddhism

As many scholars have observed, the capacity to accommodate to local norms has been one of the underlying strengths of Buddhism, a strength that allowed Buddhism to spread and take root through the diverse cultures of Asia (see e.g., Sharf 1995: 145). Just as Vajrayana Buddhism had once accommodated to the dominant Hindu culture of the Kathmandu Valley and flourished for centuries, so Theravada Buddhism selectively absorbed Vajrayana features. In his study of narratives and rituals of Newar Buddhism, Todd Lewis uses the term "religious domestication" for the process whereby certain features of the north Indian Mahayana textual tradition were selected for adoption in the Kathmandu Valley whereas others were ignored (Lewis 2000a: 3–5). The term might usefully be applied to the reverse process whereby the Theravadins selected certain features of Newar Buddhism in order to make their message locally acceptable. Once it had acquired a distinctly Newar character, people eagerly embraced it because it seemed to point the way to a wider world without requiring a radical break with the familiar. As an alternative to the intensely community-focused, and exclusivist, religion of the *baha*, the Theravadins offered the universalist, open, and internationally linked religion of the *vihara*.

The monks chose carefully where to admit local practice and where to take a stand against it. Upper-caste male members of the lay community were accustomed to being centrally involved in the running of the monastic institutions to which, through patrilineal descent, they belonged. Similarly, they expected to be centrally involved in the new Theravada viharas for which they were providing land and construction costs. Thus, the Theravadins found themselves conceding to the laity a much more prominent role in the administration of their monasteries than was the case elsewhere in the Theravada world. Given rules of commensality followed by all Newars, Hindu and Buddhist alike, many upper-caste laypeople were opposed to the monks' accepting boiled rice, the staple food, as alms from castes lower than their own, and certainly from those below the "water barrier," that is, Khadgis and below (cf. Bechert & Hartmann 1988: 23). Some upper-caste monks were themselves reluctant to accept rice from low-caste households, though Ashwaghosh and Buddhaghosh both insisted on doing so from the beginning.[16] The alms round was even more problematic in a purity-conscious society than going for *bhojan* when invited to a layperson's house. It involved accepting food from numerous different households and having it all mixed up. Nepalis were not used to giving cooked food to mendicants. Thus, although "going for alms" is a prominent feature of monastic life in Burma, once home, Nepali Theravadins, albeit that some had become accustomed to going for alms abroad, in short order abandoned the practice.[17] Instead they promoted other ways by which the laity could earn merit including sponsorship of rituals such as providing meals in the temple following Buddha Puja on lunar holy days, sponsoring *kathina* ceremonies (the presentation of robes to the monks at the conclusion of the rainy season retreat), as well as the publication costs of books, delivery of food supplies directly to the monastery, and going on pilgrimage (in the 1960s monks began to lead pilgrimages to the Buddhist sacred sites of north India and Sri Lanka).[18] People could earn merit in more routine ways too, such as providing flowers and incense for Buddha Puja and feeding monastics in their homes.

The monks initiated campaigns against practices that they identified as Hindu, principally animal sacrifice. In this they were following the lead of Tibetan Buddhist monastics; Kyangtse Lama and his followers had done the same in Kathmandu in the 1920s. Though the monks never preached explicitly against the lifelong performance of *sraddha* rituals to the ancestors, both Vajracharya and Brahman priests blame Theravada influence for the fact that that many Buddhists stopped doing *sraddha* beyond the second year after a death. Mahayana and Vajrayana divinities were not permitted in Theravada monasteries. However, the Theravadins endorsed certain Vajrayana practices such as staging plays based on Buddhist stories and illustrative of Buddhist themes, and they made the month of Gunla (roughly equivalent to August), traditionally a time of intense devotional activity, a period of daily preaching both within the monastery and in public spaces. In fact, the tradition of observing Gunla as a Buddhist holy month was probably descended historically from the observance of *vassavas*, or rains retreat, when monks are supposed to stay in one place and focus on instructing the laity.[19]

The monks encouraged the singing of devotional songs, of the sort that Mahapragya had composed, at public events, a practice that, although a standard component of Newar Buddhist devotionalism, was less common in the Theravada Buddhist world. There was a place for hymn-singing in traditional Newar Buddhism, but the texts were ancient and either in archaic Nepal Bhasha or in "Hindi" (i.e., old dialects from north India); the instruments were also ancient. By contrast, the modern *bhajan* groups made use of the harmonium and tabla; the hymns were in the vernaculars (Grandin 1989: 94). The lyrics, written by Mahapragya, Amritananda, Pragyananda, Subodhananda, Dharmachari, as well as by many laypeople, were published in handbooks that went through numerous reprints. Stimulated by regularly scheduled competitions, these hymn-singing groups proliferated and were soon a prominent feature of Buddhist community life. One did not have to be a regular Theravada supporter to participate; but the hymns were undoubtedly a way to spread the Theravada message: through, for example, the songs' focus on the historical Buddha to the relative exclusion of other divine figures and their frequent invocation of Buddhism as something that needs to be revived and adapted to modern times.[20]

Theravadins As Ritual Specialists

Compared to traditional Newar Buddhism, Theravada Buddhism is indeed "stripped down," more Protestant in flavor; but it is by no means devoid of ritual. The three fundamental practices of the Theravada tradition are (1) Buddha Puja, a rite of devotion to the Three Jewels (*triratna*), that is, the Buddha himself, the Teaching, and the Monastic Community; (2) taking the Five Precepts (*pancasil*), and more elaborately, (3) the protective rite of *paritrana*. In Nepal, Buddha Puja, which replaces the traditional Newar Buddhist rite of *nitya puja*, is performed daily in all viharas. Although it is open to the public, generally only a handful of *upasaka*s attend. By contrast, on lunar holidays (full moon, no moon, and the eighth day of the lunar month), several hundred may be expected at large and popular viharas. As reflective monks are themselves aware, the practice of *paritrana* is the Theravada replacement for Newar Buddhist protective rituals in which the Vajracharya priest chants *mantra*, *dharani*, and other verses and reads or recites sutras such as the *Pancaraksa* in order to invoke the benevolent powers of Buddhas and bodhisattvas (who may themselves be deified versions of mantras) on his patron's behalf.[21] Lay devotees began to invite the Theravada monks to their homes to chant *paritrana* texts in a rite of protection against evil. When a family member celebrated a birthday, for example, the monks would recite the *Mangala Sutta*; when someone in the household died, they would be called to the house to chant the *Marananussati Sutta*, and so forth. Although many laypeople were uneasy about monastics begging for alms in the streets, they felt comfortable feeding them in their homes where they could "control" conditions, that is, ensure that rules of commensality were followed.

The possibility also emerged for the monks to assume certain functions of traditional *purohits*. Instead of calling their Vajracharya priests, some householders began, on occasion, to invite Theravadins to perform life-cycle rituals such as the naming ceremony (*namakarana*), and first rice-eating ceremony (*annaprasana*) (performed at five months for girls and six months for boys). In 1956, Pragyananda offered a "Buddhist" alternative to caste initiation/puberty ritual (*bratabandha/kayta puja*) in which *buddhamargi* boys of non-priestly ("lay") castes have their heads shaved and, dressed as mendicants, "go out into homelessness" before being "caught" by their maternal uncle and returned to householder life. In the Theravadin version, young boys come to the vihara, have their heads shaved, don monks' robes, take the Ten Precepts, and spend a few days studying the *dharma*. A small, but slowly increasing number of parents found this substitute rite, termed *samanera pabbajja*, attractive, for much the same reasons that in Burma boys' initiation rituals are sometimes moved from a vihara to a meditation center (Houtman 1984). For some, it allows them to mark their sons' transition to manhood without spending exorbitant amounts on a feast for hundreds of relatives and friends as expected when the traditional *kayta puja* is performed. For others, it offers a solution to the problem of what ritual to perform for the offspring of a mixed-caste marriage (if the father is a Vajracharya or Shakya and the mother from a lower caste, sons are barred from initiation in their father's *baha* or *bahi*). The Theravadins' *samanera* rite is also attractive to families lacking a mother's brother (*paju*) or those on bad terms with the mother's brother (the maternal uncle plays a crucial, and economically not insignificant, role in the traditional *kayta puja* rite). Finally, at death too, the monks were and are in demand. By the 1960s, some laymen were beginning to call monks from Ananda Kuti Vihara to chant at the banks of the Vishnumati river when a relative of theirs was cremated.

The most common pattern, in regard to rituals both at puberty and at death, rather than a complete boycott of the traditional Vajrayana rituals, was to sponsor both kinds of performance, at different times. In the case of the more serious Theravada supporters, however, the Vajrayana rituals were done in the most minimal fashion possible, kept up as community and family custom, but not seen as involving any profound religious commitment or meaning. The loss of patronage was of course noticed and bitterly resented by practicing Vajracharya priests.

The Recruitment and Training of Novice Monks

The lay community was expanding rapidly, but there were few recruits to the monks' order. It is true that a continuous history of contact with Tibetan lamas meant that the possibility of renunciation in a Buddhist tradition had never entirely disappeared from the Kathmandu Valley. Nonetheless a lifelong vow of celibacy was unacceptable to most Newar males. Even for those who were attracted to it, the systematic

After cutting off the boys' topknots to convert them from householders to monks, Pragyananda Mahasthavir delivers a sermon to the new monks, January 1984, in Manimandap Vihara, Lalitpur. Gyanapurnik stands at right. (David N. Gellner)

religious training by which a raw recruit was turned into a monk was impossible to come by in Nepal. Indeed, until 1964, when Buddhaghosh established Buddhist Saturday schools for the laity and, with his colleagues, began to produce textbooks for them (the *Bauddha Pariyatti Siksa*), formal instruction in *buddha dharma* was unavailable. A young boy joining the Order had no option but to attach himself to a senior monk and learn whatever his guru chose to teach him. But despite these uncertainties, a few poor boys were convinced that monastic life offered a calling and opportunities that were otherwise unobtainable.

At the Fourth World Fellowship of Buddhists Conference, which was held in Kathmandu in November 1956, six months after the celebration of the two thousand five hundreth birthday of the Buddha, much was made of Nepal's role as the birthplace of the Buddha and of Nepali Buddhists' need for outside support. Amritananda began to travel

The new monks receive their first *dana* from their families. (David N. Gellner)

abroad both to the West and to Buddhist countries in order to firm up ties and forge new ones with people and institutions who might provide such support. In 1959, he went to the Soviet Union, China, North Vietnam, and Mongolia and returned convinced that Buddhism was flourishing under communism. He brought back half a million rupees to start a Buddhist high school for the sons of the laity.[22] But little was done to develop the education of novices and they continued to spend most of their time in the Kathmandu Valley cleaning the rooms, cooking the food, washing the clothes, and massaging the limbs of their teachers. They read the vernacular translations that were available, they memorized and learned to chant sutras in Pali, and they waited for arrangements to be made for them to study "outside," usually in the same Burmese or Sri Lankan monastery where their guru had studied.

Gyanapurnik Mahasthavira

Bhikkhu Gyanapurnik, who today is abbot of Vishwa Shanti Vihara, a seminary for novices in Kathmandu, was fairly typical of recruits in the early days. Like Amritananda, but twenty years later in 1939, he was born Hera Lal to poor Shakya parents in Tansen. Gyanapurnik's paternal grandparents had migrated there from Uku Baha in Lalitpur at the beginning of the twentieth century. As a child in the late 1940s, his mother began taking him to the vihara that Theravada missionaries had recently established in their town. Hera Lal had learned to read from an elderly *vaidya* who was fond of children, and, by the age of ten, he was intensely interested in studying further. He started to attend the new vihara school and there encountered a monk named Buddhaghosh, who had just returned from religious studies in Burma, and his chela, a novice named Sudarshan:

> Sudarshan was a few years older than I and he seemed quite grown up. He had a certain air about him which impressed me. Buddhaghosh let it be known that he needed a boy to work for him so my mother sent me to live in the vihara. I didn't really understand what the monks did, I only knew that they earned merit. I decided that I wanted to earn merit too and that the best way to do so was to follow the monks and do as they did.

In between performing domestic chores, Hera Lal began to study *buddha dharma:*

> I learned to chant and I memorized verses. I read Hindi—there were no Tripitaka books in the Nepal Bhasha in those days—and I started to learn Pali in Burmese script because that's how my guru had learned it. And to meditate . . . I learned to recall the qualities of the Buddha which was a meditation practice being taught at that time.

After a few months, Buddhaghosh left Tansen for Sumangal Vihara in Lalitpur, taking Hera Lal and Sudarshan with him. There he taught the *dharma* to laypeople, including a few children—among them the future Dhammawati (see Chapter 4)—until, in the winter of the following year, 1949–50, he decided to return to Burma to resume his studies, which had been interrupted by World War II. Once again, he took both his chelas with him. Hera Lal's parents gladly gave their consent:

> They were so poor, they hadn't the money to educate me themselves, and my mother in particular wanted me to be a monk. . . . She was very devout. . . . Eventually she became a nun and died in the vihara in Tansen.

Guru and chelas set off via Sarnath and Bodh Gaya to Calcutta where, while they tried to obtain passports, they stayed in the headquarters of the Maha Bodhi Society in College Square. But the government official whom they dealt with, convinced that Buddhaghosh had kidnapped eleven-year-old Hera Lal, refused to issue travel documents and after six months they were obliged to give up and go home.

For the next five years, Hera Lal cooked and cleaned for his guru, ran errands for him, and accompanied him when he went into the countryside to teach; and in between times, he learned to read, write, and speak both Pali and Sanskrit. "There were six of us young boys living in Sumangal Vihara and for some time every day we spoke Pali which is quite close to Nepali. After a few years I became quite fluent." As an exercise, his teacher would have him translate parts of Pali texts into Nepal Bhasha, foreshadowing his prodigiously productive career as a translator. With Buddhaghosh's other chelas, he debated doctrinal issues in public on festival days and sometimes as a group they chanted sutras and gave expositions of the dharma on the radio.[23]

It was 1956 by the time Buddhaghosh, Sudarshan, and Hera Lal set out again for Burma. Hera Lal obtained a passport without difficulty, and, after two-day passage from Calcutta, they reached Rangoon where the Sixth Buddhist Council was in session.[24] Hera Lal recalls:

> The Burmese monks were amazed that I could speak Pali—they could read and write that language but they couldn't speak it. They said I must have

a gift for languages, and I suppose that if I have any gift at all, that's what it is.

Within days Hera Lal took ordination as a novice and a new name, Gyanapurnik ("full of knowledge"):

> My guru had wanted to ordain me in Lalitpur, but I asked him to let me wait because I didn't want my friends to see me with my head shaved and wearing robes (*civara*). I knew they'd laugh! Theravada monks were so few in Nepal in those days, and as for samaneras as young as I was then—there were none. But in Burma there were thousands of us. . . . Nobody laughed at me there.

Recruitment and Training of Nuns

In this early period, virtually all the nuns, like the monks, were from upper-caste backgrounds and most were either widows or had suffered marital breakdown.[25] The position of women in Newar society has been the subject of some controversy. Newar women have often been depicted as having a high degree of freedom and as not suffering from the restrictions habitual in high-caste Parbatiya homes.[26] But in fact, these depictions were more true of women from Maharjan and other middle- and low-caste backgrounds. High-caste Newar widows did (and still do) have great difficulty remarrying, unless their husband died young and before there were children. For men, by contrast, remarriage after divorce or the death of a spouse was not problematic, and taking a second wife was also not uncommon and barely criticized, especially for the rich. Remarriage was difficult for upper-caste Newar women because it was possible only by eloping, which was both extremely risky and stigmatized (it did nonetheless happen on occasion). Young widows would be more likely to take this option, despite the stigma. Older, childless widows had little option but to live out their lives in a marginal position in their deceased husband's household. Divorced women were also in an awkward position: they would be obliged to return (or stay) in their natal home, where they and their offspring were likely to be resented by their brothers' wives and children.

Now the nuns' Order, which asked little more of recruits than that they understand the inevitability of suffering (*duhkha*), offered an alternative, at least to a few. This was not yet seen as a *respectable* alternative, however. With the exception of Dharmachari and a few others who had a smattering of education, nuns were regarded with suspicion if not derision by the laity. Raising their status would be a long-term project.

A start in this regard was made with the move from Kindo Baha to Kindol Vihara. The nuns' living conditions improved, and, although some still went daily to perform domestic tasks for the monks at Ananda Kuti, they had more freedom to do as they chose. But still no provision was made for their training. Although samaneras might initially spend several years in the Valley, in due course almost all went abroad to study in monasteries in Burma or Sri Lanka. By contrast, the nuns might go abroad on pilgrimages but very few stayed abroad to study. Some might know how to read—or at least "decode"—the words of certain basic religious texts, but how much they understood of what they read is another matter. Most lived and died with little formal knowledge of the *dharma.* As one nun recalls, "They learned some *Jataka* stories by heart, and to chant a little of this and a little of that for Buddha Puja. But really, most knew no more than the ordinary lay people knew." In the belief that the work earned them merit, they performed services for the monks, which full ordination vows, had they been permitted to take them, would have prohibited.

Although widows and divorced women continued to "take refuge," by the 1950s a few young single women were beginning to ordain, albeit over great parental opposition. Fathers in particular were unable to reconcile themselves to the idea that their daughters were making a lifelong commitment. A nun who is in her fifties recalls:

> I was determined not to marry, but my father was equally determined that I should. Even when later on he saw my shaved head and my pink dress, he couldn't accept that I was a nun. He kept on telling me, "Now take off that dress and put on a sari and come home!" But I knew what that meant: as soon as I got home, he'd get me married, and I wanted to be free.

"I wanted to be free," echo almost all the nuns who ordained as adolescents and young women. They wanted to be free from the *duhkha*, which comes as agony in childbirth, domination by mothers-in-law, quarrels between sisters-in-law, fights with husbands over other women, and domestic drudgery. The early monks were also fleeing family life, but their experiences and their motivations were perhaps less uniform. In their cases, at least the more prominent ones, the pull factors of carving out a religious career were as important as the push factor of family unhappiness.

Dhammadinna Guruma

Dhammadinna who, like Gyanapurnik, was born in 1939, recalls that she saw ordination as an escape, at least in the short run, from bitter family disputes and burdensome responsibilities, and, in the long run, from marriage. A slight, fair-skinned woman whose original name was Chameli Shakya, she has been a nun for almost forty years. "As far back as I can remember, I was sure of one thing," she says. "I was terrified of going to another house . . . I was afraid of being as unhappy as my mother." Her mother, Nani Maya, had given birth to fifteen children, seven of whom died in infancy:

> But having so many babies die wasn't even the worst of it. What made my mother's life so painful was my father's attitude. Instead of being sympathetic when one child died after another, he was furious that she didn't bear him a son. In fact her first two babies *were* sons but both of them died very young, and after that she had twelve daughters: twelve girls, one after another. . . . Five of them died too. I was the first child to live past its second birthday, and as the eldest survivor, I was my mother's chief helper and confidante. As for my father, I was *his* chief helper and confidante too. My parents didn't love each other but they both loved me and competed for my loyalty.
>
> I remember how it was each time my mother gave birth to a daughter: my father's anger and disgust and my mother's desperation. Ours was a very large joint family, one of the largest. Our house was enormous, it spread over three courtyards (*choks*). There were sixty or seventy of us under one roof: my great-grandfather and his two sons and their families, and their sons and their families. . . . So many women, and all of them had sons except my poor mother. At least three times my father made plans to marry a second wife and each time my mother became deeply depressed. From when I was quite young she looked to me to change my father's mind. I'd tell him that it was *his* karma to have so many daughters, not just my mother's, so how did he know that his new wife wouldn't only have daughters too? And I'd tell him, none of us children wanted him to get married again and if he did, his new wife, whoever she was, would have to deal with our resentment. . . . I'd threaten him that we'd make her life so difficult, she'd run away! And my father listened. He didn't respect my mother, but young as I was, he respected me. He'd say, "I'll never marry again without your permission," and since I never gave it, he never did. Finally, at forty-six, after she'd been to every pilgrimage place in Nepal asking for a son, my mother gave birth for the fifteenth time to my little brother, Amrit. You might expect that coming after so many sisters he'd be spoiled and turn out badly, but it wasn't so. He grew up to be a very fine man.

> As for me, I was seventeen when Amrit was born and by then I'd already spent too much time watching my father abuse my mother. And my dread of marriage didn't go away just because my mother had given birth to a son!

Because for so many years he had no male heir, Dhammadinna's merchant father, Hera Ratna Shakya, treated his eldest daughter like a son. In contrast with his neighbors who, if they let their daughters study at all, withdrew them on completion of elementary school if not before, he sent Dhammadinna to secondary school, and when she had trouble with her studies he ungrudgingly spent money on tutors. Meanwhile, he also involved her in his business. He traded in brass pots, a traditional Shakya occupation, and from when she was in middle school he had her weigh and price the pots and help him with his accounts. Often when he left the shop in the afternoons he would leave her in charge. In short, by the time she began to receive marriage proposals at age fourteen or fifteen, he had become dependent on her and almost as ambivalent about her marrying as she was herself:

> When a proposal came, he'd take my particulars together with the boy's to the astrologer (*joshi*) to see if they were compatible. If they weren't, then negotiations went no further and I was thankful. But if they matched, I'd get hold of the astrologer's report and burn it!

Curiously, Hera Ratna didn't seem especially bothered. Although he acknowledged that his daughter was growing up by giving her gold ornaments to wear at feasts, he never made a concerted effort to get her married. Knowing that it would be many years before Amrit would be old enough to join him in the business, he planned to keep Dhammadinna at his side.

Hera Ratna was a devotee of the Tibetan monk, Sunam Tenzing Rinpoche, whose disciples included a sizeable number of Shakyas from Kwa Baha; Hera Ratna's wife, Nani Maya, was a traditional Vajrayana Buddhist. But Dhammadinna's aunt Surya Lakshmi and her cousin Chini were devotees of the Theravada monk Pragyananda, the abbot of Sumangal Vihara. One day Surya Lakshmi took her niece to meet him. Impressed by him, Dhammadinna decided that she too wanted to learn *buddha dharma*, but she was so busy in the house helping her mother with her younger siblings and in the shop helping her father with his business, as well as doing her schoolwork that she rarely had time to go to the vihara. On one of the few occasions when she did go, however, she unburdened herself to Pragyananda, whereupon he asked if she and her cousin Chini would be interested in going to Burma to study. Both girls were aware that women who did not marry and stayed in the parental home were resented by their brothers' wives when, once the head of the family was dead, they became financially dependent on their brothers. Although, in Dhammadinna's case, it was hard to imagine her baby brother grown up, let alone married to a wife who resented her, she understood that one day she might no longer be welcome in her own home. Even more important, she longed to escape the parental battleground. Both girls accepted Pragyananda's offer and having, through subterfuge, obtained their fathers' signatures to their passport applications, set off for Burma in the autumn of 1960. Their parents believed they were going to finish secondary school in Burma. When, from the safety of their Moulmein nunnery, they wrote home requesting permission to be ordained as nuns, their fathers were appalled. Only after a delay of several months and a visit to the parental home by a delegation made up of ten prominent members of the Nepalese Sangha, did their fathers concede defeat and sign the necessary forms whereupon in due course the girls took *pabbajja*. Chameli became Dhammadinna and Chini took the monastic name Uppalavanna. They stayed in Burma until 1966.

At Moulmein they joined Dhammawati, a distant cousin (on her mother's side) of Dhammadinna. As the first Nepali nun to receive a religious education abroad, she had arrived in Burma a decade earlier. During her long years of training, she had become convinced that women and men have equal spiritual potential and, by the same token, that nuns, whether or not they are fully ordained, are equal to monks. In 1963, Dhammawati returned to Nepal resolved to prove her point.

Charisma and Education: Dhammawati and the Nuns' Order after 1963

For three decades or more, Dharmachari had been the most prominent Theravada nun in Nepal. But well before her death in 1978, she was eclipsed by a charismatic new female leader named Dhammawati. Dhammawati returned to Kathmandu in 1963, after a thirteen-year stay in Burma, and set about educating the post-Rana generation in the dharma. Although she attracted many devotees of both sexes, she became particularly popular with younger women. They admired and identified with her determination to do as she—and not the men in her family or the monks of the Sangha—thought fit. The story of her courage and persistence in overcoming the resistance of her father and older brother, with the help of her mother and other female friends, and how she succeeded in reaching Burma and acquiring a monastic education, is the principal theme of the well-known, and almost mythic, published version of her life ("Beloved Daughter": *Snehi Chori* in Nepali, *Yahmha Mhyāy* in Nepal Bhasha).[1] It has had a profound influence on many Newar girls.

Dhammawati, whose original name was Ganesh Kumari, was the only surviving—and by her own account, indulged—daughter of Harsha Man Shakya and his wife Hira Thakũ. At thirteen, she was "a handful" and, hoping that contact with a monk would have a steadying effect, her mother, an early convert to Theravada Buddhism, brought her to Sumangal Vihara in Lalitpur where Buddhaghosh was holding daily classes for fifty to sixty people, including a few children (Hera Lal Shakya, who would later take the ordination name of Gyanapurnik, was also one of his students). Ganesh Kumari had learned to read and write Nepal Bhasha with a tutor at home; now, with Buddhaghosh, she read selections from the scriptures in Nepal Bhasha and soon in Pali, for which she showed a precocious aptitude. One of the texts she studied was a Nepal Bhasha translation of the *Dhammapada* by Satya Mohan Joshi. When, after just one year, Buddhaghosh let it be known that he was about to return to Burma to resume his training, she was stunned. "I thought, 'I've had just a glimpse of nirvana—and now it's vanished! Will I ever see it again?' " To add to her dismay, she learned that her father was negotiating her marriage, and even though her mother was doing her best to slow down the proceedings, she realized that sooner or later she would be married off—whether to this particular young man or to another, it hardly mattered. Her older sister had died, weakened by overwork and childbirth. "That's what first turned me against marriage. The very thought of it terrified me!" When a visiting Burmese monk named Dhammabuddha suggested she return with him to Burma where arrangements could be made for her to study, she leapt at the idea: "My mother explained to me that this meant I would have to ordain as a nun. She asked, 'Do you understand what that means?' Really, I didn't understand, but whatever ordination might be, I assured her I was ready for it."

Ganesh Kumari's determination to study Theravada Buddhism owed much to her mother's influence. Despite the fact that her husband preferred traditional Newar Buddhism, Hira Thakũ, Ganesh Kumari's mother—along with her friend Lakshmi Maya Shakya, whose younger son later became Bhikshu Ashwaghosh—was one of the earliest followers of the Theravada. (Ashwaghosh was and has remained to this day one of Dhammawati's staunchest supporters.) Hira Thakũ became pregnant for the last time, with Ganesh Kumari's younger brother, Moti Kaji, when Ganesh Kumari was ten, and at the same time that her oldest son's wife became pregnant with her first child. The two babies were born within days of each other. The fact that Hira Thakũ and her daughter-in-law were manifestly fertile at the same time was a matter of considerable shame, since the cultural expectation was that the older generation's sexual activity should cease once their grandchildren were being born. This shame may have played a role in Hira Thakũ's enthusiasm for a new form of Buddhism that emphasized the importance of celibacy and that was, explicitly and implicitly, a critique of the Vajrayana Buddhism that was so intimately entwined with Newar culture.[2]

These family matters—the death of Ganesh Kumari's older sister, her mother's reasons for seeking out the Theravada—play no part in the novelistic account of Dhammawati's early life in *Snehi Chori*. Ganesh Kumari's ardent desire to study the dharma and to go to Burma to do so once Buddhaghosh was no longer in Lalitpur are taken as given. The story is a poignant one. Ardent determination overcomes all obstacles, especially the obstacle of family love. Long passages dwell on the attempts of Ganesh Kumari's father and eldest brother to prevent her from going, and on her mental and physical toughness to meet all the challenges. Ganesh Kumari never hesitates or doubts in her vocation, except very briefly when she realizes she will have to shave off her long hair of which she was proud.

With the help of her mother and her second eldest brother, Ganesh Kumari evaded her father's attempts to intercept her, and made her way across the Mahabharat mountains and down to Chandramani's vihara in Kushinagara where she shaved her head herself. Her father dispatched Bhikshu Amritananda, already, at age thirty, effectively the leader of the Nepalese Sangha, to bring her back to Kathmandu. But Ganesh Kumari refused to go with him and, with a shaved head but not yet ordained and without a passport, set off with Dhammabuddha for Burma.

After a long and hazardous journey, which included a trek through the jungles of Assam with a party of elephant traders, encounters with Nationalist Chinese escaping from the Communist Revolution, and a spell in a Burmese jail, Ganesh Kumari reached Rangoon where she stayed for six months in the household of an upasaka, a high government official who befriended her, while waiting for her father's permission for ordination.[3] When this, together with sponsorship by a local family was at last secured, she entered Kemarama nunnery in Moulmein, the town in Lower Burma in which her teacher, Buddhaghosh, had also studied. She would remain there, with only one short visit home, for twelve years.[4] Despite being very young and very far away, she insists she wasn't homesick. She recalled:

> I had a one-track mind. I'd come to Burma for one purpose only: to learn. I was burning to learn—anything, whatever they were prepared to teach me! To me, *duhkha* (suffering) meant being prevented from studying the *dharma*.

In Burma she was much impressed by the independence of Burmese women:

> Here in Nepal, you hear the same stories all the time about the bitterness between mother-in-law and daughter-in-law. In Nepal daughters-in-law eat leftovers, they're treated like servants by everyone else in the house. But in Burma young couples live separately from the parents, they have their own households.

The status of the nuns whom she knew in Kemarama and other nunneries was much higher than that of the Nepali gurumas. Although Burmese *thilashin* studied exclusively with other nuns, the course they followed was identical to that of the monks: they sat for the same examinations; and the monks respected them as teachers and scholars. Dhammawati—as Ganesh Kumari had become at ordination—was particularly impressed by Daw Pannyachari, the abbess of Kemarama, whose counsel, she observed, was sought by many prominent monks.

Dhammawati was the only Nepali nun studying in Burma until, in the late 1950s, she was joined at Kemarama nunnery by Ratnamanjari, a Shrestha woman fifteen years her senior, from Bhojpur in eastern Nepal.[5] A third nun, Kamala Rajkarnikar from Kathmandu soon followed and, in 1960, Dhammadinna (Chameli Shakya) and Uppalavanna (Chini Shakya) arrived from Lalitpur. In 1962, Dhammawati completed the Dhammachariya, the highest level of Burmese monastic education, in record time. During her stay in Burma, only three nuns passed, one of them being her abbess, Daw Pannyachari, and the other, her closest friend, Daw Gunawati. Invited to remain at Moulmein where her reputation as a preacher and scholar was established, she was tempted, but after only a year on the teaching staff she decided she could serve the *dharma* better in Nepal and returned home in November 1963 (LeVine 2000). She was twenty-eight years old.

Dhammawati returned home with Ratnamanjari and her Burmese friend, Daw Gunawati.[6] Their first major decision concerned where to live. They had three options: to stay with their own families (Gunawati would join Dhammawati in her parental home and Ratnamanjari would live with her brother); to move in to Kindol Vihara with Dharmachari; or to lodge with sympathetic laypeople. After trying the first option, they rejected it because Dhammawati's father was constantly after her to disrobe and get married; the second option they also rejected, because, unlike the Kindol nuns, they had never been married. In Burma never-married nuns usually live separately from the formerly married, and that was how Dhammawati and her friends wanted to live:

Dhammawati Guruma in her bedroom in the old Dharmakirti, February 1998. (Sarah LeVine)

> Nuns who have once been married, especially those who have children, have deep attachments. They tend to talk about their families a lot. . . . Widows talk about their husbands, about love and so on, which bothers those of us who are single. We'd rather not hear that kind of talk.

And so, taking up the third option, they found lodging in private homes.

Fighting the Asian Disease

"Coming home was like going from heaven to hell," Dhammawati recalls many years later. "Nepali monks had a very bad case of the 'Asian disease.' " By this she means, that, like men throughout South Asia, they viewed all women, regardless of their accomplishments, as inferior to men. From the outset, her main challenger was Bhikshu Amritananda who, years before, as her father's envoy, had tried and failed to bring her home from India. Amritananda had been trained at Nalanda in north India and, more important, at Vajirarama Vihara in Colombo, where he had spent a long stretch in the late 1930s and about a year a decade later while in exile from Nepal. Unlike Buddhaghosh and Pragyananda, both of whom had studied in Burma where the status of scholarly *thilashin* was relatively high vis-à-vis monks, Amritananda seems to have adopted the view of ordained laywomen as definitively inferior creatures that was widely held by Sri Lankan monks at that time. Although in the early part of the twentieth century "modernist" Sri Lankan monks had been supportive of female renunciants' desire to study and preach, by the 1940s the monastic establishment had adopted a more conservative stance. They believed that, like the Roman Catholic missionary nuns they encountered in Sri Lanka, *dasa sil mata* should serve the lay public as nurses, teachers, and social workers. Scriptural study and public preaching were seen as inappropriate activities for mere "ordained laywomen."

The nuns' first major confrontation with the monks occurred a few months later when the widow of a prominent merchant asked Dhammawati—along with several senior monks—to to preach at her husband's funeral. But the monks, led by Amritananda, objected to a nun being on the same program as themselves:

> They sent Bhikkhu Sudarshan to tell me so.[7] But I believed then and I believe now that the bhantes had another reason for excluding me: they were scared people would like my preaching better than theirs!

Although Dhammawati backed out of the main event, she gave three discourses on her own in honor of the dead man. She also wrote a letter to the Sangha, quoting chapter and verse to show that in the Buddha's time monks, nuns, upasakas, and upasikas had all been permitted to preach on the same occasion, and so it should be in modern times. "I was determined to stand up to those bhikkhus!" But her friend Gunawati advised her that if she insisted on confrontation, the monks could make life difficult for her; arguing her point would get her nowhere; it would be better to prove her worth through her work in the community. Although she felt deeply wounded, on this, as on other occasions, Dhammawati heeded her friend's advice. Dhammawati admitted that the characteristic she most valued in Daw Gunawati was her composure: "I was a hot-head but she was reflective. That's why I invited her to come to Nepal with me. I trusted her judgment and I knew I couldn't always trust my own."[8]

The difficulties she encountered in her first year back home convinced her that she and her companions must live as independently as possible of the monks. "The bhantes could stop me from preaching in their viharas," she says, "but they wouldn't be able to stop me from preaching in my own." With donations from her brothers and other relatives and a few upasikas she purchased, for the princely sum of three thousand rupees, a plot of land measuring just ten by fourteen meters. It was in the courtyard of Shrigha, an ancient stupa in Nagha Tol, Kathmandu (the courtyard is better known to foreigners under its Tibetan name, Kathe Simbu), and adjacent to the vihara of her old friend Bhikshu Ashwaghosh. There she built a single-story house, which she called Dharmakirti (literally "glory of the dharma," Dhammawati glossed it as "where dharma work is done").[9] Over time, this modest structure acquired a second story, bathrooms, and storerooms. A puja hall was constructed in what was originally the garden and a sliver of land was purchased for a kitchen and library. Each addition had a sponsor or a group of sponsors—Dhammawati and her family financed the construction of one third-floor room in memory of her mother—whose contribution was acknowledged in nunnery publications and whose names, following ancient tradition (Barnes 2000; Schopen 1997: 5), were engraved on plaques and installed above the door of the rooms built with their donations. The importance of Uday support for Dhammawati is underlined when one notes that over half the contributions to the infrastructure of Dharmakirti between 1964 and 1999 came from individual Uday donors.[10]

Rather than registering the nunnery as the property of the Sangha—as Amritananda instructed her to do—she registered it in her own name as founder and abbess.[11] Amritananda strongly objected to her calling it Dharmakirti *Vihara* on the grounds that although historically, bhikkhunis (fully ordained nuns) had lived in *vihāra*, meaning "settled abodes," the Nepali nuns were *anāgārikā* (homeless ones), and thus had no right to call their building a *vihāra*: it could be called merely an *ārāma*. Over the years, his lay supporters repeatedly pulled down her signboard and just as often Dhammawati had it replaced.

Dhammawati had passed the Dhammachariya exam in Burma and, as not only the first Nepali nun but also the only Nepali monastic thus far to have done so, her academic qualifications were of central importance in her struggles with the "bhantes." In 1965, no monk had yet attained that qualification.[12] Thus, although they might regard her as inferior by virtue of her sex, by virtue of her scholarship they were forced—albeit grudgingly—to respect her:

> Amritananda worked very hard on his translations and he never thought twice about telephoning me at midnight to ask the meaning of a Pali word or phrase. He even acknowledged to me that I was better trained than he was. But, mind you, he only admitted this in private. Publicly, he always set himself above me.[13]

Spreading the Dharma: the Nuns Put Their Program in Place

Dhammawati, Ratnamanjari, and Daw Gunawati were soon joined, on their return from Burma, by Kamala and Dhammadinna. Together, these five women set about launching their own program; although it replicated that of the monks in many respects, in time it would go well beyond it. Their objective was straightforward and heroic: they would teach *buddha dharma* to whomever had an interest in hearing it, and gradually they would change Newar Buddhist society for the benefit of all and in particular for women.[14]

Ritual Performance

The nuns, like the monks, offered Buddha Puja in their vihara and *paritrana* in upasakas' homes. Buddha Puja, which was scheduled five times a month (a shorter version was offered each morning and evening), followed the form with which they had become familiar in Moulmein. This had six basic components, although others, notably singing devotional songs and meditation, were added later:

(1) Following the recitation of *namo tassa bhagavato arahato sammā-sambuddhassa* (obeisance to the truly fully enlightened *arhat* lord [Buddha]), participants took refuge in the Buddha, Dharma, and Sangha.

(2) The laity took either Five or Eight Precepts (for a twenty-four-hour period).

(3) Fruit, flowers, and water were offered at the Buddha shrine (the laity received the fruit and flowers as *prasad* at the end of the puja).

(4) The three "daily" *paritrana* (protection) sutras—*Karuniya-metta*, (loving kindness), *Bojjhanga* (attainment of knowledge), and *Hetu-patthana* (causing the aspiration for enlightenment to arise)—were chanted, followed by sutras specific to the day of the week.[15]

(5) A sermon was delivered by Dhammawati, or in her absence, by Dhammadinna or Daw Gunawati. The themes of their sermons would generally be taken from the *Buddhavamsa* or *Jataka* and *Dhammapada* commentary stories on which they would elaborate in order to teach some aspect of Buddhist ethics. Each had her personal favorite. For one it was the story of Vessantara, which emphasizes the virtues of generosity; another was particularly attached to stories of the Buddha as an animal in his former lives, whereas the third most loved stories that featured Shariputra "because he was closest to the Lord."

(6) The final component of Buddha Puja was the giving of *dana*: the nuns would sit in a line with their hands in their laps and their devotees would give them minute sums of money. (Dhammadinna remembers that in the early years the "take" might be no more than two rupees, which even in those days did not go far between five nuns.)

During the month of Gunla, Buddha Puja were conducted every day and it was the sermons that Dhammawati delivered in this season that established her reputation as a preacher. She would emphasize the layperson's duties (*kartabya*): to listen to teachings given by monks and nuns; to fulfill their responsibilities as husbands and wives, parents and children, teachers and students, and masters and servants; and to oppose blood sacrifice. She also spoke frequently about women who were prominent in the early Sangha, especially Mahaprajapati, who continued doggedly to pressure the Buddha until finally he admitted women to his order; the Buddha's mother, Maya Devi; Yashodhara, his wife; and Sanghamitta, who brought Buddhism to Sri Lanka. "Our minds are equal to men's minds," she repeatedly declared. "It is only our society that keeps us back." Soon hundreds of people, the majority of them women, were flocking to hear her preach.[16]

Once the nuns were established in their new nunnery, they started to receive requests to visit the homes of devotees to chant *paritrana* sutras to comfort the sick and the dying and console the bereaved, and to celebrate special occasions. After unwinding a ball of white thread of which all who were present would take hold, the nuns would recite the appropriate *paritrana* sutra, which members of the household would follow in their handbooks.[17] At the conclusion of the recitation, the thread would be broken up into short pieces, which the nuns would tie round the wrist of each family member. If the visit were before noon, the nuns would be offered a meal, after which one of them would discourse on a theme relating to the sutra they had just chanted. Following this, family members might ask questions. Dharma talks given in an intimate household setting were at least as important for creating trust and building the community as were those delivered to hundreds in the vihara.

Teaching Children

The Dharmakirti nuns directed their attentions to women whom they saw as having been ignored in the Newar Buddhist community as well as by Nepalese society as a whole. Children provided an equally important focus however. Although by the 1960s more children—at least in urban areas—were going to school than in Rana times, the large majority, especially girls, still had no access. During their first year back in Nepal, the nuns taught in a school that Bhikshu Sumangal had opened in Gana Baha, an old site on the edge of the old city core whose owners had donated it to the Theravadins. When Sumangal left to study in Japan in 1964, he handed the school over to Dhammawati and as soon as Dharmakirti Vihara was habitable she moved it there:

> We took in the children who were hanging around our courtyard. As there were no schools for poor children in those days, and no work either, they just played most of the day. The first week we had 20 boys and girls, but soon word spread and we found ourselves with 150 children! We had no

> particular model in mind. We just thought that the first thing children needed to learn was the alphabet, and from that everything else would follow.

In summer, school began at 6 A.M. (in winter, when it was cold and dark, at seven) and ran until 9 A.M. The nuns taught reading, writing, arithmetic, and *buddha dharma*, for which Dhammawati began producing materials designed specially for children. At around the same time, Dharmashila was also starting a school in Pokhara (McHugh 2001: 125–126).

An Uday woman who attended the Dharmakirti school in the late 1960s recalls, "My older sister would drop me and my little brother off at the vihara every morning and we'd just stay there till she picked us up. I loved going there, the gurumas were like members of our family." Dharmakirti was one of several Buddhist schools established by monks and nuns; however, gradually, as new government schools opened up, the Buddhist community no longer looked to monastics to teach their children the three Rs. But whereas the other monastery schools were soon taken over by the Ministry of Education and lost any trace of their original affiliation, the Dharmakirti school remained in business for fourteen years. When eventually the nuns did close it down, they replaced it with a *buddha dharma* Saturday school (Saturday being the day of rest in Nepal). Although the monks also ran Saturday schools for children, the Dharmakirti school had a special program for young adolescents. One former student remembers:

> The children came in the morning and twenty-five of us older girls and boys came in the afternoon. The gurumas explained what the sutras meant and we memorized and chanted them. Now and then some bhantes would come to teach us too. We had to take our studies seriously because we had quiz competitions with teams of children from other Saturday schools that the bhantes ran. Dhammawati Guruma used to tell us girls that we were just as talented as the boys.

Adolescents and Young Adults: The Buddhist Study Circle

Believing that all Buddhists should be able to read the scriptures for themselves, since the earliest days of their mission the Theravadins had been teaching laypeople—a few men, but mostly women—to read. Sometimes they did so one-on-one, and sometimes they would gather several students into informal classes. From the labored forming of *devanagari* letters, students would progress to reading Jataka stories. The Dharmakirti nuns also taught their share of laypeople to read, but they soon discovered that young people who were in or had recently graduated from secondary school were also interested in learning *buddha dharma.* In 1970 some laymen, with the help of Buddhaghosh, founded the Nepal Young Men's Buddhist Association. However members were all in their twenties or older and almost all male (despite the name it did not actually exclude women). In 1971, the nuns took an important step when, with the help of Ashwaghosh Bhante, they started the Buddhist Study Circle (Bauddha Adhyayan Gosthi). The original group, which numbered only a couple of dozen members, rapidly expanded to more than a hundred. Although the program was designed for adolescents, once in the group, people tended to stay on, so that thirty years later many of the original members, now middle-aged, still attend regularly. One Uday woman, looking back to her adolescence, said:

> My father and his brothers were very interested in Tibetan Buddhism and they often called lamas to the house, but the lamas came to perform rituals not to teach the dharma. My grandmother was a devotee of Dharmachari Guruma, and sometimes I went to Kindol with her. In those days Dharmachari had a lot of lady devotees but she didn't seem to want to teach younger girls. Her chelis were all much older than I was. I thought, I want to learn too, but where to go? Then the gurumas started the Buddhist Study Circle, and my cousins and I—we were all in secondary school at the time—began to attend. . . . It was like having our own club.

She and others like her came to hear a wide range of speakers, and to read and discuss texts that Dhammawati and others had translated from Pali and Burmese into the vernacular. Though young men also attended the Study Circle, young women felt particularly welcome there. Starting in 1972, the Study Circle published a magazine titled *Dharmakirti*, with Aswaghosh as editor. Initially it came out once a year for Buddha Jayanti. In 1983, it began to be published once every two months, and from 1990 it became a monthly magazine like the monks' *Ananda Bhoomi*, and again, like *Ananda Bhoomi*, it had articles not only in Nepal Bhasha and Nepali, but also in English. Because the Study Circle had a predominance of women, there are more female than male authors in the early issues of *Dharmakirti* (P. Tuladhar 1999). The Study Circle became a prodigious publisher of books and pamphlets as well: a total of 195 as of 1999, many authored by Ashwaghosh and Dhammawati as well as other nuns.[18] The monks, notably Amritananda, Pragyananda, Buddhaghosh, Aniruddha, Gyanapurnik, and Sudarshan, published many books as well, but there were complaints that they were too difficult and so Dhammawati decided to write a series especially for Dharmakirti in language that ordinary people could understand. She had already written some simple little books for children and now she began to write a series for adults, eventually producing a seven-level *pariyatti* syllabus for use in classes that were held in Dharmakirti on Friday afternoons.

Dhammawati's main objective has been to make the dharma accessible to as many people as possible. Moreover, she has become increasingly demanding in this regard, both of her students and of herself, as their teacher. Whereas in the early years she taught only "the basics" (i.e., the *Dhammapada*, *Buddhavamsa*, *Jatakakatha*, *Sigalovada Sutta*,[19] and *paritrana* suttas), more recently—since vipassana meditation has become popular in the community—she has taught courses on the *Satipatthana Sutta* and, in the spring of 1998, a two-month course on Abhidhamma. For this she produced Nepal Bhasha translations of selections from the Pali together with her own commentary, and Dhammadinna was available every afternoon to explain the texts to confused—and sometimes almost despairing—students.

Many of the younger recruits to the nuns' Order were formerly members of the Buddhist Study Circle. One nun (a Manandhar by background) belonged to the Circle for several years before deciding to ordain in her late thirties:

> Slowly I was making my mind up and, finally, I told Dhammawati Guruma that I wanted to shave my head. She warned me that the vihara was very crowded and, if I came, I'd have to share a very small room with two other nuns. But I said I had made up my mind and somehow they squeezed me in.

Not all would-be recruits are accepted. Another member of the Study Circle, an Uday then in her early twenties, remembers telling Dhammawati how much she dreaded marriage and life in a strange household:

> I begged her to give me the precepts. But Dhammawati told me that life in the vihara could be as full of competition and jealousies as life in a joint family. So I was wrong to think that by becoming a nun I'd avoid that kind of *duhkha*. And anyway, she said she didn't think I was suited to be a nun. . . . I was too independent-minded! She said that although I'd find marriage difficult, I'd find being a nun even harder. . . . So I told my parents, "All right, go ahead and arrange my marriage." And they

> did. But I kept on going to the Study Circle. . . . I still go when I have the chance, and I've been married eighteen years.

Teaching in the Countryside

In 1950, the Dharmodaya Sabha had announced that one of their objectives was to build a vihara in every town or village that had a sizeable Buddhist population and to have one or two monks in residence to provide religious instruction and free medical care. In the final years of Rana rule and in the years immediately following the restoration of the monarchy, monks and nuns established dozens of outposts in Newar diaspora settlements. Given the shortage of manpower however—in the early 1950s the entire monastic community numbered only about fifty—few of the new viharas had a monk in permanent residence. Most stood empty for long periods whereas others were abandoned altogether and communities that had momentarily coalesced around a teacher quickly fell apart. What had once identified itself as a missionary movement was being rapidly transformed into a much more narrowly focused organization. Urban institution-building was now the first priority. Whether to continue missionary work or not was up to the individual.

In the month of Gunla in 1972, although busy with daily devotions; teaching *buddha dharma* to people of all ages; and running a circulation library, a weekly clinic, and a hospital visitors' program (not to mention cooking, washing clothes, and cleaning the nunnery[20]), the Dharmakirti nuns started going out, along with some of their Study Circle students, to teach in villages in which no monastic had been seen in years. On arrival, they would gather a group of children together in a house, a courtyard, or under a tree and teach them the alphabet along with the fundamentals of Buddhism. After a few days, they would have to move on to another village. Ideally, they would return the following year and slowly the seeds they had sown would germinate, a community would begin to form, and the vihara would be repaired or a new one built.

By the 1980s and 1990s, there was less demand for basic literacy, but in 1995 some of the younger nuns and a few lay volunteers, led by an astonishingly energetic nun named Dhammasangha, started a *buddha dharma* program in government schools. From initial forays in the towns of Lalitpur and Kirtipur, they extended their activities to a number of Valley villages, including Kokhana, Harasiddhi, Lubhu, Bungamati, Chapagaon, and Balambu. In the spring of the following year, Dhammasangha started teaching in Khungai, a village a day's bus-ride from Kathmandu on the edge of the Lumbini Garden.[21] Nowadays the population of this particular village—as of the entire district—is Hindu and Muslim. Dhammasangha explained:

> The Buddha was born there, he grew up not far away at Kapilavastu, and after enlightenment he continued to teach in the area. But Buddhism vanished many centuries ago and all we see now are the ruins of places where Buddhists once lived. It's very important to bring the dharma back, and because children are more open-minded, it's easier to start with them than with adults.

She made friends with the local headmaster, who was eager for any help he could get for his dilapidated school set in the midst of wheat fields. If the help consisted of having the children take refuge in Buddha, Dharma, and Sangha, so be it. Any attention from outsiders was better than none, he said. So every day for six weeks in late winter and early spring, in her pink dress with a straw sun hat on her head, Dhammasangha bicycled four miles out from Buddha Vihara at Lumbini to the school. Determined as she was, she admitted to being daunted by the task she had set herself. Many parents forbade their children to attend classes on Buddhism, and the mother tongue of those who were permitted to come was a dialect of Hindi; there were no Buddhist books in their dialect and many did not speak or read Nepali, and she was well aware that the main reason why some of the one hundred children who enrolled in her classes did so was to get the free pens and notebooks that she handed out. Nevertheless, they did the homework assigned to them and took the test at the end of the course and, by 2002, enrollment had risen to 350. The school buildings were newly whitewashed, Dhammasangha had exchanged her sun hat and bicycle for a helmet and motorcycle (gifts of an admiring Taiwanese donor), and a shrine, housing a large Buddha image (donated by Dhammasangha's family), had been erected in the school yard. Although so far, as she admitted, she had made no converts, there was a new awareness of Buddhism in the villages surrounding Lumbini.

Nuns As Ritual Specialists

Since 1956, several viharas in Kathmandu and Lalitpur had been offering *samanera pabbajja* as a Theravada alternative (or addition) to *kayta puja*, the traditional non-priestly Newar boy's puberty rite (see pages 65–66). In 1966, for the first time two Uday girls went to stay at Dharmakirti as an alternative to *barhay (barha) tayegu*, the Newar girl's prepuberty rite, which is performed a few years after the mock marriage ceremony (*ihi*), and before the onset of menses.[22] Traditionally, a group of three or four girls will spend twelve days hidden from male eyes and the sun in a darkened room, a liminal period in which they are ritually transformed from children into incipiently sexual adults. On the twelfth day, dressed in elaborate costumes, they emerge into the sun and after pujas have been performed in the household and at the neighborhood Ganesh temple, their new status is celebrated with a feast. On the grounds that girls wasted their time playing with their friends during *barhay tayegu*, and that the ritual had nothing Buddhist about it, Dhammawati devised a rite, modeled on a similar one in Burma, which she called *rishini pabbajja* ("the ordination of a sageess") in which young girls, dressed in distinctive dark red robes, spend the prescribed twelve days in the nunnery conforming to the nunnery schedule and keeping the Eight Precepts.[23] This means getting up at 4.30 A.M. for meditation and Buddha Puja, and spending most of the day learning *buddha dharma* and memorizing Pali sutras. Although, unlike their traditional age-mates, they were permitted to see both men and the sun, they took the Eight Precepts and so were subject to other restrictions, the most difficult being the ban on eating after midday. The *pabbajja* experience, Dhammawati believed, would encourage a sense of independence and teach the girls the virtues of self-control. The first few years it was offered, the cost of the program was covered by the sale of Dharmakirti publications; but more recently, as food and children's tastes have become expensive ("they want instant noodles, oranges, and Coke!"), the nunnery has had to impose a daily charge. Even so, this is still very cheap compared with the traditional post-*barhay* feast for scores, or even hundreds, of people, which most parents find exceedingly burdensome.

Rishini pabbajja, like *samanera pabbajja*, was soon taken up by other nunneries, and these days several of the larger monasteries offer it as well. In January 2000, eighteen girls were secluded along with six boys under the supervision of an elderly monk and a good-natured nun in Shakyasingha Vihara in Lalitpur. The most popular time for "sending children to the vihara"—as the rite is often called—is the midwinter school holiday. However, children no longer stay the full twelve days; in fact, five is the usual limit and some go home after only two. "At only nine and ten years of age, they're already taking daily tuition [i.e., their parents are paying for extra private tutors] and the parents don't want them to miss a single session," Dhammadinna comments regretfully.

How much these young girls learn about *buddha dharma* is questionable. A secondary-school girl who was eleven when she went through *rishini pabbajja* for seven days with nine others, remembers that, aside from telling them Jataka stories, the nun in charge had the group spend hours each day memorizing *paritrana* sutras: "She didn't actually teach us anything. . . . Often she'd go out of the vihara, leaving us with one of her chelis. When she returned, she'd have us recite passages. But she didn't explain what they meant." Nevertheless, she concedes that she enjoyed her week in the vihara: "Two of my cousins were also in the group and we had a lot of fun."

Today, Theravada monks can in principle offer alternatives for all the major traditional life-cycle rites. Acting as a ritual officiant in this way, as distinct from providing a blessing by reciting protection verses, marks an untraditional and modernist extension of the Buddhist monastic role, at least in the Theravada understanding of it (Gombrich 1988: 208; 1995). To date, nuns have never been invited to conduct

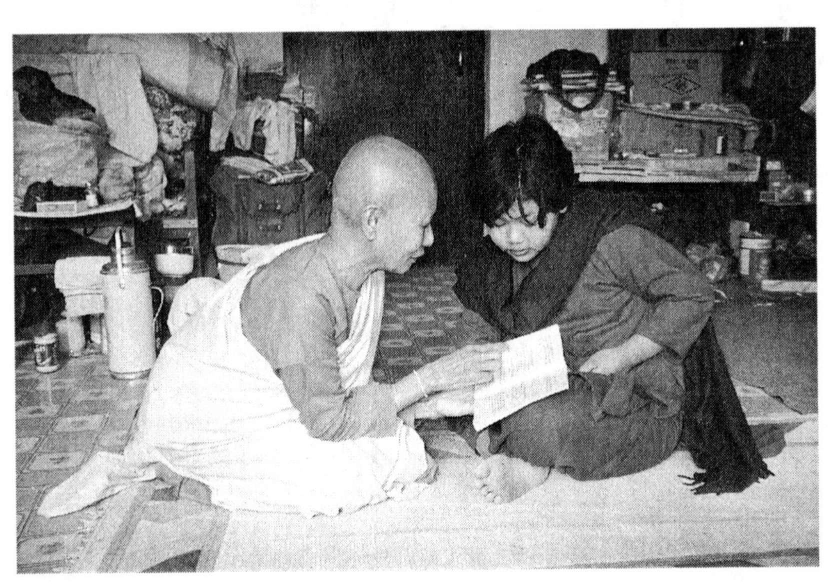

Sanghawati Guruma instructing Charana Shrestha during her time as a rishini on the meaning of the Triple Refuge and the Five Precepts, Dharmakirti Vihara, 1st April 2002. (David N. Gellner)

marriages (*vivāha*) or funerals (*dāhakarma*), although they frequently chant *paritrana* at these events; it is presumably only a matter of time before they, like the monks, are asked to be the main officiants.[24] For the moment, temporary ordination for boys is still an optional extra for most Buddhists, and has replaced *kayta puja* only for about 10 percent of Uday. Other life-cycle rituals are performed by monks or nuns only in the most exceptional circumstances. The one big exception is *rishini pabbajja*, the nuns' innovation, which has been extraordinarily successful. It has replaced the traditional performance of *barhay tayegu* for almost all Buddhists and has started to make considerable inroads even among castes that are either ambivalent about Buddhism (like Maharjans) or predominantly Hindu and very ignorant of Buddhism (like most Shresthas).

Temporary ordination, a long-established tradition in Thailand and Burma, was not offered to adult men until 1974 when the Theravadins introduced it at Buddha Vihara, Lumbini.[25] Since then, there have been several occasions on which, to mark the visit of an eminent foreigner, or the inauguration of a new vihara, as well as the birthdays of senior monks, scores of upasakas have taken temporary ordination.[26] For example, to celebrate the eighty-fifth birthday of Pragyananda, eighty-five young men shaved their heads, took the Ten Precepts, donned monks' robes, and lived in Shri Kirti Vihara for a week of dharma study and meditation. Again, in July 1999 in Shakyasingha Vihara, sixty-five laymen took the Ten Precepts at *pabbajja* ordination; immediately afterward, twenty "novices" had the 227 Patimokkha rules read to them and took full ordination vows.[27] In 2001, temporary ordination became part of the annual Buddha Jayanti celebrations in Lalitpur.

In Burma, married women and widows have long been able to take temporary ordination, that is, take the Ten Precepts and stay in the nunnery for periods of one week to several months; since 1986, Nepali women too, have had the chance to take temporary ordination. Waist-length hair is considered essential for a Newar married woman; even very modern Newar women keep at least shoulder-length hair. At every meditation retreat, a few housewives cut their waist-length hair and shave their heads, thereby earning great merit as well as attracting ambivalent attention for months to come.

Pilgrimage

As noted above, in the 1960s monks began leading groups on pilgrimages to the holy sites in north India and Sri Lanka. Groups could

Nuns leading a procession of monastics and lay people around the archaeological site at Lumbini as part of the inauguration ceremony for Gautami Vihara, February 1998. (Sarah LeVine)

number more than two hundred people, the majority of them housewives who had the time to travel, and might be on the road for up to a month. By the 1980s, Dhammawati was also taking her devotees on pilgrimages not only in South Asia but to Thailand and to Burma as well. A favorite Burmese destination was Kemarama nunnery in Moulmein where Dhammawati and several other Nepali nuns had been trained and where their abbess, Daw Pannyachari, warmly received pilgrim groups until her death in 1999. In India, pilgrims would stay in Burmese and Maha Bodhi Society rest houses close to the sacred sites and in nunneries in Buddhist countries. Meanwhile Dharmakirti was beginning to host groups of foreigners coming on pilgrimages to the great stupas of the Kathmandu Valley.

Chandrawati: Daughter of Dharmakirti

Chandrawati's easy openness and warmth belies an intense, closely guarded religious life. A handsome twenty-three-year-old, she maintains that since age seven, when she began to accompany her mother to vipassana sessions in Sumangal Vihara, her primary interest has been meditation. She spent three successive long winter holidays in a nunnery near her Lalitpur home studying the dharma and meditating. The fourth winter, when she was ten, instead of doing *barhay tayegu*, she took the Eight Precepts and donned a *rishini*'s red robe. Unlike most *rishini*, she also shaved her head, and when the holidays were over and it was time to go home and begin the new school year, she asked to be allowed to stay permanently in the nunnery but, as she recalls, "the place was poor and the nuns couldn't afford to feed me." Back home again, she refused to exchange her rishini dress for a school uniform. She wanted to be a nun, she told her parents, and she had no more interest in lay life. Her mother's elder sister, a devotee of Dhammawati, brought her to Dharmakirti in which at that time, in the mid-1980s, only adult nuns were living; however Dhammawati, impressed by the child's precocious conviction, agreed to take her, and after shaving her head again and exchanging her red *rishini*'s dress for a nun's pink one, received her, still aged only ten, into the Dharmakirti community.

Chandrawati's mother, Ratna Devi, was born in Bhaktapur, the third daughter and youngest child of poor Shakya parents. Her mother died giving birth to her and she was raised by her father, who attended teachings at the Theravada monastery and took his three small daughters with him. "We've always held tightly to Buddhism," Ratna Devi explains. As a widower, he was eager to get his daughters settled and he married them off very young. Given his poverty, he had difficulty finding husbands for them in Bhaktapur and though his eldest daughter was married in her home city, his second daughter went to Kathmandu and the youngest to Lalitpur. Ratna Devi's husband, Shanta Man, was an icon-maker; more than a decade older than his wife, he was equally impoverished. Forty years later, his financial situation has not markedly improved. He still makes statues of the Buddha, which he offers—with few takers—for sale in a cramped shop overseen by his eldest son, Nirmal.

Not long after she came to her married home, Ratna Devi began attending Sumangal Vihara every new, full, and half-moon day and every Wednesday. Her piety has had a great impact on at least four of her seven children: Chandrawati, her fifth child and second daughter, was the first to ordain; her second son is now studying as a monk in Sri Lanka, and her youngest daughter, Khemachari, ordained at thirteen and after two years in a Lalitpur nunnery joined her sister Chandrawati in Dharmakirti. Ratna Devi's youngest son also ordained as a novice but after a few years in a Kathmandu monastery disrobed and got married.

Why Chandrawati decided to become a nun is not altogether clear. Her mother says of both her nun daughters, "The seeds were sown in their previous lives. They had no choice, they had to do it." Chandrawati herself says she wanted the freedom to meditate; meditation, as she had experienced it in the nunnery, made her feel *sānti* (peace) and *ānanda* (joy), and, like many others, she maintains that at home there was always "too much going on." Indeed, when she was nine and ten years old there may well have been a great deal "going on." Her mother, according to her own and others' testimony, was in a perilous state of mind, precipitated, it appears, by a pilgrimage she made on foot with her sister, a famous medium of the Buddhist goddess of smallpox, Hariti, to Gosainkund. This lake, which lies above four thousand meters in the Langtang Mountain Range, is sacred to Shiva. While Ratna Devi was meditating at the lake, she became possessed by Shiva himself. Whereas up to this point she had been a devoted member of the Theravada Buddhist community, on her return from Gosainkund she stopped going to Sumangal Vihara. As Chandrawati explains, "She was afraid she might get possessed in the vihara, and then the monks would tell her off." Having withdrawn from the monastery, she embarked on a devotional course all her own: every morning for the next several years she went to the Bagmati River, which flows along the northern edge of Lalitpur, and there she would build small chaityas out of sand on the river bed, one hundred thousand of them, according to her calculation:

> Or maybe even *two* hundred thousand altogether! Every morning after cooking rice for the family I'd go to the river and build those little chaityas, and every evening I'd leave them there for the Lord to take away in the wind or the rain. And the following morning I'd come down to the river again and start building chaityas in a different spot. I never asked anyone to help me. How could anyone help me? They would have had to fast first, and go through as much hardship as I had. No, I worked entirely on my own.[28]

It was during this period of frenzied activity that Chandrawati ordained. In Dhammawati she seems to have found a nurturing maternal substitute, and in the nunnery, a structured environment in which, shielded from her mother's anguish, she could finish her schooling, meditate for half an hour morning and evening, and, from time to time, attend ten-day vipassana retreats.

Meanwhile, at home, Ratna Devi was continuing to go to the river each day to make chaityas while being possessed by a host of different gods and goddesses including Ganesh (a son of Shiva), Kali (the terrifying form of Shiva's wife, Parvati), Dakshinkali (a Nepalese form of Kali), and Julum Bhaju (son of the Hariti Ajima, the demoness-turned-goddess of smallpox, who is believed to protect young children from disease) all of whom, as she is quick to point out, "are one and the same—they just appear to be different." But one day, her visits to the river stopped and, in an abrupt shift, she made a shrine on the second floor of her house and began to treat patients. Eight years later, she still sits in her shrine room every morning between the hours of nine and eleven, waiting for patients to appear. "They only come from the *tol* [the immediate neighbourhood]," she hastens to say. Her practice has certainly not made her rich. "Nobody gives me money as *dana*. Only biscuits and fruit and little things."

Chandrawati finished secondary school in 1994 and then went to Sala Santi Suk nunnery in Thailand for religious studies. Half an hour's bus ride outside Bangkok, Sala Santi Suk is a serene, flower-filled place. Although it is right beside a highway, the sound of traffic is so well-muffled by a thick stand of trees that one would think one was far out in the country. Founded in the 1960s, thirty years later it housed about seventy nuns, only eleven of whom were students. Chandrawati remembers being happy there. She was confident that, through her mother, the goddess Hariti was "protecting" her; she was with her best friend Khemavati who had entered Dharmakirti the same year she had; and she became very close to Lamduwan, the middle-aged nun who was assigned as her "local mother." "She didn't have much education but she was very kind. And she came from a rich family and was very generous to me. She and I and Khemawati and Khemawati's local mother shared a room the whole time I was in Santi Suk." Possibly the most important factor contributing to her contentment was that she had more time each day than she had had in Nepal for meditation. Santi Suk was both more spacious and much quieter than Dharmakirti, and behind the nunnery was a "forest"—actually a few acres of fruit trees and bamboo—in which several meditation huts had been built:

> Each hut was intended for only one person. You went in and stayed there all by yourself, just coming out for meals and to go to the toilet. Those retreats were the best experiences I had in Thailand.

The full dharma course took nine years, but after only four both Nepali nuns returned to Kathmandu, Khemawati because her parents were ailing and needed her help, and Chandrawati because of problems following a gallstone operation. "I just wasn't recovering from the operation, and when Dhammawati Guruma, who happened to be visiting, saw my condition, she said I should come home, I'd be better off in Kathmandu. So I came." For some months following her return she continued to suffer excruciating pain, but by summer she was in good enough health to attend a ten-day retreat at Budha Nilkantha from which she returned in a state of euphoria. She didn't seem to regret having had to break off her studies at Santi Suk and evinced little desire to go back. She wanted to go to college with other young people her age, and to learn to speak better English, which she'd almost forgotten in Thailand. But for the present, she felt she should be available to help her mother, who was in poor health:

> Three of my brothers are married, but two of them live separately from my parents, and my youngest brother's wife, though she lives in the same house, doesn't want to help. My eldest sister's married far away and my other brother's a monk in Sri Lanka. So that leaves me and my little sister. My little sister's only in Class Six, she still has four years of school of secondary school. . . . But I've finished . . . so I'm the one who'll be going home.

And she did go home, but fortunately her mother soon recovered whereupon Chandrawati returned to Dharmakirti, enrolled in an art school in Kathmandu and began teaching Buddhism to children in nearby villages on Saturdays. The following year her brother, who was a monk in Sri Lanka, arranged for her to enter a Buddhist college near Colombo. On a short visit home during the winter of 2004, she appeared poised, confident, serene; and her English, the medium of instruction in her college, was much improved.

Thus far, we have seen how a new form of Buddhist practice changed the lives of men and women who became monks and nuns. It is time now to examine the impact of the Theravada on their lay supporters.

CHAPTER FIVE

The Changing Buddhist Laity

Whether someone—a monk or a nun—is a member of the Theravada Sangha is clearly marked by the ritual of ordination and their dress.[1] If a monk is unacceptable to the Order for some disciplinary reason, as happened to Mahapragya when he returned to Kathmandu as a Bauddha Rishi (Buddhist sage) in the 1960s, this will be shown by refusing to allow him to sit in line with other monks. Where the laity is concerned, however, the boundaries are not so clearly drawn. Who is to count as part of the Theravada lay community? Anyone who occasionally visits a monastery? Anyone who has at least once invited monks and/or nuns to their house? Anyone who has ever taken the Triple Refuge from a monk or nun? Is it right to consider the entire household as adherents when only one or two members participate regularly? The fact that there is no easy answer to these questions shows that the "lay community" is an amorphous body: it certainly exists, but it is not easy to define.

By contrast, in traditional Newar Buddhism there is a more precise criterion, namely the domestic priest: any household with a Vajracharya domestic priest (*purohit*) can be classified as a part of the Buddhist laity. Furthermore, only Vajracharyas and Shakyas may fill the role of temple priest in the viharas of traditional Newar Buddhism, which are called *baha* and *bahi*. (Both roles are hereditary.) Thus Vajracharyas and Shakyas constituted the clergy, and all those castes with Vajracharya priests constituted the laity of Newar Buddhism. (As patrons of Vajracharya priests, Shakya and Vajracharya households simultaneously formed part of the laity.) However, this apparently objective criterion masks considerable variations in commitment to Buddhism, with some castes being strongly committed and others only weakly. There is also considerable variation both within castes and within some families. Now that there are different forms of Buddhism on offer, the fact that a Buddhist household has a Vajracharya priest is no guarantee that its members are supporters of Vajrayana Buddhism.

In the same way, though the influence of Theravada Buddhism spreads very widely, as its supporters intend, there are many different degrees of involvement. The story of the growth of the lay community is therefore the story of a small group of (frequently interrelated) activists, and a much larger pool of less active, part-time, and irregular supporters. Both groups were at the beginning entirely drawn from the Newars, as were all the monks and nuns. Indeed, one can say with even more precision that they came almost entirely from the upper castes, which were traditionally aligned with Buddhism, namely, the Vajracharyas, Shakyas, and Uday.[2] In addition, the upwardly mobile Manandhars (oil-pressers) in Kathmandu played an important part in Theravada activism. Later on, Maharjans (Jyapu) and others came to play a significant and increasingly crucial role. The only major figure in the early period who came from a different, non-Buddhist background was Mahapragya.

The struggle for the freedom to practice religion was related in complex and sometimes contradictory ways to movements for political and cultural revival. It is notable that Newar Buddhists were not prominent as political or ethnic nationalist leaders in these spheres. Such leaders tended to be Shresthas of one kind or another. Of the four official martyrs who were executed in 1941 for organizing a political party (the Praja Parishad) and plotting against the Ranas and who are remembered each year on Martyrs' Day, a national holiday, three were Newars (all from the large Shrestha bloc) and one was a Thakuri. Pushpa Lal, the founder of the Nepali Communist Party in 1949, was also a Shrestha. On the whole, political reformers were not primarily concerned with pushing religious reform, and vice versa, even though there was some overlap and they sometimes came from the same backgrounds.[3] There was also a difference, perhaps not so clear in the early years, between religious revivalism, on the one hand, and Newar cultural-linguistic nationalism, on the other. Like the political activists, both groups were subject to political repression by the Ranas; both sought political freedoms the Ranas had no intention of granting. Some individuals, such as the poet Chittadhar Hridaya, were supporters both of religious reform and of Newar cultural revival, and Dharmacharyya was a foundational figure in both movements; in the Rana period and on occasion thereafter the two movements were natural allies. Ultimately, however, they were destined to go different ways because their basic aims were different. One movement sought to *preserve* the language and culture of the Newars, the other to *change* a fundamental aspect of traditional Newar culture as well as to take a universal religious message to all Nepalis, regardless of ethnicity.

In the complex ideological situation that has emerged from the 1950s and 1960s, Buddhist laymen and laywomen have a wide series of choices. In an interesting article that deserves to be better known, Todd T. Lewis has presented the results of a questionnaire survey on belief among the Uday of Asan, Kathmandu, and analysed the worldviews of seven of them in detail in terms of a two-dimensional graph (Lewis 1996a). He places the traditional Mahayana/Vajrayana Buddhism of the Newars in the center as the default option. The horizontal axis represents movement toward Theravada in one direction, or Tibetan Buddhism in the other. These are indeed exclusive choices: no one practices both kinds of Buddhism as a virtuoso (though occasionally a major donor, such as Gyan Jyoti, gives substantially to both). It is only relatively nonaligned lay supporters or households—who constitute the majority, of course—who call both Theravada monastics and Tibetan practitioners to hold rituals in their homes. Lewis's vertical axis opposes secular ideologies to religious pluralism or ecumenism. The latter

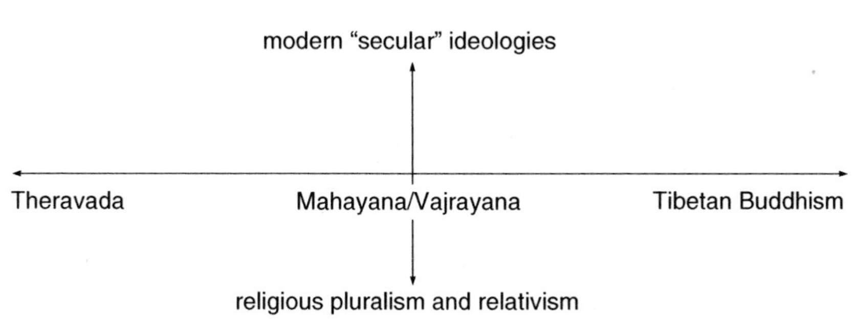

Chart 5.1 A representation of the Newar Buddhist ideological field (after Lewis 1996a: 244).

was perhaps more common among the older generation, or among generations now gone by, who were influenced by Gandhianism. There are few prominent Newar activists today who combine reverence for Hindu holy men with a strong allegiance to Buddhism; but for all that, there are, even now, born Buddhists who prefer Hindu forms of spiritual practice, as well as, vice versa, those who are born Hindu but have a preference for Buddhism.

The Role of the Sahuji

Once the opposition of the Ranas to new forms of monasticism was made very clear by the expulsions of 1926, lay efforts to support monks had to be discreet. But, at the same time, lay commitment to the teachings of Kyangtse Lama and his followers remained high. In three traditional monastic-temple complexes in Lalitpur, at Kwa Baha, Uku Baha, and Chikã Bahi, preexisting dharma halls were made over in Tibetan style and were used for Tibetan religious observances (for more, see Chapter 9). Later on, individuals supported the Theravada monks when they entered the Valley in the 1930s and 1940s, but the vast majority of Newar Buddhists continued with their traditional religious observances, anything else being strongly discouraged by the regime. In this context, support by rich laymen was crucial for the survival of the monks.

The prime task of Theravada Buddhist laypeople was and is the support of monks and nuns. Today there are many monastic buildings, more than enough to house the Sangha. (The problem, rather, is a shortage of personnel to service the smaller settlements.) This was not always so, and the initial effort of the lay community was to provide them with places to live, monasteries that would then become the focus of lay religious activity. (Meditation centers were a later development: see Chapter 8.) The principal monasteries are shown in Table 5.1. Who were the principal donors for these monasteries? In the case of the larger monasteries in Kathmandu and Lalitpur, they were wealthy businessmen, but why were they interested in supporting Theravada Buddhism?

In the 1920s, rich Buddhist Newars were those who made a success of trading in Tibet. Most of them supported Tibetan Buddhist institutions while in Tibet, and many of them continued this practice when back in Nepal. As previously noted, Dharma Man Tuladhar (Dhama Sahu) played a key role in making the visit of Kyangtse Lama to Nepal the success that it was, and he renovated Kindo Baha, which was the prime base of operations for the Theravada monks and nuns in the early years. Later, when the monks were expelled from Nepal and ended up in Kalimpong in the late 1920s, and again at the time of the second expulsion in 1944, the key figures supporting the movement were Bhaju Ratna (1882–1956) and his son Maniharsha Jyoti (1917–93), who were Kansakars (part of the Uday caste, who are principally artisans and traders). Maniharsha's younger brothers by Bhaju Ratna's second wife, Gyan Jyoti (1922–2004) and Dev Jyoti, would eventually become important Buddhist lay supporters as well. They were based in Kalimpong because at that time much of the trade with Tibet passed through there from Calcutta, rather than via Kathmandu.[4] As noted in Chapter 2, Maniharsha became the treasurer of the Dharmodaya Sabha, which was established in Sarnath in November 1944 in response to the Ranas' expulsions of four monks and four novices in July of that year.

Bhaju Ratna did not start out rich. In 1917, the year Maniharsha was born, a fire destroyed the entire stock of Bhaju Ratna's cloth shop in Kel Tol in the heart of old Kathmandu. Unable to repay his Marwari wholesaler, Bhaju Ratna moved from Kathmandu to Kalimpong where he started a hotel and restaurant for Nepali traders, and it was in this establishment, from the mid-1920s until the 1940s, that Mahapragya and other Nepali Theravada monks would frequently stay. Thanks to his support of Buddhist mendicants, Bhaju Ratna would become known as Dan Bir, "hero of charity." Meanwhile, Maniharsha was going to school in Kalimpong, after which he went to stay in Calcutta at Dhama Sahu's *kothi*, both to learn business and to study commerce at Calcutta University. During this period, he worked for Dhama Sahu as a cook (S. M. Tuladhar 1995: 123). For his entire formative years, Maniharsha stayed outside Nepal. Although he became fluent in Hindi, Bengali, and English, in addition to Nepali, according to one account he was less than fluent in his native tongue so that at one point, hearing him speaking a mishmash (*khicari*) of different languages, his father decided to send him back to Nepal for a while so that he would learn to speak Nepal Bhasha correctly (Maniharsha 1995: 766). However, according to another account, that of his elder sister, Maniharsha refused to go back to Nepal until he had passed his "Matric" and until he had enough money to repay what his father owed the Marwari wholesaler. This resulted in his having to go through the *kayta puja* ritual in Kathmandu at an embarrassingly advanced age (L. Tuladhar

Table 5.1 Some important Viharas and their donors

Vihara name	Place	Dates of founding and renovations	Donor(s) of land	Principal donor(s) of buildings
Ananda Kuti	Swayambhu, Kathmandu	1941; 1951; 1977	Government	Lay supporters
Gana	Gana Baha, Kathmandu	1961	Local government (public land)	Local lay supporters
Shrigha	Shrigha, Kathmandu	1943	Bhaju Ratna Sahu (Kansakar)	Bhaju Ratna & others
Vishwa Shanti	Naya Baneshwar, Kathmandu	1985; 1995–7	Chaitya Maya Shakya	Malaysian devotees
Sangharama	Kathmandu	1981	Local government	Dwarika Das Shrestha, Ratna Maya Shakya
Antarashtriya Dhyan Kendra (IBMC)	Shankhamul, Kathmandu (but walking distance from Lalitpur)	1985	Chaitya Maya Shakya	Many donors, including Gyan Jyoti Kansakar, Thai Sangharaja
Buddha Vihara	Bhrikuti Mandap, Kathmandu	1977	Badri Maya Manandhar	Lay supporters
Dharmachakra Ashram	Bagh Bazaar, Kathmandu	1970; 1994	Asha Ratna Tandukar	Lay supporters
Sumangal (Old name: Yangamangal, foundation from 12th century)	near Uku Baha, Lalitpur	1943; 1996	Members of lineage *baha:* late Harsha Man Shakya's family and others[a]	1996: 300 donors (largest donation in name of Ram Bahadur Manandhar)
Shakyasingha	Thaina, Lalitpur	1957, 1989	Harsha Bir Singh Shakya	Kul Narasingh Shakya; renovation in 1990: many donors, plus Thai money

Manimandap	Patko, Lalitpur	1975	Bahi *sangha*	Devotees, led by Gyanapurnik, Hera Kaji, Kaludai, and others
Nagar Mandap Shri Kirti (or Shri Kirti)	Kirtipur	1976, 1988–95	local government (public land), plus Dhan Lal Maharjan	Local people, Thai Sangharaja, Thai Airways
Muni	Bhaktapur	1953; 2002	Local *baha sangha*	Local lay people; renovation in 2002 with Thai donors
Samaskrita	Bhaktapur	1973	Local *baha sangha*	Local lay people
Dhyankuti	Banepa	1973	Purna Maya & Krishna Maya Manandhar	Ashwaghosh and Sanu Ratna Sthapit
Pranidhipurna	Balambu	1948, 1991	land bought by Ganesh Lal Maharjan, Suku Maharjan	1991: Sumangal, Ghunaghosh, Suku Maharjan
Kindo Baha	Kindol, Swayambhu	1926	local *baha sangha*	Dhama Sahu
Kindol Vihara, (Nirvanamurti Upasikarama)	Kindol, Swayambhu	1949	Dharmachari & others	Dharmachari
Dharmakirti	Shrigha, Kathmandu	1964, 2001	Harsha Man Shakya, Hira Thakũ Shakya[b]	1964: Keshari Laxmi and Dan Laxmi Kansakar; 2001: Bhairaja Tuladhar

[a]This Harsha Man was different from Dhammawati's father. Mahendra Ratna Shakya (1996: 2) lists the other donors as Jog Ratna, Muni Ratna, Purna Ratna, Hera Lal, Chiniya Kaji, and Chakra Ratna Shakya.

[b]I.e. Dhammawati's parents.

1995: 105). Maniharsha stubbornly resisted parental pressure to get married. His father, increasingly disturbed by his son's intransigence, adopted a Gandhian approach and undertook a semi-fast, which he kept to for seven years until finally, aged twenty-seven, Maniharsha gave in to his wishes (ibid.: 106).

Maniharsha's upbringing and education in India clearly had a deep impact on him. At a very early age he accepted Dharmacharyya, who often passed through Kalimpong in the 1920s, as his guru. (His younger brother Gyan Jyoti also remembers Dharmacharyya as his first guru in Buddhism.) For the rest of his life, Maniharsha ate neither fish nor meat. A photograph shows him holding a ceremonial parasol over Dharmacharyya at the Buddhist conference that Dharmacharyya organized in Calcutta in 1928 (Lacoul 1995: 109). Maniharsha, aged eleven, is still a child and Dharmacharyya himself appears extremely young. Later on, Maniharsha came under the influence of Mahatma Gandhi to such a degree that he began wearing khadi cloth, which his sisters wove for him; he would wash out the cloth himself each evening (L. Tuladhar 1995). Late in life, he accepted S. N. Goenka, the celebrated vipassana (insight) meditation teacher whom he encountered in India, as his guru also, and since 1982 his family has strongly supported the vipassana movement. Apart from encouraging his spiritual interests, his Indian boyhood and youth exposed him to middle-class patterns of frugal hard work. Despite his great wealth, unless he had women or children with him, his practice was to travel second class. It is reported that he never wasted a minute, using every spare moment to write letters or to meditate (Maniharsha 1995: 769).

Maniharsha began to do business on his own account during the Second World War, recycling scrap metal from Tibet at a time when metal was in short supply; in addition, he and his brothers started an import-export business between Calcutta and Lhasa (Maniharsha 1995: 766–767). In 1962, he founded the first iron and steel mill in Nepal and later, the first, and so far only, cement factory in the Kathmandu Valley. (It is now closed.) Although in all he started up twenty-two different manufacturing and service businesses (S. K. Joshi 1995: 386–387), despite a potentially remunerative market for cigarettes and alcohol, he refused to invest in them and neither smoked nor drank himself.

The first cohorts of Theravada monks relied heavily on the financial support of Bhaju Ratna and his sons for many of their activities. As the organization's first treasurer, it was Maniharsha who bankrolled not only the Dharmodaya Sabha but its monthly magazine, *Dharmodaya*, which, during the years that it appeared (1947–60), was effectively the only mouthpiece of Newar culture and religion, and as such was eagerly consumed in the Valley.[5] Although famously hospitable to Buddhist monastics in Calcutta and Kalimpong, the support he gave to the new Theravada movement, and later to vipassana, in Nepal itself was even more important.

Some of Maniharsha's views on the different forms of Buddhism can be gleaned from an interview that was published in 1988. The interview hints not only at his motives for his continuing support of the Theravada movement but also at a certain dissatisfaction with the spiritual level and conduct of some of its monastics. Asked about the situation of Buddhism in Nepal before 1951 he replied:

> In order to understand the situation before 1951, let me give you the example of the fight between the Uday and the Gubhaju, which had been going on for generations. The spiritual preceptors of the very religion which had brought in the change of opposing caste discrimination were themselves presuming to introduce a religious fine upholding petty caste distinctions! . . . It was against this degraded form of religion that the Ven. Dhammalok and others rebelled by becoming Theravada monks and unmasking the corruptions of Vajrayana Buddhism.
>
> [On meditation:] In fact meditation is not just a Theravadin practice, but is done in their own way by Lamas and Gurujus as well. But, just as when one sends children to college without first sending them to school, they won't understand the teaching, so [their meditation traditions] became more or less hidden. Theravada is the first level of Buddhism, it is the religious equivalent of the foundations of a house. Mahayana is the higher level, like the top floor of the house. Our Gurujus are expounding the most profound scriptures without first having learned their ABCs, like someone who can't walk being made to run off in a hurry. What benefit can this bring anyone? That's why it's necessary to first to take to heart the basic truths and facts of Buddhism through teaching vipassana meditation.
>
> "What place do you think it is appropriate to give to traditional Mahayana and Vajrayana Buddhism in society in today's context?"
>
> The Gurujus of today are just doing social rituals (*karmakanda*) in the name of religion. Such customs are really only life-cycle rituals (*samskar*) or traditions (*samskrti*), not religion (*dharma*). Religion is really only about what people have to do to achieve the practice of morality and wisdom. Gurujus do their recitation and rituals, with their dharanis and mantras, without making sure that they match. And in order to save themselves time, they shorten everything. They may be preserving religion in doing so, but their hope that the meaning will be preserved, and that the

> work accomplished will be the same, is baseless. . . . Given that Buddhism was founded by the Buddha in order to oppose Brahmanism, priest-ism (*purohitvad*), and theism (*isvaravad*), what kind of Buddhism is it that, in the Buddha's name, sets up gods and a high lord (*isvara*) and has a priest worship them?
>
> "Do you have anything to say about the life conduct of today's monks?"
>
> In today's Nepal many [Theravada] monks are no less than the Gurujus. To earn enough money and rice by doing *paritran*—is that not on the Gurujus' level? What difference [is there] from householder Gurujus if all [the monks] do is build up their bank balance and just live in one place? Who can say that they won't . . . in the near future [become] guardians of monasteries like Gurujus, if they go on like this? (Jyoti 1995)

Jog Maya: All Dharmas Are Good

Jog Maya's experiences illustrate how far, over the last sixty or seventy years, the average Buddhist householder has moved in the direction of the Theravada Buddhism that Maniharsha did so much to encourage and support. Born in 1913, Jog Maya, a gracious white-haired lady, grew up in a large Lalitpur family that belonged to a distinguished Shakya lineage. The men of the family were traders in Tibet, to which her father went off when she was so young that on his return ten years later she failed to recognize him. Her well-to-do family performed the prestigious ritual of Panchadan when she was four years old and sponsored the Samyak festival in Nag Baha when she was fourteen. A few years later, just before the joint household split up, they underwrote the renovation of the monastery of Na Bahi.

Jog Maya's father would sometimes invite Tibetan lamas to perform rituals in the home, but all the regular family rituals were performed by Vajracharyas; furthermore her mother, who was frequently ill, was a devotee of Karunamaya, the most important bodhisattva-god in the Newar Buddhist pantheon. Jog Maya had only one sibling, a younger sister, Chaitya Maya, who, because she never married, inherited most of her father's extensive landholdings. A convert to Theravada Buddhism, Chaitya Maya eventually donated much of her inheritance to the Theravada Sangha. In old age, though continuing to live in her own home, she shaved her head herself and adopted nuns' dress.

Jog Maya is very unusual for a woman of her generation in that, as a girl, she learned to read. In her childhood, as she explains, few people thought that a girl needed to study, so although—from her male cousins—she learned to read print, she never learned to read handwritten materials, to write, to do maths, or to speak Nepali. "It was only in my daughters' childhood that girls started to go to school," she points out.

At fifteen, she was given in marriage; but her husband's home was near her natal home and she visited her family frequently. "In those days," she recalls, "there were many religious stories aimed at instructing women about their wifely duties. You were taught to treat your husband as equivalent to Swayambhu and that the highest religious virtue (*dharma*) was to serve him." As a young married woman, however, she spent long periods of time separated from her husband. As he had no son of his own, Jog Maya's father took his son-in-law into his business, and, soon after she got married, Jog Maya saw her new husband leave for Tibet where he stayed for almost seven years.

Jog Maya gave birth to seven children of whom five—four daughters and one son—lived to adulthood. Altogether, she has seventeen grandchildren and twenty-three great-grandchildren. Her husband's death in 1983 was, and remains, very hard for her; but she hopes that religious stories that suggest that meritorious practice of religion is rewarded by being reunited with your husband in a future rebirth will apply to her too.

Jog Maya took Tantric Initiation (*diksa*) twice, the first time on her own at age twenty-five while her husband was away in Tibet, and the second time, twenty-five years later, with her husband. Although she has kept up her daily Vajrayanist practice throughout her adult life, in no way has she been an exclusivist. For example, after her husband's death, in addition to the full complement of Vajracharya rituals, she had both Theravada and Tibetan monks perform funerary rites. Again, astonishingly, at seventy-seven, she attended her first ten-day vipassana meditation course and, but for her age and infirmity, would consider taking a second course. These days, though she doesn't sleep too well and isn't strong enough to walk around visiting temples and monasteries as she once did, she is free, since she long ago handed over all household responsibilities to her daughter-in-law, to devote much of her time to reading religious books and reciting mantras.

Asked whether the Vajracharyas denounced the Theravada monks in the old days, she replies: "Yes they did, though they shouldn't have. Whatever dharma you feel like doing, whatever dharma it occurs to you to do, whatever dharma you like, you must do. My husband never took the Precepts, either from the Theravadins or from the Lamas in the Gompa. He would just give *dan* to them and say [to me], 'You go and do it [take the Precepts].' " As a traditionalist, he would take care of the *stupa* at I Bahi, which his father-in-law had renovated, covered with cement, and endowed with land, to pay for its annual repainting.

Jog Maya's tolerance of all sincere dharma allows her to approve both of her eldest daughter, who married into a family of virtuoso practitioners of Tibetan Buddhism, and of her youngest daughter, whose husband's family produced Dhammawati, the leading Theravada nun of the present generation. One day Jog Maya remarks:

> With all the different religions [we have] here, it is like buying vegetables in Mangal Bazaar! Some like the Shravakayan [Theravada], most Mahayana, and so on. . . . The Mahayanists say it is very meritious to light ghee lamps, whereas the Shravakayanists say one shouldn't do that. Just light a candle, give *dan*, and read the *paritran*, and that's it. Nevertheless, the Shravakayanists do one thing wrong, which is to criticize other people's practice. This is a sin (*ma tyo*). If someone is one-pointed in his devotion to Mahadev or Narayan, that is fine. After all, Lokeshvar takes different forms for different people.

Krishna Bir, Farmer, Palace Servant, Student of Philosophy: Theravada Is the Best Way

As noted above, the early converts to Theravada Buddhism were drawn almost exclusively from Buddhist Newar upper castes. In the case of males, even though very few had been to school, most had received tutoring at home. Theravada Buddhism in its modernist form places great emphasis on making religious material available in the vernacular so that the laity may read it for themselves. Because people belonging to middle and lower occupational castes were most unlikely to be literate, this was one reason why they were slower than the more privileged upper castes to become involved in the new movement. One exception is Krishna Bir Maharjan of Lalitpur who, without benefit of either formal education or tutoring, had managed to "pick up" reading at the age of eight or nine. A slightly built, carefully dressed man who is now in his late eighties, he has been wholeheartedly involved in the movement for almost sixty years. His first exposure occurred in the mid-1940s when a friend took him to Sumangal Vihara. Although at that time the abbot, Pragyananda, was in exile in India, his devotees continued to do Buddha Puja and to receive occasional visits and instruction from less prominent monks who had gone into hiding in outlying villages. By the time Pragyananda returned from India in 1946,

Krishna Bir was a committed Theravadin. Like virtually all Buddhist Newars, he continued to worship his lineage god (*digu dyah*) and to call Vajracharya priests to his house to perform life-cycle rites, but in other respects he soon gave up traditional religious practices, notably performing animal sacrifice during the autumn festival of Dasain.

Born into a simple peasant family, he had little land of his own. As a youth, he worked as a laborer for other farmers but in 1937, aged twenty-two, he took a job as a storekeeper in one of the Rana palaces and remained there for the next seventeen years. His daily wage was two *manas* of rice, plus some lentils, all of which, because his employers fed him at work, he would take home. In addition, he received four rupees per month. After leaving the Ranas' employ in 1954, he worked at various jobs, including—until they installed one of their own people—being the gatekeeper at the Chinese embassy.

Krishna Bir and his wife had five sons and two daughters; their fifteen grandchildren include two grandsons who ordained as Theravada monks and several who have received a university education. Although unschooled himself, in the mid-1950s, when the post-Rana government first introduced adult literacy classes in Lalitpur, Krishna Bir—perhaps because local government officials viewed him as a fitting role model—was appointed chairman of his neighborhood literacy committee.

Recalling how his first contact with the Theravadins occurred, he says, "My friend Chabi Lal, who was a servant at Sumangal Vihara, used to talk with me about the doctrine of the Five Skandhas underlying the Four Elements. I thought that this sounded very logical and that, in comparison, the other religions I knew about were quite superficial. So one day he took me to Sumangal Vihara." Until then, Krishna Bir had been a devotee of the gods of Mahayana Buddhism. He had worshipped the Five Buddhas, the Five Taras, the Five Protections (Pancharaksha), and the 108 Lokeshvaras, and periodically he would bathe in the Bagmati River (in order to purify himself). But now he began to understand that religion could also be about improving one's behavior (*sil*) and about training the mind (attaining *samadhi*). Just as reading the scriptures is higher than simple worship, so this ethical and psychological path is higher than either of the others. He explains:

> One way of spreading the dharma is by making a chaitya. Ordinary people will have *gyan* (knowledge) if they see it. Chaityas, temples—all of them are a kind of sign showing the way [to *gyan*]. Ashoka made as many chaityas and monasteries as there are dharma scriptures. That is one

> way of spreading the dharma. To help people to understand the dharma, you have scriptures for the learned and statues for ordinary people. Householders have to support the monks and the monks have to enlighten the householders.

Krishna Bir's Rana employers became aware of his preference for Theravada Buddhism and of his objection to animal sacrifice. So even though they required him, like all their employees, to contribute a goat to the annual worship of their lineage deity, they did not force him to slaughter chickens or to finish off animals that were brought wounded and dying from the hunt as other servants were sometimes required to do. He is proud of the fact that in the early 1950s he was able to persuade the twenty-seven families belonging to his death *guthi* to give up performing animal sacrifices at their annual feast.

Krishna Bir feels that the traditional Vajrayana Buddhism of the Newars, and especially of his own Maharjan community, has been contaminated by Hinduism. This is because throughout the century of Rana rule Maharjans were under pressure to conform to Brahmanical practice, and, even after the Ranas were ousted and the pressure eased, his community continued to mix Hinduism and Buddhism, especially with regard to animal sacrifice, which Buddhism categorically forbids. The traditional caste initiation of a Maharjan boy (*kayta puja*) is, in his view, another obviously syncretistic feature:

> The boy worships the Buddha, the Dharma, and the Sangha and takes alms from his mother. He's instructed to say, "After taking alms from my mother and father, I'll go off to the forest to be an ascetic." It is the family priest who teaches him what to say and do. Next they go for *puja* to the neighborhood shrine of the god Ganesh and then the boy's maternal uncle brings a sacrificial animal, a goat or a sheep, and the Vajracharya priest makes the dedication. On the one hand the priest has the boy worship the Buddha, the Dharma, and the Sangha, and then the very same priest then has him *sacrifice* to Ganesh! It isn't consistent with Buddhism and that's why Vajracharya priests here do their best not to do it. In the cities people have come to understand [what Buddhism is], but in the villages it is still going on a lot.

Krishna Bir's introduction to meditation came in 1971 when a visiting Burmese monk taught him to do *kesaloma* (meditation on the parts of the body, meant to generate detachment from it). For some years afterward, he practiced under the tutelage of Sumangal Bhante and Buddhaghosh Bhante. Although some old people still do *kesaloma*, since 1980 he himself has been practising vipassana, which he first learned from the Burmese nun Daw Pannyachari, who that year gave an introductory course in Dhyankuti Vihara, Banepa; later on, he learned from Mahasi Sayadaw, who came from Burma to lecture in Lalitpur the following year. But S. N. Goenka, whose course Krishna Bir attended in 1982, was the teacher who created the vipassana "wave":

> Before that, young people who came to a monastery [to meditate] were very self-conscious and people would tease them that they were trying to behave like old people. At that time, those lay people who did meditation were unusual. But Goenka is himself a Marwari and so he brought in Hindus and made vipassana acceptable to everyone. He is very charismatic and because of his reputation even very rich people came to learn from him.

For many years after his conversion, Krishna Bir continued to attend Sumangal Vihara. Later, his friend Chabi Lal, having opened a bookshop and become quite wealthy, sponsored the renovation of Manimandap Vihara, which was carried out under the direction of Gyanapurnik, who at the time was the resident monk. Krishna Bir started to go regularly to Manimandap, but when the International Meditation Center (IBMC) opened at Shankhamul in 1989 (see Chapter 8), he switched again. Almost every morning of the year he meditates there between 6 and 7 A.M. For more than a quarter of a century, he has also belonged to a group that discusses Buddhist philosophy every Monday evening in Bakhum Baha; he has himself written a lengthy manuscript on the doctrine of dependent origination that he would like to publish. But though he has been reading and discussing Buddhist books for most of his adult life, he believes that meditation is more important than study:

> There's a lot more *gyan* to be gained from studying than from just looking at statues, and again, a lot more from meditation than from studying. The benefits come much more quickly. The Lord Buddha once told [a man] off for just coming to see Him. Their two bodies were just the same, He said [so what was the point of this visit?]. Meditation was what [that man] should have been doing!

The point of meditation, Krishna Bir says, is to obtain *gyan* in *this* life—to really understand that this existence is impermanent, painful, and lacking in essence. Good works (*kushala karma*) improve your prospects for the *next* life.

His services to the community have brought him widespread recognition, and on the walls of his living room hang certificates and testimonials from many organizations including the Marxist-Leninist Party—of which he has never been a member. In old age, he would like to have become a monk; his old friend Chabi Lal, who introduced him to Theravada Buddhism so many years ago, renounced at the age of seventy, but in his own case he had to remain at home to care for his wife who suffered a stroke and was bedridden for several years until her death in 1999. Only once has he taken temporary ordination and, given the physical rigors of monastic life, which at his age might prove too much for him, he regretfully concedes that he probably will not be able to do so again.

Financing the Sangha: The Donors' Committees

Every Nepalese vihara was founded by a particular lay donor or group of donors, and when the original benefactors withdrew or died, others were found to provide support; but at the beginning, they were not organized into formal committees or other organizations. Dynamic monks like Amritananda raised large amounts of money abroad and never had to produce accounts showing how it was spent. To some extent, the same system operates even today. According to an Uday woman who is on the donor's committee of a monastery:

> The treasurer never sees that money. When construction work is being done, the abbot (*pramukh*) either supervises the work—and pays the laborers him or herself, or delegates the responsibility to a chela. The donors' job is to *give* money, and that's the end of it. The bhantes and gurumas are secretive and not only about how they spend money but about most other matters as well. And they get away with it because they wear the robe, and laypeople respect them. Even when they disapprove of something the bhantes and gurumas do, they give them the benefit of the doubt. And so even though they may be privately critical, they say nothing. Instead they just drift away. Their excuse is that, as businessmen, they don't have the time to give to vihara affairs. But the truth is, they don't want to make trouble by pushing in where they aren't welcome.

Because of criticisms about accountability—even Amritananda was burlesqued for the alleged size of his bank balance in the satirical newspapers printed once a year for the Gai Jatra festival—there have been more and more attempts since 1990 to produce formal accounts showing how money is spent. Many monasteries have a donors' committee (*dayaka samiti* or *dayaka sabha*), which is composed (optimally) of wealthy laymen and laywomen whose primary role is as contributors. Some members have always taken administrative positions and today's officers, who always include a treasurer, may be female as well as male. Government regulations require that contributors be given receipts but, because most donations are made personally to the abbot or abbess rather than to the vihara, the treasurer may not be informed when contributions are made, let alone how they are spent. However, when the treasurer himself collects money to cover the running costs of the monastery, this money at least will appear in the accounts. In the early 1990s, an attempt was made to form a central committee, based in Dharmachakra Ashram/Vihara in Bag Bazaar, that would oversee all the different donors' committees of all the different monasteries, but this provision has remained a dead letter. Nor has the Dharmodaya Sabha's committee, set up for a similar purpose, been much more successful.

Activist monks have attempted to resist donors' committees as an unnecessary restriction on the the abbot's freedom of action. Thus, Sudarshan did not allow one to be set up in Shri Kirti Vihara. Laypeople could become life members of the monastery for a payment of 105 rupees, a not inconsiderable sum in 1976 when the vihara was founded, but that gave them no role in running it. Instead, in order to avoid problems after his death, Sudarshan ensured from the beginning that the monastery was registered in the name of the Akhil Nepal Bhikshu Mahasangha. He set up seven separate bank accounts, each requiring at least two or three signatures, to cover the following expenses:

- utility bills;
- meals when there was no invitation from laypeople;
- stipends of one hundred rupees a month to resident monks and nuns (an idea copied from Thailand);
- maintenance of the building;
- maintenance of the *uposatha* building, where the relic of Yashodhara (the Buddha's wife) is kept;
- expenses when resident monks or nuns are sick;
- running the Shri Kirti Bauddha Kendra (Buddhist Center), which organizes activities such as flood relief, camps for training Janajati Buddhists, publishing, flood relief, and so on.

Sudarshan's foresight seems to have paid off in that there have been no major financial problems in his vihara following his death. This contrasts with what had happened after Bhikshu Sumangal died in 1999. His brother had been his manager and so his monastery, Buddha Vihara, as well as all the bank accounts and a house near the IBMC in Shankhamul, were in his name only. By Nepalese law all such assets go to the "relatives" (*santan*), which meant that complex and sensitive negotiations with Sumangal's family were necessary to avoid a messy court case and to ensure the transfer of the monastery and its assets to the Sangha.

Financing Nunneries

Securing financial support is a perennial problem for the nuns. In Burma, Dhammawati and her companions had been accustomed to going on the alms round twice a month. In Nepal, following the repeal of the old Law Code in 1955, there was no longer any legal or state backing for restrictions on commensality. But when the newly returned nuns tried going for alms in Kathmandu, they soon discovered that a change in the law had not changed people's attitudes. Encountering apathy, suspicion, and sometimes overt hostility, the nuns soon abandoned it. ("People would shout at us, 'Why are strong young women like you *begging*?' "[6]). On lunar days, they conducted Buddha Puja in the vihara and afterward received donations. When invited to chant in private homes, they would be given lunch and small sums of money; but most meals were taken in the nunnery. Today, the five paisa coins they received as *dana* in the 1960s have been replaced by one or two rupee notes. But the adolescent nuns especially dislike having to sit in a row, heads bowed, after Buddha Puja, waiting for those lowest denomination banknotes to fall into their laps, and as often as possible avoid doing so. "The old gurumas tell us we must do it so the upasakas can earn merit, but it makes me feel ashamed," one said, echoing the sentiments of her companions. In any event, the amount of money the nuns receive on ordinary occasions is inconsequential even today, and it is rapidly consumed by personal expenditures such as bus fares, toiletries, pens, and notebooks. (However recent their ordination, monks still routinely receive five times as much *dana* as the most senior nuns, and day-to-day donations do not match the generosity shown in the alms round when fund-raising for a particular purpose.)

As noted in previous chapters, the support of nuns' (and monks') families and relatives was crucial to the survival and growth of the Sangha, especially in the early years. For nuns coming from well-off families, this extends beyond the provision of housing and food to buying land and building viharas. It was in fact two of Dhammawati's brothers who made possible the purchase of the land on which Dharmakirti now stands.

The *Sahujis* and the Nuns

For major expenditures, the nuns have turned again and again to a group of businessmen, some of whom are the sons and grandsons of those long-ago Calcutta and Kalimpong *sahujis* who supported the first Theravadin missionaries. In the early years, the most generous supporter of the nuns was Maniharsha Jyoti, who was the key supporter of the Theravada movement generally. He became involved with Dharmakirti through his wife and sister, both devotees of Dhammawati. The original building backed on to a butcher's shop, and, when Maniharsha heard that the odor issuing from it was so bad that one hot day Daw Gunawati had fainted, he bought the shop, demolished it, and presented the site to Dhammawati, who built a kitchen and a library on it.

In Dharmakirti, just as at all Buddhist holy sites, whether Theravada or Vajrayana, the majority of devotees were women. Although Dhammawati invited some women to take positions of responsibility, she also sought male participation. Laywomen might sell their gold bangles and donate the proceeds to the vihara for a specific purpose, but few commanded substantial resources.[7] For long-term financial support, Dhammawati knew she needed the support of their husbands. The long list of male donors who regularly attend her sermons and dharma talks and who go on the pilgrimages she leads abroad testifies to her success in earning the respect of the business community. Her talents as a teacher, her scholarship, her prominence as a community leader and, most especially, her accessability have combined to win their admiration and devotion.

Of the revival of the nuns' Order in Sri Lanka, Elizabeth Nissan has noted the importance of the social status of its leaders: the fact that Catherine de Alwis in particular was highly educated and came from a prominent Sinhala family was crucial to her fund-raising success and the survival of her movement (Nissan 1984). Similarly, it is as an upper-caste woman whose family is known and respected (though not especially wealthy) that Dhammawati has been able to win the confidence of some of the most influential male members of the Buddhist community.[8] These men have competed for positions on temple committees and contributed to the publication of dozens of Buddhist books and pamphlets that Dhammawati and her team produced; they have also contributed to temple construction projects in Kathmandu and Lumbini, medications for clinics, and an endowment fund to provide for routine nunnery expenses.[9]

Supporting Monks and Nuns in the 1990s

Exact numbers of monks and nuns are hard to establish. There are almost twice as many novices as young nuns studying abroad (roughly forty-five novices to twenty-three nuns),[10] where their expenses are covered by local sponsors and the monasteries in which they are housed. Furthermore, all Vishwa Shanti Vihara novices are supported by the Chinese-Malaysian devotees of their abbot Gyanapurnik, whereas two other monasteries, Shri Kirti and Shakyasingha, regularly receive funds from Thailand.[11] As the scope of the nuns' work has widened, securing funds to pay for projects, including the education of adolescent nuns who tend to come from modest backgrounds, has become increasingly time-consuming. One upasika who, as a child in the 1970s, remembers Dhammawati coming with a group of nuns to chant in her home whenever a member of her family celebrated a birthday, observes that these days the Dharmakirti nuns in particular are so busy performing rituals, for which they receive *dana*, that one is lucky if one can book them even once a year. Aside from scheduled appointments, they may be called out to chant three times in a single twenty-four hour period.

Padmawati, like her guru Dhammawati, is a compelling preacher. She is developing an economic base for her new nunnery, Mayadevi Vihara, which one day may be on a par with Dharmakirti. She too comes from a loyal and relatively affluent family that has given generously to her projects. But because her family members, generous as they are, cannot finance them alone, like her mentor she spends a great deal of time and energy developing and maintaining her "donor network."[12] Although a few donors are members of the old upper-caste *sahuji* families, most are businessmen belonging to farming and occupational castes, many of them Manandhars like herself. "They like to drop in at the vihara and talk to me whenever they feel like it," she remarks. Officially, they come to discuss difficulties they encounter in their meditation practice; but in reality, she says, "mostly they're here to talk about personal matters. I can't send them away because if I did, they'd be offended." Until the construction of her temple is finished, Padmawati says she'll have to sit and gossip, and wait for them to take themselves away of their own accord. She adds with a wry smile that, even when the construction is finished, she'll still have to sit and gossip because then she'll need more donations to maintain what their *dana* helped build.[13]

Whereas Westerners flock to Tibetan monasteries in the Valley and some nuns at Swayambhu have begun to attract donations from Europeans and Americans (Kerin 2000), the Nepalese Theravada community is small and little known outside Nepal. Most Westerners who wish to study Theravada Buddhism or to practice vipassana meditation go to Southeast Asia or Sri Lanka, not Nepal. Again, unlike the Theravada monks who are old hands at the game, to date the nuns have attracted relatively small sums from Asian Buddhists and little from Westerners.[14] Although the nuns' Order has fewer recruits than the monks', nuns still outnumber monks, because of a much lower dropout rate. A majority of today's novice monks are drawn from farming and occupational-caste families who look to the Sangha to provide their sons with the education that they cannot afford to give them themselves. Sooner or later, the majority disrobe. By contrast, a number of recruits from impoverished rural backgrounds notwithstanding, the Nepali nuns' Order continues to attract privileged urban women willing to share their resources with their protégées.[15] Just as nuns in medieval Europe shared their incomes with poor "nieces" (McNamara 1996: 276), so also do Shakya, Tuladhar, and Manandhar nuns "adopt" young recruits from poor backgrounds whose ordination ceremonies they sponsor, whose food and clothing they provide, and whose educational expenses they underwrite. Now, as in the past, the senior nuns look to their own community, whose support they must work hard to retain.

Central to the success of their fund-raising activities is their ability to develop and maintain relationships with individual devotees. The fact that they have confined their efforts to their own community may be to their advantage. Local people see them as responsive to their needs and opinions and, accordingly, reward them with both trust and money. In recent years, as the lay community they serve has grown, the nuns, like the monks, have been in dire need of funds to repair and extend their quarters and to build new facilities. But whereas the monks have looked to Buddhists in Japan, Burma, and—especially—Thailand, the nuns have raised considerable sums at home.[16] Ironically, the monks have found that their success in attracting funds from abroad has damaged—perhaps permanently—their relations with the Newar laity, some of whom, feeling slighted and ignored, have distanced themselves from the bhantes and transferred their trust and their *dana* to the gurumas.

The Dharmodaya Sabha and the Organization of Buddha Jayanti

As described in Chapter 2, the Dharmodaya Sabha, the Buddhist Society of Nepal, was founded at Sarnath in 1944 by exiled monks and their lay supporters at a defining moment for the development of Buddhism in Nepal. It was intended as an umbrella organization that would include all Nepali Buddhists. Chandramani Mahasthavir was its first president and Amritananda its secretary, and its treasurer was Maniharsha Jyoti Kansakar, who was for half a century the Sangha's most generous financial backer. Once the Rana regime had fallen, a branch of the organization was opened in Shrigha Vihara in Kathmandu with Pragyananda as president and Amritananda as secretary. One of its first tasks was to organize Buddha Jayanti in Kathmandu. Meanwhile, its influential journal, *Dharmodaya*, continued to be published from Kalimpong; 164 issues came out between 1947 and its demise in 1960 (J. N. Shakya 1996: 49).

The first Buddha Jayanti ever celebrated in Nepal was organized by Dharmacharyya in his home city of Lalitpur in 1926. The next celebration, and the first in a continuous sequence, was organized by Bhikkhu Dhammalok in Kindo Baha in 1937, with an exhibition of Buddhist pictures that he had brought back from China. Thus began the celebration of what has come to be, from the Theravada point of view, the most important festival of the year. (The way in which it was used to forge links with the King was discussed in Chapter 3.) Modeled on the celebration of Wesak in Sri Lanka and other Theravadin countries, the festival has come to be accepted by all Nepali Buddhists as a major event in their calendar. Lay Buddhists in Lalitpur find no problem in observing this festival as well as the traditional Mataya local pilgrimage during the month of Gunla, which is also supposed to celebrate the Buddha's attainment of enlightenment.

The first of the uninterrupted sequence of Buddha Jayanti celebrations in Lalitpur was held, as in Kathmandu, in 1952. That year, and for the next two years, the Lalitpur festivities were organized by the

Taremam Sangha, the bhajan-singing group from Kwa Baha. Adapting a procedure followed at more traditional festivals, a procession was taken out along the usual city circumambulation (*pradaksina*) route, with bhajan groups from different localities of the city. Each year after 1954, a different city neighborhood undertook to organize it, and from 1962 a bank account was established with funds to support the organizers. In 1970, when it was Uku Baha's turn to take responsibility for the festival, the organizers donated a Buddha statue, which has been used ever since in the celebrations (G. B. Shakya 2001). In 2001, Dharma Duta, whose life story is given below, chaired the committee for the Nag Baha neighborhood, which had undertaken to organize the festivities for that year. He had the idea of ordaining one temporary monk for each year that the festival had been celebrated, recruiting mainly from Nag Baha itself, if possible. Thus the following year, in 2002, when the organizing locality was I Bahi, fifty-one monks were ordained; and the year after that it would be fifty-two, and so on. The temporary monks sleep and do meditation in the evenings in IBMC, but return to the organizing locale for instruction and meditation during the day.

The Buddhist aim of having Buddha Jayanti accepted as a national holiday was quickly accepted by the state. King Tribhuvan declared it a public holiday in 1951, and, as described in Chapter 3, his son, King Mahendra, promulgated a ban on animal slaughter throughout the kingdom on the occasion of Buddha Jayanti in 1956, when Nepal hosted the Fourth Conference of the World Fellowship of Buddhists. The Dharmodaya Sabha played the leading role in organizing the conference and greatly expanded the scope of its operations. Kloppenberg (1977: 310) notes that after 1956 and Amritananda's triumphal visits to Mahayana countries in 1959, the expected growth failed to occur. She ascribes this to a cooling of lay enthusiasm in "normal" political times, leaving only the committed core of monks and Theravada supporters, and to the fact that Maniharsha, at that time their leading donor, still lived in Kalimpong. Another important factor must have been the abolition of multiparty democracy in 1960 and the introduction of the Panchayat regime with its emphasis on Hinduism and its banning of any organization not specifically authorized by the state. Any attempt by the Dharmodaya Sabha to organize all the Buddhists of the kingdom would have met with government disapproval after 1960; and government cooperation was needed in order to develop Lumbini. Although Maniharsha himself denied that there was any connection to political developments, it is surely no coincidence that there was no attempt to keep the Dharmodaya Sabha's journal going after 1960.

Amritananda succeeded Chandramani as president of the Dharmodaya Sabha in 1972 but the organization remained fairly inactive until the late 1980s when, like many cultural, religious, and ethnic movements, and following the loosening of the Panchayat regime's controls, it began to try and organize on a national level. The Dharmodaya Sabha has in fact been one of the most successful movements in this regard. Since 1990, there has been a conscious attempt to overcome its Theravada origins and the dominance of Theravada supporters within its hierarchy. Its presidency—a largely honorary post—has rotated in three-year stints between Tibetan Lamaist leaders, eminent Vajracharyas, and Theravada monks. Branches have been set up in many districts and heavily attended three-day conferences have been organized every two years in different parts of the country, at which rituals, dances, and hymns representing all three kinds of Nepalese Buddhism, as well as many ethnic and folk traditions, are put on. As is usual in such conferences, prominent politicians are invited to be present as guests on the opening day.[17]

Since 1994, the Dharmodaya Sabha has had a twelve-member donor's committee (*dayaka samiti*) whose purpose is to monitor how major donations from foreign sources for Buddhist purposes are spent. Given the secretiveness of the senior monks and nuns with regard to financial matters, however, they have met with many frustrations. Lay recipients of foreign funds for religious purposes have hardly been easier to monitor. For example, funds received from a Japanese donor for a *pariyatti* program in a Kathmandu Valley village "disappeared" into the pockets of the upasaka who was supposed to be helping to organize the program.

Educating the Laity

The first curriculum for teaching Buddhism, *Bauddha Pariyatti Siksa*, was modeled initially on Burmese government textbooks. It was put together, and first taught, in 1962 in Trishuli by Bhikshu Buddhaghosh. He was aided by Dharma Ratna "Trishuli," a Shakya from Kwa Baha, Lalitpur, and a largely self-taught Buddhist scholar and social activist, whose family had long traded in Trishuli. The following year, the textbooks were adopted by the All-Nepal Bhikshu Mahasangha and introduced to the Kathmandu Valley and elsewhere. The books and ten-level curriculum, modeled on Burmese and Sri Lankan curricula, were revised continually by a team of monks and some laymen, headed by Buddhaghosh. They translated many texts from Burmese, Sinhala, and Pali into Nepal Bhasha and Nepali. They also wrote numerous textbooks from scratch. In 1985, a committee consisting mainly of monks was set up to oversee the program. From 1990, the textbooks started to be published in Nepali as well. Intended for lay children and adults, the course was nonetheless followed by novices who were waiting to be sent abroad as well as by nuns who had never had the opportunity to study outside Nepal or whose religious training abroad had been truncated. Students are required to take examinations, involving just one paper at level one, increasing to six papers at level ten. There are no formal classes beyond level five, the point at which most laypeople conclude their studies.

The first book introduces the Triple Refuge and the Five Precepts. This is followed by lists of the karmic disadvantages of breaking the precepts, with illustrative stories. The final section of the book gives the basic outline of Shakyamuni Buddha's life story. Book two introduces the Eight Precepts, praise verses to be offered to the Three Jewels, the *Mangala Sutta* and *Maitri Sutta*, and it ends with a more detailed account of the Buddha's path to enlightenment. The third book again begins with the Eight Precepts, and then introduces the ten unproductive actions (*akusala karma*) and the *Ratna Sutta*, and returns to the qualities of, and praise for, the Three Jewels. The book concludes with a collection of well-known stories about the Buddha. All the teachings are imparted by means of stories. Fourth-level books include readings from the *Sigalovada Sutta* (which outlines the duties of a householder); and at the fifth level, Pali grammar is introduced. From the sixth level on, the degree of difficulty of the material rises exponentially, but, as noted, few laypeople proceed beyond level five.

The exams at the first level ask for the meanings of words such as "*nirvana*," "*sthavira*," and "*pravrajya*," ask the student to complete the Pali text of the Five Precepts; and pose questions such as, "In which Buddha's time did Shilavan Brahman live? a) Subbabhibhu, b) Padmottara, c) Bhagavan Buddha, or d) Vipashwi?" By level three, the student is asked to give the meaning of well-known Pali verses, to explain how many unproductive actions there are (giving both the Pali and their meanings), and to explain the Eight Precepts.

Singing for Salvation: The Role of the Gyanmala Bhajan

One of the important ways in which lay religiosity in a largely Theravada idiom has developed is through the singing of hymns in the vernacular, that is, in Nepal Bhasha. The fact that there is, in itself, nothing necessarily or essentially Theravadin in the act of singing such hymns means that the participants include both the most ardent Theravada activists and other Buddhists who have a much more variable and ecumenical attitude toward Buddhism. In fact, lay Buddhists of all the types identified by Lewis and shown in Figure 5.1 can happily combine and share in the practice of singing devotional hymns. However, the manner of the bhajan groups' recruitment, as well as their preference for the vernacular, marks them as modern, not to say modernist: they are, unlike more traditional hymn-singing groups, "open, inclusive, assimilative, and innovative" (Grandin 1989: 179).

This modern style of hymn-singing in a self-consciously Buddhist idiom began in 1937 at Swayambhu. Two years later, Dhammalok brought to Nepal copies of the first Gyanmala hymn book that Bhikshu Pragyabhivamsha had had printed in India. Initially, it was known as the "Bhajan Mala" (garland of bhajans or hymns) and had no editor's name on it, for fear of the Rana censors. Subsequently, Amritananda argued that simple devotion (*bhakti*) was not enough: the hymns must also impart the Buddha's teaching (*jnān/gyān*) and the name was changed to "Gyanmala" (Gyanmala 2003). The first Lalitpur bhajan group was set up in 1939 by members of Kwa Baha and named the Taremam Sangha (D. R. Shakya "Trishuli" 2001: 1). Nine years later, in 1948, there occurred a famous incident in which the Taremam Sangha joined with Hindu singers organized by Tulsi Meher to sing Buddhist songs and "Hare Ram" around the city of Lalitpur as a protest against the political repression of the Ranas; the police arrested about 150 people on that occasion (ibid.: 2). Influenced by the example of the Taremam Sangha, by the time Rana rule came to an end, five or six similar groups had sprung up in Lalitpur.[18]

Many further printings of the first Gyanmala hymn book followed, on an almost yearly basis. Shortly after the monks were expelled by the Ranas in 1944, a Gyanmala group, singing lustily, led a procession from Swayambhu to Jana Baha in the center of Kathmandu. When it reached Jana Baha, the group was surrounded by the police, who seized as many copies of the hymn books as they could; a court case followed, in which the singers were accused of encouraging conversion from Hinduism to Buddhism and ridiculing Nepali, the national language. The case was heard by Padma Shamsher, the Rana prime minister, who decided to reject all the charges (Pradhan 1997: 2–3).

In 1951, with the fall of the Rana regime, the Gyanmala group set up a formal organization and dedicated themselves to hymn recitation, the protection of Swayambhu as a sacred site, and humanitarian service. In the 1960s, the group took the lead in organizing pilgrimages to Buddhist holy sites in India. After 1990, Gyanmala was refounded as a national organization with a new constitution. It inaugurated a series of conferences to be held every three years in different places in Nepal.

As noted above, even though they do not participate in singing hymns themselves, monks, particularly Dhammalok and Amritananda, were at the forefront of encouraging hymn singing and composing hymns in the vernacular in the early years. Later, the most prolific author of songs was Bhikshu Subodhananda. Many hymns composed by laymen are not even explicitly Buddhist, simply calling on Nepalis to "awaken," to "stand up," to learn, to resist superstition, and so on. But even this reinforces the Theravada modernist view, which is that the old way of following religion is no good in the modern era and must be replaced.

The expansion of Gyanmala as a national organization means that its membership is by no means restricted to Newars. Many new hymns in Nepali have become popular. One particularly moving one, composed by Biswa Shakya from Pokhara, calls on the Buddha to come and bring peace to Nepal.[19] The fourth national Gyanmala convention was held in Dharan, in east Nepal, in January 2003. A working paper lists the issues that at least one activist felt that the conference should be discussing:

1. The unauthorized distribution of different editions and versions of the basic Gyanmala song book and the spread of a purely devotional orientation as opposed to the *gyān* or wisdom that is supposed to be promoted by the hymns should be tackled;
2. Hymn books record the authors of the lyrics, but not the composers of the melodies, so books recording both should be printed;
3. There is an urgent need to translate the Gyanmala books, not only into Nepali, as is already happening, but into other languages of Nepal, such as Gurung and Tharu;

Bhajan singers accompanying the pilgrims to Lumbini during the inauguration of Gautami Vihara, February 1998. (Sarah LeVine)

4. The Gyanmala organization should pay particular attention to encouraging the participation of women in singing *bhajans*;
5. A record should be kept of the numerous Gyanmala tapes and CDs available;
6. Just as in the Rana period the early composers were not afraid to produce songs calling for political change, so too, in today's climate of violence, the Gyanmala groups should be raising their voices for peace.[20]

Dharma Duta, Community Organizer Par Excellence

Dharma Duta, a stalwart of the Theravada movement, lives with his wife and two of his three sons, their wives, and their children above his tailor's shop in Lalitpur. Although he often speaks in a rather gruff manner and was educated only up to class six, there is no doubting the sincerity of his attachment to Buddhism. He is vice president of the donor's committee of one of Lalitpur's monasteries and is very active both in the sale and distribution of the Theravada Buddhist magazine, *Ananda Bhoomi*, and in teaching Buddhism to children.

Dharma Duta's first contact with Buddhist teachings, other than the Vajrayanist ones traditional in his family, was with the Kwa Baha hymn-singing group, the Taremam Sangha, which he first joined as a fourteen-year-old. In 1955, when he was twenty-three, his elder sister, who had married into the family of one of the first Theravada laymen in Lalitpur, took him to meet Pragyananda Bhante in Sumangal Vihara, and it was then that he began to study Buddhism seriously. As a young man, he had many discussions with the famous Buddhist sage Mahapragya. Dharma Duta first met him when, having been "ensnared by a woman's wiles" as Dharma Duta puts it, he was living as a householder in Kalimpong. Later on, when Mahapragya renounced a second time and returned to Kathmandu, keeping his hair long and dressing in a maroon Tibetan-style robe, he lived for a time in Sumangal Vihara in Lalitpur. For three or four years, he came regularly to Dharma Duta's house, up to two or three times a week, to talk about *buddha dharma* and in particular, to explain the meaning of the bhajans that Dharma Duta and his friends sang in their Gyanmala group, some of which Mahapragya had himself composed. It was he who helped Dharma Duta to understand the verse: "Don't blame your *karma* for what happens to you. You're the one who made it so." "In other words," says Dharma Duta, "by living according to the *sil* [good conduct] you can change things for the better."

From Pragyananda Bhante, who was his guru for many years, Dharma Duta learned a great deal about *sil* but much less about *dhyan* (meditation):

> In those early days it was thought that meditation was only for the most devout, and not for people who were busy earning their living, like me. Sometimes the monks might teach meditation on the body (*kesaloma*) to a young man who, infatuated with some unsuitable girl, decided he needed to be cured of his infatuation. Only it never seemed to work!

Then Goenka came and after that "meditation was no longer for the elite," he says. "Now it could be for anyone who was interested." He himself meditates daily between 5 and 6 A.M. in summer and 6 and 7 A.M. in winter. "And many other laypeople who never would have meditated in the past, do likewise," he adds. Ordinarily he just "watches the breath" (*anapana*) meditation; he only does "insight meditation" (*vipassana*) when he's on a ten-day meditation retreat.

On Buddha Jayanti in 1971, Dharma Duta organized the first public dharma quiz competition. This turned out to be quite a success, and so the following year he organized another. Quiz competitions between teams fielded by local clubs and libraries involving several rounds leading up to a final attended by hundreds of children and parents have since become annual citywide events. In 1975, following an embarrassing incident during a visit to the primary school near his house by the famous Sri Lankan monk Narada Mahathera, Dharma Duta arranged for the children to receive *buddha dharma* instruction. As he recalls, Narada asked the largely Buddhist student body if they knew the names of the five ascetics who heard the Buddha's first sermon in the Deer Park at Sarnath. To the chagrin of their teachers, not one child knew the answer. To remedy the situation, Dharma Duta invited monks and nuns, using the *pariyatti* texts that Buddhaghosh Bhante had recently started to produce, to teach the children on a regular weekly basis. Dharma Duta, who himself passed the sixth level *pariyatti* exam, still teaches the children when no monk or nun is available.

One achievement of which Dharma Duta is particularly proud is his success, in 1976, in persuading the Maharjans who live in a nearby courtyard to give up sacrificing a buffalo to the local Ganesh shrine on the occasion of their annual death *guthi* feast. The sacrifical beast would always be killed by the traditional Newar method: the sacrificer would cut the animal below the neck, pull out the artery, and squirt a jet of blood onto the statue of the god, a method that greatly prolonged the animal's suffering. Because the Maharjans feared divine wrath if they failed to placate the god with sacrifice, Dharma Duta stood before him and offered a *kisli*[21] with the words, "If punishment/misfortune (*dosh*) should befall anyone [in this community] as a result of the abandonment of the customary sacrifice to Lord Ganesh, that punishment should not befall any member of the death *guthi*, but only Dharma Duta Shakya." Convinced of the efficacy of the oath, the members of the death *guthi* gave up the buffalo sacrifice.

Now that his sons are all married and earning a living, religious activities are Dharma Duta's first priority. After an early morning hour of meditation, he goes to the monastery where he is vice president of the donor's committee and where, because the president himself is ailing, he shoulders the major administrative responsibility. After taking his main meal of the day at home, he goes out again to deliver Buddhist publications. He frequently travels to the Indian city of Varanasi to buy Buddhist books which, together with many locally produced magazines and pamphlets, he offers for sale in the community. Almost any afternoon he may be encountered in the lanes of Lalitpur, a heavy bag of books in each hand. In the late afternoon, there may be a Buddhist event to attend or a *pariyatti* class to teach, and the whole of Saturday is taken up with religious activities of various kinds of which the one closest to his heart is *bhajan*-singing. He has always liked the songs about nonviolence (*ahimsa*), especially those condemning animal sacrifice, and he believes that, at least in the early days, he was the only member of his hymn group to take the words really seriously. Aside from singing in Kwa Baha five times a month and every day during the holy month of Gunla, his group is invited to sing at many Buddhist functions in the Kathmandu Valley and occasionally far beyond. In 1987, he was one of eleven members who paid a three-week visit to Japan, where they traveled round the country singing Gyanmala hymns.

Dharma Duta has received public recognition as an innovator and yet his views regarding women remain decidedly conservative. Because he believes that they cannot live without ornaments and entertainments and are less capable of self-discipline than men, he is opposed to women taking bhikkhuni ordination. He concedes that some women have become learned and accomplished teachers of Buddhism; nevertheless, in his opinion the intermediate status of anagarika, or ordained laywoman, that comes between the status of laywoman and fully ordained nun, is perfectly appropriate for them.

CHAPTER SIX

Organizing and Educating the Monastic Community

The Dharmodaya Sabha is supposed to be the national organization for all Nepali Buddhists. All Nepali Theravada monks belong also to the Bhikshu Mahasangha, which was founded by Amritananda in 1951.[1] Because at that time no nuns were fully ordained bhikkhuni, they were excluded, as they continue to be to this day. The original purpose of the Mahasangha was twofold: first, to resolve disputes over ritual practice that arose between monks ordained in different lineages and trained in different traditions and, second, to deal with major disciplinary violations. For the most part, monks proved unwilling to change practices that they had been taught abroad. Thus today, just as in the 1950s, there is no uniformity of dress, and in other respects too, the abbot of each monastery continues to follow the practices and traditions of the institution where he received his training. With regard to lesser disciplinary violations, monks are required, as the Vinaya specifies, to gather twice each month in the *uposathagaras* of Ananda Kuti Vihara in Kathmandu or Sumangal Vihara in Lalitpur in order to recite the Patimokkha rules, confess violations—or have them pointed out by others—and where necessary, have the appropriate punishment indicated by the most senior monk present.[2] But the attendance rule has proved impossible to enforce. Monks fall ill, they travel outside the Valley, and they have to deal with emergencies, all of which regularly prevent some from participating in this early morning ritual.

The Mahasangha executive board, composed of the fourteen most senior monks (only about half of whom still participate), has shied away from taking major disciplinary action. It is also in a difficult position, because it cannot take action unless a formal complaint is received, and, although there have been plenty of rumors of misconduct, in most cases no one ever comes forward to make a complaint. Laypeople have, by and large, been philosophical, maintaining that the Order is too small to withstand internal conflict. Be that as it may, the failure of the Mahasangha to take action has had a debilitating effect not only on the personal standing, as fields of merit, of particular individuals, but on the standing of the Order as a whole.

Physical violence is another issue that the Nepali Mahasangha, like Sanghas in other countries, has been unable or reluctant to tackle. One case involved a monk who became mentally ill while studying abroad. After a year in a foreign psychiatric hospital, he was not much improved but returned to Nepal where he took up residence in the monastery in which he had lived as a young monk and of which, following the death of the founder, he claimed he should be abbot. As the other monks were afraid of him, the monastery gradually emptied out, and it was only after he had made several attacks on those who were courageous—or foolish—enough to remain and had verbally abused leading monks that the Mahasangha executive committee finally voted to expel him. Even so, as there is nowhere else to send him, he continues to live in the monastery.

All nuns also belong to the Dharmodaya Sabha, but although they themselves refer in speech to their "Sangha," meaning "Order" or "community," the nuns' Order did not formally exist until 1994. Before that time, each nunnery was autonomous with regard to discipline. Only in 1994 did Sushila Guruma, the most senior nun by ordination, register the Anagarika Sangha as a "nongovernmental organization," with herself as president and Dhammawati—whom she did not consult prior to registration—as vice president. Sushila, who came from Bhojpur in eastern Nepal, where Mahapragya taught intermittently for many years, took the precepts from Chandramani in Kushinagara in 1944. Unschooled, she learned to read only after renunciation and subsequently learned Pali well enough to be able to translate and publish several Jataka stories. She spent most of her adult life at Tana Vihara in Lalitpur, and in her eighties she looked twenty years younger; until not long before her death aged 86 in 2001, she was quite active in the community. But because she was of the "old school" of nuns who revered and waited on the bhikkhus—in her case, Buddhaghosh Mahasthavira at Sumangal Vihara—other than on formal occasions she and Dhammawati had little to do with one another. Thus, the Anagarika Sangha has largely remained a paper organization. Despite this, because the senior nuns were all trained in Burma; or at least spent some months as visitors in Burmese nunneries, and because nuns have only recently started to go to Sri Lanka or Thailand, the community of nuns has achieved much greater uniformity of practice than the monks.

Monastic Life Today

In 1999, there were well over one hundred Nepali monks and novices including about fifty novices who—officially—were studying abroad; but many of these novices were no longer in touch with their preceptors and so were believed to have disrobed. Meanwhile, an article published in 1999 gives a figure of 121 Nepali nuns, of whom 23 were studying abroad.[3]

There are ninety-eight viharas in the country as a whole, of which eighty-one are monasteries and seventeen are nunneries.[4] Occasionally nuns reside in monasteries, but monks never reside in nunneries. Of the monasteries, thirty-one are in the cities of Kathmandu and Lalitpur, two are in Bhaktapur, and the rest are widely scattered throughout the Valley and beyond. Much the largest monastic population is to be found at Vishwa Shanti Vihara in Kathmandu, which in 1999 had five monks, twenty-four novices, and two young nuns. By 2004, there were four monks, thirty-one novices, and three nuns. The next largest monasteries in 2004 were Gana Mahavihara (three monks, eleven novices), Shri Kirti Vihara (four monks, two novices), and Ananda Kuti (two monks, four novices) (Kondanya 2004). Many house only one or two monks, and many more in the capital as well as in provincial towns and villages stand locked and empty. Fifteen nunneries are in Kathmandu and Lalitpur, and one each is in Bhaktapur, Bungamati (four miles south of Lalitpur), Balambu (a village four miles west of Kathmandu), Tansen (in the western hills), Pokhara, and Lumbini.[5] The two largest are Dharmakirti, which in 1999 housed seventeen nuns, and Kindol Vihara with twelve; seven nunneries had only one nun each. By 2004, Dharmakirti had risen to eighteen nuns, Kindol had fallen to seven, and ten nunneries had only one nun (Kondanya 2004).

Physical structures vary widely from the truly magnificent (Shri Kirti in Kirtipur), through imposing (Vishwa Shanti in Naya Baneshwar) to deteriorating (Sangharama in Dhalko, northwest Kathmandu) and decrepit, of which there are many examples.[6] The basic structure consists of a courtyard containing a *chaitya*.[7] Facing into the courtyard one sees a shrine with a Buddha image,[8] living quarters for the monks or nuns, and a gathering place for the laity. However some, including Shrigha and Dharmakirti in the densely crowded center of the city, are built as a single block in which each floor is dedicated to one particular activity. The larger viharas have many facilities including guest quarters, classrooms, and libraries. Unlike the densely ornamented traditional Newar baha-temple courtyard, most Theravada viharas, in accordance with modernist Buddhist tradition, are starkly plain, with the exception of the Thai-style Shri Kirti Vihara, mentioned above. Of the older viharas, Ananda Kuti, with its shrine, stupa, and Bo tree set around a wide courtyard on the forested northwest flank of Swayambhu hill, is the most elaborate. Maintenance is a problem in most monasteries where continual use and pollution take a heavy toll. Buildings shoddily constructed in the first place soon begin to deteriorate. Monks are reluctant to dirty their hands, or unable, due to advanced age, to do physical work themselves; few laypeople routinely volunteer their labor; and materials are expensive. Nuns are much more likely than monks to perform routine maintenance tasks from sweeping floors and collecting garbage to whitewashing walls; but whereas a few nunneries that were built by wealthy families for their daughters are well-appointed and maintained, others are in poor condition. The brick walls of Tana Vihara, a traditional *baha* that was restored and given to Sushila Guruma and a few companions fifty years ago, are crumbling away. The original donor's family is trying to raise money to rebuild it, but the next monsoon season could reduce it to mud. By 2000, after decades in punishing service, Dharmakirti, in the center of old Kathmandu, was literally sinking into the ground. The ten adult nuns who lived there were crammed into a few small rooms, and the seven adolescents who slept on mats on the floor of the dharma hall would roll up their quilts on awakening and stuff them into one corner. Fortunately, twelve Dharmakirti nuns were studying abroad or the nunnery would have been intolerably overcrowded.[9]

Monastics' personal possessions vary widely in quantity and quality, reflecting their standing as a field of merit and family support. The bright room of Gyanapurnik Mahasthavira, the abbot of brand-new Vishwa Shanti, has large west-facing windows through which, on a winter day, the sun pours in; his bed is handsome; his reading chair was custom-built to provide support for his bad back; the floor of his

Nagar Mandap Shri Kirti Vihara, Kirtipur (often just called Shri Kirti Vihara, or even Kirtipur Vihara), built in the Thai style in Kirtipur's Naya Bazaar. (David N. Gellner)

reception room is covered with thick Tibetan carpets, gifts of a lay supporter who owns a carpet factory; his tiled bathroom has shiny modern fittings. Although, prior to its reconstruction in 2002, the windows of Dharmakirti Vihara were small and let in little light, the floorboards were uneven, and the walls were a streaky gray, Dhammawati had accumulated just as many possessions as Gyanapurnik. She owned a dozen modern appliances including a TV which, lacking interest as well as time, she rarely watched.[10] Her sloping floor had wall-to-wall carpeting to keep out the winter cold and laid on top of it, in front of the gilded Burmese Buddha image, was a handsome Indian rug. There were reading lamps; a low but comfortable bed; quilts; cushions; blankets; a sewing machine; long shelves crammed with books; and heaped in one corner, waiting to be redistributed to the poor of Nagha Tol, dry goods, fruit juices, and laundry soap donated by devotees who stopped by each day to pay their respects to their guru. Like Gyanapurnik, Dhammawati had an attached bathroom. The fittings weren't

The gold-leafed statue of Pragyananda Mahasthavir in front of Shri Kirti Vihara. (David N. Gellner)

shiny and the porcelain of the sink was chipped, but her bathroom in the new Dharmakirti is every bit as state-of-the-art as Gyanapurnik's. By contrast, Mudita, a nun in her fifties, lives sparsely in Kindol Vihara, where the grass in the courtyard grows high and the wooden steps leading to the upper floor sway dangerously as one climbs them.

Most of the smaller nunneries are headed by nuns from well-to-do families who attract donations from a wide circle of relatives and are

The new Dharmakirti Vihara after its rebuilding in 2003. (David N. Gellner)

thus able to provide for their pupils as well. Kamala Guruma, who left Dharmakirti for a vihara that her parents built for her in the southern part of Kathmandu, houses and provides for five younger nuns. Meanwhile, in the large house that her wealthy family built for her in Lalitpur and to which her brothers recently added a stupa, a miniature reproduction of Swayambhu, Uppalavanna Guruma supports young nuns who are waiting for arrangements to made for them to study abroad.

Nuns who live alone, whether they are elderly women whose companions of an earlier time have died or younger women who have chosen this lifestyle, almost always have family backing. By contrast, monks who live alone, either because they are old and their chelas, if they once had some, have deserted them or because they are young and have not yet managed to find any, barely scrape by. Whenever there is a *bhojana dana*[11] following a community event such as the Buddha Jayanti celebration at Ananda Kuti Vihara, a *puja* honoring a senior monk, a *kathina* ceremony at the conclusion of the rain retreat, or a visit by a foreign dignitary to the meditation center at Shankhamul, certain monks can be counted on to find their way there so that, after the ceremony is over, they may receive donations and partake of the sumptuous meal. In doing so they are following much older patterns of religious mendicacy, upheld by the Vajracharyas and Shakyas in their ritual role, now largely defunct, as monks, which is acted out at the annual Panchadan festival (Gellner 1992: 180–188), and by Brahmans, who used to be fed by the Hindu elite on special occasions.

Recruitment Patterns: Change and Continuity

The Monks' Order: Caste Composition

As we have seen, the Buddhist revival movement in Nepal originated among members of the Newar Buddhist upper castes. All the monks and nuns of the first generation were Shakyas, Udays, or Manandhars, with the exception of Mahapragya, a Shrestha. Although in the 1950s the movement was beginning to attract recruits from farming and occupational castes, thirty years later, in a study carried out between 1978 and 1982, Tewari (1983) found that 66 percent of the monks and 69 percent of the nuns were still Shakyas, Udays, Vajracharyas, or Shresthas, that is, upper-caste. Only 23 percent of monks and 13 percent of nuns were Maharjans, with occupational castes and a few non-Newars making up the rest. In 1989, Locke and Hartmann, in separate studies, found that the proportions of monks (69 percent) and nuns (70 percent) of upper-caste origin were virtually identical, and the proportions of Maharjan origin was very close as well (monks 14 percent, nuns 16 percent). Unlike Tewari, however, they also looked at the novices separately from the monks, and found that only 39 percent were of upper-caste origin, whereas 32 percent were Maharjan and 29 percent were from occupational castes or non-Newar backgrounds. In other words, although the caste composition of the Order had not changed very much in forty years, given the backgrounds of its newest recruits, the monk's Order was poised to change quite dramatically.[12] Indeed, the trend that Locke and Hartmann had noted was emphatically confirmed in the following decade. Between 1989 and 1995, very few upper-caste boys took novice ordination, and between 1995 and 2000, none did so. All new recruits at this time came from Newar farming and occupational castes or from Janajati backgrounds, notably Tamang and Tharu. After 1995, suddenly upper-caste boys started to join again.

How should one interpret these changes in the background of recruits to the Sangha? First, they reflect a major change in the opportunity structure of Newar society. Until the 1970s, only those who by local standards were well-to-do could afford secondary let alone a university education for their sons; thus, the Order offered opportunities for study and travel as well as prestige to poor boys who, albeit that they were from upper-caste backgrounds, would not otherwise have had access. As a Shakya monk who is now is his forties readily admits, "As a child I'd go to the vihara with my father, so I was used to the monks. When I was thirteen years old [1973], one of them suggested I become a novice. I thought, well, why not? I knew that most novices studied abroad, and I thought, 'I'd like that!' " But as the economy has diversified over the past thirty years, many more parents have been able to educate their sons themselves; again, the explosive spread of secondary and tertiary education since 1980 has provided new possibilities for people of quite modest means. In the first decades of the Theravada movement, Shakyas and Udays dominated the monks' Order, and even thirty years ago devout upper-caste parents might send a son to the monastery in the hope of securing a prestigious career for the boy and earning merit for themselves; but although poor Shakya families still exist, most have prospered, especially in the curio business. Meanwhile, as merchants, Udays who were already well-to-do benefited greatly from the opening up of the economy and opportunities to pursue secular education abroad. Thus today it is largely farming and lower (occupational) caste parents who push their sons to ordain. Asked, in 1997, why they decided to take *pabbajja*, young novices (aged eleven to fifteen) almost uniformly spoke of the *duhkha* of householder life and their desire to escape it, a notion that presumably they had been taught in Saturday school. Closer questioning usually revealed that ordination had been their parents' idea.

As young men from middle and lower castes, most of whom are from rural backgrounds, rise through the ranks to assume leadership roles once exclusively held by their caste superiors, the prestige of the Order declines. From its early days, the Theravada lay community has been headed by a tight-knit group of wealthy upper-caste merchants and businessmen who willingly supported the Sangha because the monks were their "sons" who had grown up in the city, in Yetkha Baha or Asan Tol in Kathmandu, and in Uku Baha or Ila Nani in Lalitpur and whose families were known and respected. With rare exceptions, today's major donors are still from the upper castes. On the one hand, they would no longer dream of sending their own sons to the monastery, but on the other, it appears that some may not be very comfortable with the idea of rustic and/or low-caste monks being in command.

This decline in high-caste recruitment may possibly have already gone into reverse, as well-endowed monasteries in Thailand have started to offer comfortable accommodation and the chance of education to those who ordain, at least temporarily. The deteriorating political and economic situation in Nepal, as a consequence of the Maoist insurgency, combined with Thailand's allure as a developed country, may well combine to produce a resurgence in high-caste male recruitment. In July 2003, thirty-four novice monks aged between thirteen and twenty, all Newars, arrived in Thailand for monastic training in different Thai monasteries, as organized by Bhikshu Vipassi. Twenty-four, that is, more than two-thirds, were Maharjans, and these were nearly all from Kirtipur or Chapagaon (where Maharjans take the surname Desar). However, among the others there were four Shakyas (three from Lalitpur, one from Bhaktapur), three Vajracharyas (two from Kathmandu, one from Lalitpur), one Shrestha (from Kathmandu), one Nakarmi (from Kirtipur), and one Khadgi (from Kathmandu).[13] Comparing castes and origins, it is striking that the Theravada laity in outlying settlements such as Kirtipur and Chapagaon is now dominated by Maharjans, whereas high castes are still strong in the big cities. The strength of Maharjan involvement in Theravada Buddhism in the villages of the Kathmandu Valley is confirmed by the research of Kesav Lall Maharjan (forthcoming) in Nakadesh, near Thimi. He reports that Theravada there has had a big impact on village life, that the aims of the Buddhist activists are supported even by those who are not members of the Theravada organization in the village, and that they have encouraged their sons and daughters to ordain and go abroad for a Buddhist education, in the hope that maybe 10 percent will continue as monastics and return to lead Buddhism in the village.

Another major change also underway is the spread of Theravada Buddhism to the non-Newar groups known as Janajatis, especially to the Magars and Tharus. In the political and cultural ferment that led up to and followed the People's Movement of 1990, some Newar Buddhist intellectuals in Kathmandu made contact with ethnic leaders of the various Janajati groups. Some of these groups, such as the Tamangs and Gurungs, had a long and deep connection to Tibetan Buddhism. In the case of the Tharus, Ramananda Prasad Singh had written his pamphlet *The Real History of the Tharus* in 1988 in which he argued that the Tharus were descendants of the Buddha's tribe; he had already started his campaign for the Tharus to become Buddhists.[14] Some Magars were looking around for an alternative to Hinduism and thought that Buddhism might provide it. In order to encourage these connections, some scholarships were organized by Bhikshu Sugandha in Thailand. In 1991, three Tamang boys, one Gurung, one Magar, and one Tharu left to train as monks. They were told that they did not necessarily have to remain monks forever, if they could not maintain the vocation after receiving their education in Thailand. Of the six, three have since disrobed, but three are still monks, and may use their Thai education in due course to have an impact on their home communities. These six monks were the first of quite a few Janajatis who have become samaneras.

The Souvenir issue of *Shanti Sandesh*, published by Vishwa Shanti Vihara in November 2003, listed all the monks, novices, and anagarikas present in the monastery. There were six monks: Gyanapurnik, the abbot, was born a Shakya, as described in Chapter 3; of the other five, four are Maharjans by origin and one is a Bahun. Out of the thirty-six samaneras, twenty-two were Newars (eleven Maharjans, five Vajracharyas, three Shakyas, and three Shresthas) and fourteen (39 percent) were non-Newars (six Tharus—four from Siraha, two from Saptari; four Magars, two Tamangs, one Chetri, and one Limbu [all but the Chetri would be considered "Janajati"]). This proportion of non-Newars is much, much higher than has ever been the case before in

Theravada institutions in Nepal: previously there was only ever one or two non-Newar monks present. If these samaneras remain and continue as monks, it will signal a major change in the nature of the Nepalese Sangha and lay community too. Already it means that Vishwa Shanti Vihara is a much less purely Newar institution than most other Theravada monasteries. So far, however, this particular change—actively recruiting Janajatis to the Sangha—is confined to the male half of the Order: although there are a few Janajati nuns in Dharmakirti, there has been no attempt to reach out and missionize young female Janajatis (e.g., Tamangs).

The Nuns' Order: Caste Composition

Patterns of recruitment for monks and nuns were beginning to diverge by the 1980s and more recent figures have borne this out. Of seventy-five nuns resident in the Valley in 1999, forty-five (60 percent) were upper-caste (Vajracharya, Shakya, Uday, and Shrestha), twenty-six (34 percent) were Maharjans or non-Newar, and four (5.3 percent) were Manandhars, who, as we have seen, were traditionally low but already upwardly mobile and often educated by the late Rana period. Although a few Shakya nuns are from impoverished backgrounds, the majority are well-to-do. Some Maharjan nuns are also from families that are comfortably off. By renouncing lay life, nuns officially give up all claim to parental property; but by the same token, they become fields of merit for their extended kin group who are often generous in their support. In recent years, recruits to the nuns' Order have tended to come from higher-caste and better-off families than the monks. Furthermore, although the younger nuns may look to the nunnery to finance their education, most of those who ordain as adults have completed secondary school, if not several years at university. In sum, whereas upper-caste, well-to-do parents would be opposed to a son's ordination, they are likely to take a different view in the case of a daughter. Rather than losing her to another family as they would if she were to marry, they keep her, as it were, and at the same time they, as well as she, earn prestige and merit to which, as they support her projects in the nunnery, they add over the years.

Motivations for Joining the Nuns' Order

Unlike Roman Catholic Orders, which look for clear indications of a spiritual vocation, the Theravadins only ask that, through personal experience of suffering, candidates understand and accept the Four Noble

Truths. Spiritual qualities will be nurtured by monastic training in due course. Recruits to the community of nuns in the early decades were almost exclusively of widows and rejected wives. By contrast, in 1999, only sixteen (21.6 percent) of nuns in the Valley were widows or once-married. Although most of them, including a Kindol nun who had ordained with her husband when both were in their seventies,[15] were very old, the two widowed nuns who took care of Gautami Vihara in Lumbini were only in their forties. Both were from Kathmandu, and while their husbands were alive they had been devotees of Dhammawati. One, a round-faced Maharjan woman named Vivekachari, had children about whom she chatted cheerfully. Illiterate, she was nevertheless extremely useful at Lumbini for, as another nun observed, "You don't need to know how to read and write to do dharma work." Her companion was childless; a longtime serious meditator, she had specifically requested placement in the meditation center.

Like Bartholomeusz's Sri Lankan *dasa sil mata* informants (1994: 132–136), almost all the older never-married nuns stated that the most important reason they had renounced was to escape getting married. A desire to study *buddha dharma* was also mentioned often, if sometimes as an afterthought. Whereas until thirty years ago girls were being married off in their early teens or even younger, as levels of education rise, today's urban Newar girls often do not marry until their mid-twenties or later. One nun, who grew up outside Kathmandu and is now only in her early forties, reports running away from home before she reached menarche in order to avoid marriage.[16] By contrast, some of the younger nuns who were just as averse to marriage were able to spend their teens and twenties studying and, by the time they reached their thirties, had managed to convince their families of their determination to stay single. By then, however, they themselves had begun to look ahead and imagine what their lives would be like after their parents died. "My brothers were always good to me," says one, "but my friends warned me, 'Right now, you have a purpose—taking care of your mother. But once she's gone, your sisters-in-law could resent you.' I saw that in other houses that's what happened." After attending Dharmakirti for more than a decade, she decided the time had come to ordain.

A lively and highly intelligent young woman, Silawati became a member of the Buddhist Study Circle as a teenager and decided she wanted to ordain when she was still in secondary school. "I admired Dhammawati Guruma and I wanted to do dharma work, as she did."

Her well-to-do Vajracharya parents did their utmost to dissuade her. "No one in my family except me was interested in Theravada—everyone thought I was crazy!" But eventually her parents gave their permission. "They saw my mind was set." She then spent four years in Taiwan at Fo Guang Shan Monastery, from which she returned speaking fluent Chinese. Now she studies computer science and spends her Saturdays and college vacations teaching *buddha dharma* in the countryside. Her friend Parami, an attractive young woman of about thirty who is active in her family's business, has been a member of the Buddhist Study Circle for several years. As a college student, she too, made up her mind not to marry. She has stuck to her guns and her parents appear resigned to her decision. As a close friend of several Dharmakirti nuns, she has observed them in their daily lives and has decided to join them. "There's no room for me at the moment, but I'm on the waiting list."

Some of the younger nuns say that they ordained because they wanted more time for meditation. At home there had been so many distractions: family crises of all sorts and, even on the best of days, so much noise, what with telephones ringing, music playing, the TV blaring, and someone in the household always wanting something from them. On their visits to nunneries, they envied the gurumas their tranquil surroundings. Only after they ordained did they realize how little peace and quiet the gurumas actually have. "But still, at least if I'm lucky," says one with a grin, "I get an hour for meditation morning and evening, which isn't as much as I'd imagined I'd be getting, but it's more than I had in my house."

For a few nuns who ordained in childhood or adolescence, the decision was made for them. This was the case with two orphaned girls who were brought to Dharmakirti after their mothers deserted the family. Again, Kindol Vihara houses three young sisters. Their grandmother had ordained there after her husband died and she brought the girls into the nunnery with her because her son and daughter-in-law had five other daughters to feed and educate. Interviewed at the ages of ten, eleven, and fourteen, they claimed that they had wanted to ordain because on frequent visits to their grandmother they had found the nunnery so peaceful compared with the crowded tol where their family lived, but it seemed that they had had little choice in the matter. Most of the nuns who ordained at a young age, however, reported that, after being sent to the vihara for *rishini pabbajja*, they had refused to go home and had pressured their parents to let them ordain.

In the early years, recruits to the both orders were taking a leap into the unknown. Today, by contrast, most recruits have grown up in Theravada families. As children they went to the vihara with their mothers; they saw monks and nuns come to their homes to chant *paritrana*; they attended Saturday school in the vihara; many of the boys underwent *samanera pabbajja* and most of the girls did *rishini pabajja* there as well. Some have close relatives who are major contributors and several have monastics in their immediate families. Indeed, of seventeen nuns living in Dharmakirti in 1999, eight had sisters or first cousins who were nuns and four had brothers who were monks.

Sunita Makes Up Her Mind

In the summer of 1999, Sunita, a beautiful college student aged eighteen, is thinking about becoming a nun. She's sure of three things: she doesn't want to marry or have children; she wants to study *buddha dharma*; and she wants to do social work, specifically, to establish homes for old people whose families are unable or are unwilling to take care of them. She plans to set up a chain, one in every city in Nepal.

Why is she so interested in helping old people? Her closest friend, she says, is her paternal great-grandmother, Vishnu Kumari, aged 94. Her deceased great-grandfather was a gravel contractor whose business, given the building boom in the Kathmandu Valley, flourished and since his death has continued to flourish under his sons and grandsons. Vishnu Kumari is a devout Buddhist who "loves" to go to viharas. "Even now, at her great age, she keeps on going hither and thither." She also loves to give away money. Sometimes she gives cash but more often she contributes sand and gravel for the construction or renovation of viharas. "As a donor, her name is inscribed in many temples," Sunita says proudly. "Right now she's building a vihara in her town and I don't see her as often as I used to. This new vihara's keeping her so busy that she hardly ever comes to Kathmandu."

Sunita was five years old when her mother died of meningitis. "One day she fell sick, and she kept on getting sicker and sicker, and then, after two weeks, she was dead." She left four children aged seven, five, three, and two. Sunita's father, Dev Lal, has not remarried. ("We asked him not to, and he never has.") He was the oldest son and most wayward member of his family. "As a boy, my relatives say he was really wild," his daughter says with a smile. "He dropped out of school after

Class Two and never went back. He can read and write, but only a little. Having so little education didn't matter much then. In his generation, not too many boys studied for long. As a teenager, he ran away to Kathmandu and became a lorry driver. . . . He used to say that for him, driving a lorry was like riding a horse or an elephant!" At first he drove for other haulage contractors, but then he bought his own lorry and after a while, a second. He eventually became quite well-to-do.

> My mother's home was in the same town as my father's. They'd got to know each other there and had fallen in love. My father's family was Buddhist, and my mother was a Shrestha and a Hindu. There was no chance of their getting married with their parents' approval, so they eloped to Kathmandu.

When Dev Lal was left a widower, he had no one to turn to for help with his four young children. "My father put all of us children in his lorry and wherever he happened to be going, he took us along." But after six months, Dev Lal's parents sent one of his younger brothers to live with him and his children in Kathmandu. "After that, we didn't go out in the lorry any more," Sunita recalls. "We stayed in our house in with my uncle and went to school." However, they received no religious education. "I suppose, if we'd thought about it, we'd have said we were Hindus," says Sunita with a shrug:

> At least, we celebrated Dasain and Tihar, just like everybody else. But we had no altar in the house. . . . In recent years my father began going to Buddhist temples, but I don't remember him doing so when I was a child. When I was finishing primary school, my great-grandmother came to live in the city and I'd see her going off to visit temples. Most of them were Vajrayana, though now and then she'd visit a Theravada vihara too. Once she took me to the vihara in Balambu. I think that's when I first became aware that my family was really Buddhist. And after that, I began to notice Theravada nuns in the street. There was one in particular whom I'd see when I was on my way to tuition. . . . I liked her pink dress, and I'd always hope to run into her.

Sunita was growing increasingly curious about Buddhism:

> One of my father's uncles is a Theravadin. Just about every morning he goes to Swayambhu to sing with the *gyanmala* group, and his children all attend *pariyatti* classes in Ananda Kuti Vihara. I thought the classes sounded interesting, something I'd like to try, so I asked them to bring application forms for us and my sisters and brother and I enrolled. The others didn't like the program and soon they stopped going, but as for

> me, I liked it a lot. Those monks are very good teachers: they really know how to talk to children.
>
> There was one monk in particular who taught public speaking: he even had us give speeches in English. At school that year I happened to have a really good English teacher. I improved a lot and so I found giving speeches in English wasn't all that hard after all. But some of the passages we were reading in Nepal Bhasha I found very confusing. When I told the bhante, he suggested I go to Dharmakirti and ask the nuns there for help. So I did. That was the first time I remember actually speaking to a nun.

After passing SLC (School Leaving Certificate), Sunita wanted to study science, but the private college in which her father enrolled her had already filled its quota of science students and to her great disappointment she found herself in the commerce program. "They told me I was lucky to be admitted as so many kids want to study commerce—that's the prestigious course these days. But I got so bored with those business courses that after one term I simply stopped going."

She sat at home until one day her father suggested that, instead of wasting her time until the next academic year when, with luck, she might gain acceptance to a science course, she make herself useful. Having sold his trucking business profitably, Dev Lal had begun going regularly to Mayadevi Vihara, which Padmawati had recently begun to build. He felt comfortable there in part because, like himself, Padmawati was a Manandhar from a small town outside the Valley. Almost every day he did odd jobs for her. Then in the spring of 1999, he brought along his daughter Sunita, who soon found herself cooking and cleaning the vihara, assisting the doctors in the weekly clinic, and helping two teenaged nuns with their schoolwork. In between times she studied *pariyatti* and practiced meditation:

> When I was a child and I saw statues of the Buddha with his eyes closed, I'd think, "He must be meditating . . . that's what I want to do!" But no one in my family meditated, not even my great grandmother . . . she only did *jap* with her prayer beads.

It was only when she came to Mayadevi Vihara and went to work for Padmawati that she found someone to teach her meditation. "I liked it so much—the tranquility it brought—that after only one month, Padmawati Guruma asked me if I'd like to go on a retreat at Budha Nilkantha. Well, I jumped at the chance."

Most of the time during the ten-day retreat she felt light and strong and utterly peaceful. In the past, whenever people got annoyed with her, she'd get at least as angry and upset as they were. But after the retreat, she noticed that she didn't get as angry as before.

Plenty of people give Sunita advice about ordination. Some, including the doctors in the clinic where she works on Saturdays, suggest she wait to make her decision until she's finished college. Middle-aged upasikas look at her in awe and, somewhat envious, urge her to go ahead. Her sisters are astounded at the thought of her becoming a nun. Her father says it must be *her* decision.

In November 1999, her mind is made up. She takes six precepts[17] and exchanges her college-girl salwar kameez for a red rishini dress. In a letter, she writes:

> In three months' time I will take *anagarika pabbajja*. I did think about waiting until I'm older but I'm already sure this is the life for me, the only life that will allow me to go forward. I want to live simply and think deeply, and I want to help people—children, poor people, old people. That is my ambition. I don't believe I'd find any happiness in married life. In marriage there is so much tension, with one thing leading to another in a continuous chain of trouble. There may be moments of joy and happiness, but they pass in an instant. What I need is peace . . .

Ordination: "Going into Homelessness"

A recruit to the monks' Order who is at least seven years old and has his parents' permission undergoes the first ordination rite, which involves having his head shaved, donning monk's robes, and receiving the Ten Precepts and an ordination name from his monk preceptor. From that day on, until he takes higher or full ordination at age twenty, his preceptor is responsible for his maintenance, making sure that he observes the *sekhiya* training rules and teaching him *buddha dharma*. Although a novice may receive the precepts from a single monk, according to the Vinaya, the nuns' first ordination rite (*samanerika pabbajja*) requires the presence of both a monk preceptor and at least one fully ordained nun (bhikkhuni) of whom none officially exist in the Theravada tradition. Thus, Nepali nuns followed a non-canonical ordination procedure that evolved haphazardly over the years after Chandramani Mahasthavira gave the precepts to the first three Nepali female renouncers in 1931. The precepts had to be received from a monk, but that was the only requirement. Sometimes a nun (anagarika) would be present and sometimes not. One ordinand might receive the precepts on the very same day she requested ordination whereas another might have to wait for several months for parental or spousal permission. Sometimes the ritual was followed by *bhojana dana* offered by the ordinand's parents or sponsors, other times not. The first *garudhamma* stipulated that all nuns, regardless of length of time since ordination, were subordinate in status to even the most junior monk. As "ten-precept laywomen" Nepali nuns were not subject to this rule; nevertheless they complied with it, albeit in a fairly minimal fashion: on meeting a monk who was senior to her in age or ordination, a nun would kneel and then prostrate herself to him three times; but she would only nod her head and press her palms together on her breast as a gesture of reverence to a monk who was her junior in age or ordination.

The Code of Conduct of the Nuns' Order (Nepal Byapi Anagarika Sangha)

As anagarikas, Nepali nuns do not vow to observe the *Bhikkhuni Patimokkha* rules or even the training (*sekhiya*) rules. Nevertheless, over the years, each abbess, taking the Patimokkha into careful account, devised a code of conduct on an ad hoc basis and had her community observe it. But by the early 1990s, it became clear that a more formal arrangement was necessary. Although child and adolescent ordinands had usually undergone *rishini pabbajja* and spent several months in the nunnery observing the rules of the house prior to ordination and studying *pariyatti*, this was not the case with adult women. Most ordained within a few days of coming to the nunnery, had studied little if any *pariyatti*, and had a great deal of trouble adjusting to the deportment rules. Laywomen were also starting to spend time in the nunnery as temporary ordinands as well as meditators (*yogis*) during vipassana retreats. In 1993, in order to formalize procedures that had developed piecemeal over many years, as well as to address these new situations, Dhammawati drew up a list of rules, which, she emphasized, were not set in stone but were to be reviewed every six months and revised when necessary. And in fact they have been through several revisions. One version went as follows.

1. Prior to *pabbajja* ordination, new recruits should spend three or six months in the nunnery as a rishini wearing a red robe (*kaleji vastra*).[18]
2. New members of the Sangha must be accepted by the ten most senior members of the Anagarika Sangha coming together and the most senior doing the *pabbajja*.[19]
3. The precepts can only be given by a fully ordained monk.

4. Those who were ordained earlier must take precedence over those who were ordained later, regardless of age.
5. Each new anagarika must be under the guidance of a senior anagarika.
6. If one of the four chief precepts has been broken and the robe is to be set aside, ten anagarikas must come together so that she [the delinquent] can be removed from the Sangha. If the mistake has been acknowledged, they may also grant forgiveness.
7. If an anagarika took ordination in Burma, Thailand, or Sri Lanka, on her return to Nepal reports from her preceptor and her guru in that foreign country must be lodged with the Anagarika Sangha and an ID issued to her.
8. Without an ID she will not be accepted as a member of the Sangha and she cannot be invited by a householder to *bhojana dana.*
9. When it is necessary for an anagarika to go to the home of a householder other than for dharma business, it is forbidden that she scrutinize/comment on the faults of anyone in that household.
10. Without good reason, no anagarika should visit a householder's home.
11. Anagarikas must wear pink and orange dresses with a brown scarf worn over the shoulder.
12. Anagarikas may not use colored sweaters, scarves, or socks given by donors, nor may they use embroidered scarves. They may only use gifts of clothing which are pink, orange, or brown.
13. When accepting contributions from donors for the construction of her own nunnery, an anagarika is forbidden to hand over any money that remains to her relatives. This is a major sin.
14. If an anagarika passes away, all anagarikas must assemble at her place. Anyone who does not come must pay a one-hundred-rupee fine to the Sangha.
15. The assembled Anagarika Sangha will chant *paritrana* and do *puja* on behalf of the dead anagarika.

16. Having entered a room with a monk, an anagarika may not close the door unless she is accompanied by a female friend.
17. An anagarika may not go up to the roof of the nunnery with a monk unless she is accompanied by a female friend.
18. An anagarika may not travel with a monk unless she is accompanied by a female friend. To go alone is to invite censure to the monk.
19. An anagarika should not cause a scholarly monk's status to fall by behaving in such a way as to bring him disgrace.
20. Anagarikas should come together in their nunneries every Friday to discuss these rules and make sure that they are properly understood.
21. If any anagarika fails to abide by these rules, she must put on the yellow robes of a probationer.
22. Meditators (*yogis*) must study for at least ten days before taking temporary ordination as anagarika.
23. *Yogis* may not be invited to *bhojana* outside the vihara.[20]

As noted above, prior to the formulation of these rules, recruits had not been asked to meet any requirements except that they had some understanding of the Four Noble Truths. The first new rule, however, focuses on the need for preparation. Recruits may no longer move immediately from lay to renunciant status but must undergo a probationary period in which (although this is not spelled out in the document) they learn to observe a code of conduct that is promulgated by the *sekhiya* training rules of the *Bhikkhuni Patimokkha*, study the fundamentals of Buddhism, and learn to chant two or three sutras. They proceed to ordination when their abbess deems them ready.

Only one of the twenty-four rules (number three) (the Ten Precepts must be given by a fully ordained monk) directly acknowledges the authority of the monks' over the nuns' Order. But although an ordinand must have a monk as her preceptor, before receiving the precepts from him she must first be accepted into the nuns' Order; that is, nuns, not monks, are the gatekeepers. On ordination day, she has her head shaved and is received into the community by the ten most senior nuns, who present her with a pink and orange dress.[21] When she has changed into it, she goes to the dharma hall to receive the precepts and a new name from her monk preceptor. For the first three days she keeps all

Ten Precepts, but on the fourth day she drops the tenth, which prohibits handling money, and in its place vows to send loving kindness (*metta*) to all sentient beings. Every ordinand must be equipped with the necessities of monastic life, including three dresses, underclothing, and a trunk in which to keep them, as well as a bed and bedding; and these days *pabbajja* is always followed by *bhojana dana*. In short, ordination is expensive, although the parents of well-to-do nuns may pay for everything, many cannot afford to do so and therefore sponsors must be found. Usually the abbess and some of her devotees are eager to cover the *pabbajja* expenses of a poor ordinand because an ordination ceremony provides monastics as well as laypeople with an unparalleled and paradigmatic opportunity to earn merit.

Whereas some of the rules listed above are taken directly from the *Bhikkhuni Patimokkha*, others address purely contemporary concerns. The four that deal with the etiquette of working and traveling with monks (rules seventeen through twenty) are of particular interest. The concern is to help a nun keep her vow of celibacy (fourth of the Ten Precepts) and to protect her own—not just the monk's—reputation in the eyes of the lay community. Today, nuns and monks are finding themselves together in circumstances that the ancients could never have imagined. They work together to run programs for children, translate scriptures, edit publications, and co-author books. Pretty, young nuns may need to be tutored in Sanskrit by handsome young monks. Invited to attend conferences and to run meditation retreats halfway round the globe, monks and nuns may spend and weeks together in foreign places. In short, opportunities for romantic entanglements abound. Dhammawati is aware that nuns need "protection" from their own desires, not just from the desires of monks, so she ruled that a nun should always have a "female friend" (*sathi*) with her (rules sixteen, seventeen, and eighteen). But, given the exigencies of daily schedules, allowances have to be made. Thus, if no one is available to sit beside her during her Sanskrit tutorial, a nun may still meet with her male teacher—provided she keeps the door wide open. Although she may not board a city bus—even a crowded one—with a monk if she is unaccompanied, having let the monk board the bus, she may take the next bus and travel to the same destination. But traveling abroad with a monk unchaperoned is one rule that should not be waived under any circumstances.

Although in the early years at Kindol Vihara the monks were constantly interfering with the nuns, once they were no longer sharing quarters the nuns became increasingly adept at evading the monks' authority, particularly their efforts to involve themselves in disciplinary matters. The Anagarika Rules concede that a nun must take the precepts from a monk; but from then on her behavior is the concern of the nuns' Order alone. Should she break a rule, she is to be disciplined by her own community. Thus, if she violates one of the four most important precepts (not to kill, steal, lie about her spiritual attainments, or have sexual relations), she must disrobe immediately with no possibility of reinstatement. But before she returns to lay life, a quorum of ten nuns should be assembled to acknowledge her "defeat" and to offer her forgiveness should she request it. The presence of a monk is not required. As Dhammawati observes, "Yes, the bhikkhus are over us, and they tell us that if we have a problem we can't solve we should take it to them. But we've never done so because we've been able to solve our problems ourselves." As for the future, she and her colleagues have every confidence that, as in the past, they will be able to solve whatever problems arise without the "help" of the bhikkhus.[22]

Training a New Generation

Although many attempts to formalize the training process have been made, after seventy years a satisfactory system is still to be devised. Until the 1980s, senior monks and nuns, naturally enough, assumed that what a religious specialist required was specifically *religious* education. But because there was no Theravada training center in Nepal, novices and young nuns would have to be sent abroad. During the U Nu years, Burma opened its doors to foreign students, including a few Nepali nuns as well as monks. Following the military takeover in 1962, however, foreign monastics were barred from studying in Burma and, although those who were already there were permitted to finish their courses, conditions deteriorated rapidly.

After Burma was closed to foreigners, alternatives were hard to find. Kosala, who ordained as a novice monk in 1970, remembers:

> My aunt was a nun, and I used to visit her in the nunnery next door to Shakyasingha Vihara, where Pragyananda lived. I was attracted to him. Although he was already in his seventies, he was still very lively. I knew from my aunt that he had no novices to help take care of him, so one day I went to him and said, "I want to shave my head." When he asked me why, I said, "Because I want to be your chela." He said, "That isn't a good enough reason. You don't yet understand that life is *duhkha*, so I

> can't accept you." And the fact was, he was right! I didn't know what *duhkha* meant. Even so, he let me live in the vihara and I became his *kappyakar*. This meant I received the money upasakas gave him as *dana*, and I ran errands for him in the bazaar. Meanwhile I learned to chant, and every lunar day I'd take the Five Precepts. After some months I convinced Pragyananda Bhante that I was beginning to understand what *duhkha* was, and then he gave me the precepts. As my preceptor (*upajjhaya*), he had to teach me to behave properly. No more grabbing big balls of rice and stuffing them into my mouth, and no licking the palms of my hands! I couldn't run any more, and I had to wear my robe correctly. All of this was hard at first, especially the rule against running! I'd often get punished for that, which meant cleaning the latrine. My guru was responsible for teaching me *buddha dharma* as well as feeding and clothing me.

Kosala learned *anapana* meditation, along with the laypeople who came to the vihara early every morning. He began by sitting for ten minutes and even that was difficult, but the length of time he could concentrate increased rapidly and after six months he could do so continuously for four hours: "One morning I saw a radiant light which seemed to me like a miraculous reward for my hard work. But when I told my guru he said the purpose of meditation wasn't to see visions, it was to purify the mind. He said I should simply note the light and let it pass away."

When Kosala went to live in Lalitpur, he dropped out of school in his village. A year later he started attending a school near the vihara:

> I was the only samanera in that school, in fact I was probably the only one going to school in all Nepal at that time. By sending me, a samanera, to school, my guru was breaking new ground. To start with I knew nobody and I felt very shy in my robe with my shaved head while all the other boys were wearing their uniforms. The following year I passed my SLC and I also passed level five of *pariyatti*,[23] which was as high as you could go in those days. Then I was stuck because at that time monks in Nepal weren't going to university. For some years I just stayed in the vihara and took care of my guru until eventually he arranged for me to study in Thailand.

Sugandha, a city boy from Kathmandu, remembers the training his guru put him through while he was waiting for arrangements to be made for him to go abroad:

> My guru made me mash up all my food together—bananas, milk, curds, rice. And I had to eat the mash out of a new clay bowl that wasn't even dry yet. I remember thinking, "This is dog's food! I may be from a poor

family, but I'm not that poor!" The stink from that bowl was disgusting—I can smell it still. He made me eat that way for many days. Meanwhile, all the other monks were eating normal food off nice metal plates. But then I remembered the story of the Buddha when he first went out for alms and none of the laypeople would give him anything because the idea was new to them. Finally, the Buddha saw some food that a housewife was throwing away because it was four days old and mold was growing on it. So he asked her if she would throw it into his bowl, which she did, and he ate it. Then I said to myself, "If the Buddha could eat moldy four-day-old food, then surely I can eat food that's fresh and doesn't even have mold on it."

Sugandha admits, from a distance of thirty years, that tough as it was, his guru gave him excellent training.

Training Abroad: Novice Monks

At sixteen, Suman Bhante found himself headed for Sri Lanka where his guru, Ashwaghosh had been trained. "My father had died the year before and although my mother was happy I had a chance to study, she was very sad to see me go. We didn't meet again for nine years." After a few weeks in the bhikkhu training center at Mahagama, a suburb of Colombo, Suman was sent to Mathara, several hours' bus-ride away, to learn Sinhala before entering the Buddhist University:

I was with three Nepalis my own age, and four Bangladeshis who were a good deal older than we were. They had a lot of trouble with Sinhala, but we Nepalis were preaching in it after six months, and with good accents too. Because we were fair-skinned, people knew we weren't Sri Lankans, but all the same, they loved us because we came from Nepal, the birthplace of the Lord Buddha.

After completing a bachelor's degree in Buddhist Discipline and Doctrine, Suman took a second bachelor's degree in Sanskrit and Paḷi, and a diploma in English as well. In the meantime, he was also busy preaching, teaching, meditating, chanting *mahaparitrana* in all-night sessions, and doing social work in the tradition of the Sarvodaya Shramadana movement.[24]

In Sri Lanka, monks try to do everything! It isn't like here in Nepal where most monks specialize in only one thing, translation or teaching, for instance . . . and some don't seem do anything much at all. There aren't many monks in Nepal and the few that there are live scattered about in different viharas. Some ordain late in life and receive no proper training.

> They never master the *sekhiya* rules—they wear their robes carelessly, and they eat sloppily, and nobody corrects them. Then again, in Nepal, monks make confessions only twice a month, but in Sri Lanka they have to confess each night. As novices, we all touched money, which is a violation of the tenth precept. And so every night we each had to confess to a friend.

Suman took *upasampada* when he was 20, after completing his first bachelor's degree:

> My preceptor was the Ven. Piyadassi. He's a very well-known monk who has written dozens of books and taught the dharma in Japan and Australia as well as the United States. When I met him, he already had forty-five chelas, and because he traveled so much, he had little time. If he happened to be in the vihara on a Sunday, we chelas could go and consult him about any questions we might have, but the only formal instruction we received was from his assistant. I didn't see him very often, but even so I learned a great deal from him. In fact, he was the best teacher I ever had. He was a kind and lovely monk and he was a genius with children. I also liked working with children—especially village children. After all, I'd been a village child myself . . . He taught me a lot about how to deal with them, how to get them on my side so they'd listen to me. In his whole career he's only had five Nepali chelas, so I was very lucky to be one of them.

After further educational stints in Thailand and Taiwan, where he found the discipline in the Buddhist monastic university severe and "militaristic," Suman returned to Nepal where he was asked by the lay supporters of a Lalitpur vihara to come and live there and use it as his base. In a few years, his warm and charismatic personality, and his fluent preaching, attracted large numbers of laypeople and forged a large community based on his monastery. He has taught them to chant in Pali so that considerable numbers are now able to participate fully in Buddha Puja every holy day. As choreographed by Suman, the Buddha Puja at his vihara includes the following Sri Lankan verses in praise of the Three Jewels:

> *Namāmi Buddham gunasāgaran tam*
> I do obeisance to the Buddha, an ocean of good qualities.
> *Sattā sadā hotu sukhī averā*
> May all beings always be happy and free from hatred.
> *Kāyo jigucchо sakalo dugandho*
> The entire human body is disgusting and malodorous.
> *Gacchanti sabbe maranam aham ca.*
> Everyone must die and so must I.[25]

Now Suman too, in the Sri Lankan tradition he admires, is trying to do "everything." This includes preaching, teaching adults and hoards of children, chanting *paritrana*, tutoring novice monks and young nuns in Pali and Sanskrit, and leading pilgrimages to India and Thailand. But because most of his cohort have disrobed, he admits he often feels lonely.

Training Abroad: Nuns

Between 1966 and 1980, no Nepali nuns had the opportunity to study abroad. Their only recourse was to learn what they could from the senior nuns or, failing that, on their own. According to a nun who went to live in Dharmakirti in 1976:

> Dhammawati Guruma was going out all the time, she was too busy to teach me and so were the other nuns. Gunawati Guruma, who after all was also a qualified Dhammachariya, was always cooking and cleaning and helping laypeople. So I cooked and cleaned too, and memorized sutras, and I studied *pariyatti* on my own and tried to understand what I was reading.

When, in 1980, after a lapse of fourteen years, Dhammawati was at last able to arrange for two young nuns to go to Burma, their parents bought their airplane tickets and gave them money for expenses, and they entered the country on visas that needed to be renewed every three months. The following year, they were joined by four other young women. Padmawati recalls:

> The first three months we were in Mahasi Sayadaw's meditation center in Rangoon. That first month was terrible. . . . We'd had a taste of vipassana the previous year when Daw Pannyachari came to Nepal to teach us. But in Rangoon we were meditating fourteen hours a day!

At the conclusion of the retreat, they went to Moulmein where the other two nuns from Kathmandu were studying:

> We were assigned a teacher who was supposed to teach us Burmese, but I, for one, never managed to learn much of the language. For one thing, we six Nepalis shared a room and we talked Nepal Bhasha all the time. We were supposed to be studying Abhidhamma, but again, speaking for myself, I didn't learn much because I didn't understand what the teacher was saying. And then, after one year, the government canceled our visas, we couldn't get any more extensions, and we were forced to leave.

It was not until the late 1980s that the Burmese military regime began issuing long-term visas to foreign monastics, at which point a half-dozen Nepali nuns went to study in institutions in Rangoon and Sagain, as well as in Moulmein.

The First International Conference of Buddhist Nuns, which took place at Bodh Gaya in February 1987, had several important consequences for Nepali nuns. The conference, which brought together seventy monks and nuns and eighty laypeople from twenty-six countries, focused on issues of central importance to Buddhist women in general and Buddhist nuns in particular. These included education, and Dhammawati, who went to Bodh Gaya accompanied by an interpreter from the Dharmakirti community, made contacts that led to opportunities for foreign study. In 1989, the first of several nuns went to Sala Santi Suk in Thailand; in the 1990s, others went to Vajirarama in Sri Lanka and Fo Guang Shan in Taiwan. Arrangements were made on a case-by-case basis. Once a place in a foreign institution had been secured, each young woman required a local sponsor to assume financial responsibility for her during her stay in the country; her family contributed what they could to her travel expenses and Dhammawati and other senior nuns raised the balance from the community.

The education a young nun receives abroad varies depending on the country and institution to which she is sent as well as on her talents and motivation. The first task is to learn the local language. Whereas monks who have studied in monasteries to which foreigners have been coming for decades report that language instruction is reasonably effective, this is not the case for the nuns, most of whom study in much smaller and more insular institutions. Educational aids, including dictionaries and grammars, may be entirely lacking. Uttara, a young nun who went to Burma in 1997, described the tutor who was assigned to her as kind, but too busy:

> To begin with, we met every afternoon and she taught me the alphabet and words for many things, which I'd write down and memorize. But after a short while she left for Sagain for a month's meditation, and when she came back to the vihara she didn't have time for me . . . Luckily, Burmese is not so difficult for Newars.

Or perhaps Uttara has a talent for languages. In any event, when visited by LeVine four months after her arrival in Rangoon, she appeared to speak Burmese quite effectively.

Dhammasevi, a graduate degree-holder who spent nine months in Sala Santi Suk in Thailand in the mid-1990s, was similarly ambivalent about her experience. She admits that she was lucky in that both she and the abbess, who prepared her for taking the precepts, knew English, so they could communicate reasonably well. But her main purpose was to learn Thai as quickly as possible so that she could get on with studying the dharma, and with that she had little help. Chandrawati, who arrived at the same Thai nunnery aged eighteen after finishing secondary school in Kathmandu, was surprised by what she found there:

> First of all, there were very few nuns my age. In Thailand, nuns shave their heads when they're older, so almost everyone was a lot older than I. Some of them studied the dharma, but most worked like servants for the monks in the monastery next door, or else they meditated in the orchard. There were a good many nuns whom I hardly ever saw because they meditated every night and slept in the daytime! As for social work—I never saw nuns going out to work in the community. Unless they went to work for the monks, they stayed in the vihara.

Chandrawati was surprised too—if not shocked—by the fact that all the dharma talks were given by monks. "Even the learned nuns didn't give them, and when we went to chant in the homes of laypeople, after *bhojana dana* we'd read aloud dharma talks from books that monks had published!"

Unlike the Nepali monks who study abroad, the large majority of whom are enrolled in Buddhist universities, few nuns pursue university-level courses. Theoretically, Thai Buddhist universities now admit nuns, but few if any Thai nuns have enrolled thus far. An alternative, the Maechi College, which opened in Bangkok in 1999, is expensive, and courses require a high level of proficiency in written Thai; thus far only one Nepali nun—who had already spent four years in a Thai nunnery and is from a wealthy family who could afford to pay her tuition costs—has been accepted. A lower-level *pariyatti* course specifically designed for maechi takes nine years, and to date, no Nepali nun has completed it. Sri Lankan nuns, long excluded from Buddhist universities, are now being admitted also and two Nepalis have enrolled. The Buddhist International University for thilashin, which opened in Rangoon in 2000, does not charge tuition, and one Nepali nun recently finished the three-year degree course there and a second has enrolled. Several nuns have studied at Fo Guang Shan Monastery in Taiwan, where they report that although language teaching is good, religious instruction leaves much to be desired; thus, after attaining some proficiency in Chinese, they returned to Kathmandu. Two Nepali nuns recently completed the Burmese Dhammachariya course, which takes a minimum of eleven years, and a third is in her final year. But few Nepalis set their sights so high; rather, after following the government *buddha dharma* course for five or six years, they return home.

In general, Nepali nuns are less excited about foreign education than their male counterparts. This reflects the fact that very few of them are admitted to university courses, and again that, other than in Burma, nunnery-based religious education is inferior to the religious education that monks receive. Many nuns spend time abroad, but aside from being exposed to foreign ways in great Asian cities such as Bangkok, Colombo, and Taipei and acquiring a certain cosmopolitan "polish," for most, the main benefits are making foreign friends and learning another language, which from time to time they have an opportunity to practice with foreign pilgrims in Nepal.

Secular Education for Nuns

From the earliest days, the senior nuns recognized the need for formal *religious* training, but they were even slower than the monks in seeing the need for secular education. By the 1980s, however, the nuns' Order was starting to attract a more diverse group of recruits than in the past. Though some, as before, were formerly married women, the majority were adolescent girls and single women. These recruits had a different notion from their elders of what preparation for the renunciant's life required: coming of age as they were in a rapidly developing location, the Kathmandu Valley, they wanted as much secular education as their talents warranted, which in many cases meant continuing their education long after ordination through university.

For Dhammawati, the 1987 Bodh Gaya conference marked a turning point in her thinking. It was not just a question of making contacts that would help her chelis acquire a religious education abroad. Since she knew no English, she had to rely on an interpreter. Exposed for the first time to Western feminist ideas of individualism, self-realization, and gender equality, she realized that "out there" were Chinese, Taiwanese, Korean, exiled Tibetan, and Sri Lankan Buddhist women whose views on a range of topics were closer to her own than those of her much esteemed Burmese teachers. Frustrated by her inability to communicate directly with any of them, she did an about-face: in order to engage in the momentous changes that Buddhist women, both lay and monastic, were working to bring about, she conceded that Nepali nuns needed secular education as well as religious training. From that point on, instead of discouraging young recruits from continuing their studies, she began pressuring them to remain in school. This meant that, with their shaved heads and pink and orange dresses, they studied in settings in which, at least at the outset, they would be objects of great curiosity to their classmates. Furthermore, although single-sex schools existed in Kathmandu and Lalitpur, Dhammawati decided that the young nuns should study in coeducational schools:

> These girls are very young. They think they want to renounce the world but really, what do they know? If they have no contact with boys and men until after they grow up and go about their work in the city, they will be unprepared. Much better that they sit with boys in the classroom now and discover what they feel about them. Only then can they make a commitment to the homeless life. If they find they can't, then they should go back to their parents and get married in the usual way.

The older nuns all have specific responsibilities whether it is teaching, running meditation sessions, or editing publications; but aside from taking turns to prepare breakfast, doing their laundry, and learning to sew their own clothes, the "work" of the young nuns is to go to class and do their assignments. "Let us chant *paritrana* for the laypeople," say the older nuns. "They'll have plenty of time to chant later on."

Today's young nuns, like their male counterparts, are expected to

Nuns doing their homework in Dharmakirti Vihara, February 1998. (Sarah LeVine)

complete secondary school and pass the SLC. Those who fail SLC are expected to take it again and again until they pass. As Dhammawati remarks:

> It's our responsibility to give them enough education so that they can support themselves. If they stay with us, then we need competent women, and if they leave us, without a good education, what can they do?

Experiments in Samanera Education

Kosala Bhante, who passed his SLC in 1973, was the first novice monk to be allowed to attend secondary school after ordination. Over the next decade, as secondary education became the norm in the Valley, the rule was adopted that novices had to pass SLC before going abroad. Once there, however, they were exposed to the tradition of short-term ordination. In Thailand in particular, novices saw many of their cohort disrobe after a few years and soon they were following suit. "My guru sent his chelas abroad in droves," says Kosala, sitting alone in his monastery in Lalitpur, "and very few came back to the vihara." Some of the more enterprising ex-monks found ways to remain abroad in countries that, during the Asian economic boom, offered much better opportunities than their homeland; others, often to the dismay of the lay community, disrobed on their return. As Kosala remarks, the Order has been hemorrhaging monks: "Perhaps one day, when all the old monks have died and all the young ones have taken off their robes, I'll be the only monk left in Nepal."

There have been several attempts to deal with the problem, mainly by keeping novices in Nepal until they are older and—it is hoped—less likely to be dazzled by the excitements of foreign capitals. The first experiment was made by Ashwaghosh who, with the help of two donors, opened his Bhikkhu Training Center in Kathmandu next to the Vishnumati River, in 1982. His goal was to provide his ten chelas with a combined religious and secular education. "Two upasakas had given us the building," a former student recalls, "but our teachers needed salaries. Only two were laymen, and the rest were monks, and although the monks didn't require salaries, they did need bus fare and other things. So we went for alms to raise the money. After two years, the Center closed for lack of funds and we all moved out to Dhyankuti Vihara in Banepa, which was another vihara that Ashwaghosh Bhante had established." Somehow Ashwaghosh was able to see his students through, but after he had sent them off to university in Sri Lanka, he gave up his experiment. A year later, in 1985, Gyanapurnik returned from abroad to launch another training center in Vishwa Shanti Vihara (World Peace Monastery) whose construction, on land donated to the Sangha in Naya Baneshwor, he supervised. He himself had been one of the first monks to graduate—aged forty—from university in Nepal. Now he brought a small group of novices into the new vihara, his idea being that they should receive all their education in Nepal—religious training from himself, and secular training in government schools and university—and only go abroad after graduation.

The group had completed the program as planned by the early 1990s, but Gyanapurnik decided against taking on another as his health was poor and he wanted to concentrate on his translation work. Things turned out differently however. After traveling to Malaysia as a translator for U Pandita Sayadaw, the Burmese meditation master in the 1980s, he began going there on his own to teach meditation. Soon he was attracting many devotees, some of whom approached him with a proposal. They explained that although the Theravada tradition was winning a substantial following among Chinese Malaysians, thus far their community had produced no monks and, given the business orientation of their young people, was unlikely to do so. They offered to raise funds with which to build a seminary in Kathmandu in which Gyanapurnik would train Nepali monks, some of whom might eventually come to Malaysia to minister to the Chinese community. "They said that they could hardly understand a word when Thai monks spoke English—and the Burmese monks weren't that much better—but they understood my English very well," Gyanapurnik recalls. "They thought that if I could speak good English, then surely other Nepalis could too." Despite misgivings, Gyanapurnik agreed to their proposal and within a year they had raised US$200,000.

In February 1997 a greatly enlarged Vishwa Shanti Vihara took in its first group of fifteen novices aged ten to fifteen, selected on the basis of a written exam and an interview from an application pool of sixty boys whose parents had responded to a newspaper advertisement. Over the objections of a good many people, Gyanapurnik also admitted eight girls; however the group had dwindled to two just three months later. Students attended a school in the vihara that was established as a branch of government secondary school in the city center; academic subjects were taught by devout lay teachers (for minimal remuneration), and *buddha dharma*, Sanskrit, and Pali were taught by monas-

Gyanapurnik Mahasthavir and his novice pupils in Vishwa Shanti Vihara, March 1997. (Sarah LeVine)

tics. Students lived tightly disciplined lives within the high walls of the vihara. Training rules forbade music, TV, and all physical exercise other than sweeping the courtyard. Although family members could visit, students were rarely permitted to go home. They only left the building to attend monastic functions and, every full-moon day, to go on the alms round in Buddhist neighborhoods. Gyanapurnik had tried and failed to reintroduce this practice with his first group of students in the 1980s; a decade later however, the alms round proved a success and these days the novices, who, with their black Burmese begging bowls, walk barefoot in single file, heads bowed and eyes downcast, through the ancient courtyards of Lalitpur and Kathmandu, routinely collect enough rice to last them a month.[26]

Samanera Dipaka: Will He Stay the Course?

Dipaka had taken *pabbajja* ordination only a few weeks before LeVine first encountered him in the late winter of 1996–97. Thirteen years old and slight for his age, he was still a smooth-skinned child, albeit one

Novices and young nuns performing walking meditation in Vishwa Shanti Vihara, March 1997. (Sarah LeVine)

Novices from Vishwa Shanti Vihara being taken on the alms round, led by Ven. Bodhigyana, October 1997. (Sarah LeVine)

with adult preoccupations. Like his companions—the nineteen boys and girls who made up the first cohort of novice monks and nuns admitted to Vishwa Shanti Vihara—he was new to monastic life, but his deportment already appeared more "monklike" than the others. He managed his voluminous ochre and rust-colored robes a little more skillfully than they did; he seemed a little more careful to keep his gaze respectfully lowered and to move in a disciplined manner befitting a novice. Although many months later he would confide that to begin with he had found almost every aspect of life in the monastery difficult, to a visitor he appeared self-contained and confident of mastering the myriad rules and practices that henceforth would order his life. He was eager to learn whatever the monastery offered him, and he wanted to be helpful to the senior monks and to his companions, as well as to outsiders in whose presence an initial caution was quickly banished by a trusting smile. At ordination, his "home" name had been replaced by a monastic name. "You are like a lamp [*dipa*]," his abbot had told him, "so Dipaka is you shall be called!"

The youngest of four children, Dipaka was born in Kirtipur, a hilltop town just two miles southwest of Kathmandu. His father, Jagat, was a Napit (barber) who pursued his traditional caste occupation. (At one time, he was also employed by the police.) He cut the hair and beards of the *jajmans* (patrons) he had inherited from his father, and his wife, Bekha Maya, cut their toenails. Their sparsely furnished house, just a stone's throw from a wide pond where neighborhood families washed their clothes and bathed, was built on four floors connected by narrow ladders. Most of his family's food needs were supplied by his own small acreage just outside the town. Growing up in the 1960s, a time when only a small minority of Nepalese children were attending school even in town, he himself had completed secondary school and his wife, Bekha Maya, elementary school. Now, as parents, they were determined that their children should study as far as their talents took them.

From an early age, religion had been Dipaka's main preoccupation. Like many similar small Newar castes, in their personal religion Napits sometimes prefer Hinduism, sometimes Buddhism, and sometimes practice both equally. Whereas Dipaka's father's family had regarded themselves as Hindu, his mother's family preferred Tibetan Buddhism. At marriage, she brought her religious culture with her; but when her youngest child, Dipaka, was an infant, she had undergone a conversion to Theravada Buddhism and become a devotee of Sudarshan Bhante, the abbot of nearby Shri Kirti monastery. Her husband had followed her lead and soon the two were spending much of their time in the monastery in devotional activities and performing services for the monks. As their children grew older, they started attending Saturday school. "But it wasn't a case of our telling them to go," Bekha Maya recalls. "They went of their own accord."

While attending Saturday school, Dipaka became convinced of the veracity of the Four Noble Truths. One afternoon in the monastery, he talks about his childhood determination to escape the *duhkha* of the householder's life and to absolve himself from—and avoid accumulating more—*pap* (bad karma). When he was living in his parents' house he had many friends, some of them wild and heedless boys whose favorite pastimes were killing birds with slingshots and truanting from school to play cards; he admits that he too found these pastimes attractive and that had he remained in lay life he might have taken the same path as his friends. By killing defenseless creatures who are also sentient beings, he would have taken on a great burden of bad karma. Again, playing truant from school and spending his time gambling would also have brought him suffering. The monastery, he believes, will both protect him from himself and provide him with the discipline and wisdom he needs to help others protect themselves. But although he talks animatedly about *duhkha* and *pap* (suffering and sin) and his desire to avoid them, there remains a sense that may be repeating lessons he has learned from his monk teachers.

At the age of ten, Dipaka went on his first vipassana meditation retreat. Although he had been introduced to vipassana in Saturday school, sessions there never lasted more than thirty minutes. Then one day his dharma teacher asked him if he would like to attend a retreat at the Budha Nilkantha meditation center, and off he went. Whereas adult retreats last ten days, children's retreats generally last only three; and whereas adults observe Eight Precepts and do not eat after midday, children may eat rice and fruit in the evening. In other respects, the adults' and children's programs are the same: from 4 A.M. until 9.30 P.M., child meditators follow a schedule of silent sitting meditation interspersed with brief periods of instruction.

Dipaka reports that the retreat was the most compelling experience of his young life:

> I began to understand how my mind works. I saw how thoughts come like insects and buzz around and distract me, but I also saw that it was possible to control my mind.

From that point on meditation assumed a steadily increasing importance for him. The following year, and the year after that he returned to the meditation center.

Ordination

Just a few months after his third retreat, Dipaka heard that a seminary was about to open in Kathmandu and he decided to apply for admission. Though his was a devoutly Buddhist family, he felt that home life did not allow enough time for meditation. Indeed, the previous year his father, Jagat, seeking peace and quiet, had himself ordained for one month in the Kirtipur monastery. Hoping that life in the seminary would be more conducive to contemplation, Dipaka took and passed the written entrance examination, was interviewed, and was accepted as a novice in Vishwa Shanti Vihara. A few days later, his head was shaved and, as his proud parents looked on, he took the Ten Precepts and donned Theravada robes.

At first everything was new and exciting, but after a few days he began feeling strange and out of place. He missed his parents, his brothers and sister, his friends, his house. So he walked out of the monastery gates, jumped on a bus and went home. But within a day or two he realized that things at home hadn't changed and neither had he: his friends were still killing birds, missing school, and gambling; furthermore, such a life was as attractive to him as ever and he was just as afraid as ever of being ensnared by it. Hard as monastic discipline might be, he decided that he would be happier in Vishwa Shanti Vihara than at home, surrounded by temptations that he wasn't at all sure he could resist. So he told his parents he was going back to the monastery.

For a while after his return, he was extremely homesick. He found doing without supper very difficult and hunger as well as aching unhappiness prevented him from meditating properly in the evening. There were so many rules to learn about how to eat one's food and wear one's robes and walk and talk and sit, and his companions fought a lot—not as much as boys at home used to fight perhaps, but nevertheless, he found it upsetting. ("Even if you aren't involved yourself, you're affected by the atmosphere.") As the weeks and months went by, however, some of the rules that at first had been so difficult to keep became easier. He got used to fasting after midday and he missed listening to music and playing football less than before. In the monastery school, he had able and attentive teachers, several of whom had recently returned from posts in British Army Gurkha schools in Hong Kong. He soon realized that in the disciplined atmosphere of the vihara he was doing much better than he had in his chaotic class in his old school. Toward the end of his first year in the monastery, he conceded that in general things were going well. But he still found one vow—not to lie—difficult to keep. Though he no longer told "big" lies, he still lied about small things. If you lied to protect someone else, that wasn't necessarily a sin, but sometimes he couldn't stop himself from lying for his own advantage and that was definitely a sin. The senior monks were very vigilant, and if they caught you in a small lie you had to clean the latrines as punishment; if they caught you in a really big lie you would be expelled. ("Some of us spend a lot of time cleaning the latrines, but no one's been expelled so far.")

Invited to review personal changes that had occurred, he volunteered that he was no longer lazy. Although the monastery timetable was extremely demanding—the novices got up at 4 A.M., and they followed a schedule of devotions and chanting, homework, schoolwork, and housework with hardly a moment's break until they fell into bed at 9.30 P.M.—his powers of concentration had much increased through meditation. Now, he said, he could focus much better on the task at hand, whatever it happened to be. For example, when he was supposed to be sweeping the monastery courtyard, that's what he concentrated on doing. He didn't think about other things at all, and as a result he performed this essentially boring task meticulously. Another big change was that he'd become a vegetarian. Most monks in Nepal do eat meat when laypeople give it as *dana* (according to the Pali Vinaya rules, a monk may eat meat so long as the animals from which the meat comes have not been slaughtered on his orders specifically). But Dipaka suspected that eating meat and eggs disturbed his concentration, and so had given them up. As a result, he found that he could concentrate better and his overall health was better too. With a glowing smile, he announces, "I'm happier now than I've ever been in my life."

In 2002, Dipaka passed his SLC exams and, now aged eighteen, entered university in Kathmandu. How likely is he to remain in the Order for the long term, let alone fulfill the hopes of his sponsors by becoming the resident monk and meditation teacher in a Malaysian vihara? Although Vishwa Shanti Vihara has continued to be inundated with mostly male applicants,[27] the success of this educational experiment remains in the balance. Lay teachers report that, by requiring

Raising the Status of Nuns: The Controversy over Bhikkhuni Ordination

As discussed previously, the Bodh Gaya Conference on Buddhist Women in February 1987 had a profound impact on Dhammawati Guruma's views with regard to secular education for nuns. It was through contacts she made there that she began to find places for her chelis in foreign training institutions other than in Burma. The central focus of the conference, however, was the status of nuns vis-à-vis monks, and strategies for improving it. Although education was much discussed, the issue that received most attention was the exclusion from full ordination of Tibetan nuns (Willis 1984), who take the thirty-six novice precepts,[1] and of Theravada nuns, including the Nepalis, who, as "eight-" or "ten-precept laywomen," occupy a liminal space between upasika and bhikshuni. Of the roughly sixty thousand Buddhist nuns in the world, it was estimated at the time that less than ten thousand—those who belonged to the Chinese, Korean, Taiwanese, and Vietnamese traditions—were fully ordained.[2] Before describing the contemporary situation in further detail, however, we need first to go back to the earliest days of Buddhism.

A great deal has been written about the inception of the bhikkhuni Order, and many questions have been raised about the trustworthiness of the traditional "historical" accounts. An adequate treatment of this and other issues would require a thorough study of all existing *Vinayas* in all languages, with their ancillary literature. In this instance, however, only material drawn from the Pali *Vinaya* will be discussed because it is mainly with the representation of bhikkhunis and the evolution of their order as portrayed in the Pali canon that Nepali nuns identify.

Despite a doctrinal emphasis on soteriological inclusiveness, many scholars have argued that early Buddhism in India was marked by a profound ambivalence toward women.[3] For the first five years after he founded his order of mendicants, the Buddha did not admit women. It is not known whether this was because no women requested admission or because he rejected those who did. Male renouncers belonging to numerous religious sects abounded in north India at that time and female renouncers also played a part in sectarian life.[4] Nevertheless, when his aunt, Mahaprajapati Gotami, who had raised him from infancy, asked to be admitted to the order, the Buddha refused her. Mahaprajapati and a large number of the Buddha's female relatives then cut their hair, donned ochre renouncer's robes, and followed him from Nigrodha Park near the Sakya capital of Kapilavastu to Vaisali where they sought the help of Ananda, the Buddha's chief disciple. Ananda intervened on their behalf twice, but still the Buddha refused them. When Ananda then asked whether women were capable of attaining enlightenment, the Buddha admitted that they were. Ananda pressed home his advantage by reminding the Buddha that Mahaprajapati "was the Lord's aunt, foster-mother, nurse, giver of milk" (Horner 1952: 354). At this point, the Buddha retreated from his original position and, albeit reluctantly, agreed to receive his stepmother and her Sakya companions into his Order.[5]

In the Sangha's earliest days, a desire to leave the householder's life in order to seek enlightenment was all that the Buddha had required of a male renouncer. Indeed, he is reported to have ordained his first disciples simply with the command, "Come, O monk!" But even though he had agreed that in terms of spiritual potential women and men were equal, he insisted that, as a condition of their admission, Mahaprajapati and her companions agree to abide by eight "Chief Rules," *attha garudhamma*, each of which was "to be honoured, respected, revered, venerated, never to be transgressed during her life":

1. A nun who has been ordained (even) for a century must greet respectfully, rise up from her seat, salute with joined palms, do proper homage to a monk ordained but that day.
2. A nun must not spend the rains in a residence where there is no monk.

3. Every half month a nun should desire two things from the Order of monks: the asking (as to the date) of the Observance day, and the coming for the exhortation [i.e., to be taught].
4. After the rains a nun must "invite" before both Orders in respect of three matters: what was seen, what was heard, what was suspected.
5. A nun, offending against an important rule, must undergo *mānatta* (discipline) for half a month.
6. When, as a probationer, she has trained in the six rules for two years, she should seek ordination.
7. A monk must not be abused or reviled in any way by a nun.
8. From to-day admonition of monks by nuns is forbidden, admonition of nuns by monks is not forbidden.[6]

Mahaprajapati gratefully accepted the rules. Ananda reported this to the Buddha, who then made his famous prediction that, because of the acceptance of women into its monastic path, Buddhism would now last only five hundred years, whereas otherwise it would have lasted for one thousand years. He went on to compare a religion that accepted women in this way to, successively, a household with few men and many women in it that is easily overpowered by robbers, a rice field attacked by mildew, and a sugarcane field attacked by red rust. Finally the Buddha concluded:

> Even, Ānanda, as a man, looking forward, may build a dyke to a great reservoir so that the water may not overflow, even so, Ānanda, were the eight important rules for nuns laid down by me, looking forward, not to be transgressed during their life. (*Cullavagga* X.1.6; Horner 1952: 356)

The Buddha was certainly anxious that, by admitting women to his Order, they might corrupt his monks. Bearing in mind the injunction of the Laws of Manu that "reprehensible is the son who does not protect his mother after her husband has died,"[7] we may imagine that he was also concerned about his ability to ensure his stepmother's physical safety and well-being. Furthermore, with the admission of women, the Sangha suddenly increased dramatically in size and overnight he had to design an institutional structure to accommodate this expansion.[8]

The Buddha had rejected the brahmanical view that only males could pursue a religious vocation leading to the attainment of enlightenment. Nonetheless, his ideas about women remained ambivalent. He repeatedly warned his monks to be wary of them:

> Monks I know of no other single form by which a man's heart is so enslaved as it is by that of a woman. Monks, a woman's form obsesses a man's heart. Monks, I know of no other single sound by which a man's heart is so enslaved as it is by the voice of a woman. Monks, a woman's voice obsesses a man's heart.
>
> Monks, I know of no other single scent . . . savour . . . touch by which a man's heart is so enslaved as it is by the scent, savour and touch of a woman. Monks, the scent, savour and touch of a woman obsesses a man's heart.
>
> Monks, I know of no other single form, sound, scent, savour and touch by which a woman's heart is so enslaved as it is by the form, sound, scent, savour and touch of a man. Monks, a woman's heart is obsessed by these things.[9]

Elizabeth Harris has argued that modern scholars and feminists may have placed too much emphasis on the Buddha's misogynist attitudes.[10] Although textual evidence for them can be found, other passages support a quite different view, namely that, rather than advocating male domination, early Buddhism advanced the status of women and rendered male-female distinctions irrelevant. Thus the Buddha, even if it was he who formulated the Eight Chief Rules, may not have viewed them as etched in stone. In any event, within a rather short period, three of the eight (rules three, four, and five) were relaxed allowing for the partial evasion of three others (rules one, seven, and eight). Eventually only two remained (Horner 1975: 123–137): rule two, which required nuns—for their own protection—to spend the rainy season retreat in close proximity to monks; and rule six, which prescribed the form of the bhikkhuni rite of ordination (*upasampada*).

In the early years of the Sangha, provided a man was at least twenty years old and had spent an undetermined—but often very short—period as a ten-precept novice (*samanera*), he could take full ordination as a bhikkhu. By contrast, rule six of the *garudhamma* required that a woman spend two years as a six-precept novice-probationer (*sikkhamana*). During this time, she would receive instruction from an experienced (*vyatta*) and competent (*patibala*) teacher.[11] It seems that the Buddha introduced this probationary period not because he believed that women needed more training than men but, rather, because a large majority of female recruits were formerly married women who might be pregnant or nursing infants, in which case they would need two years to see their offspring through infancy to an age at which they could give them into the care foster parents. When her two years were up, the candidate took full ordination (*upasampada*) as a bhikkhuni. But whereas a male novice (*samanera*) received full ordination from monks alone, a *sikkhamana* required "double" ordination, first by a quorum of nuns and, second, by a quorum of monks. A quorum was specified as ten monks or nuns in "central lands," which were defined as areas where the Buddhist teaching was well established, but only five were required "on the borders," that is, in remote areas. The rite administered by nuns appears to have been the more important of the two. During this ritual, the candidate was asked two sets of questions, twenty-four in all. The first, which was almost identical to the set posed by monks to male novices, focused on health and legal status:

> Do you suffer from any diseases like leprosy, boils, eczema, consumption, epilepsy? Are you a human being? Are you a man? (Or, Are you a woman?) Are you not a slave? Are you free from all debt? Are you a king's servant or a soldier? Have you obtained permission from your parents? (Or, from your husband?) Are you at least twenty years of age? What is your name? Who is your preceptor?

The second set focused on sensitive gynecological issues:

> Are you a woman with no sign of female sex? (*nāsi animittā*)? Are you a woman with under-developed signs of female sex (*nāsi animittamattā*)? Are you a woman with no menstruation (*nāsi alohitā*)? Do you have perpetual menstruation (*dhuvalohitā*)? Are you always wearing a pad (*dhuvacolā*)? Are you always oozing (*paggarani*)? Do you have an extraordinarily long clitoris (*sikharani*)? Are you a she-eunuch (*itthipandaka*)? Are you an amazon (*vepurisikā*)? Are your two organs joined (*nāsi sambhinnā*)? Are you a hermaphrodite (*ubhato-byañjanakā*)?[12]

Having answered satisfactorily, the candidate would receive her robes and begging bowl from her female preceptor (*upajjhaya*) and vow to live according to the code of conduct of the Order. Only then would she go to a monastery to take the same vow in the presence of ten monks. This second rite, in which the monks did not ask the candidate any questions, appears to have been largely pro forma (Findly 2000a).[13]

At the time that women were first admitted to the Order, a code of conduct (*patimokkha*) governing daily life, including the alms round, relations with monks and the laity, building construction, and so forth, was in the process of evolving for monks. Of the rules that had already been formulated, 181 were immediately applied to nuns. Over time, only 46 additional rules were formulated to govern monks' behavior, bringing the total to 227 (in the Pali recension, more in others), whereas a further 130 rules emerged to govern the behavior of nuns. Hüsken (2000b) suggests that although nuns had to accept many more rules, a large proportion of which were aimed at regulating their interactions with males, it might be argued that these were formulated in order to protect rather than to penalize them. In any event, the *Bhikkhuni Patimokkha* ultimately totaled 311 rules, which nuns were required to recite in the presence of monks every fifteen days.[14] By contrast, the monks' bimonthly Patimokkha recitations did not require that nuns be present.

Subordinated to monks though they were, the *Mahaparinibbana Sutta* nonetheless records that the Buddha's unambiguous inclusion of the nuns' Order in the "four assemblies"—monks (*bhikkhus*), nuns (*bhikkhunis*), laymen (*upasakas*), and laywomen (*upasikas*)—of the Sangha. Both despite and because of the discipline that was imposed on them, women were able to enjoy a much greater degree of freedom within the Buddhist Order than in lay life. During the Buddha's lifetime and in the period shortly after his death many became poets, celebrated preceptors, and teachers (Blackstone 1998; Findly 2000a).

The Development, Decline, and Disappearance of the Bhikkhuni Order

The first epigraphic record of nuns is found in Emperor Asoka's edict on splits in the Order dating from the mid-third century B.C.E., which was inscribed on pillars at Kausambhi, Sanchi, and Sarnath (Bloch 1950: 152–153). The edict mentions both an order of monks (*bhikkhu-sangha*) and an order of nuns (*bhikkhuni-sangha*) (of which his daughter Sanghamitta, who is credited with establishing the nuns' Order in Sri Lanka, was a member). Thereafter, there are numerous mentions of the nuns' Order in donative inscriptions on chaityas and religious buildings, as well as in cave dwellings in Sri Lanka (Paranavitana 1970: cxvii), indicating that many nuns had the resources to become sponsors. Sometimes their names appear alone, sometimes, in the case of larger projects, they are listed with those of monks and laypeople (Willis 1992; Schopen 1997: 30–32).

In his account of his travels in early fifth century India, the Chinese monk Fa-Hsien noted that "the *bhikkhunis* for the most part make their offerings to the tope (stupa) of Ananda, because it was he who requested the World-honored one (the Buddha) to allow females to quit their families (and become nuns)" (Legge 1965: 45). Hsüan Tsang, who traveled through India in the seventh century, also observed nuns making offerings to the stupa of Ananda at Mathura (Li Rongxi 1995: 68). I-ching, who visited the subcontinent in 671–695 C.E., noted that he encountered nuns at Nalanda, at that time one of the great centers of Buddhist learning. However he also recorded that "nuns in India are very different from those in China. They support themselves by begging food, and live a poor and simple life" (Takakusu 1982: 80). Inscriptions indicate that new nunneries were established in many parts of the subcontinent during the third century C.E. but that thereafter, although here and there kings and merchants continued to make grants, nunnery endowments were sharply reduced (Dutt 1962; Lévi 1937). By the time I-ching came to India, many communities of nuns may have already fallen on hard times.

Both the *Dipavamsa*, a fourth-century Pali chronicle, and the *Mahavamsa*, which probably dates from one hundred to two hundred years later, place great emphasis on the summoning by Mahinda, the missionary monk and son of the Emperor Asoka, of his sister, Sanghamitta, from Pataliputra to Sri Lanka; on her arrival, bearing a sapling of the Bo tree from Bodh Gaya; and on her founding of the nuns' Order. But whereas the *Dipavamsa* often refers to bhikkhuni—many of whom were of royal birth or from prominent families—as teachers and spiritual virtuosi,[15] the *Mahavamsa* makes little mention of them. This may indicate that by the fifth century the nuns' Order was in decline in Sri Lanka, as in India. Nevertheless, beginning in the seventh century, there is inscriptional and literary evidence of a spate of nunnery endowments, the latest one, by King Mahinda V in the early eleventh century (Hettiaratchi 1988: 104). Thus, even though the nuns' Order seems always to have been much smaller than the monks', there clearly were periods when it was vigorous and not in decline.

Ultimately, however, the lower status of nuns vis-à-vis monks took its toll. Excluded from playing public roles, they were regarded by the laity as inferior fields of merit and less worthy recipients of *dana*. With rare exceptions, nuns seem to have been upstaged by pious laywomen who, as donors, devotees, and even teachers, are much more frequently mentioned in epigraphic texts and documentary records. In any event, lacking prestige and leadership, the Bhikkhuni Sangha seems to have vanished from India around the turn of the first millennium (i.e., three hundred years before the great monasteries of the north were laid waste by Muslim invaders) and in Sri Lanka a century later.

One case of the nuns' ordination being taken overseas is known. In 433 or 434 the *bhikkhuni upasampada* was introduced by nuns from Sri Lanka to China (Heirman 2001), where the lineage survived—a fact of considerable significance to the Theravadins of today. But this historical connection was not remembered in Sri Lanka and there is no evidence that the nuns' ordination rite was transmitted anywhere else outside South Asia.[16] By the time the nuns' ordination lineage was in need of renewal in Sri Lanka, Chinese Buddhism had long since been "domesticated," meaning that the Chinese, having studied and performed rituals, including ordination, entirely in Chinese, no longer knew Pali or retained any connection with South Asia. In fact, there is no evidence that the nuns who went from Sri Lanka even took Pali texts with them, and the textual tradition in China may derive entirely from Sanskrit and northwest Prakrit originals.

In short, the two voyages by nuns from Sri Lanka to China in the fifth century were a one-off and there was no regular contact between the two countries. When the monks' ordination disappeared in Sri Lanka around 1100 and was revived from Burma, the nuns' ordination tradition could not be revived in the same way. Nevertheless, some women in Southeast Asia and Sri Lanka continued to live the religious life, but they did so in ignorance of similar Buddhist women in other countries. The ordination statuses available to Buddhist nuns in different Asian countries before the modernist and feminist campaign began can be summarized as in Table 7.1.

The Modern *Upasampada* Movement

In modern times, the movement to establish full ordination for nuns was launched by a few highly educated, mostly Western women of the Tibetan and Theravada traditions. They realized that, if Buddhism was to expand, particularly in the West, it would need to attract thoroughly competent recruits and these recruits would need to have equal status with their male counterparts. Although by the 1980s both traditions of Buddhism were making advances in Western countries, especially among women, the focus of both had been teaching meditation to laypeople. Economic support had gone mainly to meditation centers and to the male—predominantly Asian—monastics who presided over them or else, in the case of the fast-growing Tibetan Buddhist com-

Table 7.1 The statuses available to Buddhist nuns before the campaign for full bhikkhuni ordination

	Sri Lanka, Thailand, Burma, Laos, Cambodia	Nepal among Theravadins	Tibet	China, Taiwan, Vietnam, Korea	Japan
10 precept "mother"/ *maechi* / *anagarika*	√	√			
sramanerika (novice) (10 precepts)			√	√	
bhikkhuni (fully ordained nun) (348 rules)				√	
bodhisattva vow (in Tibet: 36 rules)			√	√	√

Note: the term *biku* is sometimes used in Japan as an equivalent of *sō* meaning "Buddhist priest" and likewise *bikuni* is used as an equivalent of *nisō* ("female Buddhist practitioner") or of *ama/ni* ("Buddhist nun"), even though there is no *bhikkhuni upasampada*.

munity, to refugee institutions in India and Nepal. Lacking full ordination status, Western female renouncers, who had day-to-day responsibility for most meditation centers, were strictly subordinate to their male teachers and, receiving little or no financial support from the population they served, eked out a living from mostly marginal jobs in their local communities. Women of the caliber needed to build a sound institutional base for Buddhism in the West would only be willing to join an order that was strongly committed to social and gender equality. Full ordination for women and the status this conferred in the eyes of lay contributors was, they believed, essential to that commitment.

One of the three principal organizers of the 1987 Bodh Gaya conference, the American Karma Lekshe Tsomo (originally Patricia Zenn), had received Tibetan *sramanerika* ordination in Dharamsala in 1977 and *upasampada* in Taiwan in 1982. The second organizer, the German-born Jewish American *dasa sil mata* Ayya Khema, founder of a meditation center at Parrappaduwa, Sri Lanka, had been considering taking full ordination according to Chinese rites for several years. The third, Professor Chatsumarn Kabilsingh, was the daughter of Voramai Kabilsingh, a Thai *maechi* who had taken *upasampada* in Taiwan in

1972 and seventeen years later was still the only fully ordained Thai nun belonging to the Theravada tradition.[17] The tone of the Bodh Gaya conference was set by the Dalai Lama in his speech at the opening session. Three years earlier, in 1984, responding to pressure from some Western nuns, His Holiness had opened the Institute of Dialectics in Dharamsala, hitherto exclusively male, to everyone, regardless of sex and race (Havnevik 1990: 195). Now, speaking about the role of women in Buddhism and of women in Tibetan Buddhism in particular, he encouraged nuns not only to study the Dharma but also to take full ordination. In the Buddha's time, he said, from a religious perspective a "central Buddhist land" was one in which all four categories of disciples—bhikshus and bhikshuni, and upasakas and upasikas—existed:

> [I]n the case of Tibet, since there are no *bhiksunis*, it cannot be considered a fully qualified central land in religious terms. It has been considered as a central land in that *bhiksus* exist there, but to be precise, there must be *bhiksunis*. . . . Since the journey was very difficult in early times, *bhiksunis* were not able to come to Tibet. . . . These days we find that there are *bhiksuni* lineages in some parts of the world, such as the Chinese lineage. Speaking personally, as a Tibetan Buddhist, if an authentic *bhiksuni* lineage like this could be established within the Tibetan tradition, this would truly be something to be welcomed. (Tsomo 1988a: 41, 44)

Following the conference, the International Association of Buddhist Women, Sakyadhita (Daughters of the Buddha), was established. Although numerous international Buddhist organizations existed, notably the World Fellowship of Buddhists (founded in Sri Lanka in 1950) and the World Buddhist Sangha Council (founded in Sri Lanka in 1966), these were male organizations. Sakyadhita was the first organization to encourage the cooperation of Buddhist nuns and laywomen belonging to different traditions. Its objectives were: 1. to create a network of communications among Buddhist women of the world, 2. to educate women as teachers of Buddhism, 3. to conduct research on women in Buddhism, and 4. to work for the establishment of the Bhikshuni Sangha where it did not currently exist.[18]

Since Bodh Gaya in 1987, Sakyadhita has organized seven international conferences of Buddhist women to each of which the Nepali nuns' Order has sent delegates: Bangkok in 1991, Colombo in 1993, Leh in 1995, Phnom Penh in 1997, Lumbini in 2000, Taipei in 2002, and Seoul in 2004. Between sessions devoted to scholarly presentations on research topics as well as to discussions of broader issues, Buddhist nuns and laywomen—and a few monks and laymen—have had the

Opening session of the Sakyadhita conference in Lumbini, 1st February 2000. The chief guest, the Minister of Sport, Sharad Singh Bhandari, is seated in the centre. To his left are Dhammawati Guruma and Karma Lekshe Tsomo. (Sarah LeVine)

---

chance to develop networks, which have led to fruitful exchanges.[19] In the fourteen years since the first conference, progress has been made in all four areas that were identified as concerns in 1987; but nowhere have advances been more striking than in Nepal, where innovations that seemed inconceivable only a short while ago have become almost routine.

Single Ordination or Dual Ordination?

Although full ordination of nuns solely by monks, without the participation of nuns, is found today in Korea, Hong Kong, and Vietnam, and is regarded as valid in those communities, in the Vinaya, the dual ordination procedure stipulated by Rule Six of the *garudhamma* (first by a quorum of nuns and then by a quorum of monks) is seen as preferable, as it often was historically. In 429 C.E., the first group of three Sri Lankan nuns to reach China encountered Chinese nuns who had been ordained by monks alone.[20] In 433 or 434, another larger group of nuns arrived from Sri Lanka, and the first "dual" bhikshuni ordination to be conducted in China took place in Nanjing, the capital of the Southern Song dynasty.[21]

Subsequently, although higher ordination for nuns continued to be carried out by monks alone in some places, dual ordination was widely viewed as ideal (Tsomo 1988b: 221; Li 2000). Tibetan and Theravada nuns who today hope to establish full ordination lineages in their own countries, in order to ensure its validity, tend to take the dual ordination of China and Taiwan. This requires the presence of ten bhikshuni teachers (*acarya*) and ten bhikshu teachers (*acarya*); heading each group must be a preceptor (*sila upadhyaya*) and two instructors (*dharma-* and *karma-acaryas*), all of whom have been fully ordained for at least twelve years. (The other seven "witnessing" *acaryas* may have been ordained more recently.)

Help From Afar

Dhammawati returned from the 1987 Bodh Gaya conference perplexed. She had learned that a few Tibetan-tradition nuns had taken *upasampada* from Chinese monks and nuns in Taiwan and Hong Kong, and, more important from her own perspective, that a Theravada nun from Thailand had been fully ordained in Taiwan.[22] She had devoted her life to promoting the interests of women and had sought and had taken a leadership role in her own community; she nevertheless regarded herself as a Theravadin for whom the *Tipitaka* (the Pali Canon), much of which, as a girl in Burma, she had committed to memory, was the only source of truth. Her own esteemed Burmese teachers, as well as the senior Nepali monks with whom she had been struggling for decades, believed that the bhikkhuni ordination lineage had disappeared many centuries ago and that, once dead, it could never be revived. But at Bodh Gaya, she learned that more than fifteen hundred years ago a bhikkhuni ordination lineage had been transmitted by Sri Lankan nuns to China where it had survived unbroken down to the present. She also learned that the dual ordination rite by which many contemporary Chinese nuns and a few Tibetan nuns—and a single Theravada nun—had been ordained, was not a specifically Mahayana ritual, as the leading Theravada monks claimed. Rather, despite minor variations that reflected historical circumstances and not doctrinal differences, it was the same in its essentials as the long-defunct

Theravada dual ordination rite.[23] Furthermore, at various times in history when their own ordination lineages had died out, Thai and Sri Lankan monks had requested new transmissions from other Buddhist countries. Similarly, because the bhikshu ordination lineage had died out in Nepal in the time of the Malla kings, twentieth-century Nepali Theravada monks had had to ordain outside the country for decades. Indeed, aside from the fact that the Rana government had forbidden religious conversion, it was twenty years before there were enough monks to conduct the *upasampada* rite in Nepal. Even then, the requisite ten who were gathered in one place would be drawn from several different lineages from several different countries. If the monks had imported ordination lineages from abroad, why shouldn't the nuns do so too?

More troubling yet to Dhammawati was the idea that the *garudhamma* might not be *Buddhavacana*, that is, the Buddha's own words, at all, but rather additions to the *Bhikkhuni Patimokkha* made by misogynist monks after the death of the Buddha and before the final codification of the Vinaya.[24] Yes, she could understand the logic of dual ordination:

> There are those questions about pregnancy and menstruation and parts of the body between the neck and the knees which a female ordinand is required to answer; and those a monk shouldn't ask.

But the rest could be asked by a monk. And how essential were those gynecological questions anyway?

> When a woman asks for ordination, all she need give are her statistics: name, date of birth, family name, and so on. Did the Lord Buddha decide those questions were necessary, or was it some of his disciples after his parinirvana? . . . I began to wonder: How could the Lord Buddha, who had just admitted to Ananda that women were as capable as men of attaining enlightenment, insist that all nuns, however long they had been ordained, acknowledge the superiority of all monks, even those who had only been ordained for a day? Or that nuns shouldn't criticize monks, even in private and to each other, when laypeople are free to criticize them, and do so all the time?

When, in the spring of the following year, 1988, a group of Taiwanese nuns from Fo Guang Shan Monastery near Kaohsiung in Taiwan came to visit Dharmakirti, Dhammawati's confidence in the authenticity of the *garudhamma* had gone from scepticism to disbelief. In the end she settled on compromise:

> Even if all the eight rules were actually laid down by Lord Buddha, our times are very different from his. There are many rules of conduct that the monks don't keep any more because they aren't practical. For instance, there's one that prohibits them from traveling in a vehicle, and another that forbids them from buying medicines and requires them to drink urine when they're sick . . . So many of those old rules have been discarded. Why shouldn't the impractical *garudhamma* be discarded too?[25]

At the end of their stay, the Taiwanese visitors invited a delegation from Dharmakirti to attend the consecration of Xilai Monastery, Fo Guang Shan's new US $30 million outpost and the largest Buddhist temple in the Western world, in Hacienda Heights, a suburb of Los Angeles.[26] They were told that, in celebration of the consecration, *upasampada* would be taken by more than two-hundred Chinese monks and nuns, and, in addition, by some Tibetan and Theravada nuns. In November 1988, having informed the monks that they were going to Taiwan, Dhammawati, Daw Gunawati, Dhammadinna, Dhammavijaya, and nineteen-year-old Pannyawati, left for Taipei.[27] But instead of staying in Taipei they flew on to California.

The Fo Guang Shan Order, which represents a melding of Cha'n and Pure Land traditions, was established in Taiwan in the 1950s by Master Xingyun, a refugee from the mainland. By the 1980s, he had become one of the best known as well as the most controversial teachers in the island. His Order, which espoused "humanistic Buddhism," of which gender equality was an important feature, had attracted several thousand monastics and a large lay following.[28] Fo Guang Shan had very considerable financial resources raised from an increasingly affluent community.

For fear of antagonizing the government of mainland China, Taiwanese Buddhists and Tibetan refugee Buddhists had held aloof from each other for many years; but as Tibetan Buddhism began making inroads among the Taiwanese laity, senior members of the two hierarchies began to make contact. This led, in 1982, to four Western nuns belonging to the Tibetan tradition receiving full ordination at Hae Ming Temple in Taiwan.[29] In 1988, Master Xingyun decided to offer the Chinese ordination rite to Theravada as well as Tibetan nuns so that they might eventually establish Fo Guang Shan ordination lineages in their own countries, thereby extending his own influence, as well as that of his order.

Xingyun chose to offer the ordination at Xilai, which he envisioned both as a center for Chinese American Buddhists and as the flagship of his mission to the West. To mark the monastery's consecration, 250 male and female candidates from sixteen countries were to undertake Triple Altar Ordination there. This rite, which had been transmitted to Taiwan from the mainland after the Communist takeover and was conducted for the first time in Taipei in 1953, is so named because the ordinand undergoes three different kinds of ordination over a period of up to three months, first, novice (*pravrajya*) ordination for *sramaneras* and *sramanerikas*; second, full (*upasampada*) ordination for bhikshus and bhikshunis (both are authorized by all extant versions of the Vinaya); and third, *bodhisattva* ordination, which is an exclusively Mahayana rite. Every year, ordinands from all over the island of Taiwan would meet at a different temple for the ceremony. For each of the three ordinations, female candidates would first make their vows before ten bhikshuni acharyas and then again, together with the male candidates, before ten bhikshu acharyas. By 1988, about three-thousand monks and seven thousand nuns had undergone the rite.

In addition to Taiwanese monks and nuns, candidates at this first bhikshuni ordination ceremony on American soil included a handful of Tibetan-tradition nuns—some were refugees living in north India and others were Europeans and Americans—and some Theravada nuns. Among the latter were Ayya Khema, who had been one of the organizers of the Bodh Gaya conference; five Sri Lankans; and three nuns from Nepal led by Dhammawati. When Dhammawati fell ill soon after her arrival, her training was "speeded up," and after taking bhikshuni *upasampada* from ten Chinese nuns and a quorum composed of both Mahayana and Theravada monks, she flew to Bangkok for surgery. Daw Gunawati, realizing that she was not prepared, were she to become the first fully ordained Burmese nun, to face the hostility of her preceptor and his colleagues in the Burmese Sangha, left California for Thailand with Dhammawati. Of the three Nepalis who remained, Dhammadinna and Dhammavijaya donned dark brown Chinese robes and completed the training. Following *upasampada*, they spent two more months studying English and seeing some of the sights of California. Pannyawati, at nineteen, was too young to take *upasampada*; however she was able to stay on in California for a year and, on turning twenty, was fully ordained.

When the new bhikkhunis returned to Kathmandu, the senior monks, who by now had learned of the California ordination, followed Amritananda's lead and studiedly ignored their change of status. They continued to refer to them as "anagarika" and did not invite them to join the Sangha. Furthermore, they let it be known that in their view, because they had been ordained by Chinese rites, they should publicly announce that they were no longer Theravadins and should wear Chinese robes and adopt Mahayana practices such as prostration and chanting the name of Amitabha in Chinese.[30] By not performing these practices, the senior monks argued, the nuns were deceiving both their former Theravada gurus and their new Chinese gurus. Only two monks openly backed the nuns: Ashwaghosh, who had supported the Dharmakirti nuns from the beginning, and Sumangal, who had handed over his school to Dhammawati soon after she returned from Burma in 1963 and had quietly encouraged her ever since.

But Dhammawati and her colleagues changed neither their dress nor their behavior. "Why should we change anything?" they demanded. Yes, they had taken ordination from the Chinese who were Mahayanists; but long ago the Chinese had received the precepts from nuns from Sri Lanka whose ordination lineage, they believed, had descended from Theravada. "We're still Theravadins." Ordination had not changed their allegiance. They had simply taken back what they had lost.[31] Though after the death of Amritananda in 1990 his colleagues did not modify their opposition to *bhikkhuni upasampada*, Dhammawati remained uncowed. "All things are impermanent," she observed, "including the old bhantes. Eventually they too will pass away and the younger monks will have a different attitude."

The Bhikkhuni Ordination Movement in South and Southeast Asia

Apart from the Nepali Theravada and the Tibetan refugee communities, only in Sri Lanka has the full ordination movement thus far gained adherents. The fact that a few *dasa sil mata* began to push for *upasampada* in the 1980s reflects certain factors that differentiate the Sri Lankan Buddhist community from those of Burma and Thailand. First, the movement includes a number of prominent laywomen, notably Drs. Hema Gunatilake and Kusuma Devendra, both university teachers. Second, a few senior monks, most of whom are foreigners, have been supportive of the nuns' efforts to improve their situation generally.[32] Third, as Salgado has noted, the three thousand-odd *dasa sil mata* "are very independent creatures. . . . Since many nuns are reluctant to join it, thus far the establishment of an All Lanka Silamata Organization has failed to provide a sense of unity" (Salgado 2000a: 30–33). Junior nuns (*gollas/golayas*) who are widely dispersed across the island, tend to resist the authority of their preceptors; many leave them and go off to found nunneries of their own (Salgado 2000b: 179). The objective of most *dasa sil mata* is not social service, as with the followers of Sudharmachari described in Chapter 1; rather, it is to be free of lives ordered by kinship obligations in order to "do as they please," which, since the introduction of vipassana meditation in the 1950s, usually means, following the lead of some highly venerated monks, "leaving for the forest" in order to realize arhatship through meditation (Bloss 1984; Nissan 1984; Gombrich and Obeyesekere 1988: 252–295).[33] Given their lack of organizational structure, the *dasa sil mata* hardly constitute a community, let alone one with a unified outlook. Thus Bartholomeusz (1994: ch. 9) reports that in 1988, although most Sri Lankan nuns, like the overwhelming majority of Sri Lankan monks, were opposed to full ordination, when the Fo Guang Shan order invited eleven nuns to California, the conservative majority were totally unaware of the invitation, and even if they had known about it, they could have done nothing to prevent the small group from accepting. In fact, only five of the eleven who went to Los Angeles actually became bhikkhuni; the other six, complaining of homesickness and discomfort in the dry California climate, returned without receiving ordination.

During the 1990s, as interest in full ordination began to grow in Sri Lanka, especially among the English-educated elite, the bhikkhu opposition, which included some of the most prominent ecclesiastics in the country, intensified. Before the third Sakyadhita conference in Colombo in 1993, Madihee Pannasiha Mahathero, head of the Amarapura Nikaya, one of the three leading monastic orders in Sri Lanka, asked the organizers to pledge in writing that the issue of *bhikkhuni upasampada* would not be raised during the conference, a request with which they did not comply. In 1996, despite public condemnation of the "inauthentic rite" by many senior monks, ten *dasa sil mata*, led by Dr. Kusuma Devendra, who by this time had taken the precepts, received *bhikkhuni upasampada* in the Korean tradition from Maha Bodhi Society monks at Sarnath in India.[34] Given the outcry that their ordination provoked in the media in Sri Lanka, the new bhikkhunis decided to remain in India for an extended period until passions cooled.[35]

The Dharma and Politics

By the 1990s, Taiwanese and mainland Chinese Buddhists were engaged in a competition for legitimacy in which the Nepali nuns, in all innocence, became involved. Chinese Buddhism, which had been decimated during the Cultural Revolution, started to revive following the death of Mao Tse-tung and the shift in economic policy. Buddhist institutions soon began to receive substantial help from overseas Chinese eager to rebuild monasteries in their ancestral communities. The opening up of communications between Taiwanese and Tibetan Buddhist hierarchs noted above spurred mainland Chinese monastics to try to secure Tibetan Buddhist allegiance to China rather than Taiwan on the grounds that their ordination lineage was purer than that of the Taiwanese "branch" lineage, and that their bhikshuni ordination rite, being closer to the source, was more orthodox. Meanwhile, both parties identified the Kathmandu Valley, in which so many Tibetan refugee monastics now live, as a contested field. When both began seeking their allegiance as well as the allegiance of the Tibetans, the Nepali Theravadins became unwitting beneficiaries of their rivalry (Li 2000: 178–190).

In March 1997, the Dalai Lama paid a visit to Taipei, and bhikshuni ordination was one of the issues he discussed with the Taiwanese hierarchs. His Holiness explained that he himself was favorably disposed but he could not endorse it unilaterally as formal recognition required the assent of the Department of Religious Affairs of the Tibetan government-in-exile. Instead of waiting for the department's decision, however, mainland and Taiwanese Buddhists both organized ceremonies to which they issued invitations to exiled Tibetan and to Nepali nuns. The mainland dual ordination ceremony took place at Guang Xiao Si nunnery and Wu Ju An monastery in Guangzhou (Canton), China, in November/December 1997. Lok Darshan Vajracharya, vice president of the Dharmodaya Sabha, was asked to select some Nepali Theravadin candidates. The five he chose (and whom he escorted to China) were all in their late thirties, had graduate degrees, and could communicate fairly well in English.[36] Together with one-hundred Mahayana monks, three-hundred Mahayana nuns, and a single American nun belonging to the Tibetan tradition, they spent six weeks at Guangzhou preparing successively for *sramanerika*, *bhikshuni*, and *bodhisattva* ordination, followed by two weeks' sightseeing in Beijing, Shanghai, and elsewhere.

On their return, they said they had been much impressed by the splendor of the newly restored nunnery where they stayed, by the generosity of their hosts, and by how strictly the pratimoksha rules are observed in China.[37] But they admitted that they had missed a lot. They had tried to understand the rules that they were about to vow to observe and the rituals in which they participated, but the English-language manual was confusing, their instructor was young and her English quite poor, and the subject matter was very complicated. "I did what I saw other people doing," said Dhammaratna. "When they did prostrations I did too. But a lot of the time I really didn't know what to do."

What, then, were the benefits of taking full ordination? Padmawati may have spoken for all of them when she said she felt she had joined a new community that recognized the equality of monks and nuns:

> In China bhikshus and bhikshunis eat together, and in the temple, they sit on the same level. You could never see that here! The bhikkhus always eat separately from us and they sit above us in the vihara, they are above us in everything. . . . But if we have confidence in ourselves they will have to accept us. One day soon, we too will eat with the bhikkhus in *bhojana dana* and we will sit beside them in the dharma hall. We might even sit above them!

Fo Guang Shan in Action: Dual Ordination at Bodh Gaya, February 1998

When the Nepali nuns set off for Guangzhou in November 1997, notice had already been received in Kathmandu that Fo Guang Shan was planning to hold an ordination ceremony at Bodh Gaya in February 1998. Master Xingyun had resigned as abbot of Fo Guang Shan Monastery in 1992 in order to found a missionary order, the Buddhist Light International Association (BLIA), with which he planned not only to focus on serving Taiwanese emigrés but also to make converts around the world. In the BLIA he relied primarily on nuns, whom he already knew from Taiwan to be effective fund-raisers and community organizers. He believed they would make better missionaries than monks. By 1997, the BLIA had established ninety-five temples, Pureland meditation centers, and lecture halls from Tokyo to Paris, Sydney to São Paulo (Chandler 1999).

The Nepali nuns were told that if they were interested in attending the ordination ceremony, they should submit an application. Apart from providing straightforward personal information, two passport photographs, and a short essay explaining why she wanted to be ordained and her future plans, an applicant was asked (in English and Chinese):

1. Would you like to receive Chinese robes, or would you prefer to wear the robes of your own tradition?
2. Would you like to receive an alms bowl, or will you supply the *patra* (bowl) and *nisadana* (bedding) of your own tradition?

Participants had to "vow to adhere to the disciplinary rules promulgated by the Buddha [this meant the 348 Dharmaguptaka as opposed to the 311 Theravada rules] and to adhere to the ordination rules and regulations during the ordination period." The last phrase was crucial: the candidates would not be required to change their affiliation or practice permanently. The signature of the applicant's preceptor was required, and because in every case the preceptor was a senior monk who was expected to refuse to give his signature, Dhammawati signed the applications. Having submitted them, however, many applicants dropped out in response to pressure from their preceptors. Dhammawati was herself obliged to turn down Fo Guang Shan's invitation to participate in the ceremony as a "witnessing" acharya. She was planning to pay one last visit to her guru, Daw Pannyachari, now in her ninety-fifth year and ailing in Moulmein, and she had received word that, were she to attend the Bodh Gaya ceremony, the Burmese Sangha would make sure that her visa application was denied.

On February 13, 1998, twelve nuns set off for Bodh Gaya accompanied by Ashwaghosh Mahasthavir and Min Bahadur Shakya, director of the Nagarjuna Institute and a "feminist" who acted as tour leader (his activities are described in Chapter 9). In Bodh Gaya they were joined by two other Nepali nuns who had been studying at Fo Guang Shan and came directly from Taiwan.[38] The group included four of the five nuns who had returned from Guangzhou only six weeks before.[39] Asked why she wanted to be ordained a second time, Dhammaratna replied that she hoped the instruction would be better than it had been in China. She added with a chuckle that at Guangzhou she had talked with a Chinese nun from Singapore who said she had already taken *upasampada* twice and had come to Guangzhou to take it a third time. "Twice is better than once," Dhammaratna remarked "and three times is better yet!" The eight first-time ordinands ranged in age from a college student in her early twenties to a nun in her seventies who, although warned that the ordination ritual, which involved innumerable prostrations, would be extremely taxing, refused to be deterred. The group flew from Kathmandu to Varanasi and thence traveled by train and bus to Bodh Gaya where, for the duration of the ceremony, ordination candidates lived with nuns of nineteen nationalities in the Chinese guest house.

Logistically, the event was an immense undertaking. It involved feeding and housing 1,500 people, including 14 monk and 134 nun candidates, a support staff of laypeople recruited from Fo Guang Shan mission communities in Calcutta and Madras, 30 nuns from Fo Guang Shan Monastery itself, members of the media, and 1,200 Chinese pilgrims.[40] Of the female candidates, 30 were ethnic Chinese, including Chinese living in Australia, Singapore, and the United States, 18 were from Western countries; and 86 were from South Asia, including 14 from Nepal, 14 from Ladakh, 20 from Sri Lanka, and 28 followers of Dr. Ambedkar from Maharashtra.[41] They represented three different traditions, namely Chinese (25 candidates), Tibetan (34 candidates), and Theravada (65 candidates). All nuns belonging to the Chinese tradition were ethnic Chinese; of the 34 nuns in the Tibetan tradition, however, 17 were Westerners, 14 were Ladakhis, and 3 were Chinese. (Three Tibetan refugee nuns who were scheduled to come from Kathmandu did not appear, and the Tibetan government-in-exile, which had not yet resolved the issue of whether Dharmaguptaka ordination was valid for Tibetan nuns, sent an observer, Bhikshu Tashi Tsering, but no candidates.) With the exception of 1 German and 2 Chinese, all the Theravadins were South Asians. Meanwhile, male candidates included 10 Taiwanese and Western novices, and 4 novices from Congo Brazzaville who, after being recruited in their home country, had learned English in South Africa before being brought to Fo Guang Shan for monastic training.[42]

Instruction through translators was provided in six languages: Chinese, English, Hindi, Nepali, Tibetan, and Sinhala; all translators were native-speaker nuns who, as beneficiaries of the mission's outreach program, had spent several years at Fo Guang Shan Monastery. When it emerged that none of the candidates from Maharashtra (who had been brought to Bodh Gaya by a Sinhala missionary monk who gave no prior notice to the organizers) understood any of these languages, a seventh language, Marathi, was added.[43] Although preparation for Triple Altar rites and the rites themselves often last up to three months, at Bodh Gaya all three ordinations were crammed into nine days. In order to squeeze the whole ritual sequence into one-tenth of the time that is often committed to it, candidates and their instructors were studying, marching, chanting, and prostrating in the highly ornamented Chinese temple and surrounding study halls from long before dawn until late at night with only short breaks for meals and devotions.

The ordination schedule included ceremonial training, instruction in the *pratimoksa* rules, repentance rituals, the ordination rituals themselves, and *sanghadana*, a meal offered by the Chinese pilgrims to the monastic community. Family members, friends of the candidates, and lay observers were permitted to attend all activities except the ordination rituals themselves.[44]

The three precept masters were headed by Master Xingyun as *sila upadhayaya*. A massive bushy-browed figure in gold and scarlet silk, every move he made was documented by a video crew for the Fo Guang Shan TV station in Taiwan. The *karma-acarya* was Wuqian, a prominent English-speaking Fo Guang Shan missionary and abbot of both Xuanzang Temple in Calcutta and the Chinese Buddhist temple in Bodh Gaya where the ordination was held.[45] The Instruction (*dharma*) Acharya was Yongxing, president of the Buddhist Association of Hong Kong through which, after 1949, Taiwanese and overseas Chinese have

Nuns requesting ordination as a bhikshuni from the Fo Guang Shan of Taiwan, Bodh Gaya, February 1998. (Sarah LeVine)

maintained contact with the mainland. Although, in order to meet orthodox standards, all three precept masters belonged to the same ordination lineage, Master Xingyun's choice of "witnessing" acharyas was interesting. The Dharmaguptaka dual ordination rite requires twenty acharyas and, in a bid to win international recognition of the Bodh Gaya rites, Master Xingyun brought together acharya monks and nuns from Malaysia, Thailand, India, Britain, Cambodia, Sri Lanka, Tibet, and Nepal, so that all three traditions, Chinese, Tibetan, and Theravada, as well as many different ordination lineages, might be represented.[46] Although the ten bhikshuni acharyas were headed by three senior Fo Guang Shan bhikshunis, the seven bhikshuni "witnessing" acharyas included four Chinese nuns, two American Tibetan-tradition nuns,[47] and one nun from Korea;[48] thus the Chinese, Tibetan, and Korean traditions were all represented.[49]

Life As a Bhikkhuni

Given that at Bodh Gaya training for ordination and the rites themselves were crammed into nine days, study of the nuns Rules of Conduct (*bhiksuni pratimoksa*) to which they vowed to conform was given short shrift. However, the four Nepali nuns who had been ordained at Guangzhou the previous December had spent six weeks reading and memorizing the rules. They had soon realized that the Dharmaguptaka *Bhiksuni Pratimoksa*, which is followed in China, overlaps very considerably with the *Bhikkhuni Patimokkha* with which they were already familiar. Unfortunately, owing to the fact that the teacher/translator who had been assigned to them in China spoke worse English than they did, discussion with their preceptor of the content was superficial and focused mainly on dietary restrictions (no meat, onions, garlic, or "pungent plants") and on the vow to save all sentient beings. ("We were instructed to brush away mosquitoes, and never to kill them.") Before they left Guangzhou, their preceptor urged them to meet twice each month in Kathmandu for an *uposatha* recitation of the rules, confession, and absolution. (A monk's presence would not be necessary.) But two years later, Padmawati admitted that they had never met. "In China the other four said, 'Yes, we shall meet!' But I said, 'We live a long way from one another. I, for one, can't offer a meeting place.' I was very busy building my vihara which at that time didn't even have a roof. 'If one of you four calls me,' I told them, 'I shall come to your place.' But they've never called me." Instead of confessing to her fellow bhikkhunis every two weeks, she confesses her violations and forgives herself each night before sleep.

Some of the rules are impossible to observe. Padmawati recalled:

> When we were in China, we talked a lot about the tenth precept in particular. We told our preceptor that none of us has a *kappyakar* so it's very difficult for us to avoid touching money. Only occasionally, with a lot of planning, can we arrange this for a single day. Our preceptor told us that in order to do the Buddha's work, it's necessary for us to touch money and so we shouldn't worry about breaking that rule.

Given how different their lives are from the lives of nuns in the Buddha's time, there are many other rules "they don't worry about breaking." Some they have disregarded without hesitation. These include the rule that prohibits a nun from studying or teaching a "worldly subject" (which once preoccupied Dhammawati). They take daily rather than twice-monthly baths; instead of eating almsfood, their food, some of which is donated and some purchased, is cooked in the nunnery and includes garlic and other forbidden "pungent plants"; when occasionally they go for alms (in order to raise money for a specific project), they receive uncooked rice (which they sell) rather than cooked rice, as their vows prescribe. The *pacittiya* rules forbid "spinning yarn" (working at handicrafts), but most are expert knitters and seamstresses; they knit winter hats and sweaters and they sew their own clothes ("Who else would make them for us?"). They travel in "vehicles"—buses, trains, cars, and airplanes and even on motobikes—rather than on foot; on pilgrimage they eat in "public houses" (restaurants) and share rooms, and even on occasion beds, with laywomen; again, while on pilgrimage, they go on sightseeing trips to "pleasure houses, picture galleries, parks, pleasure groves and lotus ponds."[50] Although some adamantly refuse to touch a man, in the event of an accident, most will do whatever seems necessary to help the injured, regardless of gender. Some even massage male backs and limbs for, as one nun observed, "Desire is in the mind not the hand. Refusing to help a man when he's hurting is a worse sin than massaging him or washing his wounds."

One "violation" that they do regret, however, is of the *sanghadisesa* rule that forbids going out "to villages alone . . . to the other side of the river alone, staying away for a night alone, or staying back from the group alone."[51] Schoolgirls and college students, elderly infirm nuns, and those studying abroad make up the majority of the Order, which means that at any given moment few nuns are available to act as chaperones. When they go into the community to teach, preach, chant, and visit the sick, they would rather go with a "friend," as the *nissagiya pacittiya* stipulate, but more often than not they have no choice but to go alone.

By 2002, forty Nepali nuns—around a third of the whole Order—had taken full ordination, vowing to live by the Dharmaguptaka *Bhikshuni Pratimoksha* while they are in the ordination venue and thereafter by the Theravada *Bhikkhuni Patimokkha*. The forty included the four who ordained in California; nine who ordained in mainland China;[52] eight who ordained (for the first time) at Bodh Gaya; and nineteen who ordained on different occasions in Taiwan. All agree that their free trips abroad (their hosts covered their expenses entirely[53]), including to Bodh Gaya with which some were already quite familiar having been there on pilgrimage, were exciting; but few would claim that being fully ordained bhikkhunis makes a significant difference in their daily lives. Although they may have spent weeks trying to memorize the *Bhikshuni Pratimoksa* Rules, it was the Anagarika Rules that ordered their lives once they were back home. Nevertheless, the invitation to take *upasampada* at Bodh Gaya was open to all of them, and they did make a distinction, albeit a subtle one, between those who, like themselves, had risked provoking the anger of their preceptors to seize the opportunity, and those who had not.

Padmawati, Theravada Bhikkhuni

Teacher, preacher, mover of mountains, like her guru Dhammawati, Padmawati is a human dynamo. On a hot summer morning, her pink nun's dress is creased from her long journey. She has just returned by night bus from India where, two days ago, she submitted her doctoral dissertation to the Sanskrit University in Varanasi.

While she was writing her concluding chapter, the temperature on the Gangetic plain hovered around forty-eight degrees centigrade. "Because of power-cuts there were no lights, no fans. It was a nightmare, but it's over and now I can think about other things." As she rattles off a list of matters awaiting her attention, Padmawati, a handsome vibrant woman in her late thirties, seems to have already recovered from her long ordeal. During most of the three years it took her to research and write her dissertation, she was also traveling back and forth between Nepal and India as she planned, raised funds for, and constructed Mayadevi Vihara, a red brick nunnery beside the Bagmati River. In June 1998, the first and second floors are nearing completion and scaffolding for the third floor is in place; but funds are exhausted and her most pressing task is to raise more money. She has plans for a clinic, a library, a guest house, and an orphanage, as well as a school where young nuns will study both *buddha dharma* and the Ministry of Education curriculum. Half-a-dozen girls in nearby villages have been waiting for months to start rishini training and finally she has time for them. Tomorrow she'll bring in the first two. At the end of this month, she'll open a clinic—three doctors have already agreed to donate their time on Saturday mornings. She extracts a sheaf of papers from her shoulder bag—six essays on Buddhist topics, which she wrote for "rest and relaxation" while writing the last chapter of her dissertation. "I want to publish these as soon as possible!" she exclaims.

What Is *Duhkha*?

Padmawati was eleven when she became a nun and in large measure her reasons for doing so then are what have kept her in the Order until now: a dread of marriage and childbirth, and a compelling interest in the *buddha dharma*.

The second child and second daughter of a Manandhar family, Padmawati grew up in Banepa, a predominantly Newar town one hour east of Kathmandu. Her oil merchant father had inherited many *ropani* of land; he was hardworking, prosperous, and respected in the town. His two daughters had already received plenty of marriage proposals. By age eleven, Padmawati had received sixteen, all of which her father had turned down on the grounds that she was too young; but to the seventeenth he gave serious consideration. His elder daughter, four years Padmawati's senior, was now of an age to be married. Although child marriage had been made illegal in 1963, many parents outside the capital still ignored the minimum age of 16. In 1971, Padmawati's father decided to marry his younger daughter at the same time as his elder daughter. By combining two wedding feasts—a common Newar practice—he stood to save a lot of money:

> But I didn't want to get married. When I was nine, I happened to be in the house when my mother went into labor with my younger brother. My father ran off to fetch the midwife but everything happened so fast! My mother was moaning and crying and then the baby came out, hands clasped together above his head. There was nobody to help her but me, so I was the one who took hold of the baby, all bloody and covered in

slime. I was terrified. After that I began noticing how hard my poor mother had to work. I'd lie in bed till eight o'clock in the morning, get up, eat the rice she'd cooked for me and go to school. But Mother had been up since three, even in the dead of winter, and I knew that if I got married I'd be getting up at three for the rest of my life as well.

Although she was still very young at the time, she was already aware that wives were dominated by their husbands. Her father is a good man, a kind and considerate man, and so far as she knows has never beaten her mother, but she even if she were lucky enough to get a husband as good as he, her life would be one of subordination and tedious and repetitive domestic work. "Such a hard life, so much *duhkha*! Well, I decided it wasn't the life for me."

Padmawati's parents were traditional Vajrayana Buddhists but her mother's sister, sent home by her husband when he married a second wife, had become a devotee of Ratnajyoti, a Theravada monk. A gentle friendly man, he lived in a small monastery a few hundred meters from Padmawati's home and almost every day after school she would accompany her aunt to the monastery to hear his dharma talks and to borrow his books. "They were simply written for ordinary people. I found them very interesting, and I wanted to learn more," she recalls. One day, just as her father had started to talk about arranging her marriage, she encountered a sociable young nun named Sudharma at the monastery. She was visiting her family who lived in the town from her nunnery in Lalitpur:

When I confided my worries to her, she asked, "Have you thought about becoming a nun? If you did, you could keep on studying *buddha dharma*, and your life would be easy, not so hard like your mother's." I told Sudharma Guruma, "Let me become a nun!" Then it was a question of how to get my parents' permission since I couldn't take the precepts without it. I had a friend at school whose brother was a monk, although at that time he was away in Thailand, studying, and she agreed to help me. We decided to tell my parents we wanted to go to the city to work. And since in those days girls from our town were beginning to do that they believed us. They knew my friend—she was a year older than I was—and they trusted her. I gave them a letter that Sudharma Guruma had prepared and asked them to sign it. My mother can neither read nor write and she just made a thumbprint. My father can't read or write either except his name, which he signed. And then I set off for Lalitpur with Sudharma Guruma. My friend stayed behind—she'd never intended to go with us. We both lied so my parents would let me go.

A day or two after I left home my parents found out what I was really up to and my father came to Sudharma's vihara in Lalitpur to look for me. But he didn't find me. By then, Sudharma and I were on our way to

> Varanasi. When we got there we went to the Burmese temple where we presented the permission letter my parents had "signed." I shaved my head myself and took off my frock and my gold earings, put on the pink dress Sudharma gave me and took the precepts from one of the Burmese monks. Though he was my *upajjhaya*, he didn't teach me anything about the dharma. He just gave me the precepts, and that was that.

A few days later Padmawati returned to Lalitpur where her parents were waiting for her. Distraught, they begged her to take off her pink dress and return to lay life.

> A lot of young nuns have faced opposition from their fathers but usually their mothers have supported their decision. In my case, not only was I very young, just a child in fact, but both my parents were adamantly opposed to my being a nun. Neither of them knew anything about Theravada Buddhism. Only ten years after I ordained did I manage to convince them that Theravada was better than Vajrayana. Even now my father can't accept that when I shaved my head I became a nun for life.

Indeed, when LeVine visited Padmawati's home one afternoon, her father was an attentive host but wept on and off for the four hours she was there. Later Padmawati remarked, "He's always like that when he sees me. He chats away to me while tears are streaming down his cheeks."

Padmawati had been in Class Five when she left home to become a nun, and on her return from Varanasi she was eager to continue her education; but although these days young nuns are encouraged to study, twenty-five years ago *pariyatti* classes were all that was considered necessary for a nun. She was dismayed therefore to discover that she was expected to spend her days in the nunnery just "eating and chanting." But because for the moment this seemed to be her only alternative to marriage, she resigned herself to staying out of school.

For the first year after ordination she lived with Sudharma and her niece Sumedha, who was also a nun:

> Those two treated me like a servant. I did housework all day long. . . . When I went to Varanasi with Sudharma she took away the gold earings I'd been wearing and my clothes . . . I suppose she sold everything and kept the money. Anyway, she decided I came from a rich family and she kept pushing me to ask my father for my share of his property. I told her I was a nun now and I didn't want any property. . . . If my father wanted to give me something as *dana*, that was up to him, but I wasn't going to ask. But she kept pushing me, pushing me about my property. And there was something even worse going on in the vihara: Sudharma did *tantra*

mantra [black magic]. She'd learned it from a Hindu yogi in Gorakhpur, and back in Nepal she did it with a certain Theravada monk. The two of them would go into a room and shut the door, and who knows what was going on in there. . . . Then sick people would come to be healed. . . . Everyone—even the old nuns—was terrified of Sudharma. People thought she'd use her powers against them, so they kept quiet. But they weren't living with her like I was. I was scared to death. So one day I just walked out, got on a bus and went home to my town. I only had three rupees but a lady gave me the rest of what I needed for my fare.

I didn't actually go to my house because I was afraid that if I did so, my parents would make me disrobe, so I stayed in the little vihara nearby, which was empty at the time. My parents came to see me and I told them I'd had a disagreement with Sudharma. I didn't tell them about her being a witch because that would have made them think even worse of Theravadins and they already thought badly enough.

After a few days, another nun showed up at the place where I was staying. She said the great Samyak festival was about to start in Nag Baha in Lalitpur and she asked if I'd like to go with her to see it. Well, I'd heard about the Samyak but I'd never seen it, so of course I said yes. But after we'd seen it—and it was wonderful to see the twenty-eight Tathagata[54] statues that people keep in their houses and only bring out every four years—she took me to a nearby vihara. And there were Sudharma and her niece, waiting for me! Sudharma accused me of telling lies about her to my parents, which I hadn't of course. Then she pushed me down on the ground, knelt on my chest—I was a small girl and she was a big woman—and while her niece held my arms, she slapped me across the face with one hand and kept her other hand over my mouth to smother my screams. This continued on and off for about two hours. . . .

It happened that a young girl who knew me—she lived in my town—came along the lane on her way to the bus park and heard someone crying. She looked into the vihara and saw me on the ground with Sudharma kneeling on top of me. As soon as she reached home she told her mother who told my parents. They rushed over to Lalitpur, but by the time they reached the place where the girl had seen me, Sudharma had taken me away. The upper part of my rib-cage was crushed but I could still walk. She took me to an upasika and told her she'd beaten me because I was a wicked girl, I'd been with a boy and now I was pregnant. Then she left me there and went back to her vihara.

But that upasika was no fool—she could see I was still a small girl. I hadn't even had my period so how could I be pregnant? Because my dress was torn and blood-stained she had another dress made for me and then her son put me on a bus and sent me home. Even then, though I was in a lot of pain, I didn't go to my house. . . . I was scared my father would make me get married, so I went to the same vihara where I'd stayed when I ran away from Sudharma, where I collapsed. My mother found out

> where I was and came and took me to hospital for a chest X-ray. When the doctor saw the film, he was astonished I was still alive. . . .

It took Padmawati two full years to recuperate from the beating, and even now in winter, if she takes a deep breath, she feels pain.

Training

After suffering such abuse at the hands of another nun who was her teacher and guardian, why didn't she disrobe?

> I didn't want to get married. . . . If I'd left, sooner or later they'd have forced me to get married. These days a few women from my caste who have a lot of education do stay single, but all this happened twenty-five years ago. . . . I was twelve years old and I hadn't even completed Class Five.

When she had regained her strength Padmawati went to Kindol Vihara in Kathmandu where Dharmachari, the famous nun, took her in.

> At seventy-four, she was still strong like a man, and she had a loud voice like a man as well. She liked me a lot but after a little while she decided Kindol wasn't a good place for me. All the nuns there were old. So she took me over to Dhammawati Guruma in Dharmakirti Vihara. At that time there were only five nuns living in Dharmakirti and though they weren't as old as the Kindol nuns, they were all at least twenty years older than I was.
>
> By then I'd been out of school for three years. I was desperate to go back to school but the Dharmakirti nuns told me that wasn't possible, arrangements couldn't be made . . . I told my uncle—actually he was a cousin of my mother's—that I wanted to study. He said, "I always wanted to study too, but I only went to Class Five. Now here I am, still too shy to speak in public because I haven't learned to speak correctly and never shall. But you're young, you still have a chance to learn." He said it wasn't good just to stay in the nunnery. "Chanting and receiving *dana* isn't a good way to spend your life. You're young and you should go to school." So with his encouragement, I decided to leave Dharmakirti. But I didn't want to go to school in my town—I was shy about sitting in class with boys and girls I'd known all my life in my pink nun's dress while the rest of them were in their school uniforms. When I told my uncle he was sympathetic. He took me to his friend who lived in Bhaktapur. I stayed with that man and his family—those people were so kind to me, just like my own family—and I enrolled in Bhaktapur Girls' High School. The headmaster let me skip three classes so I only took Classes Nine and Ten and was able to finish up in two years. There were only fifteen students

in my class—in those days there still weren't many girls going to secondary school—and all of them were Newars.[55]

In her graduation photograph Padmawati looks radiant in her nun's dress, surrounded by her classmates in salwar kameez.

I was happy in Bhaktapur. . . . But after that things were bad for me. For one thing, in Class Ten I'd developed an ulcer. The doctor said this was because I hadn't been eating properly. I would eat rice before I went to school at nine in the morning, and by the time I got back it was afternoon. Because, as a nun, I am forbidden to eat after midday, for two years I only ate one meal a day. When I passed SLC and went back to Dharmakirti, the nuns there didn't believe I had an ulcer. Sometimes I vomited blood, so they said I had TB and refused to let me eat or even sleep there. I had to rent a room from a woman I knew in the tol. I'd eat and sleep there and go to the vihara by day. Another problem was that I still wanted to study. Secondary school wasn't enough for me. I told Dhammawati Guruma I wanted to go to college and she wasn't at all happy to hear it. Mind you, since then her ideas about education have changed. But back then she still thought a nun only needed to study *pariyatti*. So for five years, that's what I did. After a while a few other nuns my age began trickling in, and we studied together and did the best we could to understand what we were reading. The senior nuns had no time to help us.

In 1980, Padmawati passed "Kovid," the tenth and highest level of *pariyatti*, and, although she still had an ulcer, the nuns started letting her eat in the vihara again—provided she kept her plate and utensils separate from theirs. That year, Daw Pannyachari came from Moulmein to teach vipassana meditation. After practicing for only a few months, Padmawati's ulcer, which the medicine she'd been taking for so many years had not cured, improved markedly. By the following year, when she had the chance to go to Burma together with three other young women, her ulcer had gone completely.

She and her companions stayed in Burma for a year, but then the government revoked their visas and they were sent back to Nepal.

Again Padmawati begged Dhammawati to let her go to college:

I said that nuns need to study everything that laypeople study, but Dhammawati Guruma said Dharmakirti was a very busy place and she couldn't spare me. She needed me to teach in the countryside and to help with vipassana retreats, which, since Mahasi Sayadaw's visit, were becoming very popular. So I taught *buddha dharma* to the children, I preached to their parents, and I cooked for the yogis; and, when I wasn't cooking and washing dishes, I was an assistant vipassana teacher.

She enjoyed teaching and preaching and she believes she was good at it. She always based her dharma talks on a story—sometimes a Jataka but almost as often on an experience she had had herself. She soon learned to gauge her audience: if they seemed restless than she would wind down after an hour; and if she had them "hooked" she might keep going for twice as long:

> But I never stopped pressuring Dhammawati and eventually she did give me permission to go to college. She wouldn't permit me to go to the campus, though. She said it wasn't good for a nun to sit in classes with men. . . . So I bought all the textbooks and studied on my own in the vihara.

Things seemed to be going well enough and she was even one of four young Nepali Buddhists selected to go on a round-the-world youth tour sponsored by the Reverend Moon in 1985 on which, after the opening conference in Barrytown, New York, she visited many great sacred sites on four continents. But as time passed, she became increasingly unhappy with the tensions and stresses of life in the nunnery. Yes, she and her companions in Dharmakirti meditated on their *kilesas*. But desire, hatred, and illusion are very difficult to uproot.

The last straw came when she took her intermediate degree exams and failed them:

> I decided I couldn't live in Dharmakirti any longer. I went to my house and was on the verge of disrobing—my plan was to go into business; I thought I'd open a mill—when my uncle, the same one who had helped me before, said to me, "Stay as you are! You've worn this dress for so many years and everyone knows you as a nun. If you want to study, then go ahead and study, but you should do so as a nun not as a laywoman."

Her cousin was studying in the Sanskrit University in Varanasi and she decided to join him. All along, her parents, although unschooled themselves, had willingly financed her education and now they agreed to support her studies in India. Life in the university as the sole nun student was certainly not easy. Until she came to Varanasi, she had lived in a tightly insulated Newar world. Even in Burma she had been with companions who spoke Nepal Bhasha. She knew little Hindi, and at first missed most of what went on in class. In the women's hostel where she stayed, she was often bothered by young men who would try to climb into her room at night; later, she lived in a guest house that housed "all sorts of people": male students and married couples, but only a few single women. Despite the financial support given her by her parents, and, as time passed and they grew up and started earning, by her brothers as well, she was often short of money. She made friends with the abbot of the Burmese monastery at Sarnath and when she was really hard up he would let her eat in the monastery in return for performing domestic chores. "Occasionally I'd receive tips from pilgrims for whom I'd acted as a tour guide. So somehow I got by. I was lucky, I always had a room to myself and some privacy."

She would get up at 4:30 every morning to pray and do meditation. She would begin, as she had since childhood, with a silent recitation of the qualities of Buddha, Dharma, and Sangha, followed by *maitri bhavana* in which she would call various people to mind and wish them health and happiness. Following her prayers, which she would recite sitting in her room or walking through the campus, she would meditate for an hour and, on concluding, send *metta* to all sentient beings, ghosts, spirits, and gods. "After breakfast I'd attend lectures and later prepare lunch on a hot plate in my room, and then I'd study until bedtime."

Dharma Work

In 1995, an elderly Shakya, whose family had owned it for generations, donated a wedge-shaped piece of land lying between a major road and the cremation ghats serving several nearby villages to Dharmakirti. Every morning for fifty years "Guruju," as he was called, had done puja at the *chaitya* his father had erected on the cremation ghats; but he and his sons considered the land behind it inauspicious. Padmawati explains:

> That's why they gave it to Dharmakirti, and not knowing what else to do with it, Dhammawati called me back from Varanasi and handed it over to me. She said I should build a branch vihara there. At that time, I was just beginning to write my dissertation, but now this place was my responsibility, so I decided I'd better move into the hut by the gate—which at that time was the only building on the property—and start trying to raise money to build a vihara.

Padmawati lived alone in the hut behind the ghats for a year:

> It was horrible. . . . First of all, there were so many funerals going on, and many of them during the night, so the mourners would come past my place, wailing. And then drunkards would beat on the door, and others came who weren't drunk, just angry that the Theravadins were planning to build on this land.

Sometimes one of her cousin-brothers would spend the night in the hut with her, and Guruju would arrive each morning before dawn to perform his pujas; but mostly she was alone there. Listening to fists beating on the door and the padlock shaking on its chain, she would meditate and try to stay calm.

Meanwhile, she was raising money and putting it in the bank. When she had 1.5 million rupees—much of it from her mother, who had her own successful craft business, and other relatives—someone happened to ask her whether she had finished building her vihara. She thought, "But I hadn't laid the first brick! I'd better get going!" She found an upasaka who was a structural engineer and was willing to do the work for nothing, and together they made a plan for the whole grand complex as she envisioned it. In the spring of 1997 they broke ground for the nunnery, which she decided to name Mayadevi Vihara.

> I hired laborers and bought materials and stored them in the small place where I was living. Once when I happened to be spending the night at Dharmakirti and there was no one there, thieves broke in and stole two lakh's [Rs 200,000] worth of lumber. . . .

In the spring of 1998, with the shell of the dharma hall up and three second-floor rooms just habitable, she moved in. Since then, whenever she has had money, she has continued the construction work, and sometimes even when she hasn't had money, she's borrowed some. "I had to borrow five lakhs for the plumbing. People trusted me and so they were willing to lend me money interest-free, but soon I'll have to start repaying them." The following year, Dhammawati agreed to Padmawati opening a bank account separate from the Dharmakirti account, into which she would deposit funds she raised for Mayadevi Vihara, and on which she could draw without her guru's signature. And in the spring of 2001, Mayadevi achieved semi-autonomous status. Although the land on which the vihara stands still belongs to Dharmakirti, the buildings are registered in the name of the seven-member Mayadevi nunnery committee. Padmawati is president and her eldest brother, her second brother (whom she delivered when she was nine), and one of her cousin-brothers are members. In the event of Padmawati's death, the committee would be charged with appointing her replacement.

To one side of the main building is a large kitchen in which devotees prepare lunch for several hundred people after Buddha Puja which, in Mayadevi, is conducted twice a month; a garden with mounds of marigolds and shasta daisies, and onions, garlic, and spinach planted in neat rows is bounded by a low-walled terrace where the laity gather. It is a pleasant spot provided one can ignore the stench of the river flowing by. There's no school yet and no orphanage, but the medical clinic—staffed by four doctors (pediatrician, gynecologist, dermatologist, and pulmonary specialist) and an acupuncturist trained in Japan and Australia—is open every Saturday morning in the building in which not so long ago Padmawati would meditate to concentrate her mind while angry villagers beat on the door. Some villagers still insist on cremating their dead six feet from the door of the dharma hall. "I've been trying to persuade them to move down the river bank but they say their forefathers used that spot, and so shall they." She adds with a smile, "I use these cremations as an opportunity to meditate on impermanence, but at night especially, the young gurumas get very upset."

Padmawati rarely wastes a moment because she cannot afford to. "Yes, this vihara is for nuns, but how will we survive here if the laypeople don't come and give *dana*?" Unlike Dharmakirti, which is in the center of old Kathmandu, Mayadevi is a long way from town, and unlike Dhammawati, who has a roster of donors on whom she has been able to count for years, Padmawati must still rely on close relatives and a handful of devotees who, though not rich, are generous with their time and resources. In order to attract new devotees to her vihara, as well as to keep the old ones engaged, she offers a densely packed program, which, because the nuns who live with her are still school girls, she runs virtually alone. Although she sometimes invites monks to give talks at the twice-monthly Buddha Puja, she gives most dharma instruction herself. She looks for laypeople to help teach the daylong dharma courses she frequently schedules and has found one or two she can rely on; but because her chelis are either at school or doing homework, only she can respond to requests to chant *paritrana*. Only she can lead meditation retreats and take devotees on pilgrimage to Namobuddha, to the Ajanta and Ellora caves in India, and as far afield as Anuradhapura and Sagain.

Busy as she is, each dry season she leaves the vihara in the care of one of her committee members and, just as she did as a young woman, spends several weeks in mountain villages teaching the fundamentals of Buddhism to Janajati people. Like her guru Dhammawati, she seems to have a talent for making complicated ideas comprehensible to the unschooled. Padmawati publishes a twice-yearly magazine; she writes a regular column in a Nepali-language newspaper and tapes a weekly radio show; she has also preached on television. Although these high-profile activities have brought prestige both to her and to her vihara, her success has tended to isolate her from her contemporaries. Relations between her and Dhammawati, which since her adolescence had never been easy, went through a particularly strained period at the end of the 1990s. At one point, Padmawati spent months trying to calm her feelings of anger and guilt in meditation. Eventually, three years after she received her doctoral degree, she was honored at Dharmakirti, together with two young nuns who had recently completed the Dhammachariya in Burma. "Dhammawati Guruma presented me with two sets of robes and thirty-three thousand rupees that she had collected from her devotees for me, and she made a speech saying how proud she was of me." Padmawati admits that to receive Dhammawati's praise and finally to be treated as an equal means a great deal to her. In 2004, Padmawati organized a celebration of Dhammawati's seventieth birthday in Mayadevi Vihara at which seventy women took temporary ordination. For daily support and companionship, however, she still turns to her "trusties," her brothers and cousins, and the odd assemblage of upasakas with whom she holds daily court in her sitting room.

The question of bhikkhuni ordination is a key issue in feminist Buddhist circles and for nuns like Padmawati: Why should nuns not receive the same respect as monks? Or is it a mistake, as the traditionalists argue, to discard the Buddha's teachings in a rush to modernize the religion? Meditation for all is another area in which bringing about equality of access is the fundamental issue at stake, but here it is the whole Buddhist community—men and women, young and old, monastic and lay—that is involved.

CHAPTER EIGHT

Winds of Change: Meditation and Social Activism

Chapters 3 and 5 showed that, given the structure of traditional Newar Buddhism in which monks had long ago metamorphosed into householder priests, the first generation of Theravadin reformers in Nepal were obliged to allow the laity a far greater degree of control over monastic institutions than was true elsewhere in the Buddhist world, even though activist monks did their best to retain autonomy and control. Half a century or so ago, Nepali Theravadins may have been ahead of their times in this regard, but other Asians have since caught up. The Sangha in Sri Lanka and Southeast Asia has expanded its focus from devotional and protective rites and monastic education to include social issues, for example education for the laity, village development, and—since the 1940s and 1950s—meditation for the laity; and in fact it has often been laypeople themselves who have taken the lead in building institutions that address these new concerns (Bond 1988; Gombrich and Obeyesekere 1988; Jordt 2001).

For several decades after the Theravada movement was launched in Nepal, the multifaceted program of the vihara appears to have satisfied converts; but by the 1980s, laypeople were beginning to develop their own agendas. This was the period when education and literacy were expanding rapidly in Nepal, especially in the urban areas where Newar Buddhists were concentrated. It was also the time when the ideology of development and modernization had became all-pervasive, pushed by the government and foreign donors alike. Laypeople expected Buddhism to modernize and adapt, and they expected to be involved in helping it to do so.

Though monastics have been centrally involved in some lay-initiated innovations, such as in the introduction and writing of the *Bauddha Pariyatti Siksa*, in other areas their role, if any, has been relatively marginal. In the early decades, the reformers focused their efforts on the Newar Buddhist community and gained adherents among those who felt alienated from their traditional religion; but the children and grandchildren of their early converts have started to engage individuals and groups outside their own ranks. Today, committed Vajrayanists, Janajati followers of the Tibetan tradition, Theravadins, and even Hindus cooperate in building new structures; and they are communicating in Nepali, the national language, rather than in Nepal Bhasha, which even many Newars are beginning to find limiting.

Meditation before 1980

In traditional Newar Buddhism, meditation for enlightenment (*dhyāna*, *bhāvana*, or *sādhana*) is a process in which the meditator, through visualization, identifies himself with his tutelary Tantric divinity and internalizes the form and the ethical sensibilities of a buddha or bodhisattva. It is an esoteric practice restricted to initiated members of certain upper castes. By contrast, Theravada meditation was in principle, like the Theravada as a whole, open to anyone of any background. The early Nepali Theravadins valued meditation for its calming effects and for the merit it earned the meditator, but in practice, until the 1980s, it was restricted to monastics who stood on the highest rung of the Buddhist hierarchy and to a few devout laypeople. Many monastics actually never meditated, so that it could even be argued that meditation was less central to the everyday practice of Nepali Theravada Buddhism in the first generation than it was and is to Vajrayana Buddhism.

One layperson who did meditate was Dhammawati's mother, Hira Thakũ. In middle age she was spending so many hours each day in meditation that family members believed her to be in a perilous psychological state. When her guru was consulted, he advised her to give up meditation and switch to chanting *paritrana* sutras to protect herself from mental breakdown. The practice to which she had become "addicted" was known as *kesaloma*, in which, by meditating on every part of the body in turn and thereby being confronted with the body's impermanent nature, attachment to the physical self is gradually reduced and replaced by an experiential understanding of impermanence, suffering, and non-self. Most monks and a few laypeople were familiar with these and other practices such as *asubha bhavana* (meditation on a putrefying body, or *anatta*, non-self), *udaka bhavana* (meditation on water, or *anicca*, impermanence), and *buddhaguna* (reflections on the virtues of the Buddha), an act of devotion to and a means of identification with the Buddha.

Vipassana Meditation

Vipassana meditation was practiced by monks in Burma from at least the second half of the nineteenth century. A key figure in the early advocacy of vipassana, both to monks and to laypeople was the reforming layman, ex-monk, and Minister of Internal Affairs under the last two kings of Burma, U Hpo Hlaing. He wrote a book on vipassana in 1871 (though it was only published much later). Ledi Sayadaw used to visit him while studying in Sankyaung Vihara (Houtman 1999: 7–8, 203). King Mindon advocated vipassana meditation for aristocrats (Houtman 1997: 310), but it was mainly the pupils of Ledi Sayadaw and Mingon Sayadaw who popularized the practice, particularly from the 1930s onward, for ordinary laypeople. The scriptural basis of vipassana was the Discourse on the Arousing of Mindfulness (*Satipatthana Sutta*) and Buddhaghosa's commentary, which explains it and gives minutely detailed directions for how to practice it.[1] Htei Hlaing, a Burmese historian of meditation wrote: " '[P]ractice' (*patipatti*) has overtaken 'scriptural learning' (*pariyatti*) in prominence and popularity. . . . [T]hese sleeping books have from their place on a shelf in a library, or from being subjects to worship while encased in a pagoda, moved to be read and studied even by little girls . . . and have all become works which are now actually put into practice" (cited from the Burmese in Houtman 1985).

No longer restricted to a handful of virtuosi, vipassana had become a practice that anyone, laypeople as well as monastics, might adopt.

When the first meditation centers were established in Burma in the 1930s, the old hierarchy was still in place: both laypeople and monks meditated, but only monks were teachers. However, as the conditions for achieving insight—"right view" or the ability "to see things as they really are," that is, as ever-changing, as suffering, and as empty of substance—were systematized, perceptions of who could be enlightened shifted and renunciation was no longer seen as necessary for the attainment of enlightenment. Rather, the only requirement for *paṭi-vedha* (realization of truth through insight knowledge) was diligent practice, which would deconstruct habits of body, speech, and mind and, with the karmic residue tying one to *samsara* erased, lead one to nibbana. The lay ethic focusing on morality and offering donations for the support of monks was refocused on the pursuit of enlightenment through the Four Foundations of Mindfulness (body, feeling, consciousness, and mind objects), "the sole way (*ekayano maggo*) for the purification of beings, for the overcoming of sorrow and lamentation, for the destroying of pain and grief, for reaching the right path, for the realization of *Nibbana*" (Nyanaponika Thera 1965: 7). Moreover, given that, according to Buddhist classification, *patipatti* is a higher form of practice than scriptural study, as laymen started to demand—and receive—recognition as meditation teachers on a footing with the *sayadaws*, the Buddhist status hierarchy of monks and laypeople (from the perspective of "pure Buddhists," i.e., vipassana practitioners) dissolved.

Although a handful of visiting foreign monastics had encountered vipassana in Burma in the 1930s (Soma Thera 1941: xiii), only in the 1950s was it introduced from Burma to Thailand and Sri Lanka, where it soon flourished among the Westernized middle class (Gombrich 1983, Tambiah 1984: 170–171, Bond 1988). It was not until 1980 that lay Buddhists in Nepal had their first exposure. All Nepali monks and nuns who spent any time in Burma since the 1940s had some experience of meditation, but those who had been engaged in serious religious training had very little time to practice. Gyanapurnik recalls having spent two weeks at Mahasi Sayadaw's Thathana Yeiktha (meditation center) when he first arrived in Burma aged seventeen in 1956, and a further four weeks about ten years later. He says that ideally he should have taken at least one three-month retreat, "but I was too busy studying."

Dhammawati, too, had little time to meditate. "It was optional at Kemarama, and I was studying so hard, I couldn't spare the time." Occasionally on the completion of a set of exams she would take a short retreat:

> We practiced *kesaloma*, and *anapana* in which you focus as you breathe on the rising and falling of the stomach. When many people are practicing together they make such a noise, they sound like bellows blowing on a fire, or even a windstorm!

Anapana is the technique that prepares the meditator for vipassana, but a decade passed before she had the opportunity to advance to the second stage.

Sumangal, the monk from whom Dhammawati took over the school in Gana Baha in 1964, spent several months in Mahasi Sayadaw's Thathana Yeiktha in Rangoon and on his return to Kathmandu began teaching vipassana to a few fellow monks. He ran a twice-weekly vipassana class at Gana Vihara from 1975 (Kloppenberg 1977: 314) but did not invite any nuns to join the group.

In December 1972, Ashwaghosh, Dhammawati, Ratnamanjari, and two laywomen attended a two-day Goenka vipassana course in Varanasi (Ashwaghosh 2000: 10). Ashwaghosh recounted how he had earlier been requested to teach meditation by two of his lay followers and had come to realize that his own knowledge and experience were quite inadequate to the task. He himself hoped—as did his lay followers—that meditation would help him control his temper in public situations (ibid.: 17–18).

The term "vipassana" can be used either with a broader, more popular meaning or in a narrower, more technical sense. Loosely and colloquially, "vipassana" is used to mean both insight meditation and the *anapana* breathing meditation that is the preliminary to insight meditation. More precisely, "vipassana" is *opposed* to *anapana* since they are different techniques and the latter is a necessary preliminary to the former.[2] Originating (as far as the modern period is concerned) in Burma, it is possible to trace the spread of vipassana throughout the world, including to Nepal, in a historical fashion. From a more ecumenical point of view, however, calming insight is common to all Buddhist traditions. Thus Batchelor writes: "In fact, *vipassana* is central to *all* forms of Buddhist meditation practice . . . Over the centuries, each tradition has developed its own methods for actualizing this state. And it is in these methods that the traditions differ, *not* in the end objective of unified calm and insight" (1994: 344).

The Introduction of Vipassana Meditation to Nepal

Very few Nepali monks and nuns and virtually no laypeople knew about vipassana before the Daw Pannyachari, abbess of Kemarama nunnery in Moulmein, taught it to the nuns of Dharmakirti and fifty lay devotees over a period of two months in 1980.[3] The following year the Burmese meditation master Mahasi Sayadaw (1904–82) was invited to visit Nepal by a handful of monks who had studied in Burma. He first led a meditation retreat for monks in Buddha Vihara, Lumbini, for which Gyanapurnik, who at that time was resident monk at the West Midland Buddhist Centre in Birmingham, England, was recalled to act as translator. Although nuns were excluded from the retreat, a few were invited—along with a select group of laypeople—to attend the subsequent series of talks the sayadaw gave at Aksheshwar Mahavihara in Lalitpur. At the conclusion of his talks, which caused a sensation in the Theravada community, Dhammawati and Gunawati accompanied him to Calcutta where he embarked for Rangoon.[4] He had promised to return, but he died unexpectedly in 1982 and his place was taken by a series of sayadaw disciples who, inheriting his mission, visited Nepal each year to lead retreats wherever space could be found—Aksheshwar Mahavihara in Lalitpur, Sugatpur Vihara in Trishuli, Dhyankuti Vihara in Banepa, as well as Dharmakirti in Kathmandu—with Dhammawati and Gunawati acting as tour coordinators, translators, and assistant teachers.[5]

Between the sayadaws' visits, these two assumed the role of teacher to the community of nuns as well as to a fast-growing group of lay practitioners. Soon every vihara of any size in the Valley was offering instruction and regular hour-long meditation sessions once or twice a week. As noted above, the introduction of vipassana brought with it a practice, already widespread in Burma, Thailand, and Sri Lanka, in which lay meditators take a form of temporary ordination. This involves taking the Eight Precepts and a vow of silence and staying in retreat for ten days or longer. Each morning the "yogis," as both male and female meditators are called, rise at 4 A.M. and from then on throughout the day and until late in the evening they follow a strict schedule of sitting and walking meditation with only a few short rest periods.

Sumangal Mahasthavir, in conjunction with Mahasi Sayadaw's most prominent disciple, U Pandita Sayadaw, and a group of businessmen led by Gyan Jyoti Kansakar (whose brother, Maniharsha Jyoti, was Dhammawati's most important financial supporter), began raising money for a permanent meditation center (*dhyan kendra*). In 1988, the International Buddhist Meditation Center (IBMC), constructed with funds from Thailand, Burma, and the local business community, opened at Shankhamul in Kathmandu on land beside the Bagmati River.[6] Here, "International" refers to its close ties with Thailand and Burma, which have provided economic support and whose ambassadors to Nepal are frequent visitors. The directors of the new institution were U Pandita and Buddhaghosh. Gyanapurnik and Dhammawati were members of the board.[7] IBMC's first abbot was a Burmese monk named U Asabachara, a disciple of U Pandita, who, since the center opened, has himself spent at least a month each winter in Nepal.[8] For some years Gyanapurnik taught meditation there, and meanwhile, the sayadaw himself continued to accept Nepali novices and young nuns as students at Panditarama, his center in Rangoon. During breaks in their studies, students were encouraged to take meditation retreats and, on completion of their training, they were expected to return to IBMC to help run the program. Even though laymen were centrally involved in the administration of the center, at IBMC, as in Burmese meditation centers on which it was modeled, monastics were clearly in charge.[9]

IBMC is within easy walking distance of the large Newar Buddhist populations of Lalitpur, to which it is linked by a footbridge, and the Kathmandu suburb of Baneshwar. There are two workmanlike concrete buildings, one containing a dharma hall and classrooms and the other, kitchens and a dining hall; above them are dormitories and quarters for monks and nuns. An office occupies a separate building by the gate and a shrine topped by a stupa faces a wide lawn surrounded by rose beds where major events take place and, while retreats are being conducted, *yogis* practice walking meditation. Meditation is the central focus of IBMC: a session is held there every morning; ten-day courses for adults and, during the school holidays, three- and five-day courses for children over the age of seven are also regularly scheduled. Nonetheless, and despite its name, community activities also take place there, including a Saturday school for children and *buddha dharma* classes for adults. On Saturday mornings, after the children's classes and the meditation session are concluded and before the abbot or a visiting monk gives the dharma teachings, several hundred children and adults, seated on the long narrow straw mats that are used for traditional Newar feasts, eat breakfast together in the dining hall. Members of the donors' committee (*dayaka samiti*) make it their business to be there and the atmosphere is friendly.[10] Although vipassana meditation may be a quintessentially individualistic practice, practitioners still feel the need for a religious setting, a replacement for the *baha* in which to socialize. The language of instruction and socializing is Nepal Bhasha, not Nepali, and few non-Newars visit the center.[11] In short, even though its abbot is a foreigner, the International Buddhist Meditation Center has become a thoroughly Newar institution.

Young girls who have taken temporary ordination in order to participate in the winter meditation and Buddhism course at IBMC, 18th January 2003. (David N. Gellner)

The Bhikshu Mahasangha had long had plans to build a guest house near the Nepalese temple, Buddha Vihara, in Lumbini and in 1995, seeing that nothing was being done to implement them, Dhammawati set about building one herself. Her International Bhikkhuni Sangha ("Gautami") Vihara, which was inaugurated in 1998, is used for conferences as well as to house pilgrims but functions mainly as a meditation center in which Dhammawati leads courses—principally but not exclusively—for women during the winter months.[12] In his old age (he was born in 1921) U Pandita Sayadaw prefers to spend a large part of his winter visits to Nepal in Lumbini, where the climate is milder than that of the Kathmandu Valley. In 1997, his Burmese devotees raised funds for the construction of Panditarama Meditation Center only a few hundred meters from Gautami Vihara.

It is Mahasi Sayadaw's "teacher monk" tradition that most Nepali monks and nuns have espoused, and it is this approach that they have taught to other monastics as well as to the laity. In their own practice, they appear to focus on the benefits that meditation can provide in this life rather than in future lives, most especially with regard to controlling the mind, calming the passions, developing restraint, and improving relationships with companions and relatives. One senior monk admitted that, although as a younger man he had been much more spiritually ambitious, in old age he hoped only that the control he achieved over body, speech, and mind would be bring him rebirth in a "good" family (by which he meant one whose members had "right views," i.e., were Theravada Buddhists). A middle-aged nun who was responsible for greeting visitors to her nunnery, reported:

> I am constantly being interrupted. Whenever somebody comes to the vihara I must stop what I'm doing and attend to them. I tell you, I used to hate that! But after years of practice I have learned to control my feelings and to switch my focus of concentration smoothly. I really don't mind interruptions anymore.

Another nun who has been practicing vipassana for twenty years, reports that she used to be full of greed (*lobha*)—for good food and robes and many other things:

> Really, anything someone else had that I didn't, I wanted. These days I'm still greedy, but not for myself any more, only for my vihara. My vihara needs so many things and yes, I'm always hoping and planning how to get them. . . . And I'm more generous than I used to be. For example, the Vinaya says a nun should only have three sets of clothes. Well, at one

> time whenever I was given more, I'd hoard them. But now I give them away to the young nuns who don't receive nearly as much *dana* as I do, and extra shoes, towels and sweaters I give to poor upasikas. . . . When I was younger I used to talk and laugh too loudly. . . . I wanted to attract attention. But now I'm quieter. . . . I don't crave that attention any more. I know this is a fruit (*phal*) of meditation.

Having experienced the fruits, she and other nuns are eager to provide instruction for anyone who is open to receiving it.

Meditation Led By Laypeople

The second celebrated meditation master to visit and teach in Nepal was S. N. Goenka. His family, Marwari Jains by background, had settled in Rangoon in colonial times and had extensive business interests. Born in 1924, as a young man Goenka suffered terrible migraines. Finding that vipassana meditation cured his headaches, he became a follower of the lay meditation master, U Ba Khin (himself a disciple of Ledi Sayadaw) in the 1950s. After the military coup of 1962, the family's businesses were expropriated, and Goenka devoted himself full time to meditation. In 1969, he left for India and settled in his ancestral town, Igatpur, Gujarat, where he established a vipassana meditation center. In 1979, he began to travel abroad to teach meditation and establish new centers. As his fame as a guru spread, he began to rework the approach he had learned from his own teacher and the traditional individualized face-to-face transmission of the "truth" metamorphosed into mass "distance" teaching and learning. Although in his early years at Igatpur he would spend some time teaching and supervising practitioners, as his following expanded, he relied increasingly on "packaged" protocols of audio—and later video—recordings, with supplementary instruction by locally resident disciple-teachers.

By the time Goenka made his first two-week visit to Kathmandu in 1981, he already had a considerable international following.[13] Coming from a non-Buddhist background, he presented vipassana as a technique that anyone, regardless of religious affiliation, could learn and use effectively. In the first meditation retreat that he led at Ananda Kuti Vihara, he taught the fundamentals of vipassana to a small group of people drawn mainly from the business community; however, for the course that he taught the following year in the newly established elite boarding school at Budha Nilkantha he received so many applicants—eight hundred for two hundred places—that selection had to be done by lottery.[14] The course was a great success, as was the course he taught in 1983. At the closing ceremony in Swayambhu in 1983, all the participants gave *dana* to ninety-five Theravadin monks and nuns, to the amazement of the Western participants in the course, who could see no connection between charity to monks and meditation.[15]

Goenka continued to teach and conduct retreats on visits to Kathmandu over a number of years until, in 1988, the same group of businessmen who had invited him to Nepal, established and guaranteed support for a retreat center, Dharmashringha, which occupies about two acres above the village of Budha Nilkantha, a few miles north of Kathmandu.[16] Unlike IBMC, it is dedicated exclusively to meditation retreats, lasting ten days or longer, for adults. The director and assistant teachers, with the exception of two nuns, are all lay volunteers and only the domestic staff receive remuneration. As demand has grown, the original small cluster of buildings has been expanded to accommodate meditators who, in the warmer months, may number two hundred in each twice-monthly session. Not all "students," as they are called (using the English word), are Buddhists. Many Hindus, not all of whom are Newars, also attend, and some Westerners as well. Today, almost all the land has been built over, leaving space only for a terrace next to the dharma hall and a few flowerbeds. Surrounded by a high fence, little can be seen of the surrounding area other than the mountains towering up behind the center and the city of Kathmandu lying far below. A peaceful, well-ordered place, in which only birdsong and the cries of neighborhood children playing nearby can be heard, it has attained almost mythic stature in the community. For some it has become a longed-for place—akin to Sukhavati heaven—where radical personal transformation is believed to be possible.[17]

At neither IBMC nor Dharmashringha is there a set fee for courses (meditators give whatever they want, and two hundred rupees, which is less than US$3, is standard); thus theoretically, almost anyone can afford to take one. By and large, both centers attract people who, although not necessarily well-to-do, well educated, or even young, define themselves, broadly speaking, as forward-thinking. But although the stated objective—to acquire "insight" and "wisdom," namely, an experiential understanding of dependent origination and to "see things as they really are"—is the same, the approaches of the two centers differ in certain important respects.[18]

One difference has to do with the level meditators are expected to reach after ten days. At the outset participants (brown- and white-robed *yogis*) in a ten-day retreat at IBMC are instructed to develop "clear comprehension" during alternating one-hour periods of sitting and walking meditation by focusing their attention on the stomach as it rises and falls with each breath. Once concentration has been established, they are instructed to observe bodily behavior (*kayanupassana*) whether they are standing, sitting, lying, falling asleep, eating, drinking, and so forth, and, later in the course, the experience of specific parts of the body. After an initial three-day period, more experienced meditators may take up the contemplation of pleasant, unpleasant, and indifferent feelings of physical or mental origin (*vedananupassana*), an exercise in which feelings are noted as they appear and disappear but are not dwelt upon. Ten-day courses, whether at IBMC or Dharmashringha, do not generally provide instruction in either the third level of practice, contemplation of the state of mind (*cittanupassana*), in which the object of observation is the condition of the mind, or consciousness, as it presents itself at any given moment, or the fourth level, the contemplation of mental contents (*dhammanupassana*), which involves the noting and examination of ideas as they come into consciousness, the abandonment of hindrances and fetters (*kilesas*), and the acceptance and internalization of right beliefs. However, at Dharmashringha, unlike IBMC, participants in the one- and three-month courses that are held for small groups of people several times a year may, if judged ready by their teachers, embark upon these higher levels. Timetables at the two centers are compared in Table 8.1.

Participants at Dharmashringa are given a pamphlet titled "Code of Discipline for Vipassana Meditation." After welcoming them and stating, "Vipassana means 'to see things as they really are'; it is the process of self-purification by self-observation," it goes on to summarize:

What Vipassana is not:

- It is not a rite or ritual based on blind faith.
- It is neither an intellectual nor a philosophical entertainment.
- It is not a rest cure, a holiday or opportunity for socializing.
- It is not an escape from the trials and tribulations of everyday life nor an asylum for disgruntled misfits.

What Vipassana is:

- It is an art of living which frees the individual from all the negativities of mind, such as anger, greed, ignorance, etc.

Table 8.1 Timetables at IBMC and Dharmashringha compared

	IBMC, Shankhamul	Dharmashringha
4 A.M.	wake up bell	wake up bell
5–6 A.M.	sitting meditation	4:30 sitting meditation
6–7 A.M.	breakfast	6:30 breakfast
7–8 A.M.	sitting meditation	break
8–9 A.M.	chankraman (walking meditation)	meditation
9–10 A.M.	sitting meditation	meditation
10–11 A.M.	chankraman	meditation
11–12 noon	lunch	lunch
12–1 P.M.	rest and chankraman	break
1–2 P.M.	sitting meditation	meditation
2–3 P.M.	chankraman	meditation
3–4 PM.	dhammadesana (dharma discourses)	meditation
4–5 P.M.	lemon water and chankraman	meditation
5–6 P.M.	sitting meditation	break: tea, fruit, cereal
6–7 P.M.	chankraman	meditation
7–8 P.M.	sitting meditation	dharma discourses
8–9 P.M.	hot water and chankraman	meditation
9–10 P.M.	sitting meditation	9:30 lights out
10 P.M.	rest	

- It is a practice which develops positive, creative energy for the betterment of the individual and the society.[19]

At Dharmashringha only sitting meditation is practiced. (Chairs are not usually permitted, though Westerners may use up to four cushions to support themselves.) For the first three days, meditators, who wear ordinary street clothes and sit from long before dawn to late in the evening in a darkened hall for up to two-hour stretches, focus their attention on the breath as it passes through the nostrils. The next six days are devoted to the closest observation of sensations as they occur in specific points in the body, and the final day to Metta Savath (meditation on loving kindness) and to sharing with all sentient beings the spiritual merit one has earned from this practice.

In both settings, IBMC and Dharmashringha, every evening meditators listen to cassettes or watch videotapes of U Pandita on the one hand and Goenka on the other from whom they receive instructions for the following day. (U Pandita's talks have been translated from Burmese into Nepal Bhasha and English, and Goenka's from Hindi and

English into Nepal Bhasha.) Recorded instruction is backed up by very short daily meetings between the meditator and an assistant teacher. But whereas at IBMC teachers meet with meditators one on one, at Dharmashringha they meet with four "students" at once, which reduces communication about personal issues to a minimum.

Lauren Leve (1999) reports that the core group of Newar Goenka devotees whom she studied in Kathmandu were highly ambitious. The "gradual path" was not for them. Rather, they were set on becoming spiritual virtuosi and, having cleansed themselves of hindrances and stripped away illusion, on achieving "stream-entry" followed by—after only four more lifetimes—enlightenment. At IBMC however—and also at Gautami Vihara in Lumbini Garden—the soteriological imperative is understood in a more modest and traditional way: given the times we live in, enlightenment is possible but most unlikely. Thus, meditation practice should properly focus on quieting the passions; controlling body, speech, and mind; generating good karma; reducing bad karma; and securing a good rebirth.

Although the restrictions that meditators must promise to observe are the same in both centers (they must take the Eight Precepts and are barred from reading; writing; eating anything other than the vegetarian meals provided by the center; and making eye contact with, talking to, or touching another "student"),[20] the atmosphere in the two centers is palpably different. At IBMC, the charge is to follow the Buddha's example as best one can, thereby earning merit and gaining a deeper understanding of the law of impermanence. At Dharmashringha rather more is expected. In tape recordings, which are played in the last few minutes of every meditation session, Goenka intones, "Many thousands of students have used these techniques successfully. Be unflaggingly diligent and you too, will surely have success!" The implication here is that any lapse in diligence will result in ignominious failure to attain even a glimmer of enlightenment—and, perhaps worse, to ejection from the exclusive group of virtuosi practitioners in Kathmandu who, acknowledging and celebrating each other's success, stand, in their own eyes at least, at the apex of spiritual evolution. There is also in Dharmashringha considerable stress given to the personality of Goenka himself, which is very different from the distant reverence with which U Pandita and the late Mahasi Sayadaw are regarded at IBMC.

Bassini, who carried out a comparative study of the two meditation centers, taking courses at both, concluded:

> [T]hroughout my stay at Sankhamul [IBMC] I felt that my identity was not questioned by means of discourses that attempted at taking over the job of thinking for me and making up my mind [as at Dharmashringha] but rather the technique was offered to me as a gift and it was up to me to decide how to dispose of it and how deeply I wished to get involved in the practice. In my view, I perceived this approach to the participants as gentler and less inspired by a machine-like model of the human physiology and production [than at Dharmashringha]. (2001: 31)

Another important difference between the two centers is that at Dharmashringha religious rituals and symbols are forbidden. It is an important part of Goenka's appeal that the technique of vipassana is open to people of all religious backgrounds. However, all forms of religious ritual are banned during the courses, which means that any traditionalist Hindu or Buddhist committed to the performance of daily rituals—or any strict Muslim, Jew, or Christian—would have a hard time attending. At the same time, as noted previously, *yogis* take the Five or Eight Precepts; these, however, are not treated as specifically religious undertakings, but as part of the technique. Thus, whereas at IBMC the cult of the Buddha is central, at Dharmashringha there are no Buddha statues and no offerings are made. Perhaps the greater stress on the figure of Goenka himself follows from this. Despite this way of presenting vipassana as a nonreligious technique, there is no doubt that Goenka is in fact committed to specifically Buddhist scriptures and to a specifically Buddhist way of viewing the world. In later life, he has devoted himself to propagating translations of the Theravada scriptures. He has not become a monk, but he has undertaken a vow of celibacy. In his view, monks and nuns do not have any special status in view of their ordination; all religious status depends on one's achievements in meditation.

These differences between the two centers are reflected in the social backgrounds of the people who use them. As already indicated, the IBMC is patronized and made use of almost entirely by Newars. At Dharmashringha, by contrast, there is a conscious attempt to appeal to everyone. According to Leve (2002: 850 n. 31), 4,311 people attended courses at Dharmashringha between 1991 and 1995, 73 percent of them from Newar Buddhist castes. Bassini analysed the background of the 112 participants of the course she took in 2001, which, if it was typical, shows a large shift away from a mostly Newar constituency: 41 percent were Newars, 17 percent foreigners, 28.5 percent Brahmans or Chetris, 4.5 percent were other Nepali hill people. Among the Newars, 4 percent were Vajracharyas, 9 percent Shakyas, 48 percent Shresthas, 11 percent Uday, 9 percent Maharjan, and 19 percent Manandhar, Nakarmi, or Ranjitkar (Bassini 2001: 59). The very high proportion of Shresthas is another indication, along with the significant numbers of Brahmans and Chetris, that Dharmashringha appeals successfully to those coming from Hindu backgrounds. Many Newar vipassana practitioners, however, never set foot in Dharmashringha. They learn the preliminaries of meditation from a monk or nun in a vihara, and if they take a retreat, it is in the congenially Newar atmosphere of IBMC or Gautami Vihara rather than in Dharmashringha.

One consequence of the explicit policy of religious nonalignment at Dharmashringha is that no monks and only two nuns have left the Mahasi fold to become assistant teachers at Dharmashringha.[21] From time, to time other nuns take retreats there but they seem to pay little attention to Goenka's recorded dharma talks; rather, they continue to practice in the "Mahasi" way for which the *Satipatthana Sutta* pro-

Taking tea after Saturday morning meditation at IBMC, March 2001. (Sarah LeVine)

vides detailed instruction. As one nun observed after the conclusion of a Dharmashringha retreat:

> Meditation is very important. A person can't proceed along the Path without it and so everyone wants to take as many retreats as possible. It's up to us to make the best use of the time that we can and that means practicing in the way to which we are accustomed. Since we sit in silence with our eyes closed, how can the teachers know we're practicing differently from what the guru teaches?

Only a few nuns who ordained at a mature age after taking several retreats at Dharmashringha as laywomen admit to being Goenka devotees. Dhammaratna, who says that she renounced lay life and a successful career in large part in order to have more time to meditate, has typically "pure Buddhist" aspirations, and although she says she hasn't experienced *nibbana* "for even a minute" thus far, she is confident that "with a lot of very hard work" she will do so.[22] Though she does not expect to become an arhat in this life—she knows that her path is still very long—she hopes to be reborn a monastic so she may keep progressing steadily toward enlightenment.

There are also supposed to be considerable, more worldly benefits for vipassana practitioners. Ashwaghosh, who hoped, as noted above, that it would help cure his short temper, concludes his long introduction to a translation of Goenka's discourses by recounting the film actress Shashikala's experiences with vipassana and how it had reconciled her to leading a respectable householder's life. Presumably, he hoped that youthful readers might listen to the experiences of a film star, even if they were unlikely to be impressed by those of a monk. Ashwaghosh also listed twelve advantages of the practice. It enables one to:

1. achieve health;
2. be able to see one's own faults;
3. understand that meditation is not for show but to purify one's thoughts and achieve one-pointedness of mind;
4. conquer anger and resist saying or doing anything angry on occasions when anger arises;
5. pursue selflessly social service and engender a feeling of renunciation;
6. work hard without talking too much;

7. avoid wasting time remembering the past or dreaming about the future, but rather to work with a full understanding of the importance of the present;
8. stop being conservative and confidently seek out the solution of problems;
9. believe firmly, in whatever context, only that of which one has personal experience of its truth;
10. decrease one's selfishness and reduce one's dependence on thoughts of "me" and "mine";
11. increase one's tolerance toward others;
12. reflect on, and be aware of, jealousy, from wherever and however it has arisen. (Ashwaghosh 2000: 24–25)

An even more modern voice recasts vipassana in the language of business manuals. Roop Jyoti, Maniharsha's son, who has master's degrees in both business and public administration from Harvard University, recounts how vipassana enabled his father to face death from cancer with equanimity. He also describes how in business enterprises vipassana

> has improved the working atmosphere, the co-operative attitudes, the discipline, and the harmony within. Managers have become more patient in dealing with business uncertainties and more tolerant in dealing with troublesome employees. Workers have become more disciplined and better capable of carrying out their tasks. . . . Vipassana does not make us unambitious, it makes us more resourceful. . . . Vipassana is an art of stress management. Vipassana is an art of people management. Vipassana is an art of conflict management. There may be more to the science of management but Vipassana can become very nearly the art of total corporate management. (Jyoti 2002: 5)

Anjali: Exemplary Upasika

Anjali, a slight, sweet-faced single woman in her thirties, is a board member of several Theravada organizations and may be seen with armfuls of papers at many community events in Kathmandu. The youngest of four daughters, her three elder sisters had all been married by the age of sixteen, and as a secondary school student she too began to receive marriage proposals. She describes herself as having been almost pathologically shy as a girl, and the prospect of marriage and having to leave her own family and adapt to another household filled her with terror. When she told her well-to-do Uday parents that she did not want to "go to another house," after some protest they concurred with her wishes (although regarded as far from ideal, women of her caste do sometimes remain unmarried). For the next few years she diligently pursued her studies in secondary school and later at medical college. In her twenties however, she attended her first vipassana retreat, and over the next decade, meditation grew increasingly important to the point that today it has become the central focus of her life. "It isn't entirely too late for me to marry—I could marry a widower perhaps, but," she adds with a trace of a smile, "I don't have time for marriage. I'm too busy meditating."

She has considered ordination but she works six days a week in a government hospital and spends much of her free time on her committee work. "If I ordained," she explains, "I'd have to give most of that up. But I think what I do for the Sangha is worthwhile and if I stopped, they'd have trouble finding someone else to do it." Another reason she remains in lay life is that her mother is old and ailing and needs her only unmarried daughter's help.

One of seven children, Anjali lives with her mother, her three brothers and her eldest brother's wife and children. Her father, a prominent physician, died in the early 1980s. Until she was about twelve years old, she and her family lived in her father's ancestral home in Asan Tol but then, leaving his brothers behind, her father moved his wife and children to a new house. As the crow flies it is only a few hundred yards from their old home; nevertheless, their lives changed radically and twenty-five years later Anjali still has mixed feelings about the move:

> I'm a very quiet person and partly that's because my father took us to live on our own. Children who grow up in joint families are very sociable and outgoing—they're used to talking to everyone, whoever's there, adults as well as children. I think that if we'd stayed in the old house I might have been more assertive, but here in the new house, I managed to get by without talking too much. When my father had guests, I'd serve them tea in silence in the sitting room and then I'd run away to the kitchen. When I reached adulthood, I still didn't know how to talk to strangers.

The house where Anjali spent her earliest years was a short distance from Dharmakirti Vihara to which her mother, a devotee of Dhammawati Guruma, went regularly. As a small child, Anjali attended the Dharmakirti school every weekday morning before going home for breakfast and on to primary school. In addition, she would go to the nunnery with her mother for *puja* on new-moon, full-moon, and half-moon days; and whenever anyone in the family had a birthday they invited the nuns to the house for *bhojan*:

> In those days there were only five gurumas living in Dharmakirti. It was quite new and they were happy to receive our invitations because at that time very few people invited them. They came very often and I felt completely at home with them.

When Anjali was about thirteen, she began to attend weekly classes for teenagers that were offered at Dharmakirti:

> But now our teacher was a monk, Ashwaghosh Bhante. He has always supported Dhammawati Guruma and the cause of women. His sister is a nun—perhaps that's why he's sympathetic to women. As a teacher, he was very kind. . . . Anyway, with him we read the *Grihi Vinaya* (Rules for Householders), the *Mangala Sutta*, and the *Dhammapada*, and books that Dhammawati had written.

Anjali was invited to join a "leadership" program in which young people prepared and delivered speeches on religious topics and social problems such as drug addiction, which was beginning to affect the youth of Kathmandu. She particularly enjoyed their outings on and the sense of camaraderie that these trips encouraged:

> Dhammawati used to tell us girls that females were equal to males and that women should claim the same privileges as men. We all read *Snehi Chori*, an account of her experiences as a young girl. In class she would tell us that when she was young she'd wanted to be a leader, and indeed, that's what she had become. "You must be brave like I was," she'd say. Later on when I got older and found myself in situations where there were very few women, or maybe I was the only one, I would remember her words.

But all too soon Anjali had to drop out of the program: her third sister, whom she followed in age, got married and Anjali's help was needed now at home. In addition, she had just entered secondary school, she had more homework to do, and she didn't have time to study *buddha dharma*.

She had assumed she would go abroad for further training when she finished the medical college:

> In those days there were many scholarships for Nepali students: they were going to the West, to the Soviet Union, Australia, all over. My father was

> a very influential man and it would have been easy for him to procure one of those scholarships for me. But he also had great integrity, and unlike many other men in positions of power who gave the scholarships at their disposal to their children first, to their friends' children second, and only then, if any were left over, to deserving students, my father put me, his own daughter, at the bottom of the list.

Although bitterly disappointed, Anjali never confronted her father on this issue. She bit her tongue and, having seen many of her classmates leave for specialist training in Europe and America, went to work as a general practitioner in a government hospital.

Her father's death, which occurred when she was in her early twenties, precipitated a psychological crisis:

> Even though we never talked much, he and I, so you could say that I really wasn't all that close to him, after his death I was devastated. I couldn't stop weeping. I thought I was losing my mind. Dhammawati Guruma came to the house to give us *dharma desana* on the seven days following his death, and listening to her voice calmed me somewhat, though when she finished speaking I'd again be assailed by grief. It was she who suggested that I take the vipassana meditation course which was to be given in a few weeks' time. She said it would ease my distress. At the time I didn't really know what vipassana was. I had actually attended some teachings which Mahasi Sayadaw gave in 1981—the only time he came to Kathmandu—but I hadn't understood what he was talking about. Later, some of my friends who had also heard Mahasi but unlike me had taken up meditation, said I should do so as well. But I told them I was too busy studying. By the time my father died, Mahasi himself had been dead for a number of years and it was his chela U Pandita who came from Rangoon, and Dhammawati was his assistant and translator.

Anjali attended the ten-day retreat with one of her sisters:

> U Pandita first taught us *anapana*, concentration on the breath. He taught us to focus not on the past or the future but on each moment and to do everything very slowly: eating, picking up a book, standing up, sitting down. . . . Until then I had been grieving for my father to the point that I couldn't think about anything else; but I concentrated very hard and after four days or so I entered *samadhi*. In that state, grief no longer touched me; I was free. After terrible pain and tumult I felt calm and in control of myself, and for several days after the retreat ended I continued to feel that way.

For the next several years, she practiced meditation in an increasingly disciplined way and whenever they were offered, she attended retreats conducted by Goenka and his assistants as well as by U Pandita. Gradually, as her preoccupation with her father—her anger at his refusal to help her, her disappointment at her stagnated career—diminished, she began to overcome her reserve:

> Meditation helps a lot. It forces you to face your fears. . . . I have no interest in going abroad now. I don't want to study further in my field. My life is full enough as it is.

The equanimity with which Anjali handles the frustrations that arise both in and outside her home is impressive. "Confrontation gets you nowhere, it only makes things worse," she says. "You must be tactful and sympathetic and bide your time. Only then might you have the opportunity to influence someone's opinion or behavior for the better." And if this approach is ineffective? She shrugs. "You have to keep on biding your time." Meanwhile, much of her energy is devoted to supporting the Sangha. Indeed, no task seems to be too demanding or too trivial for her. One finds her working with engineers on the construction of monastic buildings, organizing elaborate community events, mopping floors, supervising large groups of small children during winter holiday retreats, cooking breakfast for crowds of devotees and washing the dishes afterward, teaching samaneras to draw and paint, entertaining foreign visitors, dashing from one meeting to another, and all the while skillfully navigating her way through Sangha politics from which many others, seemingly more stalwart and resilient than she, have fled.

The Democratization of Meditation

In traditional Newar Buddhism, meditation was an elite practice to which only Vajracharyas, Shakyas, and Udays had access.[23] Similarly, for the first half-century after their appearance in the Valley, Theravada monks kept the techniques they had learned in Burma largely to themselves. Only in the last twenty years have nuns as well as ordinary Buddhist laypeople had access to practices from which caste, gender, or, latterly, lay status, had barred them. But once this formerly elite practice was "democratized," Newar Buddhists—as more than one long-term observer of the community has noted—took to it like ducks to water. Today, thousands of Newars regularly practice meditation both with others in the vihara and alone at home, and each year hundreds find ten days—and sometimes considerably longer—in their complicated domestic and professional lives to undertake a vipassana retreat. Batchelor's comment on the "elective affinity" of vipassana and modern life would seem to be borne out in modernizing Nepal too: "Arguably the emphasis on technique in many *vipassana* groups, as well as the prevailing norm of intense bursts of meditation practice during week or ten-day retreats, reflect the needs of a secular society pressured by work and family commitments" (1994: 352).

Given that a multiplicity of techniques for focusing one's thoughts and calming anxiety lay at hand, why did the Newar Buddhist laity seize on vipassana meditation rather than some other approach such as, for example, Tibetan visualizations, which were close to the indigenous *sadhana* tradition, or one of the many forms of yoga practiced locally by Hindus? That they took so readily to vipassana may reflect some of the same factors that, earlier in the twentieth century, made for the success of the Theravada mission. First, as an ancient but long-neglected meditation method, vipassana was represented by its "missionaries" as a return to what was "pure." Second, it had an egalitarian appeal; no esoteric initiation was necessary: it involved a few simple directions that anyone over the age of about seven could learn and apply with benefit. Third, the very lack of an established monastic hierarchy meant that there was no long-accepted traditional view on meditation and no conservative teachers who would feel threatened by the popularity of the new technique.[24] Fourth, it could be seen to be both Buddhist and scientific or modern.

By banning rosaries and rituals, Goenka's approach was quite radically modern: not something that could be combined with, or used merely as a supplement to, traditional duties and observances. Furthermore, Goenka gave an enormous impetus to vipassana meditation by attracting large numbers of people to it who were not from a Buddhist family background. He presented a Buddhist message in an apparently nonreligious, ecumenical way, in stark humanist and psychological terms, claiming that it is accessible to those of any religious background or none. He therefore appealed very strongly to those educated in a modern way. Goenka himself is well aware of the factors that enable him to appeal to modern-educated people, which is why, though he has taken a vow of celibacy, he has never become a monk: he wants people to understand that vipassana is for laypeople also (Ekachai 2001: 278). At IBMC, although the clientele is almost exclusively Newar, similar modernizing trends are at work: the heart of Buddhism becomes not divinity, mantra, or even compassion, but a personal experience of the nature of things.

Buddhist Cultural Centers: Aksheshwar Mahavihar and the Lotus Research Center

Individualized meditation practice is one aspect of modernization; Buddhist activism is another. On top of Pulchok hill to the west of Lalitpur sits the imposing modernist edifice of Aksheshwar Mahavihara. Originally it was Pucho Bahi, a small Newar Buddhist monastery dating back to at least to the thirteenth century (Locke 1985: 219; H. Shakya 1995: 59), occupying a site that very likely had Buddhist associations hundreds of years before that. In the 1970s, the monastery was falling down and the Sangha of local Shakyas could not repair it. The committee of all the Newar Buddhist monasteries of Lalitpur persuaded them to let it be rebuilt as a modern and ecumenical Buddhist center. Thanks to a donation of 1.3 million rupees from the Ministry of Local Development, and numerous other donations from institutions and individuals (including over one hundred thousand rupees from Lalitpur's Tibetan refugees) it was rebuilt on a grand scale, with halls big enough for large meetings and one wing as a "gompa," i.e. with a Tibetan-style Amoghapasa Lokesvara. Externally it is decorated in "Newar style," but the construction techniques and the proportions are thoroughly modern.

In the words of Asha Ram Shakya, the president of the committee for the preservation of the new institution:

> The present set-up [of the] Achheswor Maha Bihar Complex came into being [according to a] Master Plan specially designed for its reconstruction and [development] as an International Buddhist Centre with facilities [including] the Research Library, the International Buddhist Guest House, the School for teaching Buddhist Art, the Tibetan-style Gompa, the Meditation Centre, and the free medical centre with its ENT, Cardiological and Asthma clinics, [as well as] regular weekly services [offered] to school children and lay people. However, there is still much to be done. [According to] the Master-Plan, a hospital, a Buddhist Garden with a 25-foot bronze Buddha figure [in the] standing posture and an International Buddhist Conference Hall are [yet] to be completed. (A. R. Shakya 1997: 1–2)

Free medical clinics are indeed held regularly, as are meditation classes, thangka painting classes, Sanskrit classes, and lectures on Buddhism. The guest house may only be occupied occasionally, but the monastery is the natural place in Lalitpur to hold Buddhist meetings of all kinds, whether seminars, committee meetings, classes, or meditation. The original Shakya Sangha of Pucho Bahi continue to have the right to be the "god-guardians" or temple priests of the principal Shakyamuni shrine, and they continue to hold their traditional communal activities in the complex. But all other parts of it are now run in a collective way by the entire Buddhist community of Lalitpur. Because it is set up as a nonaligned Buddhist institution, any form of Buddhism may make use of its premises; but the effect of it is primarily to encourage the revival, or at least the discussion of the revival, of traditional Newar Buddhism.

One institution that often holds its meetings in Aksheshwar Mahavihara is the Lotus Research Center. This was set up in 1988, with funding from the Shishin-kai of Japan, at the instigation of Hidenobu Takaoka, a Japanese Soto Zen priest from Nagoya who speaks Nepal Bhasha well and has long had a very personal interest in the Buddhism of the Kathmandu Valley, carrying out much research and directing an important project to microfilm Buddhist manuscripts. The Lotus Research Center aims to revive traditional Newar Buddhism by encouraging research on its scriptures and practices by Newar Buddhists themselves. It holds seminars, organizes lectures, employs young people to do research, and publishes translations of Newar Buddhist scriptures from Sanskrit into Nepal Bhasha and Nepali. In 2003, it held a special conference to celebrate the fact that all of Newar Buddhism's nine holiest scriptures (the *nava dharma*) had been translated into Nepal Bhasha (five at the instigation of the Center itself).[25]

An Activist Buddhist Library: Vishwa Shanti Pustakalaya

Many of the larger *baha* in Lalitpur and Kathmandu have their own collections of manuscripts, some of which are very old. By and large these manuscripts are consulted in a purely ritualistic way, being taken out to be worshipped, and sometimes recited, during the month of Gunla. One of the expressions of the political and cultural revival movements that began toward the end of Rana rule, and immediately afterward, was the establishment of modern local libraries of printed books. Many of these modern libraries soon became dormant, however, their collections moldering away neglected and unread. In 1990, a small group of young people decided to organize a new kind of library in Lalitpur, one that focused not on preaching to the converted, to those already within the revivalist community, but on spreading Buddhism to outsiders. Their intention was to learn—and facilitate the learning of others—about the whole spectrum of Buddhist thought and practices. Though from time to time they might invite Theravada monks and Vajracharya priests to address them, theirs would be a fundamentally lay and ecumenical organization, free of institutional religious control.

They began to collect and raise funds for the purchase of books from friends, relatives, and neighbors; gradually, they put together the kernel of a lending library, which they called Vishwa Shanti Pustakalaya. However, for lack of any alternative, for the first eight years it was kept in the family house of one of the members of the group. Eventually, in a house in Nyakhachuk a large enough space was found for the books themselves, a Saturday program for library members, and the classes that board members offered in *buddha dharma*, public speaking, traditional Newar arts (e.g., thangka painting), *anapana* meditation, and an intensive English course during the long winter holiday. In addition, they run blood donation programs and health camps and organize monks to make the alms round on full-moon days. These activities have been going on for ten years without a break.

By 2003, the library had 310 members, the majority of whom were under thirty. As one board member pointed out, "In this city there are very few Buddhist organizations catering to young people. In the *baha*, the programs are all for householders and children. People our age are left out. As for the larger organizations, they're hardly any better. Despite its name, most people in the Young Men's Buddhist Association (YMBA) are close to fifty years of age."[26] Vishwa Shanti Pustakalaya is a unique organization in another very important way: membership is equally divided between men and women. Furthermore, as the same youthful board member explained:

> Women don't just cook the food for big events and clean up afterwards, which is pretty much what they do in other organizations. In ours, they play leading roles. Right now we have two or three women who've had a lot of organizational experience. But they're single and unfortunately, once they're married, we'll probably lose them. Fathers-in-law usually insist that their daughters-in-law stay in the house. Partly this is because they have domestic duties to attend to and partly it's because their in-laws don't want them spending time with men other than their husbands. From our point of view, this is really too bad. . . . It would be best for us if members married each other! Then there'd be a chance of the wife continuing her library work because her husband would be sympathetic and would support her.

Vibrant as the organization undoubtedly is, it still runs largely on the energy and optimism of its board members. Even though all their course instructors work for nothing, the library has expanded slowly. Annual membership fees (fifty rupees) are swallowed up by light bills and the rental of tents for major events; as of 2002, they had collected about fifteen hundred Buddhist publications, most of which are in Nepal Bhasha but some are in English and a few others are in Nepali; without reserves, every scheduled event and publication, including their annual volume (*smarika*) of articles on Buddhist topics and current social concerns, brought out for Buddha Jayanti, requires a new round of fund-raising to cover costs. In these bad economic times, members who go house to house collecting donations count themselves lucky if someone gives them two hundred or three hundred rupees. One library publication that has been very successful—it has been reprinted three times—is an illustrated guide to all the items used in traditional Newar Buddhist worship (Bajracharya 1994).

In 1995, just five years after they established the library, the same group of young people started a savings and credit scheme that they named SCOPE (Savings and Credit Outlay for Promoting Entrepreneurship). It lent money at 14 percent interest (compared to the banks' 18 percent) and it paid 3 percent higher interest on deposits than the banks; furthermore, the paperwork involved in a SCOPE transaction was much less complicated than that of a bank. By 2000, 75 percent of library members had enrolled, a large proportion of whom were borrowing money for house construction, small trade ventures, and medical crises. In 2001, the SCOPE board decided to require that, prior to accepting their applications, new members take a management course run by SCOPE members, so that they might understand the workings of the scheme. When asked how in fact SCOPE does work, a board member replied, "Basically, on trust. Members pay their dues because SCOPE is a *community* organization. We all know each other. A person can't renege on his commitment and keep it a secret. In no time, everyone would hear about it." SCOPE members also gave training in Solu Khumbu in 2001 so that locals there could start up a similar organization. Meanwhile, in Lalitpur and the surrounding villages, over a dozen groups have sprung up in imitation.

Spreading the Word: Buddhist Awareness Camps

In the early years of their movement, the Theravadins had seen themselves as missionaries whose primary aim was to spread a true understanding of Buddhism wherever there was a sizeable Newar population. Because of restrictions on proselytization, both under the Ranas and later under the Panchayat regime, they never sought to reach out to non-Newars or to influence groups without a pre-existing Buddhist identity. Toward the end of the Panchayat regime, some young Newar Buddhist activists formed the Yuba Bauddha Samuha in Kathmandu. One of their main activities was to try and spread Buddhism in the Newar villages of the Kathmandu Valley. This was, in a way, a continuation, by laymen and in a more modernist idiom, of the earlier work of monks like Pragyananda. Other groups also participated in this work. The Jyotidaya Sangh was founded in the village of Chapagaon with the help of activists from Lalitpur and Kathmandu. From the beginning, it linked Buddhism and development, and its yearly magazine published many articles with titles such as "Buddhism and Health," "The Four Noble Truths and Village Development," and so on. Explicit links were made with Ariyaratna's Sarvodaya teachings in Sri Lanka, and Ariyaratna has himself visited more than once, making speeches in several villages in the Kathmandu Valley.

Even before 1990, the Yuva Bauddha Samuha in Kathmandu conceived the idea of trying to recruit the Janajati groups of the middle hills to a campaign for a secular, that is, non-Hindu, constitution. They held speaker meetings in Theravada viharas to which they invited prominent Janajati activists, such as Ramananda Prasad Singh, who was already famous for claiming that the Tharus were descendants of the Buddha's tribe, the Shakyas (Singh 1988). They felt that their subsequent campaign for secularism was a failure, because the 1990 constitution continued to describe Nepal as "Hindu" despite simultaneously labeling it as "multiethnic" and "multilingual."[27]

The campaign for a secular constitution brought religious and pro-Buddhist political activists of all ethnic groups into contact with one another. One outcome of this was the Himalayan Buddhist Education Foundation (HBEF) established in 1995 with Taiwanese funding. Bhikshu Sudarshan, abbot of Shri Kirti Vihara in Kirtipur and a lecturer in the Department of Culture at Tribhuvan University, was invited to be chairman of the board and a nun became head of women's affairs, but the other five board members, and the driving force behind it, were an eclectic group of laymen: a senior vipassana instructor from the Dharmashringha Center, the presidents of two Buddhist youth organizations, a university teacher, and a Hindu businessman who was a convert to Tibetan Buddhism.[28] HBEF listed its aims in its first newsletter as follows:

1. To educate Nepalese people about Buddhist philosophy and practice and promote the morals and ethics of various people of the country, especially the young people irrespective of their caste, creed, sex, and religion.
2. To organize symposiums and seminars on Buddhist culture and religion.
3. To carry out activities directly or indirectly related to the aforementioned objectives.

This meant taking Buddhist teachings to villages in the Valley, to Tibetan Buddhist hill communities (such as Tamangs and Gurungs), and to any group simply interested in Buddhism (such as the Tharus and Magars).

The Buddhist Awareness Camp project was one of the first proposals that the HBEF funded. It involved weeklong residential "camps" (*sivir*) in towns and villages where board members and their assistants taught the fundamentals of Buddhism to up to fifty students.[29] The facts that instruction was in Nepali and in most places students were equally divided by gender were important features of this outreach program. In every site, a local coordinator, usually a religious leader, organized food, lodging, and transport for which HBEF provided funding. In Jiri, a town at the beginning of the trail that leads up to the Everest region, the local coordinator was a Tamang lama (of the Tibetan Nyingma tradition) who, at the conclusion of the course, wept as he told the teacher that until he attended the camp, he had understood his priestly role to consist solely of ritual performance and chanting Tibetan texts that he didn't understand. He tearfully admitted that he had had no knowledge of the core principles of Buddhism.[30]

In the camps—which continued to be held until the spring of 2001 when, because of the rapidly spreading Maoist insurgency, a halt had to be called—instruction was given on the meaning of the Five Precepts, the Four Noble Truths, karma, and dependent origination; some history of the local Buddhist tradition was given; and in areas following Tibetan Buddhism, instruction was provided in the Four Preliminary

Practices. In the period leading up to 2001, though camps continued to be held in Tamang, Gurung, and Tharu areas, the majority were held in Magar communities whose activist leaders had decided to reverse centuries of Hinduization and adopt Buddhism.[31] They approached Bhikshu Sudarshan and Bhikshu Ashwaghosh for guidance in performing life-cycle rites in a Buddhist idiom, and for basic Buddhist texts in Nepali. The HBEF had the life of the Buddha printed in large numbers for free distribution with the help of Taiwanese donors.

Kiran Bhai Vajracharya: A New Kind of Social Activist Buddhist

With his turned-up jacket collar, fashionable haircut, and streetwise manner, Kiran Bhai Vajracharya might easily be mistaken for a typical urban Newar youth, addicted to Western popular culture and happily ignorant of his own traditions; in fact, Kiran Bhai is a deeply engaged Buddhist. In addition to studying for a master's degree in sociology, occasionally working as a tourist guide, and assisting his goldsmith father in his workshop, he meditates for thirty minutes morning and evening; he is president of the library, Vishwa Shanti Pustakalaya; for eighteen months, he taught English to Theravada novice monks and nuns at Vishwa Shanti Vihara; and, as if he didn't have enough to fill his time, he is enrolled in a demanding Mahayana Buddhist philosophy course.

The third of four sons, Kiran Bhai was born in his family's house in one of Lalitpur's great *bahas*, but when he was eight he moved with his parents and siblings to the house his father had bought near Patan Dhoka. They moved, he explains, because the old house was too small to accommodate his father and his three uncles and their growing families. But although the move occurred many years ago, there has been no formal separation of the joint family. "We're still entitled to our own space there," Kiran Bhai notes, and his father continues to join his brothers in worshipping the family lineage deity in the old family house.

Although Kiran's father and uncles all took Tantric Initiation (*diksa*), they have not learned to perform rituals for others and none has ever worked as a priest. Instead, they have earned a living as gold- and silversmiths. By contrast, Kiran Bhai's mother is from a well-known priestly family. Her father, Kiran Bhai's maternal grandfather, was chief priest of his *baha*. "He had so many *jajman* that when new people asked for his services he had to refuse them," Kiran Bhai recalls. His eldest son, Kiran Bhai's maternal uncle (*paju*), is also a practicing Vajracharya.

Because Kiran Bhai underwent *bare chuyegu*, the traditional four-day monastic initiation ceremony for Vajracharya and Shakya boys, when he was about five years old, his memories of the ritual are hazy. Recently he and his three brothers rose to the next level in the religious hierarchy by taking consecration as a Vajra-Master (*ācā luyegu*) together; each received his own mantra, which in Kiran Bhai's case, he repeats for fifteen minutes every morning just after he gets up, followed by fifteen minutes of meditation based on the *sapta vidhāna pujā*. "Ever since I was a small child I wanted to enter the *agama* (Tantric shrine room) in our *baha*, but before *aca luyegu* how could I go there? Now I may enter. But if I had married a girl from another caste, I would have been barred." In 2002, he was married to a Vajracharya girl, like him from Bu Baha, whom he had known for about ten years. They decided to marry and approached their parents to arrange it in the traditional way.

Taking Tantric Initiation permanently commits one to the observance of numerous dietary restrictions and the performance of certain religious rituals every day for the rest of one's life. Many, if not most, young Vajracharya men are unwilling to accept these restrictions and refuse initiation; but Kiran Bhai looks forward to taking it because he aspires to the respect and admiration from the community that it will bring. Tantric Initiation would be required if he were intending to perform Vajrayana domestic rituals; learning how to do them would require a long apprenticeship however, and, despite his maternal uncle's eagerness to teach him, he feels he cannot accept his offer. Though he plans to take initiation he knows he will never work as a priest for, as he says regretfully:

> The training would take too much time, and then even when I've learned everything I need to know, I wouldn't be able to make a decent living. Gubhajus only get paid fifty or one hundred rupees for performing a *samskara* (life-course rite), so you'll find very few young men doing *purohit* work, and those who do, live poorly.

Even his maternal uncle, despite having many *jajman*, has to supplement his income by working as a goldsmith. But though Kiran Bhai is headed for a more remunerative career than that of domestic priest, he is determined to learn as much as he can about Buddhism—be it the

Vajrayana Buddhism of his ancestors, the meditational practices of the Tibetan monks of the valley gompas, or the Theravadins' Abhidhamma.

In childhood he received no formal religious education. He explains that until he completed secondary school at the age of eighteen, he was studying so hard that he had no time to learn about Buddhism. But about the time he passed his SLC exams, his brother Kishor, seven years his senior, became interested in Theravada Buddhism and it was he who introduced Kiran Bhai to the "new" movement. *Pariyatti* classes had existed in his childhood but his parents didn't send any of their children to them; it was only after Kishor became involved with Theravada Buddhism that they, like Kiran Bhai, started to take an interest. These days, from time to time they invite monks to eat in their house but this is quite new; in Kiran Bhai's childhood, monks were never invited.

Encouraged by Kishor to learn about Theravada Buddhism, Kiran Bhai began to think about attending *pariyatti* classes. But when he saw that his classmates would mostly be children many years younger than himself, he gave up the idea. For a while he focused on his college studies, but then, hearing about a dharma course that Gyanapurnik Mahasthavira, abbot of Vishwa Shanti Vihara, was offering for young adults, he decided to join. He recalls:

> I had almost no background, and to begin with I hardly understood anything. But then I began to read the books the bhante lent me and gradually I understood a bit more. Well, maybe forty percent. Yes, I'd say even now that's about the most I understand of those dharma talks! Gyanapurnik Bhante would encourage us to ask questions, but as for myself, I never did. I didn't feel I knew enough to ask good questions. . . . I was afraid to show just how little I knew. Some monks are quite difficult to understand. They hardly simplify at all, so uneducated people catch very little—just a sentence here and there. Even so, they stay to listen because they have *sraddha* (faith), and they believe that just listening to dharma talks earns you merit.

After this experience, he joined Min Bahadur Shakya's classes in Mahayana philosophy (Chapter 9). This involved four two-hour classes a week for three years, with an exam at the end of each year.

While Kiran Bhai was getting his first exposure to Theravada Buddhism, his brother Kishor and three friends were establishing the Vishwa Shanti Pustakalaya, described above. When the library first opened, Kiran Bhai was an awestruck schoolboy watching his brother and his friends build a youth organization from scratch. But, within a decade, he became secretary and then president of the library, and he is centrally involved in its many programs, including classes in public speaking, dance and theater performances, the annual citywide Buddhist quiz competition. He is proud of their achievements.

In May 1998, Viswa Shanti Pustakalaya hosted the twenty-sixth annual *buddha dharma* quiz competition involving teams fielded by twenty-four Buddhist clubs and libraries in Lalitpur. Kiran Bhai, as head of the organizing committee, worked virtually full-time during the three months before the weeklong event was scheduled. Aside from coordinating the preparation of the coursebook on whose contents participants were to be quizzed, his main task was to recruit and organize more than one hundred volunteers. In addition, he played a major role in fund-raising. To this end, he put together a handsome publication containing articles in Nepal Bhasha, Nepali, and English on the history of the quiz competition, the library, and other topics, which he and his aides sold door-to-door and in the streets of Lalitpur on festival days. He wrote invitations; designed, printed, and put up posters in public places; and begged supplies, prizes, and food. He borrowed lighting and sound equipment and hung banners across streets—barely sleeping for weeks. A few days before the competition was due to begin, there was a robbery in a house in the *baha* where the competition was to be held, and so committee members had to take turns sleeping on the library premises in order to guard the equipment being stored there. "Because of mosquitoes, none of us slept at all," Kiran Bhai recalls with a grin.

Despite suffocating pre-monsoon heat, power outages, and torrential downpours, the event drew large crowds and when it was all over, an exhausted Kiran Bhai exulted:

> The main goal of our library is to spread the dharma, and that's just what we did. Due to the rain, there weren't so many in the audience on the first two evenings, but those who did come went home and talked about what they'd heard. With family members, friends, and neighbors they discussed the questions the teams had been asked and the different answers they'd given, and then the next night more people came. The audience got larger and larger until the last night there were so many people, the courtyard was completely filled.

After he and his aides returned the sound equipment and the electric generator, the cooking pots and dishes, the chairs and trestle tables, the benches and straw mats, and everything else that they borrowed, he says, "What I'd like to do right now is take a meditation retreat," but he has no time to relax: he has exactly one week in which to study for his master's degree exams.

Kiran Bhai's first Buddhist meditation teacher was a British Theravada monk from the London-based Western Buddhist Order who several years ago happened to be passing through Kathmandu and gave some teachings to members of the library. After he left, for a time Kiran Bhai would go to the IBMC on Saturday mornings. He has also attended two ten-day vipassana courses at Budha Nilkantha during Dasain, a time when students can take time off because all the schools are closed for the holidays. He observes:

> From meditation you begin to understand the truth of impermanence. And once you've begun to grasp that, little by little the intensity of your desires starts to decrease. You learn to concentrate very well during those retreats, and for a while the sense of control over mind and body that you develop stays with you. Afterwards, when you go home, your arguments are keener for a while, more persuasive. You're able to convince your friends that Buddhism is the true way. . . . But over time, the effects of the retreat—the power it has given you—does fade. . . . The thing is, it's difficult to meditate at home . . . there's too much noise: my brother's kids, the telephone, voices of people passing in the street, car horns. And social obligations are constantly interfering, especially in the evening—feasts, weddings, family events. People are whispering in the meditation hall, children are chanting outside in the garden. . . . The best place is Budha Nilkantha. Up there on the mountain no one whispers, no one chants. All you hear are birds. How I'd love to go there now!

Although he is determined to learn as much as he can about both Tibetan and Theravada Buddhism, so far his commitment to the religion of his ancestors is unwavering:

> Theravada's very new in Nepal. Until the end of Rana times no one here had even heard of it. Everyone was a Vajrayanist, and that's still our tradition. We may go to the viharas from time to time and learn from the monks. We may go to the gompas too and study with the lamas, but how can we forget our own tradition?

Other Buddhist Revival Movements: Tibetan "Mahayana" and Newar "Vajrayana"

The beginnings of the Nepalese Theravada movement, as discussed in Chapter 2, were not in fact Theravadin at all, but Tibetan and Mahayanist. For at least a millennium, the Kathmandu Valley has had close ties with Tibet. Though Nepalese inscriptions and chronicles are silent on the subject, the Tibetan histories record that at the time of the first conversion of Tibet in the seventh century the Tibetan king Songtsen Gampo married Princess Bhrikuti Devi, a daughter of the king of Nepal, who imported Nepali craftsmen to build Jokhang Monastery in Lhasa.[1] Tibetan documents and artifacts provide abundant evidence for the continuing importance of the Valley for Tibet during the second "spread of the doctrine" in the eleventh through the thirteenth centuries. Tibetans came south to "Nepal" (which in those days meant the Kathmandu Valley) to obtain religious texts, to receive initiations, and to study with famous Buddhist teachers, some of whom were Nepali and others Indian refugees. In the other direction went Nepali scholars and translators and also, for a period that lasted several centuries, painters and craftsmen to work on monastic construction throughout central Tibet.[2]

After the Muslim invasions of Kashmir in the fourteenth century, Kashmiri Buddhism, which had played a major role in the Tibetan conversion, was destroyed. In the aftermath, existing ties between Tibet and the Kathmandu Valley—where the Muslims only invaded once and did not stay—were strengthened. Throughout the later Malla period (fifteenth to late eighteenth centuries) Newar Buddhists must routinely have encountered Buddhist pilgrims—as they still do today—both from Tibet and from communities along the southern slopes of the Himalayas at the great stupas of Namobuddha, Swayambhu, and Bauddha; at the directional stupas of Lalitpur; at Mahabauddha and Shrigha in Kathmandu; and at Chabahil in Deopatan, as well as at the many Newar monastic complexes that have historical ties to Tibet (Dowman 1982). Meanwhile, Tibetan and Bhutanese Karma Kagyupa lamas, who had come to see the Valley as a province of the Tibetan Buddhist hinterland, periodically restored the Swayambhu stupa.

Trans-Himalayan trade flourished to the great benefit of Uday, Shakya, Vajracharya, and a few Shrestha, merchants and artisans. As they traveled back and forth between the Valley and the Tibetan plateau, some lived for long periods in Tibetan towns and, leaving their Newar wives at home, married Tibetan women and had second families on the plateau (Jest 1993, Lall 2001). These wealthy laymen became patrons of Tibetan monasteries and, when they returned home, took teachings from pilgrim lamas with whom they had had contact on the plateau, called them to their houses to perform expensive rituals, and contributed to the maintenance of the stupas. Though Newar Buddhist culture is South Asian in its orientation, the esteem in which the upper-caste Buddhists held the Tibetan tradition is evidenced by the number of Tibetan texts, whether obtained on the plateau or in the Valley, still in private hands in the Valley and by the fact that many Newars use Tibetan texts for their daily devotions.

The Newar Vajracharya priests modeled themselves primarily on Tantric siddhas (saints) and on the social position of Hindu domestic priests (Brahman *purohits*). Nonetheless, as Todd Lewis (1989) has argued, for centuries they have also had exposure to Nyingmapa lamas, some of whom were celibate, but many of whom were, like the Vajracharyas themselves, married. In the mid-eighteenth century the Catholic priest Giuseppe da Rovato described *baryesu* (*bare*, i.e., Vajracharyas and Shakyas) as dressing in "coarse red wollen [sic] cloth" (i.e., like lamas) and he mentioned that that they were supposed to be celibate "but in Nepal they do not observe this rule, except at their discretion" (Lewis 1989: 31). Colonel Kirkpatrick, who visited the Valley in 1793, claimed that the "Bhanrâs [are] a sort of separatists from the Newars; they are supposed to amount to about five thousand; they shave their heads like the Bhootias [Tibetans], observe many of the religious rites, as well as civil customs of these idolators . . ." (1969: 183–184). Lewis suggests that Newar Buddhist priests not only dressed like lamas, but some may also have studied in Tibetan gompas and taken initiations from Tibetan masters. In sum, for all that they were descended from Indian Buddhist lineages and were firmly positioned within the South Asian cultural sphere, Newar Vajracharyas—and not just Newar traders—had significant contact over the centuries with Tibetan lamas.[3]

In the nineteenth century, though the large number of pilgrim guidebooks of the period testify to the continued importance of the Valley to Tibetan Buddhists, at the state level ties between Nepal and Tibet loosened.[4] This was due in part to wars between the two countries (1792–93 and 1855–56), in part to internal political conditions. The Mallas, paradigmatic Asian kings, had patronized all religions within their territory, including Tibetan Buddhism whose institutions and festivals they supported, just as they had supported Newar Hindu sects and Buddhist monasteries. By contast, the Shah kings and their Rana regents, as orthodox Hindus, were much more sharply focused on the practices and institutions of their own tradition. Other traditions were supported and tolerated only as subordinate to Hinduism and only if traditional to a defined social group.

Newar-Tibetan relations have therefore gone through several distinct phases. In the early Middle Ages, the intellectual and aesthetic flow was strongly south to north. But at quite an early stage, the Tibetans were heavily involved in organizing and paying for several renovations of Swayambhu.[5] Later, as Tibetan scholarship advanced and theirs declined, Newar Buddhists accepted that the Tibetans preserved a level of understanding, practice, and orthodoxy from which they themselves had fallen away: at least this was acknowledged in the Newar myths according to which Shankara Acharya defeats the Nepali Buddhists, but goes on to Tibet and is in turn defeated by the Dalai Lama (Gellner 1992: 86).

Newars took teachings from high Tibetan lamas, when the lamas appeared in the Valley. Tibetans ceased to look to Nepal for doctrinal or spiritual teaching, but continued to regard it as a holy site; and they acknowledged that the Newars maintained a strictness in matters such as the required secrecy of Tantric Initiation that they themselves had not been able to maintain. In short, Tibetans began to view the Valley as a peripheral area within their own religious sphere, rather than as a source of knowledge, and as a place to proselytize among peoples who shared their cultural roots. Though documentation is sparse, it is likely that some Newar men ordained in the Tibetan tradition throughout Malla times and right up to the present.[6]

Revival From Tibet

Chapter 2 described how the arrival in 1925 of Kyangtse Lama, prostrating all the way from Tibet, sparked off a major surge of Buddhist enthusiasm, leading to many Newars becoming monks or nuns. And there was a considerable rise in the foundation of Tibetan Buddhist gompas in the Kathmandu Valley, sponsored by Newars, the first such new Tibetan foundations in "Nepal" for centuries.

In the early decades of the twentieth century, only two of the four main Tibetan Buddhist traditions—Nyingma and Karma Kagyu—had representation in the Valley. Gelukpa institutions did not appear until the 1940s when a monastery was established at Bauddha, and Gelukpa monks, even today, are few in number.[7] There was no Sakyapa presence in Nepal until after the Tibetan diaspora began in 1959. Today, the majority of Newar monks who belong to the Tibetan tradition are still Nyingmapas and Kagyupas; no Newar has yet ordained as a Sakya monk, so far as we know, and only a handful as Gelukpa. In Kathmandu, whether monastics or laymen, most Newars who follow Tibetan Buddhism are drawn from the Uday and Manandhar castes, whereas in Lalitpur they tend to be Shakyas and Maharjans.

Kyangtse Lama and Tsering Norbu, the two pilgrim lamas with large numbers of Newar followers in the 1920s, paved the way for two other Nyingmapa practitioners named Pata Lama and Sonam Tendzing, who arrived in the Valley in the early 1930s, and, unusually, settled in Nepal.[8] Pata Lama built a gompa at Daman on the southern rim of the Valley, and Sonam Tendzing built his Nagi Gompa on the northern rim above Budha Nilkantha in the forest on the southern flank of Mount Shivapuri.[9] Over the next twenty years, Sonam Tendzing ordained at least two dozen monks, including several Shakyas who had been devotees of Kyangtse Lama. They included a few natives of Bhaktapur who, when they continued to do prostrations and to follow meditation practices they had learned from the lama, had been expelled from their *baha* Sangha.

By the 1940s, Sonam Tendzing had also begun to offer novice ordination (*sramanerika pravrajya*) to women, the first group of whom included a few Newars.[10] Like the gurumas, these *anis*, as Tibetan nuns are called, shared quarters with monks. But unlike the gurumas, many of whom from early on successfully resisted working for the monks, the *anis* routinely performed domestic services for the lamas; their religious role was confined to chanting and the preparation of ritual requisites. In contrast with the first generation of Theravada gurumas who, despite their subordinate position within the monastic hierarchy, were protected to a degree by their high-caste status and the resourcefulness of their leader, Dharmachari, the *anis*, as illiterate women from poor farming families, were in no position to resist these male demands and expectations.

Sonam Tendzing had two sons by his first wife, both of whom had remained in Spiti with their mother, and only daughters by his second.[11] As he had no male heir in Nepal, at his death in 1961 his devotees appealed to the Sixteenth Karmapa, Rangjung Rigpe Dorje, who himself, as well as his school, had long-standing ties with the Kathmandu Valley, to appoint a successor.[12] The Karmapa chose the well-known teacher, Urgyen Tulku Rinpoche, to be abbot of Nagi Gompa. Having taken teachings from the Fifteenth Karmapa at Tsurpu Monastery, Urgyen Tulku belonged to both Karmapa and Nyingmapa lineages and was himself the Sixteenth Karmapa's root guru. At the time of his appointment, he was living in Bauddha; he moved to Nagi Gompa and it remained his main base until his death in 1996 (Parajuli 1996).

Newar Lamas

Today there are about thirty Newar monks belonging to the Tibetan tradition, most of whom are elderly Nyingmapa lamas.[13] The oldest, the Ven. Manjushasan, was born in 1918, a Shakya from Mahabauddha, a branch of Uku Baha, Lalitpur. He is today the abbot of Jyata Baha.[14] In 1943, Manjushasan left his wife and two sons and after ordination began his monastic career with a retreat lasting three years, three months, and three days. Though his wife and one surviving son still live nearby and his wife takes the Five Precepts from him on lunar days, his daily needs are taken care of by his devotees rather than his family. He spent six years at Maitri Gompa in Swayambhu and can read Tibetan texts and has translated some of the texts for ritual purposes. However, he cannot take philosophical teachings from Tibetan lamas who teach in Tibetan or in some cases in English, because he knows neither language well. Thus, his main functions are ritual performance and teaching the dharma to local devotees. He is an effective preacher in Nepal Bhasha. He is convinced that traditional Newar Buddhism is too involved in feasting and that it needed the influence of Kyangtse Lama to end its involvement with animal sacrifice. Within the last few years, he has ordained three Maharjan sramaneras who, after living with him in Jyata Baha for some time, went to Bauddha to study under the tutelage of Manjushasan's guru, Chokyi Nyima Rinpoche, in the Ranjung Yeshe Institute in the White Monastery (Seto Gompa).[15]

Living in the White Monastery is another elderly Newar monk named Urgyen Sherab, a Manandhar from Chetrapati in Kathmandu. In contrast with Manjushasan, who had little if any formal schooling, Urgyen Sherab received a university education in India, speaks English fluently and, as Krishna Man Manandhar, was for decades employed as the librarian in the USIS library in Kathmandu.[16] His mother, an early convert to Theravada Buddhism and a devotee of Dhammalok Bhikkhu, had wanted one of her sons, preferably the younger, to ordain as a Theravadin monk. However, Urgyen Sherab's younger brother showed no interest in becoming a monk, and it fell to him to fulfill his mother's desire, which he did after he had retired, albeit in a different branch of Buddhism. He had been impressed by Chokyi Nyima and, after seeking advice, took ordination under him. Urgyen Sherab's plan is to build a monastic complex on land he has bought with a donation from a Japanese devotee at Sirubari near Nuwakot. When his five Tamang chelas whom he brought to Bauddha from Nuwakot and who are currently studying in Ranjung Yeshe Institute in the White Monastery, have completed their monastic training, he will move with them to Sirubari.[17] As he knows little Tibetan, he performs his daily practice in Nepali, and functions as a sort of secretary to his guru, Chokyi Nyima. His international ties have led to his participation in peace marches in the United States and, in 2003, to his donating a set of traditional Nepali musical instruments (*panca baja*) to the New York Metropolitan Museum of Art.

Though none of the chelas of these elderly Newar monks are Tibetan, they receive daily instruction in Tibetan and by the time they graduate from Ranjung Yeshe Institute should be fluent in the language and equipped, theoretically at least, to forge significant monastic careers. But Manjushasan and Urgyen Sherab themselves, given their lack of fluency in Tibetan and their advanced age, are effectively barred from rising in the Karma Kagyu hierarchy.

Newar Anis

It is estimated that between forty and fifty Newar women are nuns belonging to the Tibetan tradition. Most are scattered about in various

Valley gompas where they share quarters with monks for whom they may perform domestic services; their religious role meanwhile is marginal. A few live independently in private homes and support themselves through the gratuities they receive for chanting for laypeople; and about fifteen others, all school-age girls, are divided between Nagi Gompa, the Nyingmapa-Kagyupa monastery above Budha Nilkantha; and Khachoe Ghakyil Ling, a Gelukpa nunnery at the foot of Kopan hill outside Bauddha.[18]

Maya Ani, the abbess of Nagi Gompa, is a woman in her fifties and has been a nun for more than thirty years. Her father, Chaitya Raj Shakya of Bhaktapur, had heard Kyangtse Lama's teachings at Kindo Baha early in 1925 and, soon after Sonam Tendzing arrived in the Valley in the early 1930s, became his devotee. In 1951, he renounced householder life to become a monk in Nagi Gompa where he lived until his death in 1991. When, as a small child, Maya Ani first visited the gompa, Sonam Tendzing, the founding abbot, headed a community of nineteen monks, of whom twelve were Newars, and twenty nuns, including five Newars.[19] "I would see the nuns practicing *nyungne* and I wanted to do it too," she recalls, "but I was still too young, I didn't have the physical strength."[20] Before her mother married her off at age eleven, she learned to meditate on Avalokitesvara, the bodhisattva of compassion, and to read (i.e., to decode but not necessarily understand) Tibetan script. Her marriage was disastrous and in 1966, when she was nineteen, she left her husband and received permission from her oldest brother, who was now head of the family, to become a nun. By this time, Sonam Tendzing was dead and Urgyen Tulku had become abbot. As a novice, Maya Ani memorized prayers and chants, learned to prepare the altar, to make *tormas*, and to play ritual instruments. After three years, she was appointed ritual master (*umje*) and made responsible for overseeing every stage of every ritual conducted in the gompa. As a child visitor she had spent a good deal of time with her father, but after her ordination as a nun she had little to do with him. "I was always busy taking care of my guru, Urgyen Tulku," she explains. "Although I didn't speak Tibetan perfectly, I understood it well and could grasp what he was saying immediately. I was especially useful to him because I was very good at managing money and keeping accounts." When Urgyen Tulku died in 1996, his son and successor, Chokyi Nyima Rinpoche, decided to remain in his White Monastery in Bauddha, where he was attracting large numbers of students, including many foreigners. "At that time there were still a few old monks living at Nagi Gompa as well as many nuns who were senior in ordination to me," says Maya Ani, "but I was chosen as abbess because I had been Urgyen Tulku's favourite cheli."

She has not found her role as abbess easy. On the one hand, she has full financial responsibility for the gompa, which in 2001 housed, in addition to a handful of monks, more than one hundred nuns, including twelve Newars;[21] on the other, she is required to refer all major decisions—regarding the education of the young nuns in her charge, for example—to her abbot. She recalls that while Urgyen Tulku was alive many foreigners would come to the gompa to receive teachings and to take long meditation retreats; on leaving, some would give handsome donations. But after his death their numbers dwindled rapidly. Nowadays, Chokyi Nyima may occasionally send up laypeople who want Tara puja to be performed on their behalf and who, in return for the service, make donations; but he provides the gompa with no other financial help. A German who once studied with the tulku still sends five hundred rupees (worth about US$7 in 2001) each month; aside from this tiny sum, the nuns must depend on their families for supplies of rice and cooking oil and on the monetary donations that they receive for ritual performances. On lunar days, in addition to providing the midday meal, laypeople from the immediate locality offer *dana* with which the nuns whose families do not support them purchase supplies.

Maya Ani recalls that when she ordained in 1966, laypeople rarely invited nuns to perform rituals in their homes. Fortunately however, now that the few monks who remain in Nagi Gompa have grown old, the nuns' ritual role is much enhanced:

> We are called to perform death rituals, rituals to ensure a long life, for wealth, the safe delivery of a baby, success in exams, recovery from illness—in short, rituals of every kind. And because we perform them correctly, not carelessly as some monks do, they are effective. . . . So the laypeople have started to like us.[22]

In particular, they like Maya Ani who, unusually for unschooled Newar women of her generation, speaks Nepali well and can therefore communicate easily with the local people.[23] She shows little interest in sending the young nuns in her charge to school, however, even to an all-girls school.[24] "It would disturb them; they could lose their focus," she says. "They have ordained for life, and if they sat in the classroom with ordinary girls their commitment might be weakened." She admits that, at least for fund-raising purposes, she wishes she knew English, but aside from that, she has no regrets that she did not go to school. What she does regret, however, is her lack of training in debate, the most prestigious aspect of the Tibetan monastic education. She would like the young nuns of Nagi Gompa to have access to the same training that novice monks in the White Monastery receive, but admits that this is unlikely to happen. "The monks who teach the sramaneras have their hands full; they've got too many students already, and anyway, supposing they accepted our nuns, they would charge fees and I don't have the money." She adds that these are not the only hurdles: For one thing, she doubts that her abbot, Chokyi Nyima, would agree to young nuns studying alongside novices. For another, even if he raised no objection, the older nuns in Nagi Gompa would emphatically oppose the idea. "They are quite old-fashioned," Maya Ani remarks sadly.

Khachoe Ghakyil Ling nunnery, an offshoot of Kopan Monastery outside Bauddha, is the other monastic institution in which more than a handful of Newar nuns are found and presents quite a contrast to Nagi Gompa. It was established in 1972 by two Gelukpa monks, Lama Yeshe, a Tibetan, and Lama Zopa, a Sherpa, cofounders of the Foundation for the Preservation of Tibetan Buddhism and prolific authors who have become well known in the West.[25] For the first two decades of its existence, Khachoe Ghakyil Ling's drab barrack-like buildings on swampy land at the foot of the hill made a sorry contrast with Kopan's elaborate hilltop monastic complex, but, by 2001, foreign donations had transformed the nunnery. It still lacks Kopan's spectacular setting, but its massive new dharma hall, dormitory, and classroom building are impressive.[26] Today Khachoe houses about three hundred *anis* from several ethnic groups, including nine Newars all of whom are Maharjans.[27] Many had first ordained at Chobhar or in Maitri Gompa, Swayambhu, and from there been sent on to Khachoe by their abbot.

The Maitri Gompa monastery goes back to 1953–54.[28] The previous abbot, Sumati Sangh, had hoped to build a nunnery next door to his gompa, but never managed to realize his plan. Bhikshu Tsultrim, his Maharjan successor, decided to transfer the six young nuns who were living at the time in Maitri Gompa to Khachyoe Ghakyil Ling nunnery where they would benefit from the more academic training on offer. Uniformly from poor rural backgrounds, some claim that they were attracted to monastic life because they had a family member who was a nun; in most cases, however, it is more likely that it was their parents' decision to bring them to the nunnery in order to earn merit.

Newar nuns in the Tibetan tradition, studying at Khachoe Gakhyil Ling, 9th April 2002. (David N. Gellner)

Though logic and debating have been taught in a few Tibetan nunneries in India since the mid-1980s (Havnevik 1990: 118, 197), Khachoe is unique among Tibetan nunneries in Nepal in that it claims to provide its novice nuns with an education equal to the one offered to novice monks. This consists of sutra and commentary study, debate, Buddhist logic, and English. Novice nuns, who are housed in the original buildings, start out by taking Tibetan language classes from a lay teacher and by memorizing the entire ritual handbook, a task that may take up to two years. Only when they have it by heart and have been tested by their abbot, Khenpo Geshe Lhundrup, can they move into the new building and start taking courses from a monk who comes down daily from Kopan. But whereas the expenses of the novice monks at Kopan are covered by donations from the Tibetan refugee community and from foreigners who take teachings from Lama Zopa both at Kopan and on his frequent tours overseas, the novice nuns must look to their families for funds for food and routine expenses as well as school fees.[29]

At present, it remains unclear whether the two main groups of Newar Tibetan nuns face different futures or not, and it will depend on wider developments within Tibetan Buddhism. The young nuns of

Nagi Gompa receive training in ritual performance alone and are gaining respect as ritualists, although they are firmly inferior to the monks with their academic training. The nuns of Khachoe Ghakyil Ling, on the other hand, are studying Tibetan Buddhism academically and follow much the same curriculum as novice monks. However, because they are not and cannot become fully ordained nuns, unless the Gelukpa hierarchy accepts the introduction of bhikshuni ordination from China, their status within the Tibetan Sangha—educated to the same level as monks, denied the status of bhikshuni—will remain ambiguous.[30] Whether equal education opportunities will lead to equal career opportunities for these young nuns remains to be seen.

Lay Adherents of Tibetan Buddhism

After 1959, the Newar presence in Tibet almost entirely disappeared as merchants were forced to close their businesses and retreat to Kathmandu, where some of them, once reestablished in the Valley, reconfirmed their Tibetan Buddhist ties. None of these wealthy businessmen are exclusively devoted to Tibetan Buddhism. As with other Newars, they continue to call Vajracharya priests to their houses to perform life-cycle rituals. Meanwhile, their wives, in many cases, are devotees of Dhammawati Guruma or one of the senior bhikkhus who are both competent and willing to teach them the *dharma* in contrast with the Tibetan monks who in general are not. Thus, at their wives' urging, many well-to-do businessmen offer *bhojana dana* and make generous donations to the Theravadins as well.[31]

The Chinese takeover sent a stream of refugees into the Valley. Some decades later this resulted in a fever of monastery-building. In 1985, Ugen Gombo reported that there were twenty-five Tibetan gompas inhabited by about four hundred monks in the Valley. In 1992, Mireille Helffer counted sixteen gompas in Bauddha alone (Helffer 1993). Ten years later, there were probably double that number, and dozens more elsewhere in and around the Kathmandu Valley.[32] Today, newly constructed monasteries, funded in large part by devotees from Taiwan and Singapore and to a lesser a degree by devotees from Europe and North America, stand on almost every hill surrounding the city.

Newars have also contributed to this explosion of Tibetan Buddhism. Their foundations include an elaborate gompa in Kamaladi near Rani Pokhari; one on the Vishnumati River; two in Bhaktapur; and one in the village of Baregaon and another in the village of Chapagaon, both south of Lalitpur. In each case, the donor presented his new building to his guru to use as he thought fit, whether as a temple or a meditation retreat center.

Today the Newar Tibetan Buddhist community of Lalitpur centers on Kwa Baha and is headed by the sons and grandsons of some of Sonam Tendzing Rinpoche's earliest followers. Soon after his arrival in Valley, Sonam Tendzing attracted devotees not only from the Tamang villages around Nagi Gompa but also from the Shakya communities of Bhaktapur and Lalitpur. In the 1940s, some of his Kwa Baha devotees, all Shakyas with long-standing family connections with Tibet, established an organization they called the Saddharma Suraksha Sangh, or Association for the Preservation of the True Dharma, which financed the conversion of an upper hall in Kwa Baha as a shrine to Amoghapasha Lokeshvara, decorated in Tibetan style.

In 1999, Nem Ratna Shakya, a son of Dev Ratna Shakya who was one of the original members of the Sangh, offered to finance the renovation of a second shrine in Kwa Baha, dedicated to Amitabha. It boasts a series of murals depicting the Abhirati heaven of Amitabha on which Lok Chitrakar, a well-known Newar painter, and a team of young Newar artists worked for several years.[33]

Since its consecration, the Kwa Baha gompa has been tended by Newar monks belonging to the Tibetan tradition (Gellner 1992: 168): the fact that it has no resident monks and is run—in keeping with Newar tradition—entirely by laypeople, makes it unique among Tibetan monasteries.[34] By 1998, membership of the Saddharma Suraksha Sangh had increased to thirty-two; their responsibilities included the organization of numerous lunar calendar ceremonies.[35] Members regard Sonam Tendzing's lineage descendents, Chokyi Nyima and Chokling Tulku, as their gurus and continue to take Tibetan initiations from them.[36]

They have experienced difficulties in this regard, however, in that for some years their gurus did not inform them when they were scheduled to give teachings, and if the devotees heard about them and attended regardless, they would be humiliated when their guru's Western assistants demanded they pay the same high fee (US$200) that foreigners paid. Finally, in 1996 they agreed to a fee their Newar devotees could afford and relations improved. Even so, as one member of the group put it:

> These big lamas are interested in foreigners because they can pay whatever they ask. But Newars, who have been their devotees for decades,

> whose fathers and even grandfathers were their devotees, they treat differently. . . . Because in comparison with foreigners we are poor, they don't respect us.

Members also occasionally receive teachings from other lamas whom they invite to Kwa Baha, and in recent years, a layman has offered philosophy courses during Gunla; but unlike most Theravada viharas, the gompa offers neither a Saturday program nor routine instruction for children or even for adults. As a gompa officer observed, in the Tibetan tradition the role of the laity consists of *puja*, *dana*, and performing the four preliminary practices; laypeople are not expected to study the *dharma*. Nevertheless, gompa officers estimate that between two thousand and three thousand people regularly visit the gompa. "Most people in our community are Maharjans and Shakyas," one said. "But Vajracharyas have never been interested in Tibetan Buddhism. They see (Tibetan) Mahayanists as competition."

Thus, access to Tibetan lamas and the spread of Tibetan Buddhism among the Newars has been steady rather than spectacular once the initial impact of Kyangtse Lama's charismatic preaching had been absorbed. But there are signs of new departures in recent years, which indicate that it is not just Theravada Buddhism that is spreading beyond its former Newar ethnic enclave. For example, Shridhar Shamsher Rana, a grandson of Padma Shamsher, became a Tibetan initiate as Chyoki Dorje or Dharmavajra and is a disciple of Urgyen Tulku Rinpoche. Shridhar Rana was educated at St. Xavier's (the Jesuit-run boarding school in Kathmandu) and in Europe and is therefore well versed in Western interpretations of Tibetan Buddhism, as well as in Sanskrit and Tibetan. He has taken teachings from many Tibetan gurus and has attracted a number of non-Newar followers. Nanda Prasad Timilsina (Baghindrasila), a Parbatiya Brahman, likewise discovered Buddhism in Varanasi and then studied in Dehradun up to Khenpo level in the Sakyapa tradition. He now preaches Mahayana Buddhism regularly in Nepali to an ethnically mixed audience. Both he and S. S. Rana see it as a major part of their mission to translate Tibetan Buddhist texts into Nepali (Singh 1996: 41–45; Parajuli 2000).

Reforming Newar Buddhism

In contrast to those, just described, who would simply *switch* to Tibetan Buddhism, there are also activists who believe that *renewal* is possible and practicable and have made considerable efforts to revive the Newar tradition. To this end, they have used several approaches, including:

1. The retransmission by Tibetan monks of meditation practices that Nepali Buddhists transmitted to Tibet many centuries ago but have since disappeared in Nepal;
2. Ritual training for young men from priestly families;
3. The revival of important rituals that are rarely or no longer performed;
4. Public lectures on Mahayana topics;
5. Nepal Bhasha translations of Sanskrit and Tibetan texts.

In an attempt to retain young Vajracharyas in the tradition, prominent Vajracharya priests have organized training courses in ritual performance. Among them is Buddha Ratna Vajracharya from Kwa Baha, who, in 1978, at the suggestion of the Vajracharya *guthi*,[37] instructed fifteen young Vajracharya men for one hour each day over a period of several months. In 1990, he gave a second training course for which, in contrast with the first course that had been open only to Vajracharyas from Kwa Baha itself, he accepted thirty-five students from throughout Lalitpur. That year only seven or eight completed the course. In 1997, he offered his course again to thirty-five students with sponsorship from the Himalayan Buddhist Education Foundation (HBEF) supported by a Taiwanese donor. With the support of the HBEF Buddha Ratna has continued to give a course on an annual basis, even though, as he noted in 2002, over the previous five years only seven of his students were actually practicing as *purohits*.[38]

Ritual revivals, led by Vajracharyas, include the *sapta vidhanottara puja*, a rite of protection that, between December 1997 and March 2001, was performed 132 times each winter near Emperor Asoka's pillar in Lumbini. Because the Lumbini Development Trust had excluded Newar Buddhists from its management committee, an important objective of the ritual's organizers was to provide a Newar Buddhist presence at Lumbini not only so that foreign pilgrims might become aware of the Newar Buddhist tradition but also to force the Lumbini Development Trust to acknowledge its importance and give it a place in the management of the sacred site.[39] Several priests were recruited and trained to take ten-day ritual shifts, though primary responsibility for the performances at Lumbini was assumed by Vikash

Vajracharya from Kathmandu. Three hundred devotees, including eighteen elders (*aju*), one from each of Lalitpur's eighteen *baha*, some of whom had never been out of the Kathmandu Valley before in their lives, and the Gyanmala troop from Uku Baha were bused down to Lumbini to attend the 365th and final puja on March 6, 2001. The cost of transport, food, and lodging for so many people was quite easily covered given that, as one of the organizers observed, Newar Buddhists believe giving *dana* is the most meritorious of all activities. Plans to revive a second ritual, worship of the *dharmadhatu mandala*, which represents the philosophical basis of Newar Buddhist belief, were not yet finalized as of 2002; but a third traditional practice, the telling of stories (*avadana*) about the Buddha's former lives as a means of teaching Buddhist ethics, has been energetically revived.

Religious storytelling on holy days in shrines and temples had once been an important and regular feature of Newar Buddhism (Lewis 2000a: chs. 2–3); but though Badri Ratna Vajracharya had continued the practice in Jana Baha, Kathmandu, it had not been done in Bhaktapur and Lalitpur since the 1980s. Buddha Ratna Vajracharya's ritual training courses sparked an interest in lunar day traditions in Lalitpur, however, and, as a result, over a two-year period (1998–2000) on every full-moon day a Vajracharya priest would recount *Avadanas* at a sacred place in and around Lalitpur; this would be followed by a meal for up to five hundred laypeople who attended each session.[40]

Newar Buddhist revivalists are keenly aware that ignorance of the philosophical underpinnings of the rituals they perform is even more widespread among Vajracharya priests than it was a generation or more ago. Their response has been to offer courses on Mahayana Buddhism not only to young Western-educated men and women who evince an interest in their tradition but also to older people who may be largely unschooled. An important focus has been on Tantric Initiation, primarily the initiation of Chakrasamvara and his consort Vajravarahi, which, by the early 1980s, had, compared to the period before 1951, sharply declined among members of those high castes who were eligible to take it.[41] In contrast to previous initiations, which had only involved ritual performance and mantra transmission, and minimal explanation and instruction, in 2001 would-be initiates belonging to Kwa Baha heard five two-hour lectures designed to equip them to be teachers (*acarya*) of their tradition. The series began with a consideration of the Three Yanas and continued with discussions of Buddha nature, the importance of the precious human body, qualities to be looked for in a Spiritual Friend, and lastly, the Four Noble Truths. As one of the lecturers noted, it was a lot of material to cover in only ten hours. Nevertheless, the series was well received and the expectation is that it will be repeated for the next cohort of initiates.

Min Bahadur Shakya: Reviving Newar Buddhism by Studying Tibet

Min Bahadur Shakya, a short, dark-haired man who looks much younger than his fifty years, lives a double life. He devotes his mornings to teaching mathematics at the Engineering College and much of the rest of his time to the study and teaching of Mahayana Buddhist philosophy. At a time when many western-educated Newar Buddhists have turned away from their indigenous religious institutions, Min Bahadur is something of an anomaly. Though he too believes that Newar Buddhism is critically stagnant if not moribund, in his view, rather than abandon its ancient practices for Theravada modernism, the community should look to the Tibetan tradition, which historically is so closely related to their own, as a source of renewal. The revitalization of Vajrayana Buddhism should be based on the retransmission—or "downloading" to use his expression—of the deeper spiritual understandings found in Tibetan Buddhism to the younger generation of Newar Buddhists, especially the younger generation of Vajracharya priests. There are many unique features of the Newars' Buddhist tradition, which, once lost, will be lost for the whole world. It is to prevent this, and for the promotion of the whole Mahayana-Vajrayana tradition within Nepal, that he has dedicated his life.

Min Bahadur comes from a family of Kwa Baha goldsmiths with ties to Tibet. Though his paternal grandfather spent time in Lhasa and, like most Newar craftsmen and traders residing in Tibetan towns, must surely have visited monasteries and shrines for devotional purposes, he does not seem to have developed an interest in Tibetan Buddhist practice. By contrast, though he had never visited Tibet, Min Bahadur's father became a devotee of Sonam Tendzing Rinpoche in the 1940s. For the rest of his life he remained a staunch member of the Saddharma Suraksha Sangh, which, as described above, was set up to maintain the Tibetan-style gompa in Kwa Baha. As one of its officeholders, he regularly took his sons to the gompa, and Min Bahadur vividly remembers, aged three or four, gazing at the scarlet, blue, green, and gold frescoes on the gompa walls from his perch on his father's shoulders.

Though in adulthood his three brothers would take little interest in religion, in due course Min Bahadur became an officeholder in the Kwa Baha gompa as his father had been before him.[42] Min Bahadur recalls:

> When I was a boy my father would take me to visit his teachers, and though to start with I'd feel strange going to see those lamas—after all, my friends' parents didn't go to see lamas, they were mostly traditional Vajrayana Buddhists—as I grew older I got used to doing prostrations and I stopped feeling so different and strange.

After Min Bahadur finished university, he had to wait almost a year for his exam results and, during that time, he would go to libraries to read biographies of great scientists. One day he happened upon Shantideva's *Bodhicaryavatara*:

> I was captivated, and with that began my study of Mahayana Buddhism. I read Evans-Wentz's books and decided I wanted to learn to read Tibetan, so I found myself a teacher and for the next five years I studied with him.

In 1976, Min Bahadur went on a pilgrimage arranged by the Young Men's Buddhist Association, an organization that was strongly Theravada in its orientation, to the north Indian sacred places. While on that trip, he was asked to take over the editorship of the YMBA journal. Even though he was not yet a member of the organization, he accepted the assignment and joined the YMBA. Despite his Mahayanist orientation, he became secretary and later president, and over the next decade brought out eight issues of the *Young Buddhist* magazine with articles on a wide range of Buddhist topics in English:

> I realized that the great majority of YMBA members knew next to nothing about Mahayana Buddhism. They were unhappy with our own Vajrayana tradition and were looking for something else and Theravada was what they had latched on to. But the root of our tradition isn't Theravada, it's Mahayana. . . . I decided that because our YMBA members were already having an intensive exposure to Theravada thought, my purpose should be to present them with an alternative—I should try to provide a balanced outlook by educating them about the Mahayana tradition. This involved exposing them to lamas who could teach the tradition, and to texts. But this posed a very serious problem: the lamas spoke neither Nepali nor Nepal Bhasha—only Tibetan and sometimes English. And their texts were all written either in Tibetan or Sanskrit which very few Newars could read.

Because Min Bahadur spoke some Tibetan as well as English, he was able to translate for the lamas when they were invited to speak at

YMBA meetings. Eager to reach as wide an audience as possible, he generally translated their lectures into Nepali as well as Nepal Bhasha. Meanwhile, he was aware that Nisthananda's 1914 translation of the *Lalitavistara*, the Mahayanist version of the Buddha's biography, had had a major impact on the Newar Buddhist community; furthermore, he noted that following the staging in Lalitpur in 1924 of a dramatized version of the biography, several people had been inspired to take Tibetan ordination. Now, as secretary of the YMBA, he proposed that the association republish Nisthananda's translation.

Because the *Lalitavistara*'s account of the Buddha's life prior to enlightenment was drawn from the Sarvastivada tradition and differed sharply from the *Tripitaka* account, some Theravada monks vehemently opposed publication. The *Lalitavistara* account of the Buddha's life was the one popularly known in Nepal, and Theravada monks sometimes found themselves criticized by the laity for "not knowing the Buddha's life story." They tried to object on scholarly grounds, namely that Nisthananda had amalgamated various different scriptures in producing his version. But Min Bahadur continued to push his proposal until the YMBA executive committee was won over, whereupon he edited Nisthananda's translation and added an English-language introduction in which he explained that, far from being definitive, this was just one of several accounts of Shakyamuni Buddha's early life (M. B. Shakya 1997b). He and his friends raised money to print a thousand copies and it appeared under the auspices of the YMBA in 1978. Unable to prevent Nisthananda's *Lalitavistara* from being republished, the Theravada monks organized the reissue of Mahapragya's version of the Buddha's life story, which closely followed Rahul Sankrityayan's Hindi version based on Pali sources—to which Mahapragya had then applied the traditional Mahayanist title, the *Lalitavistara*. Mahapragya had composed this decades earlier and there were only eighty copies of the original printing.[43] This time, far more were printed, and many Newar Buddhists, seeking to acquire Nisthananda's traditionalist life of the Buddha, unwittingly found themselves reading a version of the Pali account. Given all this opposition to the *Lalitavistara* by senior members of the Theravada Sangha, it is somewhat ironic that this 1978 edition moved several people to take ordination, just as the Nisthananda's original had—only this time in the Theravada rather than in the Tibetan (Mahayana) Buddhist tradition.[44]

When S. N. Goenka came to Nepal to teach vipassana in 1982, Min Bahadur and some other YMBA members volunteered to assist him;

but Goenka told them that anyone who didn't hold with his views 100 percent should leave. So Min Bahadur, who disagreed with him on a number of issues, including his insistence that textual study was not important, resigned and resumed the meditation practices he had learned from his Tibetan teachers.[45] In response to what he perceived as the narrow-mindedness—if not downright ignorance—of the Theravadins, he helped to organize weekly teachings in Lalitpur by Pandit Dibya Vajra Vajracharya in 1983–84 on Shantideva's *Bodhicaryavatara* and its commentary; these were later published in Nepal Bhasha. Min Bahadur explains,

> The *Bodhicaryavatara* includes not only instruction on bodhisattva meditation but a long chapter on how to control one's mind. We published it just when vipassana meditation was becoming popular here. And all of a sudden local people realized that the Mahayanists too were offering a meditation practice, that it wasn't *only* the Theravadins who could teach them to meditate.

Meanwhile, Min Bahadur had become president of the YMBA and had been invited to attend the World Fellowship of Buddhist Youth Conference that was to meet in Japan in 1978:

> I asked myself, How can I accept this invitation? I'm a college teacher, not a businessman. I have no money for the plane fare. But I was very fortunate—I was able to get a loan from my well-wishers to pay for air travel and other expenses. Apart from India, I'd never been out of Nepal before and more important, I'd never been exposed to the views of other Buddhists. What I encountered in Japan for the first time was ecumenical thinking: I realized that there was more than one way to nirvana.

The following year, in 1982, he was invited to the International Religious Foundation's Youth Seminar on World Religion in the United States, which was sponsored by the Reverand Sun Myong Moon's Unification Church. At the conclusion of the seminar, he and the four other Nepali delegates, together with 130 delegates from the United States and many developing countries, visited some of the world's most important pilgrimage places on a two-month tour that began in Barrytown, New York, and ended in Seoul. On this and other trips he made on YMBA business, Min Bahadur developed a network of foreign contacts, perhaps the most significant of whom was a young Taiwanese scholar named Dr. Yo Hsiang Chou, whom he met in 1984 when both were delegates to a conference in Sri Lanka organized by the World Fellowship of Buddhist Youth. At that time, Dr. Yo was teaching in

Taiwan at Fo Guang Shan Buddhist University while working on a doctoral thesis that concerned Madhyamika philosophy, a topic of great interest to Min Bahadur. Their friendship deepened as they exchanged materials and met from time to time at conferences. It was on a visit to Fo Guang Shan that Min Bahadur first met Master Xingyun, at that time abbot of the monastery, whose missionary organization, the Buddhist Light International Association, has since become active in several dozen countries (as described in Chapter 7).

In the early 1980s, Min Bahadur and an Indian friend had registered an organization for the study of Hinduism and Buddhism with the Nepalese government; however, since nongovernmental organizations were closely controlled under the Panchayat regime, they decided to conceal their purpose by calling their organization "The Nagarjuna Institute of Exact Methods" so that the government would think their focus was computer science rather than religion.

For almost a decade, the center existed only on paper. Min Bahadur was busy with other things: the YMBA; a short-lived Buddhist institute named the Dharmodaya Sabha, for which he taught a course in Mahayana philosophy; a journal titled *Buddhist Himalaya* that he founded after his office as YMBA president expired; and last but not least, a year's study (1989–90) in the Bhutanese Archives, funded by SAARC (the South Asian Association for Regional Cooperation). In 1988, he decided that, even though his cofounder had drifted away, the time was ripe to bring the Nagarjuna Institute of Exact Methods to life. Using some money he had saved from his SAARC fellowship and funds from the sale of a piece of land he had inherited, he purchased a plot in Chakupat, Lalitpur, on which he planned to build a library.

Meanwhile, his friend Dr. Yo had received his doctorate and moved up from the World Fellowship of Buddhist Youth to become a vice president of the World Fellowship of Buddhists (WFB); his mandate was to channel funds for educational projects to a number of countries, including Nepal. In 1993, Dr. Yo, who had a personal interest in the revitalization of Newar Buddhism, made the first of several grants to the Nagarjuna Institute, enabling Min Bahadur to start the construction of his library and run the journal *Buddhist Himalaya*:

> As soon as the roof was on the ground floor, I moved in with my wife and children and started teaching a course on Mahayana Buddhism. Renting a hall would have cost one thousand rupees each time, and I couldn't afford that. So I did the best I could in the unfinished building with wires sticking out of the walls. I charged a registration fee but it

> wasn't much and some of the students couldn't pay so I let them in for nothing. Though at first all the students were Newars, predominantly young Vajracharyas, before long Shakyas took the lead, and people from outside our community—Tamangs, Gurungs, even some Hindus—started to enroll. By 1998, more than two hundred laypeople and monastics had taken our course. Before Tribhuvan University established a postgraduate diploma in Buddhist Studies in 1999, we were offering the only systematic course in Buddhist philosophy in Nepal. We taught all kinds of Buddhism: Theravada, the four Tibetan schools, Madhyamika, Yogachara, Vajrayana. With one exception, Vajrayana, finding teachers from all these traditions hasn't been a problem. Of course there are plenty of Vajrayana Gubhajus around but it's difficult to find one who can talk articulately about his tradition. . . . Gubhajus know how to conduct rituals but they can't explain what they mean.

For the first few years it was in operation, the Nagarjuna Institute of Exact Methods continued to receive funds raised by Dr. Yo from a variety of sources, including wealthy Taiwanese individuals and Fo Guang Shan Monastery itself. The HBEF, founded in 1995, in which Min Bahadur was a prime mover, has been described in Chapter 8.

Min Bahadur has been tireless in his support of women in the Buddhist community, and from the start, students attending courses at both the Nagarjuna Institute and the awareness camps have been almost equally divided by gender. Furthermore, though he himself is a Mahayanist and his sister ordained as a Tibetan nun, he has gone to great lengths to support Theravada nuns. He not only has encouraged them to study in his center but also on occasion has approached wealthy Buddhist businessmen to provide funding to enable them to attend conferences abroad. Moreover, he organized funding for the party of twelve nuns to travel to India to receive *upasampada* according to Mahayana rites in February 1998, and he also made their travel arrangements and chaperoned the group to and from Bodh Gaya himself. In contrast with the senior Theravada monks who remain deeply antagonistic to *bhikshuni* ordination, Min Bahadur is fully in favor of Theravada nuns being ordained by Mahayana rites, not only because it should enhance their status within their community but also because, in his view even more important, this cross-pollination might ultimately provide a bridge between the two traditions.

One feature of the Mahayana ordination rites that has especially interested Min Bahadur is the—third and final—"Bodhisattva" vow.[46] In his view, compassionate thought and action are the two central features of the Buddhist life. Moreover, he believes that his main task is to establish—or reestablish—in the Nepalese Buddhist community bodhisattva practice, specifically a meditation practice known as *bodhicitta* (Generating the Thought of Enlightenment), which he terms "the most powerful weapon against the *kleshas* that there is." He has translated into Nepali two books on *bodhicitta* authored by the Dalai Lama; sixty thousand copies were printed in Taiwan and are distributed freely in Nepal to those who are interested.

Preserving the Newar Buddhist Tradition

Although many Shakyas and Uday revere Tibetan teachers, and individual Vajracharyas may have taken teachings from them, as a group, Vajracharyas have seen their task as *preserving* the tradition that has come down to them. It is a tradition rich in ritual and providing much spiritual, social, and pragmatic sustenance to its many followers. But because it is fully embedded in a traditional caste system, and because it lacks the full-time, permanent, celibate option, and because, therefore, it provides no religious or priestly vocation either for women or for non-Vajracharyas, it cannot retain its hereditary adherents if they feel moved to renounce and become monastics. Perhaps even more seriously, it cannot retain the deepest allegiance of lay adherents when they acquire modern-style education and become reflexive about their own tradition.

Despite these drawbacks, discussed further in chapter 10, thousands of shrines and chaityas in hundreds of monasteries continue to provide a devotional focus for the Newar Buddhist community in which a substantial majority still observes traditional life-cycle rites, sponsors protective rituals, and celebrates festival in honor of buddhas and bodhisattvas as well as gods and goddesses of the Hindu-Buddhist pantheon.

Bir Bajra Vajracharya: "This Is What I Want to Do, and I Hope My Son Will Want to Do it Also."

Bir Bajra Vajracharya, the Rituals Officer (*betaju*) of Kwa Baha in Lalitpur, seeks to preserve Newar Buddhism by practicing it to the best of his ability and passing it on to others. He has been a practicing priest for about twenty years and reports that he has almost more work than he can handle:

> This is the work of my caste. My father was a *purohit* and my son will be one after me. I have never considered doing any other work because I

inherited so many *jajman* from my father. At the moment I am *purohit* for about one hundred *jajman*: sixty percent are Shakyas, twenty-five percent are Jyapus, and the rest Vajracharyas like myself. From time to time a joint household splits up and then I have additional *jajman* to take care of so I am always getting busier and busier. Luckily I have my younger brother Hem Bajra to help me with my ritual work.

After their father's death when Bir Bajra was seven and Hem Bajra was only two, the boys and their mother continued to live with their paternal grandmother. Their father's *jajman* were taken over by two distantly related *purohits*, and their mother supported the family by making curios. The brothers both underwent Monastic Initiation (*bare chuyegu*) at about seven years of age. They took Consecration as a Vajra-Master (*aca luyegu*, *acarya abhiseka*) when Bir Bajra was fifteen and Hem Bajra was ten. Consecration made them eligible to work as family priests and was the preamble to Tantric Initiation (*diksa*), which they took three years later, at eighteen and thirteen respectively.[47]

It was right after my Consecration as a Vajra-Master and after completing Class Five [i.e., the final year of primary school] that I began learning the work of a *purohit*. For the first two years, for two hours every morning, I would read and memorize ritual texts. Most important was learning to pronounce them correctly. My teachers were the two Vajracharyas who had been taking care of my father's *jajmans*. And then in the third year they started taking me with them when they went to perform rituals in different households. I would watch what they were doing and follow along in my handbook, and once they felt I knew how to perform a ritual they would have me do it on my own. Of course since they were my teachers I had to pay them a "fee" (*gurudaksina*) three times a year, on the festivals of Guru Purnima, Magh Shri Panchami, and Sarasvati Panchami. In those days we gave whatever we could afford—it wasn't like nowadays with school fees, which are set at a certain amount. At first one of my teachers would accompany me but after a while, when they had confidence in me, they would send me out alone. The fact is many of the *jajman* were elderly people who knew the rituals very well so that if I made a mistake they would notice. I can tell you that to begin with I found the work pretty hard. . . . But by the time I turned twenty I was working completely on my own. These days I know the work of a *purohit* so well that I can help younger people. In Aki Baha there's a kind of school called Vajracharya Charya Adhyayan Mandal. The head teacher is Kaji Ratna Vajracharya; then comes Mangal Raj Vajracharya, and the third teacher is myself.

In addition to performing life-cycle and other rituals for the parishioners he had inherited from his father, soon after he began to practice independently as a *purohit*, Bir Bajra began to read and recite the *Prajna Paramita*, an ancient copy of which is kept in Kwa Baha.[48] Recitations of this text, which are sponsored both by members of Kwa Baha and outsiders, require ten Vajracharyas, seven of whom are provided by the baha and three by the sponsor. Bir Bajra, who inherited the right to recite it and to a share of the income a recitation generates, has been reciting the *Prajna Paramita* on as many as three hundred mornings a year since he was twenty. By the time he got married, aged twenty-two, he was already well established in his hereditary profession:

> For me, the morning is rather busy. I get up at five o'clock in warm weather and at six-thirty in winter. Then I have to perform *nhikã puja*—after taking *aca luyegu* you must do *nhikã* every morning for the rest of your life—and recite the mantras that I received when I took *diksa*. All this takes about one hour and then, without eating or drinking anything because one must fast in order to recite, I go to Kwa Baha for the recitation (*pa thyakegu*). This takes about three hours—an hour to set up and almost two hours for the reading. I can only break my fast when I get home. These days the recitation is very popular and there's always a waiting list. We could probably have a sponsor every day were it not for the fact that recitations are forbidden during the month of Gunla (August/September) as well as on certain [holy] days during the year.

Bir Bajra's mother came from a Shakya family, which meant that though she could assist his father in all other rituals, she could not give the mantras in Tantric Initiation (*diksa*). His wife, however, is a Vajracharya by birth and has taken full Tantric Initiation. She assisted him recently in a large performance of Tantric Initiation where he was the second in charge, and there were seventy-two candidates: twenty-five couples, and twenty-two people on their own (either unmarried or whose partners did not wish to take it). If he finds that a ritual performance in a household conflicts with a *Prajna Paramita* recitation in Kwa Baha, he postpones the domestic ritual until after the recitation is over. More than two ritual engagements on a single day he cannot manage; when three are scheduled he performs two himself and sends his younger brother Hem Bajra to perform the third. Though Hem Bajra received a master's degree in business and works in an NGO, he too trained as a *purohit* and helps out when needed.

Today, though Bir Bajra continues to do some of the silversmith work that he learned as a child from his mother, most of his time is spent practicing as a priest. In addition to reciting the *Prajna Paramita* and working as a *purohit*, at the relatively young age of thirty-one, he was appointed Rituals Officer of Kwa Baha. He is in charge of scheduling all life-cycle, calendrical, and Tantric rites that occur in Kwa Baha, the most important, in his view, being Monastic Initiation (*bare chuyegu*) and the induction ritual for new monastic elders (*nayo luyegu*). Aside from scheduling a ritual, he frequently participates in its performance also, and for each one of the services he performs, he receives fees (*daksina*). In 1998, which was a relatively prosperous time in Nepal, he told us:

> In the past people were very poor, they couldn't afford to give much as *daksina*. But now some people are able to give quite a lot more. They give one hundred, two hundred, or three hundred rupees, depending on their income. Compared with a few years ago, people have begun to understand not only that ritual performance is important but that the *purohit* should be paid accordingly. Also, they have come to realize that practices our ancestors established should be kept up and so some, which had been abandoned, are once again being performed. Speaking for myself, I shall stick to uplifting my *jajman*, fulfilling their requests [for ritual performance]. . . . This is what I want to do, and I hope my son will want to do it also. Though he's only six years old, I've already begun to take him with me sometimes when I'm invited to perform rituals. I want him to learn my work. . . . If I were to give up and he didn't take my place, there would be no one to serve our *jajman*. . . . Someone in our family has to continue doing this work.

But though Bir Bajra's parishioners increase every year, the Buddhism that he practices has to fight against the modernist stereotype that it is little more than a ritually complex structure whose foundation is superstition and ignorance. The future of Newar Buddhism, which the early Theravadins set out to "cleanse," is certainly in question. Rather than cleansing it, the Theravadins have hastened its decay by drawing away the educated and wealthy members of their community who might, under other circumstances, have injected new life into indigenous Buddhist institutions. As the number of Vajracharyas and Shakyas who have taken Tantric Initiation dwindles, regular participation in and responsibility for *baha* affairs is reduced to an ever smaller circle, though this may be less of a problem in a *baha* like Kwa Baha with a very large membership. Bir Bajra's hope that his son will follow in his footsteps is exceptional; most practicing Vajracharya priests do their best to educate their sons for modern occupations that generate a living wage. Bir Bajra himself lives in a joint household with his brother who, with his modern-sector employment, can be relied on to contribute substantially to family expenses.

The Future of Newar Buddhism

Todd Lewis (2000b) has suggested that Newars who are seeking to revive their own Buddhist tradition might learn from diaspora Tibetans. The Tibetans, by taking their version of the dharma to the world, have succeeded in transforming a local tradition into a global tradition. He urges Newar Buddhists to follow the Tibetan example in the belief that they, too, will find that Mahayana doctrine, when carefully explained, has a powerful attraction for the young and educated everywhere. Lewis even has suggestions as to how such a mission might be financed.

One issue that Lewis does not mention is the place of women in the tradition. From the modern female perspective, the marginalization of women in Newar Buddhism constitutes a profound and possibly fatal flaw. Aside from wives (*guruma*) who help their Vajracharya spouses prepare ritual requisites, women can only be devotees and donors. They cannot be ritual specialists or teachers and only under most unusual circumstances can they be students of the dharma. Without the introduction of fundamental structural changes providing for the inclusion of women—of whom today, as ever, the majority of the actively engaged lay community is composed, and whose rise and importance within the Theravada movement has been described—efforts to revive traditional Newar Buddhism within the Valley would seem doomed to be small in scale and limited in their impact.

The exclusion of women is part of a larger problem, namely the continued exclusion of non-Vajracharyas, men or women, from the priestly role in Newar Buddhism and the exclusion of all but the highest castes from receiving the highest teachings and taking Tantric Initiation. When the Lotus Research Center held a big conference on the Buddhist heritage of the Kathmandu Valley in 1998, it was left to a non-Newar, Punya Parajuli, to point this out (Parajuli 1999: 275). His point was not picked up or even mentioned by any of the eminent Newar Buddhists invited to speak. It is true that, as a response to Theravada temporary ordination rituals, Badri Ratna Vajracharya has carried out a temporary ordination in Lumbini of non-Shakya, non-Vajracharya men. But there are no proposals to open the higher roles in Newar Buddhism to those who show aptitude for them, as opposed to those born into the right families.

One further problem for Newar Buddhists seeking to emulate the Tibetans, a corollary of what has already been noted, is that they lack the monastic institutions that exist even in the Nyingma and Bonpo traditions of Tibet and that are able to act as a core around which lay emigrants can gather, reconstruct, and then reach out for Western followers. Thus, there is no obvious leader of any kind, and certainly none of the stature of the Dalai Lama. Furthermore, only some Newars identify strongly with a Newar identity as opposed to a more broadly based Nepali identity; and even among those who do, they do not necessarily come from a Buddhist background. When diaspora Newars do have a strong personal commitment to Buddhism, this is more likely to be to the modernist and Theravada forms that have been described. Probably very few Newar emigrants perform a daily ritual in a traditional Newar Buddhist idiom. Newar Buddhism is not a defining feature of Nepali, or even of Newar, identity traditionally, and therefore cannot be associated with, or become a symbol of, any kind of ethno-nationalism because an equal number of Newars are Hindus and any stress on Buddhism must be divisive from an ethnic point of view.

In short, within Nepal, Newar Buddhism is defined as part of tradition and no simplified version exists that could be used by emigrants or converts. If emigré Newars wish to preserve a Buddhist identity, they are virtually obliged to resort to Theravada Buddhism, to Goenka meditation, or to transnational forms of Tibetan Buddhism. Within Nepal, Newar Buddhist activists have yet to make headway against the view that Newar Buddhism is backward-looking and superstitious. Building a dynamic transnational movement is surely impossible under such circumstances. The advantages that Theravada Buddhism has over Newar Buddhism in this respect will be explored further in the concluding chapter.

 CHAPTER TEN

Conclusion: Nepal's Theravadins in the Twenty-First Century

Monks: Ambivalence

Following the ousting of the Ranas in the winter of 1950–51, the Theravada mission seemed poised for rapid expansion. For the Newar Buddhist community, it offered a break with an elitist and overly ritualistic past and a vehicle by means of which Buddhism might play a key role, and gain substantial government support, in the modernization of Nepal. A half-century later, the early hopes for political recognition and patronage have been mostly disappointed, but nonetheless the Theravadins have a complex program firmly in place and their community is expanding beyond Newar cultural borders into other ethnic groups in the hills and the Tarai. Although Buddhists have frequently bemoaned the lack of state support for Buddhism, this lack has forced them to be active, to be self-reliant and well organized, and to seek international links. In Thailand, where the Sangha is supported by the state, such support is not always seen as a good thing: "One of the Sangha's weaknesses is its heavy dependence on state power and nationalism to protect its turf and silence its critics. This has encouraged a cry-baby mentality so that the clergy is forever demanding outside help instead of developing self-reliance—one of Buddhism's main teachings" (Ekachai 2001: 318).

A clear sign of the Nepalese Sangha's success in reaching out beyond its Newar base came in 2001 when the central committee of the Nepal

Magar Sangh, the national body claiming to represent Magars, issued an appeal to all Magars that they should return their religion as "Buddhist" in the forthcoming national census (even though there is no tradition of Magars calling themselves Buddhist).[1] Some Tharus and Gurungs argue in a similar way that they should all consider themselves Buddhist (many Gurungs have long followed Tibetan Buddhism), but such a position has yet to be adopted officially by their overarching ethnic organizations.[2]

Despite a high profile, the Theravada monastic community itself still numbers only about two hundred, of whom rather more than half are nuns (if monastic novices are left out of account). Although Newar men did occasionally become monks in the Tibetan tradition in the nineteenth century and earlier, to all intents and purposes, monasticism had died out in the Newar Buddhist community at least half a millennium before the first Theravada missionary monks appeared in the Kathmandu Valley. It might well have been anticipated, then, that it would take more than a generation or two for the vocation of permanent celibacy to become firmly reestablished. Many more men than women have "gone into homelessness," but at least one-third and possibly as many as half of all novices and monks have disrobed. Indeed, so many monks have slipped away—many of them while studying abroad—that their preceptors cannot keep count of them.

There are several factors both pulling and pushing men to return to lay life. Sexual need would appear to be one of the main reasons that adult monks return to lay life, which many left before puberty. Understandably, the men themselves are more comfortable talking about other motives. From the parental perspective, a son's role is to perpetuate the lineage, support his father and mother in old age, and perform their funerary rites; thus, although parents may gladly give a son permission to ordain as a novice and even push him to do so, once he has completed his education and reached marriageable age, many—particularly those, for example Maharjans or Shresthas, who are not from strongly Buddhist backgrounds—want him to disrobe. Pressure from families to marry is the reason for disrobing that ex-monks mention most frequently. In the case of those who have spent time in Burma and Thailand and have seen many of their companions return to lay life after just a few years or months in the monastery, a conviction that ordination does not imply a lifelong commitment is a second reason for disrobing.

A third reason for abandoning the monastic vocation is frustration with the failure of senior monks to provide those returning from abroad with meaningful responsibilities. On returning to Nepal after as much as a decade living in monastic institutions in South or Southeast Asian societies in which the monk's role, whether as scholar, teacher, ritual performer, or social worker, is relatively clearly defined and respected, they report that they find themselves in a painfully anomalous situation. As Buddhist monks in a rapidly secularizing Hindu state, they look, sometimes vainly, to their seniors for guidance. Keshab, an ex-monk now living in Thailand, recalled:

> After spending ten years in Bangkok, I went back to Kathmandu to join my preceptor, who had been living alone in his vihara. In Thailand, we would spend the university holidays teaching young people in the countryside. I was good at that work and I wanted to do it in Nepal, but it was a problem that my Nepali wasn't good enough because I had been in Thailand so long. In any case, my guru wouldn't let me go out: he wanted to keep me by his side. Being in the monastery in Nepal was very difficult. It wasn't like in Thailand where monks are free. In Nepal, they have to be at the beck and call of the laypeople. I thought: what is the point of being a monk if you are always under laypeople's power?

After two years of increasing frustration, Keshab made his way back to Bangkok where he disrobed:

> When I was a novice in Nepal, before I went to Thailand, I had received sponsorship from a lot of people. A lot of people had *invested* in me. When a Thai monk disrobes nobody cares much because there are so many thousands of monks in Thailand. But in Nepal there are very few and each one who disrobes is a big loss to the community. I didn't want to disrobe in Nepal because I knew people would be angry and I didn't want to face them.

Keshab, who later married a Thai, is one of dozens of Newars who, after giving up their vows, have settled down in the country where they were educated, where their university degrees are valued, and where, as former monks, they are respected. Although they might still make a valuable contribution to the community they will do so as upasakas not as monks and, all too often, outside Nepal.

A similar case is that of Dipaka (see Chapter 6) who disrobed in 2003 because "I wanted to be free"—free of all the rules a monk has to follow. His ambition is to study child development and education and become a schoolteacher. Nowadays, he teaches *pariyatti* every Saturday at his local vihara but, though he admits that as a boy he was addicted to meditation, now he only meditates in the vihara and never at home.

One who has stayed in the Sangha is Ashok, who was trained in Sri Lanka where he spent several years doing social work in a Sarvodaya Center. But, three years after returning to Nepal, he admits that it has been touch and go. When he first got back to Kathmandu one of the senior monks invited him to live in his substantial newly constructed vihara, but aware that, were he to accept, he would have to follow his abbot's agenda rather than his own, which was to work with the poor as he had in Sri Lanka, Ashok turned down the invitation. Offered a room in one corner of a ruinous Newar Buddhist *baha*, he accepted it over two other equally decrepit places that he had seen, because, filthy as it was, it had a latrine whereas the other two had none. The elders still often used their *baha* for *guthi* feasts at which alcohol was consumed in large quantities and most people got drunk. The government had designated the *baha* a national monument, but had donated only half the amount needed for its renovation. Ashok took up the challenge of raising the balance, which he was able to do from Sri Lankan, Thai, and Bangladeshi Buddhists in fairly short order, and restoration work began. When two of the four walls of his room were pulled down, he hung up bed sheets to shield himself from prying eyes. These provided a measure of privacy, but no protection from the winter cold.

Ashok was the first Theravada monk to live in that community and he found arousing interest and support for his projects uphill work. As people rarely invited him to their homes for *bhojana dana*, he cooked, did his laundry, and swept his sparsely furnished quarters himself; if he had no rice to cook, which happened not infrequently, he would eat biscuits that the children had brought into Saturday school. But his worst problem was that ever since his return from Sri Lanka his father had been trying to get him to disrobe and get married, even though, with three other sons and only a few acres, he had little to offer him. Thus far, to his father's disgust, Ashok had refused to comply with his wishes. But though he expressed his resolve to stay in the Order, he admitted that his decision to maintain his independence from the monastic hierarchy meant that he led a lonely and often hungry life.

Keshab's and Ashok's accounts gave of their difficulties on returning to Nepal after training abroad focus on the conservatism of the senior generation of monks, even of some known as progressives and innovators. The older monks remain very conscious of the need for the new Nepalese Theravada movement to be seen to be respectable in the eyes of the long-established and conservative monastic hierarchies of Sri Lanka and Southeast Asia. One must also bear in mind that many of the young monks joined the Sangha as novices in the first place primarily in order to gain an education. Once they have that education, many leave; and many will have been told at the outset that it is permissable to do so. The case studies published in Pannapadipo (2002) illustrate that this is frequently the case in Thailand too; and in Thailand, becoming a novice is also often the only way for a boy to escape from rural poverty, even destitution.[3]

There are other constraints on Nepali Theravada monks that are more specific to the Nepalese Sangha. These have to do with the large number of laypeople in relation to the monks and with lay rather than monastic expectations of the monk role: young and active monks are in very high demand for all kinds of religious activities, which means that they have little time to pursue their own projects. Cases of committed monastics preferring to stay in Thailand or other countries, rather than return to Nepal after their education, or, in another case, of consciously deciding to become a Tibetan Mahayanist rather than a Theravadin monk, suggest that becoming a Theravadin monk and staying in Nepal involves accepting considerable limits on one's freedom of action, which may be traced back to the relatively small size of the Order in Nepal.[4]

That even those who remain committed to the monastic vocation share some of Keshab's and Ashok's frustrations can be deduced from Bhikshu Ashwaghosh's small book, *The Life of a Monk* (2003). In order to refute the lay accusation that being a monk is easy, Ashwaghosh explains at length the difficulties of being a monk:[5]

> The monks are simply entangled in priestly functions [and] in activities that have nothing to do with their dharma-related works. For example, they are asked to take upasakas and upasikas to foreign countries on pilgrimages, bring foreign goods for them, get students admitted in schools and colleges, get jobs for their boys and girls etc. They are even involved in the job of matchmaking. Some [laypeople] come to borrow money. Those monks who do not help them in such matters are neglected. . . . [I]f they are unable to give lectures due to illness or old age, they are neglected. . . . I asked some people who had abandoned him, "Don't you go to Mahapragya nowadays?" They replied, "Now, there is no opportunity of hearing words of wisdom from him. He is unable to give sermons. Therefore, we do not go." After hearing so many words of wisdom, the people abandoned him when he was in bad health. Such is the fate of monks. (Ashwaghosh 2003: 56–57)

Ashwaghosh returns several times to the problem that monks are dependent on women to look after them, especially when they are ill. He also points out that it is humiliating for monks to have to request facilities from rich laypeople in order to provide hospitality to visiting monastics from Theravada countries (ibid.: vi).

Nuns: A Lifelong Commitment

"Shaving the head means far more to a woman than to a man," Dhammawati once remarked. "Men are frequently obliged to do it for *sraddha* [performing ancestor worship] and it grows back quickly. But women wear their hair very long and once we've shaved our heads the hair will take years to grow back and all that time we'll be looking different from other women. So we only do it if we're very serious, we've made our decision, there's no going back." So far as we could determine, only a handful of nuns have left the Order in the last thirty years. Of these, one, who is reported to have been pushed, as a girl, to ordain by her mother, eloped with a monk to India. After several years in the nunnery, two young Dharmakirti nuns decided that the renunciant life was "dull," went to their homes, and had arranged marriages; more recently, two others eloped with neighborhood boys. So unusual were these nuns, however, that the turbulence that their departures generated was distinctly recalled, sometimes after many years, by their former companions in the nunnery.

For women, ordination is more an act of emancipation than of "renunciation"—as it is for men. Undoubtedly some adult female recruits "go into homelessness" in order to have more time to meditate and to study *buddha dharma*, but all are motivated by the urgent desire to escape marriage and motherhood, which, despite the fact that women are now entering the professions in considerable numbers, is still widely regarded as the only entirely acceptable adult female role. Nuns frequently list the "Woes of Women" of which they emphasize three in particular: marriage, which requires one to leave the home in which one grew up to go as a stranger to one's husband's home and, there, to suffer emotional and possibly physical abuse from one's in-laws for an indefinite period; the pain and danger of childbirth; and the sorrow of losing children.[6] If pressed, they admit that modern contraception, improved medical care, and hospital deliveries have made childbearing and child rearing much less hazardous than it was only a generation ago. They know that whereas their grandmothers commonly had ten or more pregnancies, and were lucky if half their children survived, in the Valley today educated women like themselves often have only two children, and infant and child death has become quite rare.[7]

In short, marriage appears to arouse much greater dread than motherhood. When asked about the female reproductive system, nuns in their thirties and upward showed an astounding ignorance. They excused themselves by saying that "those things" were not taught when they attended their single-sex school, which was undoubtedly the case. Although some eagerly showed LeVine photographs of themselves as attractive—even glamorous—adolescents and young women before they "shaved their heads," they categorically denied having had crushes on boys in those years. They denied just as adamantly having had romantic attachments since ordination. "I see all men as my brothers," one insisted primly. Having been reared to repress an awareness of sexual desire until marriage, the prospect of lifelong celibacy seems to have come as a profound relief.

For the younger nuns who walk through streets—in which Hindi pop music blares and girls their own age are wearing figure-hugging T-shirts and jeans—to attend coeducational schools and colleges, the possibility of romance and the need to resist it are issues of which they are well aware. What steadies and protects them may not be monastic discipline so much as those same constraints under which the great majority of Nepali girls grow to adulthood. Dating is still unacceptable and although love marriages, usually between young people who meet in school or college, are on the increase, most marriages are arranged.[8] Thus, behavior that in any way damages one's reputation (*ijjat*) or the reputation of one's family spoils one's marriage chances. Before ordination, the younger nuns may have read romance novels and watched TV soap operas and all of them have had much more exposure than the older nuns to unrelated members of the opposite sex. Nonetheless, like their elders, they emphatically emphasized their desire to avoid marriage. They admitted they knew couples who, total strangers until the wedding, had afterward proved well suited. Even so, in their view marriage was characterized by submission to in-laws and unremitting domestic labor, not romantic love.

In discussions of other reasons why they joined the Order, nuns of all ages mentioned the importance of a relationship with a particular monastic. In the case of the older nuns, a monk had usually been the catalyst: they recalled the interest that Pragyananda or Buddhaghosh had taken in them many decades ago. But the generation under thirty more often remembered nuns who had intrigued them, had been especially kind to them, or had inspired them. The names Dhammasangha, Gunawati, Padmawati, and Dhammawati came up again and again. Aware of the dangers of idealization, senior nuns go to great lengths to alert would-be ordinands to the realities of life in the vihara: discipline is strict, rivalries can be fierce and enduring, jealousies insidious, the demands of the laity exhausting. Even so, each year there are many more applicants than the nunneries, short on space and resources, can accommodate. Those few who are accepted must take between three and six months' preparation in the vihara, depending on how many years of *pariyatti* they have already studied, before receiving the precepts. During this time, assured that if they have reservations they may leave without recrimination, they are instructed to examine their motivations for entering the Order very carefully. At the outset those who go forward to ordination may be more attracted by freedom *from* marriage and everything that householder life implies than freedom *to* pursue the religious life. Like the Tibetan nuns whom Sara Shneiderman (1999) studied in Mustang, these Theravadins see the religious life more as a source of positive communal relationship than as a path toward intellectual development or individual enlightenment. Even though they have rejected marriage and the burden of family responsibilities, thereby defining themselves as marginal to their own society, they need the companionship of like-minded women to make life on the margins tolerable, let alone a success.

In the early days, most monks, like most nuns, were from priestly and/or merchant backgrounds. But ordination no longer offers young upper-caste males unique opportunities for travel, study, and prestige. Today, most novices are from farming or occupational castes or, more recently, from Janajati communities, and most are economically disadvantaged. By contrast, although some recruits to the nuns' Order are also from poor rural backgrounds, many still come from relatively privileged families. Rather than joining the Order for the educational opportunities it might afford, they are already well educated and quite capable of earning a living in some professional field. Furthermore, although their parents might never encourage a son to "go to the vihara," they may enthusiastically endorse a daughter's decision to do so and, after she has ordained, provide her with financial support, thereby themselves enjoying social prestige and earning spiritual merit.

In recent years, options for women have markedly increased and, in the expanding middle class, single career-women are becoming more common. With bachelor's and even master's degrees and connections in government, education, and business circles, some would-be ordinands have excellent employment prospects. As college students they often come under pressure to agree to an arranged marriage, but some are determined enough to resist. Unlike their elders, the younger generation do not regard ordination as the only acceptable way to avoid marriage in youth; however, they still see it as the best solution to the problem of where and how to live in middle and old age.

The nuns' Order affords women companions with whom to tread the religious path. By contrast, young monks tend to find themselves very much alone. They note that most other members of their cohort who have thus far resisted the lures of the world seem to view Nepal mainly as a staging post to which to return from abroad in order to plan the next foreign venture. Meanwhile, their elders, most of whom are elderly and in poor health, expect them to be useful to them personally: instead of encouraging them to use the skills they have acquired abroad, they keep them on a tight rein. Dhammawati, too, has been known to pressure her chelis into working in her programs instead of launching their own. But, over time, most have learned to withstand her considerable powers of command and persuasion and have gone their own way. Furthermore, after preliminary dramas, they go with her blessing, reflecting her flexibility and willingness, unusual in monastic culture, to support the strivings for independence of her subordinates. Whereas the young monks who try to stand up to their preceptors have little to back them up, Dhammawati's chelis have wider social networks and greater resources, or, at least, access to the resources of close relatives, which together put them at considerable advantage vis-à-vis the younger monks.

Some Persisting Inequalities Between Monks and Nuns

After a protracted struggle, the Nepali nuns' Order, modeling itself on the Burmese *ngebyu* movement, has convinced the lay community that nuns are the moral and intellectual equals of monks, and, furthermore, that certain outstandingly effective nuns are worthy of greater economic support. Indeed, like Taiwanese nuns who, as Li Yuchen (2000) reports, have proved more successful at fund-raising than Taiwanese monks, in the past five years, Dhammawati and her followers have raised more from local sources for their projects than the monks have raised in fifty years. Although there are holdouts among senior members of the Sangha, many of the younger monks, like the laity, are convinced that certain nuns in particular are their equals in all respects. Indeed, they express bemusement that so many of them have taken full ordination. As one monk remarked:

> I don't understand why they did it. The *mahasthaviras* say that because *bhikkhuni upasampada* died out long ago and there's no way to revive it, *bhikkhuni upasampada* has no value for the gurumas. And they're *never* going to change their minds about that! So if the gurumas can't change the minds of the *mahasthaviras*, whose minds are they hoping to change? Do they hope to earn the respect of the laity? But they already have it! The upasakas and upasikas don't care one way or the other about full ordination. They already respect the gurumas. The truth is, they don't just respect them, they *love* them!

Nevertheless, the Nepali Theravadins continue to operate in a society in which there are considerable inequalities between men and women. These inequalities and social expectations explain why monks who disrobe and return to lay life experience it as gaining freedom, whereas for women it is becoming a nun that confers the same sense of liberation.

The nuns are far from complacent with regard to their status in the community. Despite a keen awareness that the Buddha acknowledged the spiritual equality of the sexes, most are emphatic in their desire to be reborn as males and provide a list of handicaps from which nuns, as females in Nepalese society, still suffer. Conserving the prestige they have won by "trying harder" requires never slowing down. All things are impermanent but some, and this could include the respect that the laity have for them, are less permanent than others. When the issue was raised with them individually, several highly educated nuns insisted that there was no fundamental difference between men and women; all are simply human beings. Thus "of course" they wanted to be reborn female. But when the question was put to them a year later almost all had reversed themselves. When this was pointed out to one nun in particular, she refused to believe it. "Why would I have told you I wanted to be reborn a woman? Surely, once is enough!" Upon reviewing the progress the nuns have made on various fronts with a second nun, she responded with a shake of her head, "But the progress has taken so much *work*! In my next lifetime I don't want to have to work so hard. That's why I'd rather be a monk. The bhantes don't have to keep struggling like we do." (Senior monks, who have spent so much time and energy recruiting novices and arranging for them to be trained abroad only to see most of them disrobe, might disagree.)

Despite the advances the nuns have made in raising levels of secular education, they still lag behind the monks with regard to religious training. Over the last decade, places have been found for more than thirty Nepali nuns in institutions in Burma, Thailand, Sri Lanka, and Taiwan; but aside from Burma, where monks and nuns follow the same exacting curriculum, the programs to which young Theravada nuns have thus far had access are rarely on a par with the monks'. Nepali nuns who have the grades to pursue a university course have usually chosen to do so—in Kathmandu. The recent admission of nuns to Buddhist universities that offer degree programs combining secular and religious subjects in South and Southeast Asia, such as the International Buddhist University in Rangoon, Buddhist College in Taiwan, and Maechi College in Bangkok, is welcome. But, given the need for a strong command of the local language, it is doubtful that Nepali nuns who have had their secondary education in Kathmandu could be in a position to enroll unless they were to have one or two years' in-country language training prior to enrollment.

When young people of both sexes "go into homelessness," they are likely to remain involved with their families, but women have closer ties. Both monks and nuns sponsor the ordinations of brothers, nephews, and even aged fathers; they arrange for sisters and nieces to be accepted in nunneries in the Valley and abroad, and some contribute to the support of their parents—widowed mothers, in particular—out of the donations they receive. However, unlike a monk, a nun may be called home to nurse a parent in his or her last illness. This may mean flying back from the foreign country where she has been studying to live in her natal home for an extended period until her parent's demise. During that time, she will have little contact with other members of her Order. Often, the nun in question has one if not more brothers who are married and living with their wives in the parental home. Nevertheless it seems to be a universal assumption that a daughter-in-law cannot care for her parents-in-law as well as a daughter cares for her parents; and since nuns are unmarried and have no other routine familial responsibilities, they are expected to take on the nursing role. Despite the disruption it causes in their lives, they accept it not only out of attachment and filial piety but also to strengthen future claims on their brothers for financial support.

One nun who had three sisters-in-law living in the parental home reported that whenever either parent fell ill she would be summoned. After decades trying to meet her obligations to both nunnery and natal home, she dreaded the day when she would no longer be able to balance them and would have to decide between meeting the demands of her chosen calling and those of her family. The conflict in which the pursuit of personal goals places them can be the preoccupation of both monks and nuns. They are charged to seek their own salvation with diligence. But this requires a single-mindedness that is guaranteed to generate discord. Adolescent novices and nuns express their firm belief in the possibility, even in this Kali Yuga, of attaining enlightenment in one lifetime: Their teachers have told them that in the forests of Burma live two extraordinary monks, both *arhats*. But older monastics rarely mention nirvana as a concept, let alone as a personal goal. Their meditation practice focuses on cleansing mental impurities, cravings, hatreds, and delusions in order to improve their relationships with other people, the monks and nuns they live with, the laity they serve, and, most important, family members.

As of 2004, almost one-third of Nepali nuns over the age of twenty had received full ordination according to Chinese rites. Whether they accept, disapprove of, or are indifferent to the nuns' new status, the monks continue to refer to the nuns as *anagarika*. Nevertheless, in certain important respects their behavior toward the nuns has changed. Before 1995, when an influential layman invited several senior monks and nuns to a community event and arranged for them to sit together, no nun had ever shared the dais with a monk. If the monks were surprised and upset when this changed, they had the wit not to show it at the time. Nor did they comment on it later and, now that the ramparts have been breached, seating monks and nuns on the same level has become routine at all public events, which would never happen in the long-established Theravada countries. A second significant innovation, initiated by the monks themselves, occurred when Dhammawati received her first invitation to preach at Vishwa Shanti Vihara in 1998. For decades she had invited senior monks to preach in Dharmakirti, but the invitation had never been reciprocated. In the past, whenever a monk came to preach in a nunnery, he would sit above all the nuns, including the abbess. Today the abbess sits beside him. Padmawati recalls:

> One morning, not long after the consecration of Mayadevi Vihara, I invited a certain monk to preach. I thought, 'This is *my* vihara. Why should I sit below him?' So I gestured to him to be seated and then I sat down next to him. Of course he was very surprised, but what could he do?

This was such a simple gesture, and yet it was one that Dhammawati, who, since her earliest days in Kathmandu, had avoided confrontation, had never risked making. If the monks refused to recognize her talents as a preacher or her status as a *bhikkhuni*, she learned to absorb her resentment and, on those relatively rare occasions when she was in their company, maintained a studiedly calm expression. But Padmawati, with her newspaper column and her weekly radio program, refused to observe archaic status differentials. She pushed the envelope and found, to her surprise, no resistance.

Within the Newar Buddhist community, the leadership of the nuns' Order is judged just as effective, if not more so, as that of the monks. But whereas from time to time prominent monks have played an active role in the larger society, thus far the nuns have stayed within the confines of their own community. Amritananda, abbot of Ananda Kuti Vihara, maintained a high profile from the early days of his friendship with King Tribhuvan in the 1950s and throughout the Panchayat period. Sudarshan, abbot of Shri Kirti Vihara in Kirtipur and for more than twenty years a lecturer in the Department of Culture at Tribhuvan University, was involved, as dramatist and author, in the Nepal Bhasha language and culture "renaissance." Ashwaghosh, abbot of Shrigha Vi-

Nuns sitting on the same level as a monk, July 1999. (Sarah LeVine)

hara, entered the political arena after the 1990 restoration of multi-party democracy, was very active in the movement for a secular constitution, and allied himself with the UML (the Communist Party of Nepal, Unified Marxist-Leninist, the main parliamentary opposition, which formed a minority government for nine months in 1994–5). After the first general election in 1991, he was nominated by the UML to the Upper House where he served until 1993.

By contrast, Dhammawati has never become involved in politics. The occasional march—to protest government failure to pursue the murderers of a Japanese monk in Lumbini in July 1997, for example—marks the limits of her participation. Even women's rights issues, which are periodically debated in the press and in parliament and bring members of feminist organizations into the streets, have not engaged her publicly. From her perspective, the Theravada nuns' Order is a feminist organization. From the first, her objective has been to empower women; but she has confined her efforts to the religious and domestic spheres. Prolific though her publications have been, she has been concerned exclusively with spreading *buddha dharma* and helping people to understand it and live by its lights. But if she is reluctant to venture into a wider world, her followers, who belong to a different generation, are better prepared, should they so choose, to address issues of gender equality in the wider society.

The Laity

The mass movement or sudden conversion away from Vajrayana or traditional Newar Buddhism that some of the early Theravadin activists hoped there might be has not occurred. Thirty years ago there was a small number of highly committed laymen and laywomen, often coming from related households, who provided the core of support on a day-to-day basis. The same is largely true today. What has changed is that Theravada Buddhist monastics have successfully reached out to middle and lower Newar castes as well. Maharjans, as we have seen, have come to provide a large proportion of new male recruits to the Sangha; many Maharjans have become strong lay supporters of Theravada Buddhism.

Although there has been no mass movement away from traditional Newar Buddhism, there has indeed been a major decline in the quantity of rituals performed and sponsored. Compulsory Vajrayana rituals are pared back and performed on a smaller scale or for fewer days; optional Vajrayana rituals have become a rare and noteworthy occurrence. In the past, all Vajracharya men learned how to perform basic Vajrayana rituals, even if they did not have their own patrons (*jajman*) who would call them on a regular basis: there were enough optional rituals, and rituals requiring other Vajracharyas to make up the numbers, and it was in any case part of being a Vajracharya to know Vajrayana rituals. Since 1951, there has been a massive decline in the numbers of Vajracharyas taking Tantric Initiation (Gellner 1992: 269–270). This reflects a radical secularization of Vajracharya identity. It is also connected to the fact that being a Vajrayana priest is a viable vocation only for a few today. More widely, knowing how to perform the rituals of Newar Buddhism is no longer essential to being a good Buddhist.

The gradual decline of commitment to Vajrayana Buddhism is reflected in the fact that the big local donations go to Theravada buildings. The magnificent old shrines of traditional Newar Buddhism either decline beyond repair (as with Aksheshwar Mahavihara, discussed in Chapter 9) and are replaced with modern alternatives, or are repaired with help from international agencies.[9] Another, and perhaps more significant, way in which Theravada would seem to have won the battle for Newar hearts and minds—for all that elaborate Vajrayana rituals are still being performed—is in the sphere of public discourse. Theravada activists and their way of defining Buddhism have the advantage of simplicity and clarity. Consequently, everything that Vajracharyas do is seen as "really Hindu"; most Newar Buddhists continue to perform the Vajracharyas' life-cycle rituals, but many of them are no longer convinced that they should be doing them. They concede regretfully that their Buddhism is "mixed up," "corrupted by Hinduism," and so on.

A writer who has expressed these themes in particularly clear form is B. A. Kanaka Dweep. He is in fact a Vajracharya by birth (the "B. A." stands for "Bajracharya"), but for the most part he adopts an uncompromising modernist view, according to which original Buddhism—identified as Theravada Buddhism minus later accretions—was a simple anti-Hindu philosophy that abjured all image worship; rejected gods, magic, and animal sacrifice; and treated the Buddha as a gifted individual to be remembered, not a god to be worshipped. A theme to which he also often returns is the influence of Buddhism on Christianity. Needless to say, everything to do with Mahayana and especially Vajrayana, is anathema:

> Once Vajrayana got its hands on [Buddhist doctrine] the teachings of suffering, impermanence, and non-self somehow disappeared. And gods appeared. Samvaras and Mahasamvaras with countless hands, legs, and heads—these became Buddhist gods. The teaching of the five "m"s arose and the teaching of "great happiness" [allusions to Tantric teachings on the consumption of meat and alcohol and the ritual use of sexual intercourse]. Nairatmya [the goddess] also appeared. And Buddhists who were actually Tantric Hindus were called Buddhists and were respected as Buddhists. (Kanaka Dweep 2001)[10]

The uncompromising and aggressive way in which Kanaka Dweep expresses such ideas does not make him popular. However, the underlying position or perception that Buddhism is to be defined against Hinduism, and that Vajrayana, because structurally similar to Hinduism, is corrupt, is widely shared and has become almost a kind of unthinking "common sense" among lay Buddhists in Nepal—which makes it particularly hard to combat.[11]

Thus, Theravada Buddhism provides a way of being Buddhist in the Nepalese context, which—unlike traditional Newar Buddhism—is sharply distinguishable from Hinduism. A summary of the ways in which Theravada Buddhism in Nepal is distinctive was produced by Bhikshu Sudarshan in 1998 for a Lotus Research Center conference.[12] Sudarshan took his lead from an article that the Nepal Bhasha poet Chittadhar Hridaya had published in 1950, to considerable controversy, titled "What Has Theravada Contributed to Us? What Do We Need?" Hridaya went point by point through the items that Theravada Buddhism had added to Newar culture, and in nearly every case he argued that what Theravada had introduced already existed as part of traditional Newar Buddhism. Bhikshu Sudarshan, nearly half a century later, began from Hridaya's list of nine items, and added a further eight of his own.[13] Theravada's contribution was:

1. Teaching Newars the significance of Swaya Punhi, that is, the full moon of Baisakh, in other words, the introduction of the annual celebration of Buddha Jayanti;
2. The observance of Buddhist *sila*, that is, the Five and Eight Precepts, first administered in accordance with the Vinaya by Pragyananda;
3. The introduction of *paritrana* in place of the worship of the Pancharaksha and other gods;
4. The construction of viharas;

5. The introduction of the Anagarika Sangha: "This is a fundamental contribution of the Theravada" (Sudarshan 1999);
6. The introduction of religious discourses;
7. Worship of the Buddha;
8. A new style of *chaitya* (the Lanka Chaitya at Ananda Kuti);
9. The introduction of a Buddha relic at Ananda Kuti;
10. New organizations;
11. Pilgrimage to Buddhist sites in India: "This is indeed a great contribution of Theravada tradition . . . [Newar Buddhists] have become part of [the] international movement of Theravada Buddhism" (Sudarshan 1999);
12. Hymn singing, that is, the Gyanmala *bhajans*;
13. Publication of journals and books;
14. The alms round;
15. Eradication of caste discrimination, that is, permitting monks from any background to join the Sangha;
16. Reviving Lumbini as a holy site;
17. Introducing and propagating vipassana meditation.

The tone of each article—Hridaya's from 1950, Bhikshu Sudarshan's from 1998—is very different. Hridaya recognized the sincerity of the early monks and nuns, and admired them, but he regretted what was being lost in the process, and he questioned whether the Theravadins were not just replacing one reactionary (*rudhivadi*) set of customs with another.[14] Sudarshan shows, with considerably more enthusiasm and in line with what has been described in this book, that, in every sphere of action, Theravada, far from helping to preserve traditional Newar Buddhism, has in fact displaced, or threatens to displace, it with similar practices of its own.[15]

If Theravada Buddhism had only to compete against traditional Newar Buddhism for the allegiance of young people, its task might be easy. But that is far from the case; not only are numerous other options available in the globalized religious marketplace that Kathmandu has become, but there has also been a rise of internationally derived consumerism and class formation, which makes religion, of any kind, seem like an irrelevance to many. In the Nepalese case this has been best described in an important monograph by Liechty (2003) on the basis of fieldwork in the early 1990s. He shows how fashion, the consumption of consumer goods, and films have become ubiquitous and unavoidable for middle-class youth and for those who aspire to middle-class status. Unfortunately, his analysis leaves religion almost completely out of account.[16] For many Nepalis, Theravada Buddhism, vipassana meditation, or other forms of religious activism, provide a way to combine tradition and modernity, to participate in global trends, and, as they see it, be true to their roots too.

The way in which Theravada Buddhism has been packaged and the very fact that it comes from abroad, and its clear dissimilarity from Hinduism, mean that it is ideally placed to be seen as the modern and progressive way of being a Buddhist. Furthermore, the very fact of its newness in Nepal, for all the problems that this causes its adherents, also brings some advantages. Although the monks may seem like a hindrance to the nuns' development, in fact, as noted above, they are much less of one than in the long-established Theravada countries. In Sri Lanka, it is still problematic for nuns to go on the alms round (Bartholomeusz 1994: 185), whereas in Nepal even monks are proud that the nuns of Dharmakirti raised all the money they needed to build Gautami Vihara in Lumbini by begging.[17] In Sri Lanka, conservative monks of the Theravada establishment denounced the new fashion for vipassana on the grounds that it introduced a new and scripturally unwarranted style of meditation. In Nepal, however, monks have enthusiastically championed it and encouraged laypeople to participate.[18]

Explaining Monasticism Among the Newars

The stories told in these pages are quite similar to—and took place rather close in time and space to—the Sherpa histories that Sherry Ortner has pulled together in her book *High Religion: A Cultural and Political History of Sherpa Buddhism* (1989a) and several related articles.[19] Originally—that is, from the late seventeenth century until the end of the nineteenth century—the Sherpas (just like the Newars) supported "temples run by married lamas that conducted rituals (and still do) for the benefit of a hereditarily attached clientele" (Ortner 1989a: 45). Temples such as these were probably also the norm in Kham, Tibet, at the time when the Sherpas' ancestors first left Tibet and settled on the other side of the Himalayas in what is now Nepal. At the beginning of the twentieth century, rich traders and big men with links to the Rana state began to support celibate Tibetan lamas and their

Sherpa followers, who preached against Buddhist involvement in animal sacrifice, shamanism, and bawdy public rituals. Once established in Sherpa territory, the monks began to replace such traditional Sherpa practices with "cleaned up" monastic substitutes or alternatives, new rituals that are now widely accepted and are often presented as traditional Sherpa customs. Two of the best-known rituals to be introduced in this way were the Nyungne fast and the Mani Rimdu dance drama.[20] The new practices of the monks were seen as superior to, and more Buddhist than, those they replaced or displaced, but at the same time as the culmination of them. This apotheosis was expressed also in the idiom of reincarnation: Lama Gulu who founded the first celibate monastery in 1916 was told by his Tibetan sponsor, Zatul Rinpoche, that he was the incarnation of the father of Lama Sangwa Dorje, the founder of the first Sherpa Buddhist temples in the seventeenth century, and an important local culture hero (Ortner 1989a: 133–134). Although the married lamas were displaced, they themselves mostly saw this as a good thing (ibid.: 190–191).

There are some important and significant differences between the revivalism described here among the Newars and the Sherpa movement analysed by Ortner. In the first place, the Sherpas, though defined as a separate ethnic group for the purposes of relations with the Nepalese state, never lost contact with Tibet and remained part of the larger Tibetan culture area. There is no indication that the monastery founding by the Sherpas was anything other than a continuation of the historical expansion (and occasional contraction) of what Samuel (1993) calls "clerical Buddhism." This process of expanding monasticism had been going on for centuries in those parts of Tibet where there was sufficient economic surplus to support it. Thus, there was nothing specifically modern about the motivations either of the sponsors or of the monastics involved in the original foundings of celibate monasteries among the Sherpas. Both big men and monks were following, according to Ortner, a long-established "schema" within Sherpa culture of competition between brothers, whereby one side, the originally subordinate, leaves and seeks an external sponsor, becomes rich and/or powerful, and returns to defeat his adversary. By founding celibate monasteries they were also following a clearly understood Tibetan schema of Buddhist merit-making.

Yet, if Sherpa patrons' motivations for founding monasteries were traditional, elements of the context in which these developments took place clearly showed the impact of the modern world. The Rana state took the form that it did, and adopted the extractive revenue strategies that it did, because it had become a client, with fixed boundaries, of British India (expansion through military conquest westward and eastward along the Himalayas was no longer an option). Sherpa big men acquired the power that they did because they had become representatives of the state, which was cautiously modernizing the machinery by which it extracted a surplus from the peasantry. The power that the Sherpa big men acquired simultaneously put them at odds with other Sherpas and in need of legitimation. Other Sherpas sought out new economic opportunities in British Darjeeling and later by working for foreign climbers and trekkers.

The founding of the first celibate monastery among the Sherpas in 1916 may have marked a major turning point for the Sherpas, but it was not connected to the rise of Tibetan nationalism or linked to the development of a modernist form of Tibetan Buddhism. In the wider culture area of which the Sherpas were part, such monastery foundings were, so to speak, a thoroughly traditional form of revivalism, if not quite business as usual. By contrast, the introduction of Theravada monasticism among the Newars was a more radical break, even though it did not seem like one at the outset. There was no way in which the Theravada monks who took over old Newar *bahas* would have shared the space with incumbent Vajracharyas and allowed them to participate in rituals together, as Ortner (1989a: 188–192) describes Sherpa monks doing with householder lamas at Thami monastery in Khumbu.[21] For a start, the Theravadins' tradition was never and is not now a set of ritual and liturgical practices in the way that the Vajracharyas' and the Nyingma were and are. The Sherpa monks and the Sherpa married lamas were heirs to the same rituals; the two statuses were alternative, valid ways of practicing the same tradition, although in the Sherpa context the monks always outranked the married practitioners. This is not always the case within Tibetan Buddhism in general: contrary to what Ortner suggests (1995: 382), not all tulkus are monks, and in some cases married tulkus outrank celibate tulkus.[22]

By contrast, there is no possible way, within their own institutions, that Theravada Buddhists can recognize a married practitioner as anything other than inferior to even the most junior monastic. Furthermore, though not fully aware of it, the early Newar Theravadins, by making links to the south, were indeed becoming part of a modernizing religious world. These links were reestablished only thanks to the intervention of the Maha Bodhi Society, a resolutely and thoroughly modernist organization based in Calcutta. Yet, paradoxically, Dharmaditya Dharmacharyya apart, the early founders of Theravada Buddhism in Nepal, Mahapragya, Dhammalok, and Karmasheel/Pragyananda, almost certainly saw themselves as doing much the same as the Sherpa monastic missionaries, such as Zatul Rimpoche, that is, they saw themselves as simply spreading a higher-status, and more centrally Buddhist, practice of lifelong celibacy, together with campaigns against animal sacrifice. As discussed in Chapter 2, even when the first Newars became Theravadin monks, the choice seems to have been conceptualized as a pragmatic one, dictated by the ease of learning Pali and the support they received from India and Burma, rather than as a radical change of direction. It was this kind of ecumenical attitude to different Buddhist traditions that led Mahapragya, late in life, to protest as follows:

> Some do their [Buddhist] practice through (worshipping) statues, others by following rules, some through Tantra, some through mantras . . . Although the means and the ritual conduct are diverse, the main teacher and the refuges are the same Buddha, Dharma, and Sangha. It is therefore a complete mistake for Buddhists who share the same dharma today to view each other with hatred and say "Ours is good, yours is bad." . . . Dharma was set up to purify the mind. It will not be protected by an impure mind. It is impossible for the mind to be purified by prejudice (*bhedbhāv*) and hatred (*dveṣbhāv*). (Mahapragya 1976: 2–3)

At its origin, the Theravada movement in Nepal was indeed a revivalist, arguably even a fundamentalist, movement; however, what was being revived, or returned to, was not any particular doctrine, nor any form of meditation, but simply the *practice* of monasticism: men renouncing remunerative work, sex, and family life and devoting themselves to religion. Unexpectedly, women insisted on an equal right to renounce, right from the start, and, as has been described, they have in some ways made a greater success of it, especially considering the low esteem in which they were held at the outset. The emotional force with which the founders of the Theravada movement committed themselves to the monastic path was akin to the experience that in Judaeo-Christian traditions is usually thought of as conversion (from one religion to another). By comparison, as noted, the decision on whether to be a Mahayanist or a Theravadin was a relatively trivial and pragmatic one.[23] In short, the stress was on practice, not on details of sect allegiance, not on doctrine, and certainly not on allegiance to any particular book.

The shift to Theravada Buddhism was pregnant with consequences: it may not have had to do with texts and doctrines originally, but eventually these would be implicated. The sources of Theravada—initially Burma and Sri Lanka, later also Thailand—were already long embarked on the modernization of Buddhism, of repackaging it in school textbooks and as a practice for laypeople. What the first generations of Nepali monks and nuns were to learn was, whether or not they wanted it, a modernized form of the religion. Its lay leaders were educated and inclined to a rationalist and modernizing view both of Buddhism and of life in general. When Nepali Buddhists sought to construct a curriculum for teaching Buddhism in Nepal, the models they turned to were Burmese and Sri Lankan. When lay leaders made speeches, right from the outset they inveighed against "blind faith," "superstition," and ritual. In short, the Theravada movement described here may have had a complex relationship to modernism, but it most definitely had a connection. By contrast, the Sherpa revival seems to have had no such connection.

Another difference between this account and Ortner's has to do with the place of the laity. Ortner's analysis of the founding of the first monasteries focuses in the first instance on the actions and the competition of the rich lay sponsors. She later admits that "from the Sherpa point of view the prime movers . . . were not the wealthy lay sponsors, but the religious figures involved" (1989a: 130). Some details on the sahujis who funded the early years of the Theravada movement have been provided in Chapter 5, but their background and motivations have not been at the heart of this story. It is true that among the Newars, as for the Sherpa revival, the support of rich laypeople has been crucial for the survival of the Theravada movement, both in the past and today. And certainly, as among the Sherpas, there is some competition in donations. Yet though there are occasional cases of agonistic, intra-familial competition in religious gifting, we would hesitate to say that there is a cultural *schema* for *competition between brothers* among the Newars, such as that which Ortner posits for the Sherpas and sees at work in the early foundings of monasteries.[24] Nor is there the public and competitive pledging of gifts as occurs among the Jains in India (Laidlaw 1995), though it is true that the names of donors and the amounts they have given are prominently displayed in Theravada monasteries.

Though brothers may not be expected to compete religiously, as in Ortner's Sherpa schema, religious gifting to Buddhist monks is a prominent theme of Newar culture. The sponsorship of an optional performance of the traditional ceremony of Samyak was in the past, and has again recently become, an ostentatious and specifically Buddhist way of gaining merit and prestige: this involves the casting a life-size Dipankara Buddha statue, and giving an elaborate and expensive set of alms to all the Shakyas and Vajracharyas of the Kathmandu Valley, who are considered to be the monks of traditional Newar Buddhism. One informant said that Bhairaja Tuladhar had at first considered performing Samyak, but was persuaded that it would be more meritorious to rebuild Dharmakirti Vihara (Chapter 5, n.16). In a personal interview, Bhairaja himself denied that this had been the case, and so it may well be that the perception was merely in the eye of the beholder. Nonetheless, the fact that the two kinds of donation—one a highly traditional Newar Buddhist practice, the other the paradigmatic big gift in Theravada Buddhism—were *perceived* to be substitutable is itself highly significant.

Rather than between brothers, among the Newars public religious competition occurs between localities, between cities, and even between castes. Usually this takes the relatively restrained form of maintaining the public face of a given locality when it undertakes the organization of some citywide festival. This continues in a modern context in quiz competitions for which different religious institutions field teams, and in the rivalry between different localities offering to host particular annual festivals, such as Buddha Jayanti. Only in more traditional contexts, usually associated with the chariot festival of a Hindu god or goddess, does such inter-locality competition spill over into violence.

For the Sherpa monks and nuns who became the first incumbents of the new monasteries, most of whom were middle sons or daughters of high-status families, Ortner suggests that

> monasticism creates the most perfect—and indeed most culturally valued—form of legitimation. The monk or nun is (theoretically) higher in status than even the biggest laypeople, yet at the same time (again theoretically) the monk or nun is "smaller"—materially poorer, spiritually less self-interested—than even the smallest villager. It is symbolically, as well as pragmatically, the perfect solution to the contradictions of the little big people's positions. (Ortner 1989a: 175).

For nuns, specifically those from high-status backgrounds, she argues that

> high-status women might experience the internal contradictions of the female situation more deeply than other women. That is, they would tend

> to have particularly positive self images (indeed many of them have probably been quite spoiled as children), and might thus feel much more unjustly abused than other women by the social restrictions and negative ideology constraining women generally. (Ortner 1996: 128).

Both of these interpretations, put forward with admirable tentativeness by Ortner, have some mileage in the Newar case. In the past, for marginal men from high-status backgrounds, and still today for marginal women from the same backgrounds, monasticism does indeed offer a "solution," though of course those who have taken it up are far fewer than those who have not. Her suggestion as to the motivation of those high-status women who are particularly attracted to becoming a nun is certainly pertinent. There is also the point that only women from a relatively well-off background have the resources to ensure that becoming a nun is not a one-way ticket to impoverishment.

Whatever individuals' particular motivations may have been, and whatever personal conflicts may have found their resolution in becoming a monk or nun, we hope to have conveyed how the Nepalese Theravada revival movement has seemed from the viewpoint of various participants. We argue that the original participants—Dharmaditya Dharmacharyya apart—saw it as an attempt to recapture authentic Buddhist practice. In the process, and subsequently, diverse new and modernist understandings of Buddhism were unleashed, which led to a newly prominent female monasticism and new lay Buddhist movements—all of which went far beyond what could have been imagined by the earliest monks and nuns.

Dramatis Personae: Some Prominent Personalities in the Theravada Movement

Amritananda, Bhikshu (1918–1990): born Lal Kaji Shakya in Tansen, west Nepal, he became a novice in 1936 and was one of the earliest Theravada monks. He studied and was ordained a monk in Sri Lanka in 1940. Returning to Nepal, he was the first monk to preach publicly in the Kathmandu Valley (in 1942). Because of his dynamism and charisma, he was well known and traveled widely outside of Nepal. He founded the All-Nepal Bhikshu Mahasangh in 1951 and remained its unchallenged leader until his death.

Aniruddha, Bhikshu (1915–2003): born Gaja Ratna Tuladhar, son of Dhammalok (Dasa Ratna), q.v., he became a novice-monk (*samanera*) before his father and studied in Sri Lanka and later in Kalimpong. He was the titular head of the Nepalese Sangha at the time of his death.

Ashwaghosh, Bhikshu (b. 1926): born as Buddha Ratna Shakya, his mother and Dhammawati's mother were close friends and shared an enthusiasm for Theravada Buddhism. He became a novice in 1944 and took full ordination in 1949 in Sri Lanka. He is known to many as "the communist monk" and was a nominee of the UML (Unified Marxist-Leninist) party, one of Nepal's two main political parties in the 1990s, to the Upper House 1993–5. He is abbot of Shrigha Vihara, Kathmandu, next door to Dharmakirti Vihara, and of Dhyankuti Vihara, Banepa.

Bhaju Ratna (Kansakar) (1882–1956): rich merchant involved in the Tibet trade and a generous supporter of the Theravada movement in its early years.

Buddhaghosh, Bhikshu (b. 1921): born Sapta Ratna Vajracharya in Kwa Baha, Kathmandu, he is today (2003) the highly respected abbot of Sumangal Vihara in Lalitpur and the president of the All-Nepal Bhikshu Mahasangh.

Chandramani, Bhikkhu (1876–1972): Burmese monk who spent most of his life based in Kushinagara, where the Buddha passed into ultimate nirvana. Chandramani initiated most of the early Nepali Theravadins as monks.

Chittadhar Hridaya (Tuladhar) (1906–1982): famous Newar poet and activist, author of the epic poem, the *Sugat Saurabh*, on the life of the Buddha, and many other literary works.

Dhama Sahuor Dharma Man Tuladhar (1861–1937): a rich Buddhist merchant whose support for Buddhism was very important in the 1920s.

Dharmachari, Anagarika (1898–1978): born Laxmi Nani Tuladhar, she took the precepts from Chandramani in Kushinagara in 1934 and from then until Dhammawati returned from Burma she was the most prominent Nepali nun. She founded the first nunnery in Nepal, Nirvana Murti Upasikarama (Kindol Vihara), in 1947.

Dhammadinna, Anagarika/Bhikshuni (b. 1939): born Chameli Shakya in Nag Baha, Lalitpur, she is Dhammawati's chief assistant in Dharmakirti Vihara.

Dhammalok, Bhikshu (also known as Dharmalok) (1891–1977): born Das Ratna Tuladhar, Asan, Kathmandu, he traded in Lhasa, taught Buddhism as a layman, and later became a monk, after his son, Aniruddha, did so.

Dhammawati, Anagarika/Bhikshuni (b. 1925): born Ganesh Kumari Shakya, in Uku Baha, Lalitpur. Since her return in 1963 from studying in Burma, where she passed the Dhammachariya examination, she has been the undisputed leader of the Theravada nuns. She founded Dharmakirti Vihara in 1965.

Dharmacharyya, Dharmaditya (1902–1963): the first Newar Buddhist modernist and the first Newar cultural nationalist. He was born Jagat Man Vaidya (Shakya) in Chikã Bahi, Lalitpur. He went to study in Calcutta where he became a follower of Anagarika Dharmapala, founder of the Maha Bodhi Society.

Goenka, S. N. (b. 1924): Burmese-born Indian layman meditation master. He introduced his form of 'non-denominational' vipassana meditation to Nepal in 1981.

Gyan Jyoti (Kansakar) (1922–2004): son of Bhaju Ratna Kansakar, half-brother of Maniharsha and a patron of both Tibetan and Theravada Buddhist institutions. He was a sponsor of IBMC.

Gyanapurnik, Bhikshu (b. 1939): Born Hera Lal Shakya in Tansen, he studied with Buddhaghosh in Lalitpur, in Burma, and in England. He is a prominent translator and abbot of Vishwa Shanti Vihara. He is the only Nepali monk who has passed the Dhammachariya examination.

Karmashil: see Pragyananda

Kumar Kashyap, Bhikshu (b. 1926): Born Krishna Man Shakya, as a novice, he was exiled to India by the Ranas in 1944. Today, he is abbot of Ananda Kuti Vihara and vice president of the All-Nepal Bhikshu Mahasangh.

Mahapragya, Bauddha Rishi, earlier Bhikshu (1901–1979): born Prem Bahadur (Nani Kaji) Shrestha (Khyahju), he was one of the earliest Theravada monks, having first been the leader of the five Newar Tibetan monks expelled in 1926. He fell into householderhood in Kalimpong in the 1940s but then returned to Kathmandu as a Buddhist sage (Bauddha Rishi) in the 1960s, where he taught until his death.

Mahasi Sayadaw (1904–1982): Burmese meditation master who introduced the form of vipassana meditation taught at the IBMC in Shankhamul to Nepal in 1981.

Maniharsha Jyoti (Kansakar) (1917–1993): son of Bhaju Ratna Kansakar and prominent Buddhist businessman. He played a key role in supporting the Theravada movement and, later, S. N. Goenka and his form of vipassana meditation.

Pragyananda, Bhikshu (1900–1993): born Kul Man Singh Tuladhar in Itum Baha, Kathmandu, he traded in Tibet where he met Mahapragya. He became a Tibetan monk, Karmasheel, in 1928 and two years later a Theravadin under Chandramani in Kushinagara.

Shakya, Min Bahadur (b. 1951): leading Buddhist layman, working for the revival of Newar Mahayana Buddhism.

Shakyananda, Bhikshu (1909–1997): born Chakra Dhan Shakya in Taksar, Bhojpur, east Nepal, he spent over forty years as a monk in Tansen.

Subodhanand, Bhikshu (b. 1916): born as Kul Raj Shakya in Taksar, Bhojpur, east Nepal, he was one of the monks exiled by the Ranas in 1944. He was a prolific composer of hymns in Nepal Bhasha. In 2003, as the most senior monk in Nepal, he was the Sangha Nayaka.

Sudarshan, Bhikshu (1934–2002): born Rudra Raj Shakya in Uku Baha, Lalitpur, he was famous as "the boy monk." For many years he was a lecturer in the Culture Department of Tribhuvan University, a prolific writer, and abbot of Shri Kirti Vihara, Kirtipur. He was jailed for a short time for Nepal Bhasha activities in the Panchayat period. He was a campaigner on Buddhist issues, particularly to do with Lumbini.

Sumangal, Bhikshu (1929–1999): born Bhakta Krishna Shilpakar in Lalitpur, he ordained in 1959 in Burma, obtained a master's degree in Buddhism from Rissho University, Japan, in 1972, and was among the first monks to mobilize international connections for Buddhist projects in Nepal. He established Buddha Vihara in Bhrikuti Mandap, Kathmandu, helped raise funds from Thailand and Japan for IBMC (1985), brought the Japanese healing movement Sei Mei Kyo to Nepal, and in 1993 opened an old people's home in Banepa.

Sushila, Anagarika (1915–2001): born Asha Maya Shakya in Taksar, Bhojpur, east Nepal, she received the precepts from Chandramani. After a spending a few years in Tansen, she moved to Tana Baha in Lalitpur where she was very active in the community. She was the head of the Anagarika Sangh at the time of her death.

Tsering Norbu: Tibetan Nyingma lama active in the Kathmandu Valley in the 1920s.

Complete List of Theravada Viharas in Nepal

(after Kondanya 2001: 47–48; 2002: 53–55; 2003, supplemented and rearranged).

Nunneries, that is, viharas inhabited solely by nuns, are marked with an asterisk. In some cases, it may be simply by chance that no monks reside there and the vihara was not established specifically for nuns; also, many nuns are to be found staying in viharas alongside monks. Both of these patterns are found particularly in outlying areas where separate nunneries have not been established. Further details of principal viharas are given in Table 5.1.

Many of the smaller viharas are registered in private names.

Kathmandu District

In Kathmandu

Ananda Kuti Vihara, Swayambhu

Ananda Bhuvana Vihara, Swayambhu

Antarashtriya Bauddha Dhyan Kendra (International Buddhist Meditation Centre), Shankhamul

Basundhara Buddha Vihara, Maharajganj

*Bauddha Rishi Ashram, Anam Nagar

Buddha Vihara, Bhrikuti Mandap

Buddharatna Vihara, Putali Sadak

*Dhammavasa Vihara, Khusibun, Dhalko

*Dharmakirti Vihara, Shrigha

Dharmachakra Vihara, Bag Bazaar

Gana Mahavihara, Gana Bahal

*Kindol Vihara, Swayambhu (formal name:

Nirvanamurti Upasikaram)
*Kunsa Baha, Hyumat
*Padmakirti Vihara, Kamal Pokhari
Padma Sugandha Vihara, Majipat
Pippali Theravada Buddha Vihara, Siphal
Sangharama Vihara, Dhalko
Shrigha Vihara, Nagha
Vishwa Shanti Vihara, Naya Baneshwar
*Vi. Sha. Dharmakirti Vihara, Basundhara
Outside Kathmandu
Chaturbrahma Vihara, Mata Tirtha
Charumati Buddha Vihara, Chabahil
Gautam Buddha Vihara, Panga-Kirtipur
Jitavana [sic] Vihara, Thankot
Kuti Vihara, Koteshwar
Pranidhipurna Mahavihara, Balambu
Shri Kirti Vihara, Kirtipur
*Sulakshana Kirti Vihara, Chobhar
Tokha Buddha Vihara, Tokha
Vijayarama Vihara, Balambu, Dombu
Lalitpur District
In Lalitpur
Ilay Bahi
*Jaya Mangala Vihara, Tana Baha
Mani Mandap Vihara, Patko
*Narasingh Arama, Thaina
*Pragyananda Arama, Uku Baha
*Sangharakshita Vihara, Tana Baha
*Shanti Sukhavas, Chakupat
Shakyasingha Vihara, Thaina
Sumangal Vihara, Lukhusi
*Sunanda Arama, Thaina
Yampi Bahi, I Bahi
Outside Lalitpur
*Amarapura Vihara, Bungamati
Jana Udaya Vihara, Sunakothi
Jitapur Gandhakuti Vihara, Khokna
Jyoti Udaya Vihara, Chapagaon
Punyodaya Vihara, Harasiddhi
Shanti Vihara, Kopundol
Siddhi Mangal Vihara, Thasi
Suvarna Dantapur Vihara, Lubhu
Veluvan Arama, Thecho
Bhaktapur District
Bauddha Samskrita Vihara, Bhaktapur
Muni Vihara, Hanuman Ghat, Bhaktapur
Nagadesh Buddha Vihara, Madhyapur
Pati Vihara, Thimi, Madhyapur

Kabhre-Palanchok
Bodhicharya Vihara, Banepa
Chandrakirti Vihara, Banepa
Dhyankuti Vihara, Banepa
Sudarshan Vihara, Banepa
*Kashivarna Buddha Vihara, Panauti
Purvarama Vihara, Dhulikhel
Shikhalapur Vihara, Dhulikhel
Balaharsha Kirti Vihara, Khopasi
Other Hill Districts
Ananda Vihara, Tansen (Palpa)
Holandi Vihara, Holandi, Tansen
Mahabodhi Vihara, Laharepipal, Tansen
Mahachaitya Vihara, Taksar, Tansen
Sugandha Vihara, Ridi, Gulmi
Gyanodaya Buddha Vihara, Baglung
Beni Buddha Vihara, Myagdi
Dharmashila Buddha Vihara, Pokhara, Kaski
Machhapuchhre Buddha Vihara, Ghachok, Kaski
Sugatpur Vihara, Trishuli, Nuwakot
Shakyamuni Vihara, Taksar, Bhojpur
Bodhisatva Vihara, Chainpur, Sankhuwasabha
Siddhi Vihara, Chainpur, Sankhuwasabha
Buddha Vihara, Dhankuta
Tarai Districts
Lokchakra Vihara, Dhangadi, Kailali
Buddha Vihara, Nepalganj, Banke
Kapilvastu Buddha Vihara, Taulihawa, Kapilvastu
Sri Mangala Vihara, Kapilvastu
Abhinava Buddha Vihara, Lumbini, Rupandehi
*Gautami Vihara, Lumbini, Rupandehi
International Buddhist Society Vihara, Lumbini, Rupandehi
Lokmuni Chula Vihara, Lumbini, Rupandehi
Lumbini Thai Vihara, Lumbini, Rupandehi
Mahamaya Vishwa Shanti Vihara, Lumbini, Rupandehi
Shakyamuni Buddha Vihara, Lumbini, Rupandehi
Padmachaitya Vihara, Butwal, Rupandehi
Pugatabhumi Jetavana Vihara, Siddhartha Nagar (Bhairhawa)
Chitrawana Vihara, Narayangadh, Chitwan
Pragya Vihara, Hetauda, Makwanpur
Buddha Vihara, Birganj, Parsa

Kalaiya Buddha Vihara, Kalaiya, Bara
Buddha Vihara, Dharan, Sunsari
Vayaravana Jyoti Vihara, Chatara, Dharan, Sunsari
Swayambhu Chaitya Mahavihara, Dharan
Buddha Vihara, Biratnagar, Morang
Swayambhu Chaitya Buddha Vihara, Urlabari, Morang

Glossary

Nepal Bhasha (Newari), the mother tongue of most of the subjects of this book, is a Tibeto-Burman language that for more than fifteen hundred years has been part of the Indo-European linguistic area of South Asia. Consequently, like the Semitic language Maltese, which is written in the roman alphabet and takes its complex and abstract vocabulary from Latin, Nepal Bhasha has been, until the rise of modern linguistic nationalism in the twentieth century, entirely oriented toward scriptural and prestige language forms from a different language group, in this case Sanskrit and Middle Indo-Aryan languages. Its borrowings in the sphere of religion have been overwhelmingly from Sanskrit. This means that terminology used by Theravada practitioners may vary between Pali and Sanskrit forms—*dhamma* versus *dharma*, *kamma* versus *karma*—even within a single sentence. The key point to remember is that there is a hierarchy of languages, so that any Sanskrit or Pali noun may be used in, and can be treated as a valid vocabulary item of, Nepali or Nepal Bhasha, but not vice versa. (In the same way, because of the political and cultural dominance of Nepali, Nepali nouns, and even many verbs suitably adapted, can be used in Nepal Bhasha, but not vice versa.) In both Nepali and Nepal Bhasha there tends to be a preference for Sanskrit over Pali forms. In precisely the same way there is today a widespread tendency to insert English words in educated speech (and writing) in both Nepali and Nepal Bhasha.*

* A striking example occurred in a speech by Malla K. Sundar at a press conference to

The problems of Sanskrit vs. Pali, and of consistency, also affect personal names. Some monastics prefer the Sanskritic form (Sudarshan, Dharmachari), others the Pali (Dhammawati, Kondanya); it may not be a coincidence, however, that the older monks nearly all seem to have preferred Sanskritic forms of their names. Sometimes the bearers of the names are themselves inconsistent in the way in which they anglicize their own name. In this book, an attempt has been made to follow the most common form used: thus, "Dhammalok" (Pali), rather than "Dharmaloka" (Sanskrit), in spite of the fact that he himself wrote his name in English in the latter form, because "Dhammalok" is how he is more generally known. Even where there is no switch between Sanskritic and Pali forms (thus Dhammawati, not Dharmavati), there may be other inconsistencies.†

In the text, specialist terms have been anglicized wherever possible, and the use of diacritics has been limited to occasions where it seemed likely that that they would aid in pronunciation.

Skt.=Sanskrit, P.=Pali, N.Bh.=Nepal Bhasha (Newari), N.=Nepali, T.=Tibetan.

anāgārikā/anagārikā (Skt./P.): the term used in Nepal to refer to women who take the Ten Precepts and wear monastic robes; the equivalent of Sri Lankan *dasa sil mata*, Burmese *thilashin*, or Thai *maechi*

ānāpāna (P.): breathing in and out (in the context of meditation); meditation on the breath

ārāma (Skt./P.): Lit. "rest house"; used of dwellings of *anāgārikā* to distinguish them from a *vihāra*

arhat (P. *arahant*): An enlightened person who is not a Buddha

baha (*bāhāḥ*) (N.Bh.): the colloquial term for most traditional Newar Buddhist monasteries, membership of which is by descent; the honorific titles of such monasteries refer to them as *vihāra*

bahi (*bahī*) (N.Bh.): colloquial term for a small subclass of traditional Newar Buddhist monasteries (see Gellner 2001: ch. 6 on the distinction between *baha* and *bahi*)

bhajan (N.Bh., N. *bhajan*): hymns

---

inform journalists about the activities of the Newa De Dabu (an umbrella organization bringing together all Newar cultural organizations) on November 30, 2003: "Thwa samsthāyā 'vision' 'mission' 'clear' juye māḥ" (This organization's vision and mission must be clear).

† In Devanagari, one sees, and in speech one hears, "Dhammāwati" as often as "Dhammawati."

bhante (P.): "Venerable Sir"; term of address for Theravada monks; also used colloquially as a term of reference ("the bhantes," meaning Theravada monks)

bhikkhu (P.): see bhikshu

bhikkhuni (P.): see bhikshuni

bhikshu (Skt. *bhikṣu*, P. *bhikkhu*): fully ordained monk, supposed to observe 227 rules in the Theravada Vinaya

bhikshuni (Skt. *bhikṣuni*, P. *bhikkhuni*): fully ordained nun, supposed to observe 311 rules (according to the Theravada Vinaya) or 348 (according to the Dharmaguptaka Vinaya)

bhojan (Skt.): honorific term for food, used in polite discourse in N. and N.Bh., and as a term for the main meal for monastics, eaten at 11:30 A.M. and offered by donors

buddha dharma (Skt.): "the dharma of the Buddha"; how Theravadins refer to their own religion; traditionalist Newar Buddhists are more likely to say simply "dharma" or "our dharma"

chaitya (Skt. *caitya*): the principal Buddhist object of worship in all forms of Buddhism; cf. *stūpa*

chela (*celā*), fem. cheli (*celī*) (N./N.Bh.): disciple, pupil

dāna/*dān* (Skt./P.): gifts, charity

dasa sil mata (Sinhala): Sri Lankan equivalent of *anāgārikā*

dharma desana (Skt. *deśanā,* P. *desanā*): religious discourse or preaching

dharmadhātu (Skt.): second most common form of cult object, after chaityas, in Newar Buddhism; dedicated to the bodhisattva Manjushri

dīkṣā (Skt.): initiation, Tantric Initiation, the highest ritual qualification in Vajrayana Buddhism; once taken, the practitioner must perform rituals to their personal deity every morning before eating

duḥkha (N./N.Bh. often also *dukha*, Skt. *duḥkha*, P. *dukkha*): suffering, the inevitable unsatisfactoriness of everyday householder life; what monastics are supposed to be escaping, in joining the Sangha

Eight Precepts (Skt. *aṣṭaśīla*, P. *aṭṭhasīla*): the Five Precepts plus three further undertakings: to avoid eating after midday, to avoid shows and adornments, and to avoid luxurious beds; in addition, the third precept becomes a complete ban on sexual activity

Five Precepts: see *pañcasil*

garudhamma (P.): the eight chief or "weighty" rules (see pp. 172–173), which nuns must follow in relation to monks

gelong (T. *dge-long*): the Tibetan term for an ordained monk

ghat (N. *ghāṭ*): "ford"; place on a holy river used for cremations and other religious activities

gompa (T. *dgon-pa*): usually written and pronounced *gumbā* in N.Bh. and N.; literally "holy place," monastery of temple in the Tibetan style; can also refer to a wing of a Newar *baha* done up in Tibetan style

Gubhaju (N.Bh. *gubhāju*): honorific term of reference for Vajracharyas

Gunla (N.Bh. *gū̃lā*): month in the Newar religious calendar corresponding approximately to August; a time for heightened Buddhist practice in traditional Newar Buddhism, it also falls in the Theravada *vassāvāsa* period

guruju (N.Bh.): term of address for a Vajracharya priest; also used colloquially in reference

guruma (*gurumā*) (N.Bh.): "mother guru"; traditional term of respect (used to address a Vajracharya priest's wife) which was adopted as the colloquial term, both in address and reference, for Theravada nuns

guthi (N.Bh., N. *guṭhi*): Newar socio-religious association, usually of caste equals, to carry out some social and/or religious purpose: death *guthis*, which take care of cremations, and lineage deity *guthis*, for the carrying out of the annual worship of a lineage deity, are the two most common kinds

jajmān (N., N.Bh. *jaymā*, Skt. *yajamāna*): hereditary patron of a priest or other ritual specialist

Janajati (N./N.Bh. *janajāti*): a politically correct neologism coined to translate "ethnic group" in the Nepali context. Adopted from Bengali by Darjeeling-based Nepalis, the word was unknown in Kathmandu in the 1980s and is still not recognized by many ordinary Nepalis. It is used to refer to those groups such Magar, Gurung, Tamang, Rai, Limbu, and Tharu, who would previously have been called "tribes"; whether the Newars should or should not be considered Janajati is a controversial question, but they have been included in the official government list and are members of the Nepal Janajati Mahasangh, which calls itself The Nepal Federation of Indigenous Nationalities (NEFIN) in English.

jhārphuke vaidya (N.Bh.): a traditional healer (*vaidya*, *baidde*) who makes use of brushing, mantras, and rituals, as well as loosely Ayurvedic concepts and medicines

kappiyakār (P. *kappiyakāraka*): layman who accepts gifts on behalf of a monk; hence a lay assistant who organizes financial and household matters

kathina (P. *kaṭhina*): ceremony in which new robes are presented to monks at the end of the *vassāvāsa*

kaytā pūjā (N.Bh.) (N. *vartamān*, Skt. *vratabandha*): Lit. "worship of [putting on] the loincloth"; the caste initiation ritual for a layperson, whether Buddhist or Hindu

kesaloma (P.): a form of Buddhist meditation that consists in focusing on each part of the body in turn and seeing it as non-self

kilesa (P., Skt. *kleśa*): defilements or afflictions, especially greed, hatred, and delusion

kothi (N.Bh., N. *koṭhi*): old (pre–1960) term for a large trading business

kuṭī (Skt./P.): cottage, mendicant's hut

maitrī bhāvanā (Skt.): meditation on kindness

mettā (P., Skt. *maitrī*): kindness or benevolence

nirvana (Skt. *nirvāṇa*, P. *nibbāna*): liberation from the cycle of rebirths through enlightenment; see also parinirvana

nun: used for any full-time Theravadin or Mahayana female renunciant, whether an *anagarika* or a fully ordained *bhikkhuni*

pabbajjā (P., Skt. *pravrajyā*, N. *pabajyā*): lit. "going forth"; the rite of renunciation

pācittiya (P.): 92 offences against the Vinaya rules for monks and nuns (bhikshunis), which must be confessed before the Sangha

pañcasīl (P., Skt. *pañcaśīla*): the Five Precepts, that is, undertakings not to kill, not to steal, not to indulge in wrongful sexual conduct, not to lie, and not to intoxicate oneself (most laypeople in Nepal interpret the third and fifth precepts as requiring a complete ban on sex and alcohol for the day on which the precepts have been taken)

paṇḍit (Skt.): learned man; scholar

parinirvana (Skt. *parinirvāṇa*): ultimate nirvana achieved only after death

paritrāṇa (Skt.): "protection rite"; the recitation of specified Pali verses in order to win merit and, therefore, protection for the sponsor and his or her household

paritta (P.): see *paritrāṇa*

pariyatti (P.): skill in and knowledge of the scriptures, often contrasted to P. *paṭipatti*, spiritual accomplishment or practice

pātimokkha (P., Skt. *prātimokṣa*): The collection of rules (227 for monks, 311 for bhikshunis in the Theravada Vinaya), which are supposed to be recited and reviewed twice a month

pravacan (Skt): speech; colloquially used for *dharmadeśanā*, religious sermon

prasād (Skt.): "blessing"; used for the blessed substances, food, water, flowers, that a worshipper or devotee receives in Hinduism or in traditional Newar Buddhism

pūjā (Skt.): worship, fundamental in Theravada Buddhism as it is in traditional Newar Buddhism and Hinduism; in Theravada, however, it is restricted mainly to the figure of Shakyamuni Buddha and to *stupas* or chaityas that represent him or earlier Buddhas

purohit (Skt.): hereditary priest of a patron (*jajmān*, N.Bh. *jaymā*); can be used both of Hindu Brahmans and of Vajracharyas

rishini (Skt. *ṛṣiṇi*): "sage-ess" or female sage; role invented for temporary female ordination (*rishini pabajja*); see pp. 91–93.

sahuji (N. *sāhū* plus honorific): rich businessman, moneylender

samādhi; (Skt./P.): concentration, especially in meditation

samanera (P. *sāmaṇera*; Skt. *śrāmaṇera*): monastic novice, who may, if over the age of twenty, take full ordination as a bhikkhu

samsara (Skt./P. *saṃsāra*): worldly existence, involving repeated births and deaths

Sangha (P./Skt. *saṅgha*): the Monastic Community established by the Buddha, it applies both to all Buddhist monastics as the ideal Sangha and to specific Sanghas sharing an ordination tradition or a disciplinary code; the same term (also shortened to *sā*) is used for the hereditary members of a traditional Newar Buddhist *baha* or *bahi*

sanghādisesa (P., Skt. *saṅghāvaśeṣa*): monastic disciplinary rules requiring suspension from the Sangha

sekhiya (P.): lit. "training rule"; 75 minor rules about dress and comportment to be followed by monks and nuns

sila (P. *sīla*, Skt. *śīla*): moral conduct, the essential first step on the Buddhist path
Shravakayana: The Mahayanist name for the first level of Buddhist doctrine and practice; used by traditional Newar Buddhists as a name for the Theravada
śloka (Skt.): sacred verses in Sanskrit
stūpa (Skt., N.Bh. *thūr*): sacred mound oriented to the directions, containing the remains of a Buddha; large version of a chaitya
sutra (Skt. *sūtra*, P. *sutta*): Buddhist scripture recording the words or deeds of the Buddha
Ten Precepts (Skt. *daśaśīla*, P. *dasasīla*): the Eight Precepts with one additional precept (not to accept gold or silver, i.e. money) and the seventh precept split into two separate precepts
thilashin (Burmese): Burmese equivalent of *anāgārikā*
Three Jewels (Skt./P. *triratna*): the Buddha, Dharma, and Sangha
ṭol (N., N.Bh. *twāḥ*): neighborhood of a town or section of a Newar village
Triple Refuge: taking refuge in the Buddha, Dharma, and Sangha
upāsaka (male)/*upāsikā* (fem.) (Skt./P.): layperson, a supporter of Buddhism; in the Newar context the term specifically indicates a supporter of Theravada Buddhism
upasampadā (P.): ordination as a bhikshu
uposatha (P.): holy days, twice a month, when monks and nuns are supposed to recite the Patimokkha and when laypeople take the precepts
uposathāgāra (P.): meeting hall for holding Patimokkha recitations; must be established as such within a monastery boundary (*simā*)
vaidya (Skt.): traditional doctor or healer, including Ayurvedic practitioners
vajra (Skt.): "diamond"; the symbol of Tantric Buddhism
vassāvāsa (P.): rains retreat, for the three months of the rainy period monks are supposed to stay in one place and teach the laity there
vihara (P./Skt. *vihāra*): monastery, nunnery (cf. *ārāma*)
Vinaya: the Buddhist scripture that records the Buddha's rules of monastic discipline, found both in Theravada and in Mahayana branches of Buddhism
vipassana (P. *vipassanā*, Skt. *vipaśyanā*): "insight," form of meditation started by Ledi Sayadaw and popularized worldwide by Goenka; see Chapter 8
yogi (Skt./P. *yogin*): Following Burmese usage, the term used in N. and N.Bh. to refer to meditators on a course who take the Eight Precepts for a number of days; more widely, a practitioner of yoga

Notes

Chapter 1. Introduction: The Origins of Modernist Buddhism

1. If Sri Lanka and Southeast Asia are defined as different cultural regions, the Theravada missions that brought ordination traditions from Southeast Asia to revive monasticism in Sri Lanka in 1070, 1753, and 1862 were all exceptions to this generalization.
2. On both figures, see Brekke (2002); see also, on Vivekananda, Raychaudhuri (1988: ch. 4) and on Dharmapala, Obeyesekere (1976, 1995), Gombrich and Obeyesekere (1988), and Sangharakshita (1980). Vivekananda and Dharmapala met in Chicago and quickly became friends and allies, but after Vivekananda visited Sri Lanka four years later and started openly criticizing Buddhism, they fell out (Brekke 2002: 53–60).
3. *St Louis Observer*, September 21, 1893, quoted in Barrows (1895, 1: 95).
4. See Malalgoda (1976) and Gombrich (1988: 175–6).
5. See Gombrich and Obeyesekere (1988: 203–204), Spencer (1995: 206–207), Young and Somaratne (1996).
6. On Buddhist reform in Sri Lanka, see Malalgoda (1976), Bond (1988), and Gombrich and Obeyesekere (1988).
7. Prothero (1996: 95). Olcott noted in his diaries that "Our Buddhism was that of the Master-Adept Gautama Buddha, which was identically the Wisdom Religion of the Aryan Upanishads, and the soul of all the ancient world-faiths" (ibid.: 96).
8. In a letter to his father, he wrote: "As long as life lasts I will work in accordance with the Buddhist precepts, for the progress of the world. . . . I have realized that to be head of a household, protecting home and property, bringing up children, is one of suffering. Hence I have decided to live as a brahmacharin. Though I would like to become a monk, I have decided not to do so, but instead become a brahmacharin for life. A life of a monk is

suitable for a person who is concerned with his own selfwelfare. But for those concerned with the welfare for others the brahmacharin life is suitable, useful for meaningful worldly work" (Obeyesekere 1976: 235, citing Karunaratne 1964: 46–48). As a celibate layman, Dharmapala embraced what Obeyesekere in another article (1995a) dubbed a form of Weberian "worldly asceticism." This permitted Dharmapala to engage in a wide range of activities that would have been considered inappropriate at that time for a monk; it also enabled him to evolve an ethic suitable for a Buddhist bourgeoisie. Only when he was old and sick, did he take novice ordination (at Sarnath in 1931) and full ordination shortly before his death in 1933.

9. Cited in Sangharakshita (1980: 64). Brekke points out that the idea of reviving Bodh Gaya as a center for world Buddhism had already been put forward by Sir Edwin Arnold, the author of the highly influential poem on the Buddha's life, "The Light of Asia," when he went to Sri Lanka after visiting Bodh Gaya in 1885. And in fact Dharmapala acknowledged Arnold's influence (2002: 93–94).
10. On the history of conflict over the ownership and control of the Bodh Gaya shrine, see Barua (1981), Trevithick (1988, 1999), Doyle (1997), and Brekke (2002: 86–104).
11. *Dharmaduta* (messenger of truth) is a late-nineteenth-century neologism intended to neutralize the idea of a "Buddhist" mission. The MBS's emphasis was on the revitalization and reform of Buddhist communities rather than on conversion (Kemper 2004).
12. Madame Blavatsky had died; Colonel Olcott was the "director" and "chief advisor," but he was to resign in 1896 after differences over attempts to buy the Bo Tree temple site (Prothero 1996: 158–163). For a history of the Maha Bodhi Society, see Ratnatunga (1991).
13. Although he continued to travel widely, even when old and sick, Dharmapala spent much of the rest of his life in Calcutta and was even exiled there by the British colonial government (1915–1922) as punishment for his participation, starting in 1906, in the Sinhala nationalist movement in Sri Lanka (Ratnatunga 1991: 47).
14. For a recent analysis, see Tartakov (2003). Ambedkar may also have delayed his own conversion because he wanted to lay the groundwork and make sure his conversion project was a success. For a time he considered joining Sikhism (Juergensmeyer 1988: 162; Gore 1993: 248).
15. Prothero gives Doss's name as Iyothee Thass. On Doss, see Perumal (1998).
16. Emphasis in the original. Olcott's address was published originally in the *Journal of the Maha Bodhi Society* (7.4, August 1898), cited from Prothero (1996: 140).
17. Originally published in the *Journal of the Maha Bodhi Society* (15.1–3, January–March 1907), cited from Prothero (1996: 172). For excellent summaries of Olcott's and Dharmapala's impacts on Sinhalese Buddhism, see Gombrich (1988: 181–197). Obeyesekere notes that "Olcott had little understanding of Dharmapāla's populism and little sympathy for it," but they

were alike in that "their knowledge of Buddhism came primarily from Orientalist sources" (Obeyeskere 1995: 250).

18. For the text of all twenty-two vows, see Zelliott (1996: 215), Tartakov (2003: 196–197), or Kantowsky (2003: 26). Similarly, in his *The Buddha and his Dhamma*, Ambedkar (1992: 249ff) included a section on what Dhamma was not: viz, belief in the supernatural, belief in union with Brahma, belief in sacrifices or the infallibility of books, and so forth. On Ambedkar's Buddhist legacy, see Kantowsky (2003: 111ff.) On Untouchable religious and political movements in the Punjab, most of which have not been Buddhist, see Juergensmeyer (1988).
19. See Carrithers (1983) and Tiyavanich (1997) for two important studies of these movements in Theravada contexts in modern times. The inferior position of women in Buddhism is considered in detail below. See Bartholomeusz (1994) on women's revivalism in Sri Lanka.
20. In Japanese Buddhism there was also an *anti*-monastic revival movement, led by Shinran (1173–1263).
21. In her study of the Theravada movement in Nepal, Leve (1999, 2002) has emphasized precisely the radical differences in ethos and outlook of the two forms of Buddhism.
22. Leading Newar Theravada monks, such as Amritananda, have objected to the label "Newar Buddhism," presumably because they wish Theravada Buddhism to be considered equally "Newar." On Newar Buddhism, see Locke (1980) and Gellner (1992). On Tibetan Buddhism within Nepal see Fürer-Haimendorf (1964), Holmberg (1989), Mumford (1989), and Ortner (1989a, 1999).
23. See Kloppenberg (1977: 311) for the mid-1970s, Gellner (1992: 322) and Hartmann (1993: 77) for the end of the 1980s, and Kondanya (2001) for the 2001 figures.
24. See Davidson (2002) for an examination of the Indian social background to the rise of Tantric Buddhism.
25. A Nepali was quoted as retorting, "It's like saying Mohandas Karamchand Gandhi was born in India, but Mahatma Gandhi was born in South Africa" (www.nepalnews.com.np/ntimes/may18–2001/nation.htm) (accessed June 8, 2005).
26. See Almond (1988: 73–76, 123–126), Lopez (1995, 1998), and Gellner (2001a: ch. 2) for explorations of this theme.
27. There is perhaps a paradox here in that Colonel Olcott, who contributed so much to the cause of Protestant Buddhism and its rationalist view of the world, was himself a lifelong believer in an astral plane from which he received messages from the "Mahatmas"; it is possibly less paradoxical that in 1882–1883 he spent over a year healing thousands of people in the name of the Buddha in Sri Lanka and Bengal before the Mahatmas told him to stop (Prothero 1996: 109).
28. Obeyesekere (1970); Malalgoda (1976); Gombrich (1988: 174); Gombrich and Obeyesekere (1988: 5–6).

29. See Gombrich (1988: ch. 7), Gombrich and Obeyesekere (1988: 7, 218 ff.).
30. Skilling (1995). The first recorded "sighting" of a female renouncer by a foreigner was by Joost Schouten, the director of the Dutch East India Company at Ayutthaya between 1624 and 1629. "Besides these Priests, there are a sort of old Nuns shorn, lodged in Chappels near the greatest Temples, who assist very devoutly in all their preachings, singings, ceremonies, and other Church services, but all voluntary, being tied to no rules or prescriptions" (Caron and Schouten 1986: 141).
31. Tiyavanich (1997: 281). Only in the 1950s did their status begin to improve when a handful of educated women escaped subordination to the monks by building their own nunneries whose land, construction, and maintenance costs were provided by their lay devotees or by their own families (Falk 2000).
32. "[They] are equally common with priests. They reside in a convent of nuns, or live separately in some house constructed near a *Koo* (temple), superintending the offerings, and leading a life of religious abstinence. The greater part of the *Bhi Kuni* have retained their virginity from early youth; others have retired from the scene of earthly cares at a more advanced age; in some instances, after marriage, but only when the marriage has not been productive of children. The dress of the *Bhi Kuni* is similar to that of the *Phoongrees* (monks), and their discipline in every other respect alike. Both are equally revered by the laity, and supplied with the little food necessary for their subsistence" (Foley 1835). On the claim that there were bhikkhuni in Burma, see Chapter 7, note 16.
33. On the Burmese Sangha in the nineteenth century, see Mendelson (1975).
34. *Ngebyu* stood in contrast with *tawdwet*, meaning "forestdweller." Whether or not *tawdwet* actually lived in the forest, this appellation implied a state of mind, referring to the brahmanical idea of the third *varna* or life-stage when elderly people withdraw to the jungle to a life of ascetic reflection.
35. Thaton Mingun Zetawun was one of the first Burmese monks to encourage women to study Buddhism to an advanced level. In old age he published a commentarial work in which he wrote, "Even though the order of the Bhikkhunīs is completely discontinued, some say that women should not be given ordination by the order of monks. . . . In this matter, we say that, for this very reason, women should be given ordination by the order of monks" (cited in Deshpande 1999: 11–12). The views he expressed on female ordination, among other issues, in this book aroused such controversy that it was banned both by the Sangha and by the government. Mingun was also known as U Narada Sayadaw, and he was the meditation teacher of Mahasi Sayadaw who introduced vipassana meditation to Nepal in 1981 (see Chapter 8).

Chapter 2. Theravada Missionaries in an Autocratic State

1. On the Gurkhas, see Falwell (1984), Des Chene (1991), and Caplan (1995). After 1947, the regiments were split 50–50 between the United Kingdom

and India. On the Law Code of 1854, which attempted to weld the whole country into a single over-arching Hindu caste framework and to legitimize the Rana regime in traditional Hindu terms, see Höfer (1979).

2. See Liechty (1997). For Prithvi Narayan's warning, see Stiller (1968: 43).
3. The best introduction to the Uday as a caste is Lewis (1995). See also Rosser (1966). They are known also as Urāy, Udās (in Nepali), and by their common surnames: Tulādhar, Kansakār, Sthāpit, and others.
4. The Ranas' school, later known as Durbar High School, was established in 1853 in Thapathali palace. It was moved outside to a building in front of Rani Pokhari by Ranoddip Singh Rana, who added classes nine and ten (see Thapa 1988: 118–19). In 1894, Bir S.J.B. Rana moved it to another building to the west of Rani Pokhari and permitted commoners to attend.
5. Once he returned to Nepal for good in 1936, he resumed lay dress.
6. On Dhama Sahu himself, see R. S. Shakya (1992b: 79–87). On the Swayambhu restoration, see Rospatt (2000: 628).
7. Of Dharmacharyya's journals, *Bauddha Bharata* was in Hindi and Bengali; *Himalaya Bauddha* was in Nepali; *Buddhadharma wa Nepal Bhasha* was in Nepal Bhasha; and *Buddhist India* (which came out in 1927, 1928, and 1929, and for the first two years had numerous scholarly articles by Indian and Western authors) was in English. He appears to have reused much of the same material in all of them.
8. For an influential early discussion of the evolution of Nepali national identity, see Burghart (1984). For more recent studies, see Onta (1996, 1999) and Chalmers (2003).
9. It may possibly be relevant to an understanding of Dharmacharyya's own motivation for reviving Newar Buddhism that he came from Chikã Bahi, one of the small *bahi* class of monasteries that used to maintain the religious identity and surname of "celibate monks" (Brahmacharya Bhikshu) even though they were in fact married householders, just like other Shakyas. In other words, they retained a memory and certain ritual traces of a more purely monastic, and less Tantric, practice of Buddhism; at the same time, the *bahi* were seen as having slightly inferior social standing by other Shakyas, and by Vajracharyas. Thus, Prof. Asha Ram Shakya, who also comes from a *bahi*, recalls how Dharmacharyya came to his house to tell him off for giving his surname as "Shakya," rather than as "Brahmacharya Bhikshu" (A. R. Shakya 1998: 9). On the question of *baha-bahi* differences and relations see Locke (1985) and Gellner (1987).
10. Letter dated September 24, 1930, India Office Library, L/P&S/2/3005. We are indebted to Taeko Uesugi for this reference.
11. See Toffin (1984) and Gellner and Quigley (1995). Some idea of the ways in which it was rapidly transforming into a class society on the global periphery in the 1980s and 1990s can be had from Liechty (2003).
12. The Khadgi (category five) are a special case, in that they have a special lineage of lower-caste Buddhist priests. The Kapali-Jogi (also category five) and the Sweepers (category six) find priests within their own caste (for details, see Gellner 1995).

13. See Rosser (1966), Toffin (1984: ch. 13), and Quigley (1995, 1996). An interesting contribution to the Hinduization debate is Webster (1981). On Sankhu, from which Rosser drew much of his data for his thesis of priest-switching, see Shrestha (2002).
14. On the rise of identity politics in Nepal generally since 1990, see Gellner et al. (1997) and Gellner (2001b).
15. On this, see Gellner (1992, 2001a: ch. 5).
16. See Locke (1985) for a comprehensive survey of all Newar Buddhist monasteries which documents the various different systems in use for determining duties and roles; cf. Gellner (1987).
17. The small class of *bahi* monasteries were an exception, as mentioned previously in note 9.
18. The alternative origin myth, held concurrently, is that the Shakyas are descendants of the last celibate monks, forcibly laicized by Shankara Acharya and/or by Jaya Sthiti Malla. The Nepali historian, Bhuwan Lal Pradhan, trying to systematize the myths and the historical evidence, writes: "The Shakyas of Kapilwastu continued migrating into the valley of Kathmandu at different times and in different groups" (Pradhan 1985: 9). On the different Shakya titles, see Gellner (1989).
19. Seven sons of Tansen became bhikshus between 1933 and 1963, including Shakyananda, Amritananda, Kumar Kashyap, and Gyanapurnik, but not a single bhikshu has come from Tansen since that time (C. Shakya 997: 8).
20. The hill Shakyas (and Vajracharyas) had a specific ground of grievance against the old form of Buddhism, which was that until the last decade of the Rana period they had to trek many days, at ruinous expense, to have their boys initiated at the monasteries of their forebears in Lalitpur, Kathmandu, or—more rarely—Bhaktapur, a procedure that was essential to maintain their caste status. Unlike other Newar castes, they were unable to do this by substituting hill Brahmans and their rituals in their place of residence; in order to be able to perform the ritual in their home towns, they had to build a new *baha* and have it accepted as such by Vajracharyas in the Kathmandu Valley (see *Dharmodaya* 3.9, July 1950, p. 256).
21. That it is in decline is widely recognized by Newar Buddhist intellectuals, though they do not, in print, blame Theravada for this. The decline and what to do about it has been the subject of two conferences (in 1993 and 1998) organized by the Lotus Research Institute (on which see further, below, pp. 266, 283). We do not agree, therefore, with Lienhard's judgment, when he wrote, "Since the beginning of the 20th century Hīnayāna missionary activity has begun again with the arrival of Sinhalese monks who are working to introduce Theravāda Buddhism, but their success has been limited" (Lienhard 1984: 109).
22. Hridaya (1992: 30–31). Min Bahadur Shakya lists the texts he used, in addition to the *Lalitavistara* and the *Bhadrakalpa Avadana* (the two main sources), as the *Ratnamala Avadana*, the *Gunakarandavyuha*, the *Svay-*

ambhu Purana, the *Pancaraksa*, the *Mahavastu*, the *Asoka Avadana*, the *Astasahasrika Prajnaparamita*, and the *Nirvana Sutra* (M. B. Shakya 1997b: 6).

23. P. H. Tuladhar (2002). Nisthananda's book also inspired the poet Hridaya to write his classic Nepal Bhasha epic poem on the life of the Buddha, *Sugata Saurabha*; for a translation, see Hridaya (1998). K. P. Malla (1979: 16–17) quotes Hridaya describing how books had to be published and distributed secretly; he also describes how in 1940 and 1941, the Rana regime threw dozens of Nepal Bhasha literary activists into jail—which turned out to be a "blessing in disguise" because of the large amount of poetry that was composed inside, including the *Sugata Saurabha.* A bust of Nisthananda was erected near his home in Om Bahal, just south of the Hanuman Dhoka palace, Kathmandu, in 1998.
24. Different sources give different dates for Kyangtse Lama's arrival in Kathmandu, varying from 1922 to 1925. M. B. Shakya (1983: b) gives a date of 1922; Rosser (1966: 105) writes 1923; H. L. Singh (1996: 74) has 1924; H. Shakya (1978: 338) specifies the full moon of the month of Phalgun NS 1045, equivalent to mid March 1925; and S. M. Joshi (1990: 64) gives NS 1045, which corresponds to November 1924–October 1925. There seem to be no written sources on Kyangtse Lama in Tibetan, which suggests that he was not considered a significant figure in Tibet (K. Tanaka, personal communication).
25. As often happens with such mytho-religious sites in Asia, there are similar pilgrimage sites, equally identified as the place where Mahasattva made his sacrifice, in other Buddhist countries.
26. The *ratna mandala* is an arrangement of both hands to represent Mt. Meru, the cosmic summit at the center of the world. *Guruyoga-samadhi* is meditation on one's guru as the Buddha. These are the preliminary practices for Nyingma's Dzogchen teachings. Kyangtse Lama's teachings have been rendered into Nepal Bhasha by Buddhiraj Shakyavamsha (1990); for an English translation of the Tibetan source, see Patrul Rimpoche (1994).
27. Reformist Hindus, supporters of Dayananda Saraswati Arya Samaj, were persecuted on the same charge, including Madhav Raj Joshi, and his son Shukra Raj, who was later (in 1941) hanged along with the non-Brahman members of the Praja Parisad (Joshi and Rose 1966: 51, 55).
28. His clan name, which is sometimes given as his surname, was Khyāhju (Joshi 1990: 71).
29. Although the large majority of Shresthas are Hindu, a few (Mahapragya's family not among them) are Buddhists. The details of Mahapragya's life are taken from his autobiography.
30. Mahapragya received an answer to his longstanding question, Does one have the same or different parents in every rebirth? He learned from Kyangtse Lama that they are the same.
31. According to Satya Mohan Joshi (1990: 7), who interviewed those participants still alive, Tsering Norbu "recognized Dharmacharyya's scholarship"

and handed over responsibility for his five disciples to him and requested him to teach them about Buddhism.

32. When he grew up, Kul Man Singh Tuladhar's son ordained as a Gelukpa monk and Kul Man's wife as a Gelukpa nun. After the Chinese takeover, his son left Tibet for Switzerland where father and son had a single meeting in the 1970s. The son predeceased his father by several years.
33. Chandramani visited Kathmandu and Tarai towns with sizeable Newar Buddhist populations fairly frequently, but he never lived for any length of time in Nepal.
34. This presupposes the local Buddhist myth that Jaya Sthiti Malla (reigned 1382–95) abolished celibate Buddhist monasticism in Nepal (Gellner 1992: 86–87). In fact *non-Mahayanist* monasticism, as a widely followed permanent institution and lifelong option, almost certainly died out in the Kathmandu Valley long before Jaya Sthiti's time, and Mahayanist monasticism lingered on after it, exemplified by the figure of the highly respected monk, Vanaratna, who died in Pintu Bahi, Lalitpur, in 1468 (Vajracharya 1987: 34). Monastics in the Tibetan tradition continued to visit and stay in the Valley even after that (Lewis 1988, 1989, 1996b).
35. Vajracharya (1973: 382, 507). For the Mahāsanghika, see Roth (1970: xiv–xvi); for the Mulasarvastivada, see Skilling (1994).
36. According to Locke (1985: 402), the *baha* was originally built between 1685 and 1687. Dharmacharyya made his suggestion in 1924 and the renovation occurred in 1926. (Tuladhar 2001: 58, gives 1928 as the date for the renovation.)
37. These included Nisthananda's translation of the *Lalitavistara* and the texts produced by Dharmaditya Dharmacharyya.
38. See Joshi and Rose (1966), Fisher et al. (1997), and Hoftun et al. (1999) for descriptions of the period. One of the four martyrs, Shukra Raj, was actually a religious not a political reformist (n. 27, above)
39. The eight included four monks, Pragyananda, Dhammalok, Subodhananda, and Pragyarashmi, and four novices, Pragyarasa, Ratnajyoti, Aggadhamma, and Kumar Kashyap.
40. Gubhaju (1989: 10, 12) and Adhikari and Seddon (2002: 32). For an affectionate portrait of Dharmashila, see McHugh (2001: ch. 6).
41. Ananda Kaushalyayana was vice president, Bhikkhu Mahanama was joint secretary, and Mahapragya, Dhammalok, and Subodhananda were all members (Dharmalok 1999: 125). The role of Maniharsha is considered in detail in Chapter 5.
42. Bajracharya, Bajracharya, and Lall (1992: 98–99); see ibid.: 95–111 for other letters on the controversy.
43. The original Ananda Kuti Buddha relic was stolen in 1992. It was replaced in 1995 by a relic certified by the Sri Lankan government as being of the Buddha himself.
44. Because he was outside the Valley, Shakyananda had escaped being exiled in 1944. Aside from short visits to the capital, he spent his whole life in

Tansen. At Pragyananda's death, he became Sangha Nayaka, seniormost member of the Sangha, and died in Tansen in 1998.

45. Ordinary spoken Nepali does not normally inflect for gender, and Nepal Bhasha never does. Born in the Tarai, Sushila received the precepts from Chandramani, who sent her to Tansen where she lived for some years before moving into the Valley. She told us that she did not learn to read until after she became a nun but then she became literate not only in Nepali, Nepal Bhasha, and Hindi, but also in Pali well enough to translate Jataka stories into the vernacular. In the 1950s, she moved from Tansen to Tana Baha in Lalitpur; she died in Padmakirti Vihara, Kathmandu, in 2001.
46. Kloppenberg (1976: 307–308) citing *Dharmodaya* 35 (1950). The material in parentheses may be assumed to be Kloppenberg's glosses.

Chapter 3. Creating a Tradition

1. In the thirty years between 1950 and 1980, fifteen monasteries were established in each of the Lalitpur and Kathmandu districts, five in each of the Bhaktapur and Kabhre-Palanchok districts, and three in each of the Tansen and Sunsari districts (Vipassi 2001: 146). By 2002, there were fifty-four inside the Valley and forty-four outside (see appendix 2).
2. In 1949, Pragyananda moved to Shakyasingha Vihara, also in Lalitpur, and Buddhaghosh became abbot of Sumangal Vihara.
3. An exception was Buddha Vihara, constructed close to the Asoka pillar at Lumbini in 1956 to mark the two thousand five hundredth anniversary of the Buddha's birth. Meant to be seen as an international showcase for Nepalese Buddhism, the puja hall was decorated with large murals depicting the life of the Buddha executed in traditional Newar style. Some viharas constructed in recent decades, for example, Vishwa Shanti Vihara, have elaborate paintings of scenes from the Buddha's life, which also include (in supporting roles) the great gods of the Hindu pantheon, Brahma, Vishnu, and Shiva. Mahayana and Vajrayana divinities are strictly excluded, however.
4. Mohan Shamsher had already agreed to it being a holiday for Buddhists in the Kathmandu Valley at Narada Thera's suggestion in 1948.
5. The relics were excavated from the Sanchi stupa in 1849 and removed to the Victoria and Albert Museum in London. In 1939, after lengthy negotiations, the Maha Bodhi Society recovered them and, following World War II, members brought them via Colombo to Calcutta. In 1952, after having visited Nepal and several Buddhist countries, they were interred in the new Maha Bodhi Society vihara at Sanchi (Ratnatunga 1991: 60–77).
6. Sponsorship of *mahaparitrana*, which was introduced from Sri Lanka by Amritananda in 1941 when it was chanted at Parvasthana, Swayambhu, is expensive as it is followed, the next morning, by Buddhapuja, *dana*, and a meal for all the participating monks. According to Sudarshan (1982: 5), it had been performed thirty times by 1960 and was done twelve times within one year in 1978. Consisting of the recitation of 29 suttas, it is normally

expected that as many monks as possible should be present, at least at the opening and at the end of the ceremony. The normal pattern is to invite the whole Nepalese Sangha and complete it in a single all-night session, finishing in time for the monks' *bhojan* before midday the following day. An alternative option is for it to be performed in sections over a week with smaller numbers chanting. In recent years, perhaps because of the deteriorating security situation, it is often performed in one day, starting early in the morning and breaking halfway through for the monks' meal at 11:30 a.m. *Mahaparitrana* is the only Theravada ceremony sponsored by the kings of Nepal. From the late 1990s, nuns have sometimes been invited to assist the monks, that is, they chant for a stretch while the monks rest.

7. However, the government has done nothing to implement the ban and many Chetris continue to sacrifice to their clan deities on this day.
8. Sangharakshita (1956: 133–134). Sangharakshita went on to record his sorrow that some of the Theravada modernists seemed to think that the best way to bring about a revival of Buddhism was to ridicule and condemn the beliefs and practices of traditional Newar Buddhism and to criticize Vajracharya priests. He thought this laid them open to fairly obvious countercharges: "The few dozen Hinayana bhikshus, sramaneras and anagarikas of Nepal have as yet no provision whatsoever for study, whether of secular or religious subjects. Few are able to preach even elementary Buddhism, and it appears that none of them is versed in the practice of meditation well enough to be able to instruct others" (ibid.: 137).
9. See Bond (1988: 77). Note that whereas in Nepal "Buddha Jayanti" has been adopted as the name for the annual celebration of the Buddha's birth, enlightenment, and parinirvana, in Sri Lanka the term refers specifically to the celebrations of 1956. For a description of Buddha Jayanti in Kathmandu and Lalitpur in 1989, see Kieffer-Pülz (1993).
10. Under the new constitution of 1990, it is still illegal to proselytize, and in particular to offer inducements to convert, but violations are no longer prosecuted. (For discussion of the constitutional provisions on conversion see Dhungel et al. 1998: 178–184.)
11. The others are: mental development, transferring merit, empathizing in the merit transferred, doing service (to elders), respectful behavior, teaching, listening (to religious teaching), and holding right views (Gombrich and Obeyesekere 1988: 24). At this juncture, the missionaries did not emphasize the third "good deed," mental development, commonly understood to mean meditation, which they regarded as an esoteric practice suited only to monastics.
12. The first precept, not to kill, could be kept so long as one did not personally order an animal to be slaughtered. Eating meat purchased from a butcher is not considered to violate this precept. The problem arose when, as host of a feast, one bought goats or a buffalo and had them slaughtered for one's guests. The fourth precept, not to lie, is regarded as the hardest for traders and shopkeepers. The fifth, not to drink alcohol, was regarded as the most

difficult for laymen to keep given that at Newar feasts and at many familial rituals the consumption of alcohol is required. In fact, the Pali in which the precepts are recited speaks of undertaking not to intoxicate oneself, but it is understood to imply a complete ban on consuming alcohol for the rest of the day on which the precept is taken.

13. Some Kalimpong Newars restarted *Dharmodaya* as a Buddhist monthly in Nepal Bhasha in October 1977, but times had changed and, as one among a number of such publications, it no longer had the impact of its earlier namesake.
14. There were no Theravada Buddhist books in Nepali until Amritananda launched a series of Pali-Nepali translations in the 1970s, but Amritananda was equally prolific in Nepal Bhasha, and in 1962 he was honored by Chwasa Pasa, a leading Nepal Bhasha literary organization. Ashwaghosh, like Amritananda, was trained in Sri Lanka and Varanasi, and knows some English; he too writes in both Nepali and Nepal Bhasha. Of other leading writers and translators, Pragyananda and Buddhaghosh (both trained in Burma) wrote in Nepal Bhasha; Gyanapurnik, who was also trained in Burma, writes in both languages but favors Nepal Bhasha.
15. Malla (1979). A more recent bibliography (Amatya 1998) gives similar figures: of 2,361 books printed in Nepal Bhasha, 42 percent are on religious subjects. The list includes 25 by Amritananda (including translations and edited as well as single-authored volumes), 25 by Dhammalok, 22 by Pragyananda, 69 by Sudarshan, 18 by Vivekananda, and 42 by Dhammawati. The bibliography also lists 24 works by Buddhaghosh, 55 by Ashwaghosh, and 38 by Gyanapurnik. Slightly different figures are given by Bodhigyan (2002), who lists 1,335 books in Nepal Bhasha on Buddhism: 840 Theravada, 357 Mahayana, and 138 Vajrayana. His list, which counts all the different editions of the same text, has 57 titles for Amritananda, 55 for Dhammalok, 37 for Pragyananda, 79 for Sudarshan, 18 for Vivekananda, 55 for Dhammawati, 28 for Buddhaghosh, 71 for Ashwaghosh, and 16 for Gyanapurnik. (This list only includes titles in Nepal Bhasha, so Amritananda's numerous publications in Nepali are not included.)
16. In a traditional yearly festival of Newar Buddhism, Panchadan, male (and nowadays young female) Vajracharyas and Shakyas sometimes receive alms from other castes; however, on these ritually marked-off occasions, the rice donated is either uncooked or cooked in milk; not being cooked in water, it does not transfer impurity (Gellner 1992: 182).
17. An effort to reinstate the alms round in the 1980s failed. In the 1990s, novice monks from Vishwa Shanti Vihara took it up again but on a monthly, not a daily, basis.
18. Pilgrimage was soon conjoined with tourism as devotees alternated visits to sacred sites with shopping.
19. Nepali monastics conscientiously observe the rains retreat. If possible, they should be back in their viharas by the full-moon day in July, where they will remain until the full-moon day in October. Should they be elsewhere

on the July full-moon day, they must stay in that place until the October full moon day.

20. See chapter 5 for more on the hymn groups.
21. See Gellner (1992: 326–327); for the text and ritual of the *Pancaraksa*, see Lewis (2000a: ch. 6).
22. Kloppenberg (1977: 310). The need for Buddhist education for lay boys in Nepal had been particularly stressed by two foreigners, Narada and Sangharakshita, back in 1951 when visiting with the relics of Maudgalyayana and Shariputra. Remembering the role of Christian missionaries in education in Sri Lanka, Sangharakshita warned: "Christian missionaries are already perched like a flock of noisome vultures on the ridges of Kalimpong, where this article is being written, awaiting with eagerness an opportunity of swooping down and tearing the entrails out of what they believe to be the dead body of the Buddhism of Nepal" (Sangharakshita 1952: 70).
23. At this time, the abbot of Sumangal Vihara was Pragyananda who, when he was a monk in Tibet, had learned debating. He taught the basic principles to the young people in his monastery.
24. Sudarshan was permitted to attend the Council even though technically, as a samanera, he should have been excluded. Because of ill health, he returned to Nepal shortly afterward.
25. The majority of the monks, including Mahapragya, Pragyananda, Dhammalok, and Amritananda, had also, like the Buddha himself, been married householders before renouncing.
26. See Gellner (2001c) for a summary of the discussion.

Chapter 4. Charisma and Education: Dhammawati and the Nuns' Order after 1963

1. The original biography of Dhammawati, titled *Tamichet*, meaning "Dear Daughter," was written by a Burmese monk, Ra We Thon. Published in Burma in 1963, it was translated into Nepal Bhasha by Gyanapurnik and published in 1967. The Nepali version (*Snehi Chori*) was prepared by Moti Kaji Shakya, Dhammawati's own younger brother; published in 1990, it has been reprinted many times. His privileged position in relation to the story enabled him to expand it in one or two places.
2. Dhammawati herself did not mention this pregnancy, but she did stress the importance of her mother's support at this and many other points in her career: "From the time of her own conversion, my mother wanted to ordain, but she knew she couldn't get my father's permission, and after he died, my brothers wouldn't give it. So you might say that I was her substitute. She helped me in every way she could."
3. Regardless of their age, females wishing to ordain were required to get the permission of their closest male relatives.
4. In 1960, she was given a plane ticket home by Prime Minister U Nu

as a reward for her outstanding performance in the fourth-level "Achi" examinations.

5. Ratnamanjari, who came from a Hindu family, had been converted to Theravada Buddhism by Shakya women friends.
6. Although many foreign monastics have visited Nepal for short periods, Daw Gunawati (known as Mahaguna in Nepal) is one of very few who settled there. She saw herself as a missionary and for thirty years dedicated herself to the Newar Buddhist community in Kathmandu. She became fluent in Nepal Bhasha (though not in Nepali); however, she and Dhammawati always speak Burmese together. She went back to live in Burma only in 1995 when the government deeded her some land on the outskirts of Rangoon (now Yangon) on which, with Nepali as well as Burmese donations, she has built a nunnery, the Burma-Nepal Vihara.
7. Sudarshan, who died in 2002, and Dhammawati came from the same locality in Lalitpur and were distantly related.
8. From early in her career, Dhammawati was invited to preach in Theravada monasteries in provincial towns such as Pokhara and Butwal. But it was not until the late 1990s that she would be invited to preach in monasteries in Kathmandu and Lalitpur.
9. Dhammawati's father had recently died but according to Nepalese law at that time (1964), a daughter received her "inheritance" in the form of clothing, jewelry, and household requisites at her marriage and had no further claim on paternal property. A spinster meanwhile had no legal claim at all on her father's property. According to a law enacted in 1975, a woman who was still unmarried at age thirty-five might claim a share of paternal property equal to that of her brothers; in the highly unlikely event that she married later on, she was required to return her inheritance to her brothers. However Dhammawati's father died before this law was enacted. Thus her brothers were not required to give her a share and the fact that two of the three contributed to the construction of her vihara was an indication of the esteem in which they held her.
10. For the list of donors, see Nakarmi and Tuladhar (1999: 9–11). In three instances, the donors' caste is not given or not known. If one subtracts the four cases in which donations were made by the life members' fund, the four cases where the donors were nuns, and the two cases where the donors were devotees in general, the caste breakdown of donors is as follows: 10 Uday, 3 Shrestha, 3 Maharjan, 1 Shakya, 1 Manandhar.
11. In 1988, Dhammawati reregistered Dharmakirti in the name of the donors' committee (*dāyaka samiti*).
12. Gyanapurnik Mahasthavir passed the Dhammachariya in 1966, four years after Dhammawati. In 1999, after a gap of thirty-three years, a second Nepali nun, Aganani, from Nag Baha, Lalitpur, passed and in 2000 a third, Bimalagyani, from Ikhache Baha, Lalitpur, did so too. Both were students of U Pandita Sayadaw, himself a student of Mahasi Sayadaw, the great med-

itation master. To date, Gyanapurnik is still the only Nepali monk with the Dhammachariya.

13. In later life, Amritananda was addressed as "Dr. Bhikkhu Amritananda," but his doctorate was in fact an honorary degree, awarded in 1979, by the Pali Institute of Nalanda (Lall 1986: 38). Before that, he was known as "Acharya Bhikkhu Amritananda," the title associated with the master's degree that he received from the same institute in 1955.
14. Today, the Dharmakirti community is drawn mostly from upper and middle castes, and members of lower occupational castes are also numerous; so far, there are only a few devotees from water-unacceptable castes and none from the lowest untouchable caste. The composition of the communities of other viharas appears to be quite similar. Though untouchables may sometimes attend Buddha Puja, they are rarely known to participate in other community events.
15. The following suttas were chanted: Sunday, *Avana Sutta*; Monday, *Ratana Sutta/Mattanisama Sutta*; Tuesday, *Khandha Paritta/Mora Paritta/Vatta Paritta*; Wednesday, *Dhajagga Sutta*; Thursday, *Atanatiya Sutta*; Friday, *Angulimala Sutta*; Saturday, *Anatalakkhana Sutta/Bojjhanga Sutta.*
16. Between 1974 and 1980, Dhammawati preached on all 555 Jatakas (S. K. Tuladhar 1999: 41).
17. For example, the *Mangala Sutta* for a birthday, the *Bojjhanga Sutta* in the case of illness, the *Angulimala Sutta* for a pregnancy, or the *Marananussati Sutta* for a death.
18. As of 1999, Dhammawati had thirty-nine publications, Gunawati had one, Sushila had four, Madhavi had one, and Ratnamanjari had one. Although a majority of Dharmakirti publications were produced by monastics, laypeople authored a sizeable number too. The Study Circle included many young people eager to publish their ideas and they were encouraged to do so. Of the 195 publications, 134 were in Nepal Bhasha, 57 in Nepali, and 4 in English. In most cases, production costs of individual publications were underwritten by families in memory of a deceased relative.
19. The *Sigalovada Sutta* instructs the laity in how to conduct all domestic relationships, especially conjugal relationships. Because it was designed for a lay audience, the wife is depicted as an essential support, not as a stimulator of the senses and a dangerous distraction from the path.
20. They did not employ a servant until the 1990s.
21. The Lumbini Development Trust was established by UN Secretary General U Thant in 1956 during the World Fellowship of Buddhists Conference. An area several miles square surrounding the spot where the Buddha is believed to have been born was designated "Lumbini Garden," seven villages were destroyed and their inhabitants given land elsewhere in compensation, trees were planted, and a Nepalese vihara was built close to the Asoka pillar, after which development of the site came to a halt. Only after thirty years and several financial scandals was a fresh start made; lots were parceled out to Buddhist countries interested in building viharas and construction began.

By 2000, more than a dozen viharas, many of them extremely elaborate, were completed or nearing completion and several hotels were open to receive pilgrims. However thus far, aside from the Newar Buddhist community that frequents Lumbini in the winter months and resident monks at the Burmese and Chinese monasteries, few pilgrims or tourists spend more than a day in the place.

22. Among the Newars, only Rajopadhyaya Brahmans perform *barhay tayegu* after the onset of the menses, following the pattern of the Parbatiyas' *gupha basne* ritual.
23. In July 1983, during an ordination he conducted in Dhyankuti Vihara, Banepa, where three boys were becoming samaneras and two other boys (a Ranjitkar and a Shrestha) were going through temporary ordination for five days, the Burmese Sayadaw U Thondara (Sundara) explained that there are three kinds of ordination: rishi, samanera, and bhikkhu. The first is open to non-Buddhists as rishis only acquire good conduct and concentration (*sila* and *samadhi*), whereas the other two bring wisdom (*pragya*) as well (*Dharmakirti* 13 (2) (September 1983: 26–27). On the introduction of the rishini ritual in Nepal, see Kunreuther (1994) and Hartmann (1996). Hartmann (1996: 364), on the basis of research in the 1980s, reports that "the Theravādins emphasize their low-cost policy," that is, that doing rishini is much cheaper than the traditional *barhay tayegu*.
24. In 1997, Sudarshan Mahasthavir, abbot of Shri Kirti Vihara, Kirtipur, was asked to perform the marriage of a rich Shakya bridegroom and his Chyamkhala (untouchable) bride whom no Vajracharya priest would agree to marry. Since then, he and several other monks have officiated at other intercaste weddings and even at marriages between members of the same caste. In some cases a Vajracharya priest is also present, but even when the monk is the only ritual specialist involved, the wedding is conducted in the traditional manner over a three-or four-day period. In sum, the objective in calling Theravadins is not to reduce costs, as is often the case with *samanera* and *rishini pabbajja*, but to have the couple married by a simple rite that avoids the appearance of Hindu influence. Anil Sakya (2000: 186–189) has summarized a short booklet that provides a Theravadin liturgy for marriage, which was published by a Shakya man when he arranged the wedding of his daughter with a Vajracharya. The ritual included taking the Five Precepts and Buddha Puja, and vows in which the groom undertook to honor and be faithful to his wife, and to provide her with wealth and ornaments to the best of his ability, and the bride undertook to manage household affairs, please family members, be faithful, take care of her husband's wealth, and to be skilful and industrious (as in the *Sigalovada Sutta*).
25. According to Thai custom, all males should take *pabbajja* ordination before marriage; however, today this is often ignored. In Burma, although ordination is not compulsory, as a very costly ritual, it is widely observed as a mark of social status.
26. On the visit of the Sangharaja, the Supreme Patriarch of Thailand in No-

vember 1985, seventy-three Shakya men took temporary ordination at Kirtipur to celebrate his seventy-third birthday.

27. Yogi—as such temporary ordinands are called—must bring their own bedding and are charged (usually one thousand rupees for a ten-day retreat) for food, which is cooked by nuns assisted by upasikas.
28. Making sand chaityas is a traditional, highly meritorious practice in Newar Buddhism (Gellner 1992: 224, fig. 4; Lewis 2000a: ch. 2, esp. fig. 2.3, p. 39).

Chapter 5. The Changing Buddhist Laity

1. The right of women to go through the rite of full ordination as a nun (*bhikkhuni*) is highly contested, as discussed later in Chapter 7.
2. Bhikshu Sumangal was a Shilpakar from Lalitpur. The Shilpakars form one part of a caste that likes to align itself with the Uday (on the complex relationship between them, see Lewis 1995: 76 note 20, and Pickett 2003).
3. Cf. Tanka Prasad Acharya's remark that Dasharath Chand's interest in the Hindu reform movement, the Arya Samaj, was not shared by the other revolutionaries (Fisher, Acharya, and Acharya 1997: 91). Of the four martyrs, one, Shukra Raj Joshi, was not even a member of the Praja Parishad, but the Ranas had long been trying to suppress the Arya Samajist ideas first introduced by his father, Madhav Raj (see Chapter 2, note 27). In fact it was Shukra Raj's uncle who betrayed them to the Ranas (Fisher et al. ibid.).
4. For a description of the trading year in 1958 for Newars based in Kyirong, see Jest (1993: 160–163). The Jyotis' house in Kalimpong house was inherited by Gyan Jyoti. He renovated and donated it to the seventeenth Karmapa so that he could live there after his flight from Tibet in 2001.
5. One of Maniharsha's sisters was the wife of Chittadhar Hridaya, the celebrated Nepal Bhasha poet; following Hridaya's death, in 1989, Maniharsha endowed the annual Rs 15,000 Hridaya Prize for Nepal Bhasha literature (S. K. Joshi 1995: 390).
6. Thirty years later, when the hostility that the alms round had once provoked had dissipated, Dhammawati and her chelis went out to collect money and rice, which they would sell to devotees at a lower than market price in order to raise funds for the construction of Gautami Vihara in Lumbini. These forays were outstandingly successful, and, they reported, they would regularly raise "more than $1000" for their cause. They would distribute biscuits, which they also collected, to patients in hospitals (LeVine 2002).
7. There have also been some major female donors including Champawati Baniya (Tuladhar), who owned shops and hotels, and Dil Maya Maharjan, a wealthy traditional healer.
8. Apart from Maniharsha Jyoti, some prominent donors included Hera Kaji Kansakar, who owned a store in Bag Bazaar; Kulesh Ratna Tuladhar, a former Lhasa trader; Kancha Guruju Shakya, a curio dealer; Bhim Bahadur Shrestha, a lawyer; and Sanu Ratna Sthapit, owner of the Crystal Hotel. All of the above regularly sponsored *bhojana dana* following public perform-

ances of Buddha Puja five times each month, as well as providing food supplies. In 2000, devotees generally provided the nuns' noon meal twenty days out of every month. Gyan Jyoti Kansakar, Maniharsha's younger half-brother, has also been a prominent donor, both to Theravada causes and to the Tibetan Karma Kagyu sect.

9. A distinction is made between funds donated to the nunnery as an institution and to individual nuns. For the first, receipts are supposed to be provided, and nunnery accounts are audited annually; but no receipts are required for personal donations.
10. These figures are approximate and are difficult to verify with precision. D. R. Shakya (1999: 87–89) lists 107 nuns by name, plus 5 who have "abandoned the robe." However, of his 107, 31 are deceased. The Ven. Kondanya listed 78 monks, 94 novices, and 118 nuns for 2001 and 76 monks, 187 novices, and 131 nuns for 2004 (Kondanya 2001, 2004). S. K. Tuladhar (1999: 26) writes that there are 121 members of the Bhikkhuni Sangha.
11. Shri Kirti Vihara receives the particular patronage of the Supreme Patriarch of Thailand, and a room is kept there for his exclusive use.
12. Aside from her mother, brothers, and a first cousin, major donors include several Maharjan businessmen who live nearby and come to the vihara after work most evenings.
13. Kindol Vihara, which under its founder Dharmachari was for decades the most important center for Theravada Buddhist women in Nepal, is one of the few nunneries that still houses widows and divorced women who, in the eyes of the laity, appear less worthy of donations than never-married nuns. They are protected from real want however by the fact that, after the death of Dharmachari, Kindol was divided in two for administrative purposes. Thus, whereas some of the older nuns are affiliated with Ananda Kuti Vihara, the rest look to Dharmakirti for support.
14. In January 2000, the Nepali nuns' Order received a five-year grant from a private American foundation for the education of young Theravada nuns. This is the first substantial amount they have received from any foreign source. It covers the educational costs of nuns living in Nepal and the air travel of those who go to study abroad.
15. In 1998, 70 percent of the adult Nepali nuns were Vajracharyas, Shakyas, and Udays; 21 percent were Maharjans; and 9 percent were Manandhars, who although technically from a low caste, are often from well-to-do families. On the monks, see Chapter 6, p. 137ff.
16. In 2000, Drabya Man Singh ("Bhairaja") Tuladhar, a Kathmandu businessman, donated 12.5 million rupees (US$170,000) for the reconstruction of Dharmakirti nunnery and also provided an elaborately renovated house in Asan Tol for the younger nuns to live in while the work was being carried out. Inaugurated in 2002, the new Dharmakirti is built in traditional Newar style; rising five stories, it boasts marble floors and staircases and many high-ceilinged rooms and bathrooms. Beside it is a new building housing a shrine

with a twenty-foot Buddha statue. In 2001, on their own initiative, Dhammawati's devotees raised money for the transformation of a small house, which had been donated to her on the northern edge of the city beside Basundhara Baha, into a substantial monastic complex to be used as a guesthouse for foreign pilgrims and a meditation retreat center.

17. Accounts for the fifth conference show a budget of over 1 million rupees covered principally by donations (from individuals and local and central government), registration fees, and advertising. See Guneratne (2002) and Krauskopff (2003: 229–232) for descriptions of the way in which the Tharus have attempted to build a national organization of this sort, and Fisher (2001) on the Thakalis.
18. New groups were also set up in Tansen in 1947 and in Trishuli and Butwol in 1949 (Shakya S. 2003: 4). D. R. Shakya "Trishuli" (2001: 3) lists other activities that the Taramam Sangha has been involved in since 1951: providing the first health clinic in Lalitpur; encouraging social reform; organizing performances of the *astami* and *vasundhara vratas*; reviving a twelve-year local pilgrimage called the *nyakhu jatra*, which involves the preservation of old instruments; and organizing training in the skills needed to perform them.
19. "Ignorant of dharma, ignorant of karma,/Ignorant of the essence of the Five Precepts,/Beings are drowning in violence and insecurity" (B. Shakya 2004).
20. Summary of Shakya Suren (2003: 6–7).
21. A *kisli* is a small clay saucer with grains of unhusked rice and a betel nut, offered when making an undertaking or a vow to a god.

Chapter 6. Organizing and Educating the Monastic Community

1. The head of the Mahasangha is the most senior monk (from time of ordination) and he is designated the Sangha Nayaka. Holders of this post have been Pragyananda, Shakyananda, Aniruddha, and currently Subodhananda. In recent years, the Sangha Nayaka has generally been in his eighties or older, and the position has been largely one of token leadership. Actual leadership is provided by the president of the Bhikshu Mahasangha (*adhyaksa*), who was Amritananda until his death in 1990. Since then, the presidents have been Pragyananda, Aniruddha, and then Buddhaghosh.
2. Buddha Vihara in Lumbini, built in 1956, also has an *uposathagara*, as does Shri Kirti Vihara, which was rebuilt in 1988. Junior monks report that it is only senior monks who point out the infringements of the younger monks, never the other way round.
3. S. K. Tuladhar (1999: 26). Kondanya (2001: 46) lists 118 nuns, including 8 in Burma, 3 in Taiwan, 4 in Thailand, and 5 in Sri Lanka. By the following year (Kondanya 2002: 53–54), these had become 128 nuns, with 7 in Burma, 4 in Taiwan, 5 in Thailand, 7 in Sri Lanka, and 2 in India. In 2004, there were 129 nuns with 8 in Burma, 4 in Taiwan, 4 in Thailand, and 10

in India (Kondanya 2004: 37–38). D. R. Shakya (1999) lists 16 who had at that time taken full ordination as a bhikkhuni. See also note 10 in Chapter 5 on these figures.

4. See appendix 2. See Table 5.1 for the principal monasteries and nunneries.
5. In addition, one nun was living in the monastery at Kirtipur, and two in the International Buddhist Meditation Center at Shankhamul.
6. Cultural purists and foreigners sometimes object to the construction of a huge monastery (Shri Kirti) in a style entirely foreign to Nepal in a place where it dominates the view of Kirtipur from the south and east. The original vihara was established by Sudarshan and dates from 1976; this was rebuilt, largely with Thai funds and in Thai style, on a much grander scale between 1985 and 1995. The original Vishwa Shanti was founded by Gyanapurnik in 1985 and rebuilt with Malaysian funds as a seminary for novices and young nuns between 1995 and 1997. Sangharama was built as a training center by Ashwaghosh in the early 1980s with funds donated by two devotees.
7. In the case of traditional *baha* that were donated to the Order, already existing *chaityas* would be restored, if necessary. Because the Theravada Vinaya does not include instructions, when a new vihara was built, a *chaitya* or *stupa* (sometimes, because of lack of space, placed on the roof) would be constructed according to directions given in Mahayana texts. Whether or how far a Vajracharya priest is involved in consecrating a new *chaitya* in a Theravada context depends on the wishes of the donor(s). For an encyclopedic survey of traditional Newar Buddhist *chaitya* styles, see Gutschow (1997).
8. Many images are gifts of donors in Burma and Thailand. These differ distinctly from images in the Newar style.
9. See Chapter 5, note 16, on the reconstruction of Dharmakirti in 2001–2002.
10. She explains that the TV was given to her by the parents of a girl who was sent to Dharmakirti for *rishini pabbajja*: "They wanted the children to be able to watch Hindi films, like the *Ramayana*, and the news."
11. The families who are planning to host the *bhojana dana*, which concludes all major events and often routine events such as Buddha Puja, invite—often by printed invitation—certain monks and nuns. A single family may often feed up to forty monks and forty nuns on the birthday of their household head. Following an autumn *kathina* ceremony at which the devotees of a particular vihara offer new robes to the monastic community, a dozen families may sponsor the meal to which all monks, nuns, and novices in the Valley are invited.
12. All these figures are given in Gellner (1992: 322–323).
13. At least ten of these novices disrobed and returned home within a year.
14. See Guneratne (2002) and Krauskopff (2003) on these developments in Tharu ethnicity.
15. Her husband was living in Ananda Kuti. Unlike in Thailand, where married couples may ordain in the same temple and, though they live in separate

quarters, remain in contact, in Nepal couples separate at ordination and thereafter have nothing to do with each other.

16. Another nun in her early twenties who came, grief-stricken, to the nunnery after her boyfriend died in a motorcycle accident, is one of the very few who admit to having had a pre-ordination romance.
17. The six rishini precepts are: not to kill, steal, indulge in any form of sexual behavior, lie, drink alcohol, or eat after midday.
18. Rishini dress consists of a red floor-length skirt and long-sleeved overblouse, with a red shawl in winter.
19. Another version explicitly states that if anyone initiates their followers on their own, that is, if they discard this rule, the initiates will not be accepted as members of the Sangha.
20. Another version specifies that temporary ordinands may participate in *bhojan* that are held at the vihara where they are staying but may not go for *bhojan* at donors' houses.
21. This rule was later modified: as Nepal is a "border land," only five nuns are needed for *pabbajja*. According to one informant, in very remote areas only one nun is needed, provided she has been ordained for twenty years or more.
22. After the Anagarika Rules were formulated, the nuns of Kathmandu and Lalitpur would gather at Dharmakirti on Friday afternoons to review and discuss them. Attendance soon dropped off however for as one nun said laughingly, "We learned the rules and we talked about them, and then what more was there to do but obey them?"
23. That is, the *Bauddha Pariyatti Siksa* discussed in Chapter 3.
24. Founded in 1958 by Dr A. T. Ariyaratne, who was influenced by the teachings of Mahatma Gandhi and Anagarika Dharmapala, the Sarvodaya Shramadana movement reinterpreted the Dharma to focus on social action and selfless service for humanity as the highest form of religious practice. Although originally a lay movement, Sarvodaya has had a major impact on monastic training. See Gombrich and Obeyesekere (1988: ch. 7) and Bond (1988: ch. 7; 1995).
25. The verse is recited with a different first line for the Dharma and Sangha, respectively *Namāmi Dhammam sugatena desitam* (I do obeisance to the Dharma taught by the Buddha) and *Namāmi Sangham munirāja-sāvakam* (I do obeisance to the Sangha, the renunciates [who follow] the King of all sages).
26. A second coeducational seminary was opened in 1997 by Jatila, a Burmese monk of Nepali descent, in Dharan in the eastern part of the country. His plan was to send the children, all of whom were from Janajati groups, to Burma for training as soon as places could be found for them in institutions there. Thus, the vihara he established was more of a "transit station" than a seminary. Entirely dependent on donations from the Newar community, Jatila would bring the children to Kathmandu and Lalitpur to collect alms. In 2001, Jatila, unable to extend his visa, had to close the seminary. He

returned to Burma, taking with him those of his students for whom he could find places in Burmese monasteries; the rest went back to their homes.

27. Because six of the eight original female candidates dropped out, word spread that this coeducational training institution was in fact male-dominated, and since 1998, it has received very few applications from girls.

Chapter 7. Raising the Status of Nuns: The Controversy over Bhikkhuni Ordination

1. At novice (*sramanerika*) ordination, Tibetan nuns take thirty-six precepts; however their precepts do not differ from but rather amplify the Eight or Ten Precepts of Theravada nuns (Gutschow 2004: 283 n.27).
2. In 1987 there were thought to be about five thousand Tibetan nuns, forty-five thousand Theravada nuns, and two thousand Japanese nuns. Japanese nuns take bodhisattva (highest ordination) without having taken first (*sramanerika*) or higher ordination (*upasampada*) (Tsomo 1988c: 129). Unlike nuns of the Tibetan and Theravada traditions, thus far Japanese nuns, though often keen to modernize and improve their status (Arai 1999) have shown little interest in taking *upasampada* (Tsomo, personal communication).
3. For images and stereotypes of women in Theravada Buddhism, see Kawanami (1990) and Kloppenberg (1995).
4. For renouncers in the Buddha's time, see Basham (1951).
5. According to Horner (1975: 105), this is the only instance in the Pali Canon where the Buddha is recorded admitting he was wrong. See Heirman (1997) and Hüskin (2000a) for recent discussions.
6. Horner (1952: 354–5), translating *Cullavaga* X.1.4 (the *Cullavagga* forms part of the *Vinaya* or monastic code).
7. Manu IX.4 (Bühler 1886: 328). One may assume that, although the *Manusmrti* postdates the Buddha by centuries, the attitudes it expresses broadly held good for the Buddha's time.
8. Mahaprajapati is reported to have brought five hundred women with her.
9. Anguttara Nikaya I.1.1–10, trans. Woodward (1932: 1–2).
10. Harris (1999: 49–66); cf. Collins (1997), Harvey (2000: 382–383). For a collection of misogynist stories from later Buddhist texts, with Christian parallels, see Wilson (1996). On Japan, see Faure (2003).
11. "Experience" and "competence" are identified as the two most important traits required of monks and nuns in leadership positions; five other valued traits were modesty, contentedness, conscientiousness, scrupulousness, and desire for training (Findly 2000).
12. From Cullavagga X.1.17, trans. Upasak (1975: 49–50); cf. Horner (1952: 375–376).
13. Despite the *garudhamma* directive, even in the Buddha's time there seems to have been confusion over female ordination. There are frequent references in the *Bhikkhuni Vibhanga* to the status of female novice (*samaneri*), which

a recruit achieved by renouncing lay life (*pabbajja*) and observing the ten training rules, and to that of the probationer (*sikkhamana*), who trained for two years observing the six precepts. Whether the two statuses were supposed to be held concurrently or not, and whether there was a preferred order between them, is not clear. Later, Dharmaguptakas and Theravadins took opposing views as to whether being a probationer should precede being a novice or vice versa. According to the texts, under certain circumstances, monks did not need to be physically present for *bhikkhuni upasampada*, but rather could send their assent by messenger (*Vinaya* II.277–278). Moreover, the statement (*Cullavagga* X.2.2) that "nuns should be ordained by monks" seems to be authorizing single ordination.

14. The 311 included 75 training (*sekhiya*) rules that both novices (*samanera*) and female probationers (*sikkhamana*) were required to follow.
15. See Dipavamsa 7.21–22, 12.42–43, 15.17, 16.2–3, 17.16–21, 18.11–12, 24–25.
16. Gunawardana (1979: 39) and others (e.g., Tsomo 1988d: 105; Barnes 1996: 267) have written that the Theravada nuns' ordination lineage was transmitted to Burma and survived into the thirteenth century or beyond. This idea is based on G. H. Luce's (1970 I: 105, 109–110, II: 42–43) interpretations of inscriptions from Pagan. However, the inscriptions do not use the word "bhikkhuni" or any other unequivocal term for female renouncers and Skilling (2001) regards Luce's conclusions as erroneous.
17. Two short-lived predecessors to Kabilsingh were the daughters of Narin Klueng, a Thai progressive, who were ordained as bhikkhunis in the 1920s: they were "arrested, defrocked, and temporarily jailed" (Ekachai 2001: 293). About her 1972 ordination Voramai Kabilsingh wrote, "I did not really need to be a *bhikkhuni* to do this [help all sentient beings by dedicating merit earned through meditation]. However, I wanted to set an example as there were no *bhikkhunis* and many obstacles to becoming one. I was able to show that a woman could become fully ordained" (Batchelor 2000: 58). Her daughter Chatsumarn was ten years old when voramai separated from her husband and took the precepts. Chatsumarn grew up in the family home, which her mother had turned into a temple and orphanage. Before Chatsumarn married, she told her future husband that she too intended to renounce eventually. Having separated from her husband and raised her three sons to adulthood, she took early retirement from her university and in 2001 was ordained as a novice (*sramanerika*) in Sri Lanka. Her return to Thailand with a shaved head and in Sri Lankan nun's dress caused an outcry among the bhikkhus (*South China Morning Post*, Sunday, June 18, 2001). For a while she was a frequent guest on TV talk shows.
18. See Tsomo (1999). A fifth objective of Sakyadhita, the prevention of the sexual exploitation of women by their male gurus, although not publicized, was discussed privately at Bodh Gaya and later conferences by Western women who have been much more ready to speak about the issue than their Asian counterparts.

19. Thus far, five volumes of conference papers, all edited by Karma Lekshe Tsomo, have been published.
20. The first bhikshuni ordinations in China were performed according to rites of the Mahasanghika tradition by a Kashmiri monk named Dharmagupta (Zürcher 1972: 109).
21. As the first ordination did not involve previously ordained nuns, it was not universally accepted (Ku 1991: 117). So a monk named Gunavarman sent for nuns from Sri Lanka to confer bhikshuni ordination. By the time enough Sri Lankans had arrived to make up a quorum, Gunavarman had died and so another monk, Sanghavarman, guided the ceremony in Nanjing in 433/434 (Heirman 2001: 295; Tsai 1981; Pao-chang 1981). According to Lévi and Chavannes (1916: 46) the Sri Lankan nuns followed the ordination rites of the Dharmaguptaka tradition. However, Skilling (1994) notes that it is unclear to which Vinaya lineage the nuns belonged. L. Cousins (personal communication) observes that there is no record of Dharmaguptakas within the boundaries of present-day India, apart from two inscriptions from Mathura. Rather, they seem to have been strong in what is now Afghanistan and to have proselytized central Asia and China from there. Though today five different Vinaya traditions are followed in China, the Dharmaguptaka translation into Chinese seems to have been the most reliable, and it is the Dharmaguptaka version that is followed most widely. For a discussion of dates of transmission, and the failure of the Sri Lankan connection with China to survive, see Gunawardana (1979: 37–39, 1988).
22. Voramai Kabilsingh was ordained at Fo Guang Shan Monastery, Taiwan, in 1970. Tenzin Palmo, a British nun in the Tibetan tradition, was ordained at Po Lin monastery, Lantau Island, Hong Kong in 1973. Four Western nuns belonging to the Tibetan tradition, including Karma Lekshe Tsomo, were ordained at Hae Ming Temple, Taiwan in 1982. Four refugee Tibetan nuns were ordained in Hong Kong in 1983.
23. No record survives of how Theravada ordination rites for women (*bhikkhuni upasampada*) were carried out in the past. For Vinaya codes of conduct for nuns (*Bhikkhuni Patimokkha*) belonging to six Buddhist traditions including Theravada and Dharmaguptaka, see Kabilsingh (1991) and Tsomo (1996). The *pacittiya* of the *patimokkha* include many rules regarding eligibility and instruction for ordination but, aside from a reiteration of Rule Six of the *garudhamma*, no mention is made of the ordination rite itself.
24. Doubts about the historicity of the account of the Buddha's acceptance of Mahaprajapati into his order have been voiced by many scholars on the grounds that its portrayal of women is inconsistent. See Horner (1975: xx, 105), Church (1975), Pitzer-Reyl (1984), Sponberg (1992), Gross (1993), Barnes (1996: 282), and Hüskin (2000a, 2000b).
25. Barnes (1996: 283) reports that modern Taiwanese nuns do not follow the *garudhamma* and are not expected to.
26. After the land was acquired in 1980, the Order spent several years negoti-

ating with the local community, which did not want its quiet suburb disrupted by "tourists," before they received permission to build. Xilai Monastery was much in the news when Vice President Al Gore was accused of violating campaign funding laws by accepting a donation of US $200,000 from the nuns during the 1996 presidential campaign.

27. Dhammadinna had finished secondary school and, having studied English on and off for many years, spoke it quite well. Dhammavijaya is from a Tuladhar family. In 1988, she earned a bachelor's degree and spoke some English. After ordination, she stayed for several years in Taiwan and learned Mandarin. From there she went to Magadha University in India where she received a master's degree and later a doctorate.
28. Ordination is increasingly popular among young Taiwanese women who outnumber male monastics by five to one (Tsomo 1999: 20). As Taiwan has become more and more affluent and more men can afford it, concubinage has become very widespread. Polygyny is an important reason why recruits to Fo Guang Shan, as well as to other orders, are women, many of them university-educated, who want to avoid marriage.
29. One of the four was Karma Lekshe Tsomo; having already taken *upasampada* in Korea from bhikshus, she traveled on to Taiwan to take dual ordination from bhikshunis as well.
30. This is the position of senior learned monks in Thailand also (Ekachai 2001: 221).
31. It was from Western Buddhist women that the Nepali nuns got the idea that the Sri Lankan nuns who transmitted *bhikkhuni upasampada* to China in the fifth century were Dharmaguptakas and that the Dharmaguptaka tradition was an offshoot of the Theravada.
32. See the message to the First International Conference of Buddhist Nuns from Bhikkhu Nyanaponika (a German) in Tsomo (1988a: 38).
33. Bartholomeusz (1994: 176–179) interviewed three meditator nuns who were living in caves in remote jungle areas.
34. The ten acharyas, drawn largely from north Indian monasteries, included Sri Lankan missionary monks belonging to the Maha Bodhi Society.
35. Tsomo (1999: 13). Twenty Sri Lankan nuns participated in the full ordination rite at Bodh Gaya in February 1998. Immediately after the celebration, leading Sri Lankan nuns and their bhikkhu supporters decided that they now had enough fully ordained nuns to constitute a quorum and, even though the twelve-year waiting period stipulated in the Vinaya had not expired, *bhikkhuni upasampada* was held in Dambulla, Sri Lanka, in March 1998 (Salgado 2000b). Since then, *upasampada* for nuns has been held regularly in Sri Lanka.
36. After seeing them settled, he returned to Kathmandu.
37. The aspect of the *bodhisattva* ordination procedure that astonished most of them was the practice by which the ordinand places three lighted candles on her head and allows them to burn her scalp. The alternative, to burn one's inner arm in three places, was chosen by one of the candidates. The

other four Nepalis were thankful to discover that this display of asceticism was voluntary.

38. Bhikshu Sumangal had also planned to go, but ill health prevented him.
39. The fifth nun was unable to go because, as headmistress of a primary school, she had used up all her leave in China.
40. The pilgrims earned merit by contributing to the cost and by taking the Five Precepts for the duration, as well as by their presence at the ceremony.
41. The second Thai nun to receive full ordination was ordained at Sarnath in 1996 in a ceremony that the Maha Bodhi Society arranged for Sri Lankan nuns; however, she continues to be resident in Sri Lanka. There were no Thai candidates at Bodh Gaya. One Burmese nun arrived too late to be included.
42. By 1998, the missionary arm of Fo Guang Shan Monastery, the Buddhist Light International Association, had brought monastics and laypeople from many countries to study in Taiwan. It claimed to have a presence in fifty-six countries and to have built or to be in the process of building temples in twenty of them.
43. Because none of the Maharashtrian nuns had submitted applications and communication was extremely difficult, the event organizers were never quite sure of their ordination status. It emerged that a few were married women, in which case they had to be excluded from the rites, but, in all, twenty-four of the twenty-eight who came to Bodh Gaya were ordained.
44. For activities during the ordination we draw on Yuchen Li's article (2000), as well as LeVine's notes. Though LeVine was barred from attending the ordination rituals, she obtained a copy of the candidates' manual, which was written in Chinese and "approximate" English. Documents and photos of posters from the event are reproduced in Kantowsky (2003: 100–105).
45. There are two Chinese temples at Bodh Gaya, the newer one having been built by the Fo Guang Shan mission. The mission is also making a statue of Master Xingyun which, when completed, will be the tallest statue in the world. Master Xingyun is believed by his devotees to be a bodhisattva who will eventually appear in the world as Maitreya Buddha.
46. The one Tibetan acharya was Lama Yeshe Losal Rimpoche, abbot of Kagyu Samye Ling in Scotland, who brought eleven Western nuns for ordination. Ashwaghosh represented Nepal.
47. Karma Lekshe Tsomo from Hawaii and Thubten Chodron from Seattle are both nuns in the Tibetan tradition and active internationally.
48. Kuang Woo, head of Bhikshuni Affairs of the Chogye order in Korea.
49. Although Fo Guang Shan nuns were central to the organization of the event and great efforts were made to present an international front during the ordination procedures, in the evening sessions in which the future of the bhikshuni lineage was discussed, deliberations were dominated by monks; nuns, regardless of national origin and tradition, remained virtually silent (Li 2000).
50. Dharmaguptaka *pacittiya* rule number one hundred and Theravada *pacit-*

tiya rule number ten forbid watching "singing and dancing," that is, entertainments as forbidden by the eighth precept. However nuns routinely attend performances of Gyanmala bhajans, and even participate in them themselves in their own nunneries; they sometimes also watch traditional Newar dancing when it is included in Buddhist events.

51. *Sanghadisesa* rule number seven in the Dharmaguptaka code (Tsomo 1996: 31) and *sanghadisesa* rule number three in the Theravada code.
52. Five ordained in Guangzhou in 1997 and four in Shanghai in 2002.
53. The Chinese government paid the travel expenses of the nuns who ordained at Guangzhou.
54. The statues are not just Buddhas (Tathagatas) but, more specifically, of the former Buddha, Dipankara, in whose time Shakyamuni in an earlier life vowed to become a Buddha (Gellner 1992: 183–184).
55. All her teachers, with the exception of her Sanskrit teacher, were Newars, and, although their textbooks were written in Nepali, they spoke Nepal Bhasha most of the time.

Chapter 8. Winds of Change: Meditation and Social Activism

1. The *Satipatthana Sutta* occurs twice in the Pali Canon: as the tenth Discourse of the *Majjhima Nikaya*, and as the twenty-second Discourse of the *Digha Nikaya*, in which it is titled the *Mahasatipatthana Sutta*. The second version includes a detailed treatment of the Four Noble Truths in the section titled "Contemplation of Mental Contents." See Nyanaponika Thera (1965: 9).
2. See, for example, the quotation above from Dhammawati, or the quotation from Dharma Duta in Chapter 5, p. 127.
3. The retreat took place at Dhyankuti Vihara in Banepa, as Dharmakirti was both too small and too noisy.
4. Dhammawati reported, "While we were on the train, the sayadaw was meditating all the time. When we reached Calcutta he suddenly stirred and asked, 'How many nuns are with me?' He had been so deeply absorbed in *samadhi* that he'd had no idea."
5. In the mid-1980s, Dhammawati and Gunawati took a long retreat in the Burmese vihara in Varanasi where they received instruction in teaching vipassana.
6. The land was donated by Chaitya Maya Shakya.
7. U Pandita, who is the guru of Aung San Suu Kyi and a feminist, insisted that nuns and monks be equally represented on the IBMC board. Thus, it consists of Gyanapurnik and Sudarshan (till his death in 2002), and Dhammawati and Gyanawati, a younger nun who, like Dhammawati, had studied in Burma; she also holds a master's degree.
8. Asabachara left IBMC for Washington D.C., in 1998 and was replaced as abbot by another Burmese monk, U Sujanapiya. Although both monks know English quite well, their spoken Nepal Bhasha is inadequate for

preaching purposes. Thus they give their sermons in Burmese, which is translated by young Newar monks and nuns who have studied in Burma.

9. See Houtman (1984) for a description of the administrative structure of the Burmese meditation center.
10. Once or twice a year, the abbot leads groups of (wealthier) devotees on pilgrimage to sacred Buddhist sites in India or, farther afield, to Thailand, Burma, and Sri Lanka.
11. The dominance of Nepal Bhasha began to change here (and in other viharas) in the winter months of 2002–3 when teachers of courses for children at IBMC and elsewhere reported that so many Newar children were incapable of understanding Nepal Bhasha that, contrary to their own ingrained habits, they were obliged to teach in Nepali.
12. The sixth International Conference of Buddhist Women was held there in February 2000. The three-day celebration for the inauguration of the vihara followed a traditional pattern. The great Hindu gods (i.e., Jyapus costumed as Brahma, Vishnu, and Shiva worshipping Lord Buddha) as well as a traditional Jyapu band headed a procession around the tree under which the Buddha is believed to have been born (see Wright [1972: 146] and Gellner [1992: 96–97] on this "Lumbini Jatra"). The procession included fifty nuns, twenty monks who chanted *mahaparitran* throughout the following night, and more than two hundred female devotees of Dhammawati dressed in identical brown saris. According to Daw Gunawati (1988: 21) the custom of upasikas from one vihara all wearing identical uniform saris began in Dharmakirti and spread from there to the others: the idea was both to discourage the wearing of fine clothes to the nunnery and to support Nepali industry.
13. He was invited to Nepal by a group of Newar and Marwari businessmen; Marwaris have been established in the capital for many generations and dominate much of the commercial life of Kathmandu.
14. The British headmaster of the Budha Nilkantha school was a follower of Goenka.
15. By chance, Gellner was present at this *dana*, accompanying family members of participants on the course.
16. The group that established Dharmashringha was led by Roop Jyoti and Padma Jyoti Kansakar, sons of Maniharsha Jyoti, the principal benefactor of Dharmakirti in its early years. Although its formal name is Dharmashringha Meditation Center, doing meditation there is referred to by most Newars simply as "going to Budha Nilkantha" or "doing meditation at Budha Nilkantha."
17. Although some, perhaps most, meditators hoped to get a glimpse, however short-lived, of nirvana during the course of a Dharmashringha retreat, a few overburdened housewives admitted both to us and to Bassini (2001: 33) that they experienced a retreat as a—fully defensible—break from domestic life.
18. Initial enquiries as to the differences are likely to be met with comments

such as: "There is no real difference: at IBMC you are taught to concentrate on the stomach, whereas at Dharmashringha you focus on the nostrils—that's all."

19. A similar code of discipline for vipassana meditation distributed at the Vipassana International Academy in Igatpur is reproduced in Kantowsky (2003: 207–211). The timetable it outlines is virtually identical to that given for Dharmashringha in Table 8.1.
20. "First-timers" take only Five Precepts which means that, unlike "old-timers" who do not eat after noon, they receive a light evening meal.
21. The nuns are Ratnamanjari, who was one of the first to train in Burma, and Dhammasangha, who ordained in Burma in 1981. Ratnamanjari's affiliation with Goenka may be explained by the fact that she was very close to Maniharsha Jyoti, one of the principal donors to Dharmashringha, dating from when she stayed in his house in Calcutta for several months en route to Burma in the 1950s. Dhammasangha, a serious Pali scholar, has been teaching Pali to Western students at Goenka's center at Igatpur. Sometimes younger nuns, serving as volunteers (*sathi*), help with the day-to-day physical needs of meditators.
22. Because lying about spiritual attainments is a *parajika,* behavior for which a monastic must immediately disrobe, Dhammaratna showed extreme caution and modesty when talking about her meditation experiences.
23. For some minor exceptions to this, see Gellner (1992: 269).
24. See Bond (1988: 162–173) for critics of vipassana in Sri Lanka. Cousins (1996) analyzes in detail the relationship between Mahasi Sayadaw's teaching and the canon and places his interpretation of vipassana in the context of numerous Theravada traditions of meditation.
25. For further details on the Lotus Research Center, see its Web site (*www.lrcnepal.com*). Its conferences on the preservation of Newar Buddhism are mentioned in Chapter 10. It has also produced a digital database of inscriptions and photographs of all the chaityas and dharmadhatus in the Kathmandu Valley.
26. The Nepal YMBA, modeled on Maha Bodhi Society organizations of the same name, was founded in 1970.
27. On the controversy over the constitution, see Hoftun, Raeper, and Whelpton (1999: chs. 7 and 8) and Gellner (2001b). The constitution explicitly outlawed discrimination on the grounds of religion.
28. The university teacher was Min Bahadur Shakya, whose activities are described in Chapter 9.
29. The assistant teachers included a few monastics though the majority were young laymen and laywomen who had studied Buddhist philosophy with Min Bahadur Shakya.
30. In addition to the Awareness Camps, the Himalayan Buddhist Education Foundation funded the children's programs, discussed in Chapter 4, that Dhammasangha and her team launched in Lumbini as well as many Valley villages.
31. This phenomenon has yet to be studied in detail, but Lecomte-Tilouine

(2003) provides a description of the background to the "de-Sanskritization" of the Magars, which is in fact a new form of Sanskritization, that is, Sanskritization in a new idiom and not a return to a putative tribal past.

Chapter 9. Other Buddhist Revival Movements: Tibetan "Mahayana" and Newar "Vajrayana"

1. On Bhrikuti, see M. B. Shakya (1997a). Tucci (1971: 610) expressed some scepticism about her existence: "The story of the marriage of Sron btsan sgam po with a daughter of Amsuvarman is far from being certain." Shakya does his best to counter Tucci's arguments.
2. The most complete account of the early Newar scholars who helped bring Buddhism to Tibet is given by Lo Bue (1999), though one may quibble with his use of the ethnonym "Newar"—nowhere attested until the seventeenth century—to describe inhabitants of the Kathmandu Valley in the eighth to thirteenth centuries. On Newar artists in Tibet, see Macdonald and Stahl (1979).
3. The evidence is collected in Lewis (1988, 1989, 1996b). The Rovato quotation is given in Lewis (1989: 31).
4. On Tibetan pilgrimage to the Valley, see Macdonald and Rin-po-che (1981), Wylie (1970), and Dowman (1982).
5. For example, in 1504, 1629, 1681, and 1751. In 1814 and 1918, the Bhutanese were involved both as sponsors and as ritualists. See Gutschow (1997) and von Rospatt (2000).
6. Interestingly, in 1942 a Newar monk in Lhasa, called Nawang Dorje, petitioned the Lhasa government, which in turn wrote a letter to the Rana government of Nepal requesting it to stop animal sacrifices in the vicinity of the Mayadevi temple in Lumbini and around Bauddha and Swayambhu stupas (Cüppers 1997).
7. Gelukpas only started to be a significant presence in the Valley in the 1970s after the Tibetan Lama Yeshe and his student Lama Zopa established Kopan Monastery outside Bauddha (see further below). In Pokhara also, the Gelukpa presence is, unlike the other Tibetan sects which appeal to Nepalis, ethnically entirely Tibetan (Tamblyn 2002). On Western Buddhists' interactions with Tibetans in Bauddha, see Moran (2004).
8. There is no evidence that Sonam Tendzing or Pata Lama knew Tsering Norbu.
9. Although Pata Lama eventually returned to his homeland, the gompa he built near a cave in which Padmasambhava is believed to have meditated is still visited by many pilgrims. The Shivapuri Watershed National Park, in which Nagi Gompa stands today, was established in the 1970s. Prior to that time, the area where the Gompa is located was community forest, a few hectares of which the local Tamang population donated to Sonam Tendzing.
10. There is no full ordination for women in the Tibetan tradition, as explained in Chapter 7.

11. Sonam Tendzing's second wife was a Tamang who is said to have escaped from the palace of one of the Ranas whose concubine she had been. The Ranas' practice of abducting pretty girls was so frequent and so much dreaded that many parents who lived in places through which the Ranas regularly passed kept their daughters hidden.
12. Sonam Tendzing died in a gompa he had established in Pharping on the Valley's southern edge. During his lifetime, the Karmapa paid two visits to the Valley. In 1948, en route from Tsurpu Monastery near Lhasa to Sikkim where he was based for the rest of his life, he was invited to teach in Nag Baha by the Dhakhwa family. He did so again in 1959, at the invitation of Purna Bahadur Shakya, when he lectured on Vajrayogini. His third and last visit occurred in 1972, when he inaugurated the White Monastery (Seto Gompa) established by Urgyen Tulku in Bauddha the year before.
13. Newars often refer to Tibetan Buddhism as "Mahayana" to differentiate it from Newar Buddhism (Vajrayana), on the one side, and Theravada, on the other.
14. Jyata, Jyatan, or Jyatha Baha is a lineage branch *baha* of Uku Baha (Locke 1985: 102–103). It was donated to Manjushasan and another Newar monk, Shanta Raj, in 1949 by Ratna Man and Harsha Ratna Shakya, who represented the two lineages with rights in the *baha*. It was renovated in the Tibetan style and Shanta Raj was the abbot until his death in 1997 (R. J. Shakya 2002).
15. Bka'-rnying bshad-sgrub gling in Tibetan (Helffer 1993: 117).
16. Urgyen Sherab's father, a medical assistant to King Tribhuvan, was convicted of involvement in a 1940 conspiracy against the Ranas for which he had his property confiscated and served nine years in prison. He assisted Ganesh Man Singh in his famous escape from jail. He was released at the end of Rana rule and his property was returned to him.
17. Ranjung Yeshe Institute opened in 1981 and has about 150 students studying a four-year bachelor's degree program in Buddhist Studies affiliated with Kathmandu University.
18. This is how the nunnery's name is spelt in English. The Nepali is *kopan khācyo gākhīl ling nanerī.*
19. All the non-Newar monks and nuns were Tamangs from the surrounding hills.
20. Nyungne is a Tibetan version of the *astami* (*posadha*) *vrata*, widely practiced by Tibetan Buddhists. On Nyungne, see Ortner (1978, 1999) and Vargas-O'Brian (2001); on the *astami vrata*, see Locke (1987), Gellner (1992: 221–225), and Douglas (2002).
21. The twelve Newar nuns in Nagi Gompa vary widely in age; ten are Maharjans and two—Maya Ani and a young relative of hers—are Shakyas.
22. Maya Ani noted that even though she is the abbess of Nagi Gompa, if a monk is present during a ritual, she must sit lower than he.
23. When she was a young nun, her oldest brother told her that she needed to learn Nepali, the lingua franca, in order to communicate with the Tamang people living round about the Gompa as well as with the other nuns, most

of whom were Tamang or Manangi (both hill groups practicing Tibetan Buddhism); furthermore, he took the time to teach her himself.

24. In 2000, the Arya Tara School for Tibetan nuns, funded by a Singaporean devotee of Urgyen Tulku, opened with ten students in temporary quarters near Swayambhu, in anticipation of moving to a campus still under construction at Pharping. Thus far the school has no Newar students. The director is an Italian and the head mistress is Choying Drolma, a Tibetan refugee nun who was educated through Class Eight in South India, speaks English well, and has toured the United States giving performances of devotional songs and chants.
25. Kopan Monastery was founded in 1972 by Lama Yeshe and Lama Zopa on land that had belonged to the Ranas' chief Brahman priest. It was purchased for them by an American woman named Zina Rachevsky. Lama Yeshe died in 1986; Lama Zopa continues to attract many Western students both to his teachings when he travels abroad and to courses offered at Kopan. For descriptions of Lamas Yeshe and Zopa by a Western follower, see MacKenzie (1992). On Lama Zopa's life and on Zina Rachevsky, see Wangmo (2005). Moran (2004: 72, 74) notes that "Kopan is the only Buddhist monastery in Nepal in which *Western* monks and nuns regularly function as Buddhist teachers to other Westerners. . . . Kopan emphatically exists as the hub of an *international* organization that aims primarily to bring Buddhism to the West" (emphases in original).
26. Spacious dormitory rooms were furnished with sturdy furniture, plentiful bedding, and appliances such as water purifiers and electric rings.
27. In addition to Newars, Khachoe includes *anis* from many ethnic groups: Tamangs, Limbus, Sherpas, and Tibetans, most of whom were born in Nepal of refugee parents, not in Tibet.
28. It was founded on the initiative of Sahu Bodhichitta Ratna, an Uday from Asan Tol. He consulted with abbot of Drepung Monastery in Tibet who sent five Newar monks (Shakyas and Tuladhars) from there to establish and organize the monastery. In order to increase the number to ten, five merchants became monks later on, among them Sumati Sangh, a Shakya from Bhinche Baha in Lalitpur, who later became the abbot (H. Shakya 1978: 596–597).
29. However, since 2001, Newar *anis* in Kachoe Ghakyil Ling have received educational funding from the same American foundation that supports the young Theravada nuns.
30. According to Moran (2004: 91), Thrangu Rinpoche envisaged that his nuns would take full bhikshuni ordination, at least according to a pamphlet produced in 1993, but, as far as we know, nothing has come of this.
31. To cite just one case of many, Sanu Ratna Sthapit, owner of the Crystal Hotel, is a generous donor to both Tibetan and Theravada Buddhist institutions.
32. For some details on the main monasteries around Bauddha, see Moran (2004: ch. 4).
33. Nem Ratna Shakya is probably the most generous Newar donor to the

Karma Kagyupa community. His first donation was a thousand-armed Avalokiteshvara image, which he presented to his mother's guru, Urgyen Tulku. He paid for the image with money he earned from work for then Crown Prince Birendra; later, he used money he earned from more work he did for the royal family to set up a prayer wheel below Nagi Gompa. In the 1980s, he joined up with some Newar businessmen to purchase more land in the Shivapuri Forest on which the then abbot Urgyen Tulku built an extension of Nagi Gompa. Nem Ratna then provided a flight of concrete steps up the steep mountainside to the extension. In memory of his mother, he built an elaborately muraled gompa in Chapagaon, which he donated to his guru, Chokling Tulku, Chokyi Nyima's brother. It was consecrated in 1999.

34. The fifteen or so monks who come according to a schedule to read texts in the gompa all live elsewhere. The trust fund established by the Saddharma Suraksha Sangh around 1946 for the purpose of feeding them is their only institutional support.
35. Kwa Baha calendrical ceremonies include: *uposatha* at 4 A.M. on the eighth day of the lunar month when laypeople (usually women) take the Eight Precepts for twenty-four hours; Padmasambhava *puja* on the tenth day; *sojong* on the new-moon day; and a two-day Nyungne ritual in May/June.
36. All members receive initiations for the following practices: Avalokiteshvara; Arya Tara; Ngondro (the four preliminary practices of 100,000 prostrations, 100,000 recitations of Vajrasattva, 100,000 mandala offerings to the whole universe, and 100,000 performances of guru yoga in which the practitioner visualizes his guru-deity and recites his mantra); and, once these have been completed, members may take additional initiations and practice like Phowa (the Transformation of Consciousness) from other teachers as well as from their guru.
37. The Vajracharya *guthi* brings together all the Vajracharya members of Kwa Baha.
38. Students are now drawn from all the *baha* of Lalitpur. There are no students from Kathmandu because the ritual practices of Vajracharyas in Kathmandu are significantly different from those of Lalitpur. Buddha Ratna has been hoping to find someone willing to sponsor the publication of a ritual handbook, but because thus far he has been unsuccessful in his search, he can only provide his students with computer printouts. In fact, many young Vajracharyas from Lalitpur have been taught in similar courses run by Badri Ratna Vajracharya in Kathmandu, which has led to a considerable admixture of Kathmandu traditions into the performance of life-cycle rituals in Lalitpur.
39. Newar Buddhists now have a seat on the management committee.
40. Sponsors underwrote all expenses, including the cost of buses to bring devotees to the eight *pitha* ("power places"; Dowman 1982), twelve *tirthas* (fords), and four *stupas* where Vajracharyas oversaw the ritual fasts and recited the appropriate *Avadana* story.
41. Lewis (1984: 239) and Gellner (1992: 268). Other initiations such as those

of Chandamaharoshana (*acala diksa*), Yogambara, and Kalachakra were always much less common and do not seem to be given today (Gellner 1992: 271).

42. His considerably older sister remained unmarried and in middle age became a Tibetan nun. She lived for the rest of her life in a private home near the Swayambhu stupa.
43. Amritananda, who had been Mahapragya's disciple in 1940 and had spent time in prison with him, added a preface to the 1978 reissue in which he pointed out the mistakes in scriptural attributions due to Mahapragya's reliance on Sankrityayan.
44. In 1997, the *Lalitavistara* was reprinted in Taiwan in a run of five thousand for free distribution, again at Min Bahadur's instigation.
45. His daily practice, a combination of prayer, meditation, and prostrations, which occupies him 5–7 A.M., is composed of *tekcho*, a meditation practice meaning "on the nature of the mind" or looking into one's own mind in order to understand it, a teaching he received from Urgyen Tulku; contemplating and generating the *bodhi* mind; recitation of the *Namasangiti*, a traditional Newar Buddhist prayer to Manjushri, the bodhisattva of wisdom, in which one prays to acquire his qualities; recitation of the *Bhadracari*, a traditional Newar Buddhist prayer which has both a sixty-two- and a twelve-verse version; and, lastly, 108 prostrations.
46. Min Bahadur received teaching on the Bodhisattva vow from Geshe Losang Jangpa, now deceased.
47. For descriptions of these rituals, see Gellner (1992: 266–281; 1997).
48. The *Prajna Paramita* text in Kwa Baha dates from 1225. It is cared for by a guthi made up of eleven Shakya families who take turns in sending a family member to remove it from its box before each reading and to replace it afterward. Having the text read is believed to evoke the power and blessings of the goddess Prajna Paramita herself, who fulfils her devotees' desires and needs (see Gellner 2001a: ch. 7).

Conclusion: Nepal's Theravadins in the Twenty-First Century

1. They also requested them to return their language as "Magar," even though well over half of all Magars speak only Nepali (Whelpton 1997: 59). On the way in which the Panchayat-era census takers were instructed so that Hinduism would become a default category into which all Janajatis would fall, see Gurung (1997: 520; 1998: 24–25).
2. On Tharu ethnicity and the place of Buddhism in it, see Guneratne (2002) and Krauskopff (2003). On social change among the Magars, see Lecomte-Tilouine (2003).
3. Spiro (1982: 324) reported that virtually all monks in Burma came from poor, rural backgrounds. Clearly, the predominantly urban nature of Theravada Buddhism, so far, and the fact that it is not the dominant religion of the country, make the situation in Nepal rather different.

4. It will be interesting to see whether all these considerations will continue to influence the latest cohort of novice monks to arrive in Thailand from Nepal. Moran's brief discussion of Tibetan monks in Bauddha (2004: 106–107) suggests that Tibetan monks often disrobe for very similar reasons, that it is hard for Tibetan monks trained in Bauddha to return to remote Nepali villages, and that Tibetans living in Kathmandu are now too prosperous to want their sons to become monks.
5. In an article originally published in *Ananda Bhoomi* in 1993, Bhikshu Vipassi lists the accusations made against monks as "The monks are lazy, they are pleasure-seekers (*vilāsī*), they just want money for their ritual services, they never go out to spread the Dharma" (Vipassi 1999: 107). He identifies the key weakness of Theravada in Nepal as a lack of religious education for monastics and lay disinterest in supporting it.
6. Fear of marriage is not confined to Newars or to urban Nepalis. Debra Skinner studied a multi-caste village near Pokhara: "In 1986, girls talked about education as a way of avoiding or postponing marriage, a fate that all but one of Skinner's informants dreaded" (Skinner and Holland 1996: 285). For a superb account of the suffering that marriage can bring, even in a relatively less oppressive Janajati context, see Des Chene (1998).
7. In 1960, the under-five mortality rate for Nepal as a whole was 315 per 1,000 live births; by 1990, it had fallen to 145, and by 2002 to 91. The total fertility rate in 1960 was 5.9 live births, by 1990 it was 5.1, and by 2002, 4.3 (UNICEF 2004). Fertility and mortality rates within the Kathmandu Valley, where there is a concentration of Western medical facilities, are much lower than the average for the country as a whole.
8. In the 2003 wedding season, for the first time, large numbers of Newar intercaste marriages were being celebrated with the full ritual and feast as if they had been arranged, from the very beginning, in the traditional way.
9. Ibaha Bahi in Lalitpur was paintakingly restored by the Nippon Institute of Technology and HMG Dept of Archaeology between 1990 and 1996. Kwa Baha (the "Golden Temple") in Lalitpur began charging entrance to tourists on December 15, 1997; its members may be able to fund the renovation it undoubtedly needs out of their own resources.
10. Compare this quotation to that by Gombrich in Chapter 1 p. 16.
11. The view of Newar Buddhism as "Hinduism in all but name" (Snellgrove 1957: 106) has been common among scholars with a superficial acquaintance with the Kathmandu Valley for a long time, and it is discussed in detail in Gellner (1992, especially 2, 98–104, 159, 339–340). It was the Protestant assumptions of Olcott and of nineteenth-century religious discourse more generally that influenced Dharmapala and through him modernists such as Kanaka Dweep.
12. On the Lotus Research Center, see Chapter 9. Sudarshan was asked to give a paper on "the role of Theravada in the preservation of Newar Buddhism" and his paper was indeed published under that title (Sudarshan 1999). He records his own surprise at the title he was given and in fact what he wrote

was a detailed list of how Theravada Buddhism had preserved or revived *Buddhism* among the Newars.

13. The list here summarizes Sudarshan (1999). Sudarshan followed Hridaya exactly, except that he inverted the order of items six and seven.
14. Hridaya's article provoked a response by Bhikkhu Dhammalok entitled "What Has Theravada Not Given [Us]? What Do We Still Need?" in which he responded that Theravada practices marked a real departure from what traditional Newar Buddhists did, for example, that the verses of *paritrana* recitations were meaningful, unlike the mantras of the Hundred Names of Tara (Dharmalok 1950).
15. Whether this subtlety was lost on the organizers of the conference, when they asked Sudarshan to speak on Theravada's role in preserving Newar Buddhism, is not clear. The convention that different forms of Buddhism should maintain an ecumenical attitude and not criticize each other in public is rarely flouted and when it is, it is usually by modernists criticizing Newar Buddhism. In 1986 one such case occurred when Ashwaghosh published a letter asserting that the recent World Fellowship of Buddhists Conference supported the notion that the Vajracharyas' religion was "superstitious"; some Vajracharyas responded with a pamphlet accusing the Theravadins of being even more "superstitious" (Hartmann 1996: 364). The term for "superstition" is *andhaviśvās* and literally means "blind faith." Ever since it was introduced into north Indian languages by Dayananda Saraswati in the nineteenth century (Bharati 1970: 45), it has been an essential part of modernists' vocabulary, an "antitraditional device" in Bharati's words.
16. One could also criticize Liechty for focusing entirely on status-related *consumption* and leaving to one side the key role that offices, schools, and other workplaces have in the *production* of the new middle class. However, this point is tangential to the argument being made here.
17. Over a period of years in the 1990s, the nuns went on the alms round in order to collect cash and dry rice which they later sold to their devotees (see above, Chapter 5, n. 6).
18. See Bond (1988: 162–173) on Sri Lankan critics of vipassana. Bond concludes that the conservatives overstated their case, but were right that such a style of meditation, which bypasses the meditative states called *jhanas* and the process known as *samadhi*, was rarely practiced in the past; even in the scriptures, it seems to have been considered only a minority option. Once outside their homelands, the monks of Southeast Asia appear to lose their conservatism; thus Sri Lankan monks in the United States have encouraged bhikkhuni ordination (Bartholomeusz 1994: ch. 9).
19. See in particular, Ortner's "Cultural Politics: Religious Activism and Ideological Transformation among 20th Century Sherpas" (1989b), "The Founding of the First Sherpa Nunnery, and the Problem of 'Women' as an Analytic Category" (1983; reissued as ch. 6 of Ortner 1996), and "The Case of the Disappearing Shamans, or, No Individualism, No Relationalism" (1995). See also the passages on religion in Ortner (1999). Other important

monographs on Tibetan Buddhism in Nepal are Holmberg (1989) and Mumford (1989). The bibliography on the Sherpas is too large to list here, but one should consult J. F. Fisher (1990) and Adams (1996), which anticipate some of the themes of Ortner (1999).

20. On Nyungne, see references in n. 20, Chapter 9. On Mani Rimdu, see Kohn (2001).
21. Dhammalok did have Pragyananda administer the precepts at a performance of Vajracharyas' *astami vrata* in the early days (see p. 45).
22. The absence of these subtleties from Ortner's argument is presumably what lies behind Macdonald's criticism that her account is "conditioned by American Puritanism" (Macdonald 1991: 344).
23. In an article on early Buddhism and the other renouncer sects existing in the Buddha's time, Brekke (2003) argues that the decision to renounce lay life was typically accompanied by the emotional turmoil that is associated with the term "conversion" in Judaeo-Christian traditions, but that moving from Buddhism to other sects (or vice versa), once one had become a renouncer, was not.
24. Having said that, the fact that Maniharsha Jyoti and his sons supported Dharmashringha, whereas his younger half-brother Gyan Jyoti and his family supported IBMC could be read as evidence for such competition between brothers.

References

JIABS: *Journal of the International Association of Buddhist Studies*
NS: Nepal Samvat (Nepal era, starting in 879 C.E.)
VS: Vikram Samvat (Vikram era, starting in 57 B.C.E.)
For languages, the same abbreviations are used as in the glossary

Adams, V. 1996. *Tigers of the Snow and Other Virtual Sherpas: An Ethnography of Himalayan Encounters*. Princeton, N.J.: Princeton University Press.

Adhikari, Jagannath, and David Seddon. 2002. *Pokhara: Biography of a Town*. Kathmandu: Mandala Book Point.

Almond, P. C. 1988. *The British Discovery of Buddhism*. Cambridge: Cambridge University Press.

Amatya, Purna Prasad. 1998 [NS 1118]. *Nepālbhāsāyā Vānmaya Sūci* [A systematic bibliography of the printed books in Newar language]. Kathmandu: Nepal Bhasha Academy.

Ambedkar, B. 1992 [1957]. *The Buddha and His Dhamma* (Dr Babasaheb Ambedkar Writings and Speeches, vol. 11). Bombay: Education Dept. Govt. of Maharashtra.

Appadurai, A. 1981. *Worship and Conflict Under Colonial Rule: A South Indian Case*. Cambridge: Cambridge University Press.

Arai, P. K. R. 1999. "Japanese Buddhist Nuns: Innovators for the Sake of Tradition." In Tsomo, ed., *Buddhist Women Across Cultures*.

Ashwaghosh, Bhikshu. 2000. "Bhāvanā: mero anubhav" [Meditation: my experiences; in N]. In *Bauddha dhyān (vipassanā dhyān)*, ed. Bhikshu Ashwaghosh, 1–28. Kathmandu: Dharmakirti Bauddha Adhyayan Gosthi.

———. 2003. *The Life of a Monk*. Trans. & ed. H. L. Singh. Kathmandu: Dilhari Devi, Bhushan, Roshan, & Rabin Shrestha.

Bajracharya, H. 1994 [NS 1115]. *An Exhibition of Charya Dance and the Materials Used in the Worship Rituals.* Lalitpur: Vishwa Shanti Pustakalaya.

Bajracharya, N. B, R. B. Bajracharya, and K. Lall, eds. 1992. *Amritanjali: A Homage to the Late Ven. Bhikkhu Amritananda.* Kathmandu: Anandakuti Vihara Trust.

Bajracharya, P. R., ed. 1995. *Maṇiharṣa Jyoti Smṛtigrantha* [Memorial volume for Maniharsha Jyoti; in NBh, N., and English]. Kathmandu: Nepal Bhasha Parishad.

Bandya, R. B. 1975. *Samghanāyak Bhadanta Prajnānanda Mahāsthavir yā jīvanī* [The life of the leader of the Sangha, the Venerable Pragyananda; in NBh]. Asan, Kathmandu: Tej Ratna Tuladhar.

———. 1995. "Nepālay buddhadharmayā punarjāgaranay ādhunik pravartak samghamahānāyak Bhikṣu Prajñānanda Mahāsthavir" [The Venerable Monk Pragyananda, the leader of the Sangha, as a modernizer in the revival of Nepalese Buddhism; in NBh]. In *Prajñānanda Smṛti Grantha* (Pragyananda Commemorative Volume), ed. Ven. Sudarshan et al. Lalitpur: Prajñānanda Smrti Grantha Prakāsan Samiti.

Barnes, N. J. 1996. "Buddhist Women and the Nuns' Order in Asia." In *Engaged Buddhism: Buddhist Liberation Movements in Asia,* C. S. Queen & S. B. King, 259–294. Albany, N.Y.: SUNY Press.

———. 2000. "The Nuns at the Stupa: Inscriptional Evidence for the Lives and Activities of Early Buddhist Nuns in India." In E. B. Findly, ed., *Women's Buddhism,* 17–36. Boston: Wisdom Publications.

Barrows, J. H. 1895. *The World's First Parliament of Religions: Its Christian Spirit, Historic Greatness and Manifold Results.* Chicago: Hill and Shuman.

Bartholomeusz, T. 1994. *Women Under the Bo Tree.* Cambridge: Cambridge University Press.

Barua, D. K. 1981. *Buddha Gaya Temple: Its History.* 2nd ed. Buddha Gaya: Buddha Gaya Temple Management Committee.

Basham, A. L. 1951. *History of the Ajivakas.* London: Luzac & Co.

Bassini, P. 2001. "The Healing Properties of Insight Meditation: A Self-Absorbed Anthropological Analysis of the Practice of Vipassana amidst the Newars in the Kathmandu Valley, Nepal." M.Sc. diss., Medical Anthropology, Brunel University, London.

Batchelor, M. 2000. "Voramai Kabilsingh: The First Thai Bhikkuni, and Chatsumarn Kabilsingh: Advocate for a Bhikkhuni Sangha in Thailand." In E. B. Findly, ed., *Women's Buddhism,* 58.

Batchelor, S. 1994. *The Awakening of the West: The Encounter of Buddhism and Western Culture.* London: Thorsons.

Bechert, H., and J.-U. Hartmann. 1988. "Observations on the Reform of Buddhism in Nepal." *Journal of the Nepal Research Center* 8: 1–28.

Bennett, Lynn, 1983. *Dangerous Wives and Sacred Sisters: Social and Symbolic Roles of High-Caste Women in Nepal.* New York: Columbia University Press.

Bharati, A. 1970. "The Use of 'Superstition' as an Anti-Traditional Device in Urban Hinduism." *Contributions to Indian Sociology* (n.s.) 4: 36–49.

Blackburn, A. M. 2003. "Localizing Lineage: Importing Higher Ordination in Theravadin South and Southeast Asia." In *Constituting Communities: Theravada Buddhism and the Religious Cultures of South and Southeast Asia*, ed., J. C. Holt, J. N. Kinnard, & J. S. Walters, 131–150. Albany, N.Y.: SUNY Press.

Blackstone, K. R. 1998. *Women in the Footsteps of the Buddha*. Richmond: Curzon Press.

Bloch, Jules. 1950. *Les Inscriptions d'Asoka*. Paris.

Bloss, L. W. 1984. "The Female Renouncers of Sri Lanka: The Dasasilmatawa." *JIABS* 10(1): 7–29.

Bodhigyan, Bh. 2002. *Buddhist Literature in Nepal Bhasha*. Kathmandu: PG Diploma Press.

Bond, G. D. 1988. *The Buddhist Revival in Sri Lanka: Religious Tradition, Reinterpretation and Response*. Columbia: University of South Carolina Press.

———. 1995. "A. T. Ariyaratne and the Sarvodaya Shramadana Movement in Sri Lanka." In *Engaged Buddhism: Buddhist Liberation Movements in Asia*, ed. C. S. Queen & S. B. King, 121–146. Albany, N.Y.: SUNY Press.

Brekke, T. 2002. *Makers of Modern Indian Religion in the Late Nineteenth Century*. Oxford: Oxford University Press.

———. 2003. "Conversion in Buddhism?" In *Religious Conversion in India: Modes, Motivations, and Meanings*, ed. R. Robinson and S. Clarke, 181–191. Delhi: Oxford University Press.

Bühler, G., trans. and ed. 1886. *The Laws of Manu* (Sacred Books of the East 25). Oxford: Clarendon Press.

Burghart, R. 1984. "The Formation of the Concept of Nation-State in Nepal." *Journal of Asian Studies* 44(1): 101–125.

Caplan, L. 1995. *Warrior Gentlemen: "Gurkhas" in the Western Imagination*. Providence and Oxford: Berghahn.

Caron, F., and J. Schouten. 1986 [1671]. *A True Description of the Mighty Kingdoms and Japan and Siam*. Ed. John Villiers. Bangkok: The Siam Society.

Carrithers, M. 1983. *The Forest Monks of Sri Lanka: An Anthropological Study*. Delhi: Oxford University Press.

Chalmers, R. 2003. " 'We Nepalis': Language, Literature and the Formation of a Nepali Public Sphere in India, 1914–1940." Ph.D. diss., SOAS, London University.

Chandler, S. 1999. "Placing Palms Together: Religious and Cultural Dimensions of the Hsi Lai Temple Political Donations Controversy." In *American Buddhism: Methods and Findings in Recent Scholarship*, ed. D. R. Williams & C. S. Queen, 36–56. Richmond and Surrey: Curzon Press.

Church, C. D. 1975. "Temptress, Housewife, Nun: Women's Role in Early Buddhism." *Anima* 1: 52–58.

Collins, S. 1997. "The Body in Theravāda Buddhist Monasticism." In *Religion and the Body*, ed. S. Coakley, 185–204. Cambridge: Cambridge University Press.

Copleston, Bishop R. S. 1892. *Buddhism Primitive and Present in Magadha and Ceylon*. London: Longmans.

Cousins, L. S. 1996. "The Origins of Insight Meditation." In *The Buddhist Forum IV*, pp. 35–58, ed. T. Skorupski, London: SOAS.

Cüppers, C. 1997. "A Ban on Animal Slaughter at Buddhist Shrines in Nepal." In S. Karmay and P. Sagant, eds, *Les habitants do toît du monde*, 677–688.

Darshandhari, S. 1998. "Dharmāditya Dharmācarya wa waykaḥyā kṛti: chagu adhyayan" [Dharmaditya Dharmacharyya and his work: a study; in NBh]. M. A. diss., Patan Joint Campus, Tribhuvan University, Nepal.

Davidson, R. 2002. *Indian Esoteric Buddhism: A Social History of the Tantric Movement*. New York: Columbia University Press.

Des Chene, M. 1991. "Relics of Empire: A Cultural History of the Gurkhas, 1815–1987." Ph.D. diss., Stanford University.

———. 1998. "Fate, Domestic Authority and Women's Wills." In D. Skinner, A. I. Pach III, and D. Holland, eds, *Selves in Time and Place*, 19–50.

Deshpande, M. M. Transcriber ed. and 1999. Introd. to *Milindapañhā Aṭṭhakathā*. (Studia Philologica Buddhica Monograph Series 13), 1–23. Tokyo: International Institute for Buddhist Studies.

Dhammalok, Bh., and Bh. Amritananda. 1984 [1937]. *Jñānmālā* [Buddhist Hymns; in NBh]. Swayambhu: Gyanmala Bhajan Khala.

Dharmacharyya, Dharmaditya. 1974. *Buddha-dharma wa Nepāl Bhāṣā munā* [*Buddhism and Nepal Bhasha Collected*; in NBh]. Repr., Kathmandu: Vaikuntha Prasad Lacoul.

Dharmalok Sthavir, Bhikshu. 1950. "Theravādi śāsanā chu mabila? Chu māni?" [What has the Theravada teaching not given us? What do we still need?; in NBh] *Dharmodaya* 3(12): 298–300.

———. 1999. *A Pilgrimage in China*. Trans. K. Lall. Kathmandu: Bhikkhu Aniruddha Mahasthavir. (First published 1950 in Nepal Bhasha; translated 1980 as *Pilgrimage to Great China* by S. Pathak.)

Dharmapala, Anagarika. 1893. "The World's Debt to Buddha." In *The World's Parliament of Religions*, vol. 2, ed. J. H. Barrows. Chicago: The Parliament Publishing Company.

Dhungel, S. P. S., B. Adhikari, B. P. Bhandari, and C. Murgatroyd. 1998. *Commentary on the Nepalese Constitution*. Kathmandu: DeLF.

Douglas, W. 2002. "The Fifteenth-Century Reinvention of Nepalese Buddhism." Ph.D. diss., University of Oxford.

Dowman, K. 1982. "A Buddhist Guide to the Power Places of the Kathmandu Valley." *Kailash* 4(3–4): 183–291.

Doyle, T. N. 1997. "Bodh Gaya: Journey to the Diamond Throne and the Feet of Gayasur." Ph.D. diss., Committee on the Study of Religion, Harvard University.

Durkin-Longley, M. S. 1982. "Ayurveda in Nepal: A Medical Belief System in Action." Ph.D. diss., Madison University (UMI 8224034).

Dutt, S. 1962. *Buddhist Monks and Monasteries of India: Their History and their Contribution to Indian Culture*. London: Allen and Unwin.

Ekachai, S. 2001. *Keeping the Faith: Thai Buddhism at the Crossroads*. Bangkok: Post Books.

Falk, N. A. 1980. "The Case of the Vanishing Nuns." In *Unspoken Worlds: Women's Religious Lives in Non-Western Cultures*, ed. N. A. Falk and R. M. Gross, 207–224. San Francisco: Harper & Row.

Falk, M. L. 2000. "Thammacarini Witthaya: The First Buddhist School for Girls in Thailand." In K. L. Tsomo, ed., *Innovative Buddhist Women* 61–71.

Falwell, B. 1984. *The Gurkhas*. London: Allen Lane.

Faure, B. 2003. *The Power of Denial: Buddhism, Purity, and Gender*. Princeton University Press.

Findly, E. B. 2000a. "Women Teachers of Women: Early Nuns 'Worthy of My Confidence.' " In E. B. Findly, ed., *Women's Buddhism*, 133–155.

Findly, E. B., ed. 2000b. *Women's Buddhism, Buddhism's Women: Tradition, Revision, Renewal*. Boston: Wisdom Publications.

Fisher, J. F. 1990. *Sherpas: Reflections on Change in Himalayan Nepal*. Berkeley: University of California Press.

Fisher, J. F., T. P. Acharya, and R. K. Acharya. 1997. *Living Martyrs: Individuals and Revolution in Nepal*. Delhi: Oxford University Press.

Fisher, W. F. 2001. *Fluid Boundaries: Forming and Transforming Identity in Nepal*. New York: Columbia University Press.

Foley, W. 1835. "Journal of a Tour through the Island of Rambree with a Geological Sketch of the Country, and a Brief Account of the Customs etc. of its Inhabitants." *Journal of the Asiatic Society* 1: 20–39. Reprinted in *Fragile Palm Leaves*, 4, September 1998.

Fürer-Haimendorf, C. von. 1964. *The Sherpas of Nepal: Buddhist Highlanders*. London: John Murray.

Gellner, D. N. 1987. "The Newar Buddhist Monastery: An Anthropological and Historical Typology." In *Heritage of the Kathmandu Valley* (Nepalica 4), ed. N. Gutschow and A. Michaels, 365–414. Sankt Augustin, GDR: VGH Wissenschaftsverlag. (Shortened version reprinted as ch. 6 in Gellner 2001a.)

———. 1989. "Buddhist Monks or Kinsmen of the Buddha? Reflections on the Titles Traditionally used by Śākyas in the Kathmandu Valley." *Kailash* 15(1–2): 5–25.

———. 1992. *Monk, Householder, and Tantric Priest: Newar Buddhism and its Hierarchy of Ritual*. Cambridge: Cambridge University Press.

———. 1995. "Low Castes in Lalitpur." In Gellner and Quigley, eds., *Contested Hierarchies*, 264–297.

———. 1997. "The Consecration of a Vajra-Master in Newar Buddhism." In S. Karmay & P. Sagant, eds., *Les habitants du toît du monde*, 659–675.

———. 2001a. *The Anthropology of Buddhism and Hinduism: Weberian Themes*. Delhi: Oxford University Press.

———. 2001b. "From Group Rights to Individual Rights and Back: Nepalese

Struggles with Culture and Equality." In *Culture and the Anthropology of Rights*, ed. J. Cowan, M. Dembour, and R. Wilson, 177–200. Cambridge: Cambridge University Press.

———. 2001c. "Hinduism, Tribalism, and the Position of Women." In Gellner, *The Anthropology of Buddhism and Hinduism*. (Originally published in *Man* [n.s.] 26 [1991]: 105–125.)

Gellner, D. N., and D. Quigley, eds. 1995. *Contested Hierarchies: A Collaborative Ethnography of Caste Among the Newars of the Kathmandu Valley, Nepal*. Oxford: Clarendon Press.

Gellner, D. N., J. Pfaff-Czarnecka, and J. Whelpton, eds. 1997. *Nationalism and Ethnicity in a Hindu Kingdom: The Politics of Culture in Contemporary Nepal*. Amsterdam: Harwood Academic Publishers.

Gombrich, R. F. 1983. "From Monastery to Meditation Center: Lay Meditation in Modern Sri Lanka." In *Buddhist Studies: Ancient and Modern*, ed. P. Denwood & A. Piatagorsky, 20–34. London: Curzon Press.

———. 1988. *Theravada Buddhism: A Social History from Ancient Benares to Modern Colombo*. London and New York: Routledge.

———. 1995. "The Monk in the Pāli Vinaya: Priest or Wedding Guest?" *Journal of the Pali Text Society* 21: 193–197.

———. 1996. *How Buddhism Began: The Conditioned Genesis of the Early Teachings*. London: Athlone.

Gombrich, R. F., and G. Obeyesekere. 1988. *Buddhism Transformed: Religious Change in Sri Lanka*. Princeton, N.J.: Princeton University Press.

Gore, M. S. 1993. *The Social Context of an Ideology: Ambedkar's Political and Social Thought*. Delhi: Sage.

Grandin, I. 1989. *Music and Media in Local Life: Music Practice in a Newar Neighbourhood in Nepal*. Linköping, Sweden: Linköping University.

Gross, R. M. 1993. *Buddhism After Patriarchy: A Feminist History, Analysis, and Reconstruction of Buddhism*. Albany: State University of New York Press.

Gubhaju, T. M. 1989 [VS 2046]. *Anagārikā Dharmasilā ra Uhākā Kāryaharu* [Anagarika Dharmasila and her works; in N]. Pokhara, Nepal: Dharmasila Buddha Vihara.

Gunawardana, R. A. L. H., 1979. *Robe and Plough: Monasticism and Economic Interest in Early Medieval Sri Lanka*. Tuscon: University of Arizona Press.

———. 1988. "Subtile Silk or Ferreous Firmness: Buddhist Nuns in Ancient and Early Medieval Sri Lanka and Their Role in the Propagation of Buddhism." *Sri Lanka Journal of the Humanities* 14(1–2): 1–59.

Gunawati, Mā. 1987 [VS 2044]. *Nepālay 25 dā jigu lumanti* [My memories of 25 years in Nepal; in NBh]. Kathmandu: Dharmakirti Vihara.

Guneratne, A. 2002. *Many Tongues, One People: The Making of Tharu Identity in Nepal*. Ithaca N.Y.: Cornell University Press.

Gurung, H. 1997. "State and Society in Nepal." In Gellner et al., eds, *Nationalism and Ethnicity in a Hindu Kingdom*, 495–532.

———. 1998. *Nepal: Social Demography and Expressions*. Kathmandu: New Era.

Gutschow, Kim, 2004. *Being a Buddhist Nun: The Struggle for Enlightenment in the Himalayas*. Cambridge, Mass.: Harvard University Press.

Gutschow, N. 1997. *The Nepalese Caitya*. Stuttgart: Edition Axel Menges.

Gyanmala 2003 (no author). "Jñānmālā bhajanay jñānyā khā duwāle balay" [Examining the *gyan* (wisdom) in Gyanmala; in NBh] *Sandhya Times*, August 1, 2003.

Harris, E. J. 1999. "The Female in Buddhism." In K. L. Tsomo, ed., 49–66.

Hartmann, J.-U. 1993. "Some Remarks on Caste in the Theravada Sangha of Nepal." In *Nepal Past and Present*, ed. G. Toffin, 73–81. New Delhi: Sterling.

———. 1996. "Cultural Change through Substitution: Ordination versus Initiation in Newar Buddhism." In S. Lienhard, ed., *Change and Continuity*, 355–365.

Harvey, P. 2000. *An Introduction to Buddhist Ethics*. Cambridge: Cambridge University Press.

Havnevik, H. 1990. *Tibetan Buddhist Nuns*. Oslo: Norwegian University Press.

Heirman, A. 1997. "Some Remarks on the Rise of the *bhikṣuṇisamgha* and on the Ordination Ceremony for the *bhikṣuṇis* according to the Dharmagupta *Vinaya*." *JIABS* 20(2): 33–85.

———. 2001. "Chinese Nuns and Their Ordination in Fifth Century China." *JIABS* 24(2): 275–304.

Helffer, M. 1993. "A Recent Phenomenon: The Emergence of Buddhist Monasteries around the Stupa of Bodnath." In *The Anthropology of Nepal: From Tradition to Modernity*, ed. G. Toffin, 114–131. Kathmandu: French Cultural Centre.

Hettiaratchi, S. B. 1988. *Social and Cultural History of Ancient Sri Lanka*. Delhi: Sri Satguru Publications.

Hodgson, B. 1972 [1874]. *Essays on the Language, Literature and Religion of Nepal and Tibet* (Bibliotheca Himalayica). Delhi: Manjushri Publishing House.

Höfer, A. 1979. *The Caste Hierarchy and the State in Nepal: A Study of the Muluki Ain of 1854*. Innsbruck: Universitätsverlag Wagner. (Reissue 2004, Kathmandu: Himal Books.)

Hoftun, M., W. Raeper, and J. Whelpton. 1999. *People, Politics and Ideology: Democracy and Social Change in Nepal*. Kathmandu: Mandala Book Point.

Holmberg, D. H. 1989. *Order in Paradox: Myth, Ritual and Exchange Among Nepal's Tamang*. Ithaca, N.Y.: Cornell University Press.

Horner, I. B. trans. 1952. *The Book of the Discipline* (Vinaya-Pitaka), vol. 5 (Cullavagga). London: Luzac & Co.

———. 1975 [1930]. *Women Under Primitive Buddhism: Laywomen and Almswomen*. Delhi: Motilal Banarsidas.

Houtman, G. 1984. "Novitiation: Received and Interpreted Versions." *South Asia Research* 4(1): 51–76.

———. 1985. "The Burmese *Wipathana* Meditation Tradition Self-conscious: A History of Sleeping Texts and Silent Buddhas." *Groniek* (special issue on South Asia) 92: 87–105.

———. 1997. "Beyond the Cradle and Past the Grave: The Biography of Burmese Meditation Master U Ba Khin." In *Sacred Biography in the Buddhist Traditions of South and South East Asia*, ed. J. Schober, 310–344. Hawaii: Hawaii University Press.

———. 1999. *Mental Culture in Burmese Crisis Politics: Aung San Suu Kyi and the National League for Democracy*. Tokyo: Institute for the Study of Cultures and Languages of Asia and Africa. Also available online at: *http://homepages.tesco.net/~ghoutman/index.htm.*

Hridaya, Chittadhar. 1950. "Theravādi śāsanā jhita chu bila? Chu mālā cwanā?"[What has Theravada contributed to us? What do we need?, in NBh] *Dharmodaya* 3(9): 234–238.

———. 1992 [NS 1102]. *Jhigu Sāhitya* [Our literature; in NBh]. Kathmandu: Nepal Bhasha Parishad.

———. 1998. *Sugata Saurabha: The Life and Teachings of the Buddha.* Trans. Tirtha Raj Tuladhar. Kathmandu: Nepal Bhasha Academy.

Hüsken, U. 2000a. "The Legend of the Establishment of the Buddhist Order of Nuns in the Theravāda Vinaya-Piṭaka." *Journal of the Pali Text Society* 26: 43–69.

———. 2000b. "Nonnen in der fruhen buddhistischen Ordensgemeinschaft." In *Aspekte des Weiblichen in der indischen Kultur*, ed. U. Roesler, 25–46. Swisttal-Odendorf: Indica et Tibetica Verlag.

Jackson, C. T. 1981. *The Oriental Religions and American Thought: Nineteenth-Century Explorations.* Westport: Greenwood Press.

Jest, C. 1993. "The Newar Community in Tibet: An interface of Newar and Tibetan Cultures." In *Nepal, Past and Present*, ed. G. Toffin, Paris: CNRS.

Jordt, I. 1988. "Bhikkhuni, Thilashin, Mae-chii: Women who Renounce the World in Burma, Thailand and the Classical Pali Buddhist Texts." *Crossroads: An Interdisciplinary Journal of Southeast Asian Studies* 4(1): 31–39.

———. 2001. "Mass Lay Meditation and the State in Post-Independence Burma." Ph.D. diss., Dept. of Anthropology, Harvard University.

Joshi, M. B., and L. Rose. 1966. *Democratic Innovations in Nepal: A Case Study of Political Acculturation.* Berkeley: University of California Press.

Joshi, Satya Mohan. 1990. *Kyānchyālāmā wa dondu lumanti-munā* [Reminiscences of Kyanche Lama and the Dondu Scripture; in NBh]. Lalitpur: Bodhi Prakashan Kendra.

Joshi, Sundar Krishna. 1995. "Vikāsyā swakālāy sw. Sāhu Maniharsa Jyoti" [The late Sahu Maniharsha Jyoti in the context of development; in NBh]. In P. R. Bajracharya, ed., *Maniharsa Jyota Smrtigrantha*, 386–391.

Juergensmeyer, M. 1988. *Religious Rebels in the Punjab: The Social Vision of Untouchables.* Delhi: Ajanta.

Jyoti, Maniharsha. 1995. "Dharmayā prayojan ācaraṇ sudhār khaḥ" [The practice of dharma is purification of conduct; in NBh]. In P. R. Bajracharya, ed., *Maniharsa Jyota Smritigrantha*, 535–537. (Originally published in *Nhasalā* 1108.)

Jyoti, Roop. 2002. "Vipassana: An Art of Corporate Management." *Lumbini, Journal of the Lumbini Nepalese Buddha Dharma Society (UK)* 5(1): 4–5.

Kabilsingh, C. 1991. *The Bhikkhuni Patimokkha of the Six Schools*. Bangkok: Thammasat University Press.

Kanaka Dweep, B. A. 2001. "Bauddha dharma guli bhina guli syana" [Buddhism: How far has it got better, how far worse; in NBh]. *Sandhya Times* (NS 1121 dillathwa 14): 2.

Kantowsky, D. 2003. *Buddhists in India Today: Descriptions, Pictures, and Documents*. Trans. H.-G. Tuerstig. Delhi: Manohar.

Karmay, S., and P. Sagant, eds. *Les habitants du toît du monde: Hommage à Alexander W. Macdonald*. Paris: Société d'Ethnologie, Nanterre.

Karunaratne, D. 1964. *Anagarika Dharmapala*. Colombo: M. D. Gunasena.

Kawanami, H. 1990. "The Religious Standing of Burmese Buddhist Nuns (thilashin): The Ten Precepts and Religious Respect Words." *JIABS* 13(1): 17–40.

———. 2000. "Patterns of Renunciation: The Changing World of Burmese Nuns." In E. B. Findly, ed., *Women's Buddhism*, 59–71.

———. 2001. "Can Women Be Celibate? Sexuality and Asceticism in Theravada Buddhism." In *Celibacy, Culture and Society: The Anthropology of Sexual Abstinence*, ed. E. J. Sobo and S. Bell, Madison: University of Wisconsin Press.

Kemper, S. 2004. "Dharmapala's *Dharmaduta* and the Buddhist Ethnoscape." In *Buddhist Missionaries in an Era of Globalization*, ed. L. Learman, Honolulu: University of Hawaii Press.

Kerin, M. 2000. "From Periphery to Center: Tibetan Women's Journey to Sacred Artistry." In E. B. Findly, ed., *Women's Buddhism*, 319–338.

Keyes, C. F. 1984. "Mother or Mistress but Never a Monk: Culture of Gender and Rural Women in Buddhist Thailand." *American Ethnologist* 11(2): 223–241.

Kieffer-Pülz, P. 1993. "Remarks on the Vaiśākha Festival in Nepal." In *Nepal, Past and Present*, ed. G. Toffin, New Delhi: Sterling.

Kirkpatrick, Col. 1969 [1811]. *An Account of the Kingdom of Nepal* (Bibliotheca Himalayica 1.3). Delhi: Manjushri.

Kloppenberg, R. 1977. "Theravada Buddhism in Nepal." *Kailash* 5: 301–322.

———. 1995. "Female Stereotypes in Early Buddhism: The Women of the Therigatha." In *Female Sterotypes in Religious Traditions*, ed. R. Kloppenberg and W. J. Hanegraff, 151–169. Leiden: E. J. Brill.

Kohn, R. J. 2001. *Lord of the Dance: The Mani Rimdu Festival in Tibet and Nepal*. New York: SUNY Press.

Kondanya, Ven. 2001. "Theravadian Records in Present Nepal." *The Charumati Voice* [Kathmandu]: 43–48.

———. 2002. "Bhikṣu, śrāmanera, anāgārikā tathā vihārharu." [Monks, novices, nuns, and viharas; in N.]. *Ananda Bhoomi* 30(1): 49–55.

———. 2003. "Bhikṣu, śrāmanera, anāgārikā tathā vihārharu (2600)" [Monks, novices, nuns, and viharas in the year 2600; in N.]. *Ananda Bhoomi* 31(1): 56–61.

———. 2004. "Theravād bhikṣu, śrāmanera, anāgārikā tathā vihārharu (2061)" [Theravada monks, novices, nuns, and viharas in the year 2601; in N.]. *Ananda Bhoomi* 32(1): 35–40.

Krauskopff, G. 2003. "An 'Indigenous Minority' in a Border Area: Tharu Ethnic Associations, NGOs, and the Nepalese State." In *Resistance and the State: Nepalese Experiences*, ed. D. N. Gellner, 199–243. Delhi: Social Science Press.

Ku Cheng-mei 1991. "The Mahisasaka View of Women." In *Buddhist Thought and Ritual*, ed. D. Kalupahana, New York: Paragon House.

Kunreuther, L. 1994. "Newar Traditions in a Changing Culture: An Analysis of Two Pre-pubescent Rituals for Girls." In *Anthropology of Nepal: Peoples, Problems and Processes*, ed. M. Allen, 339–348. Kathmandu: Mandala Book Point.

Lacoul, V. P. 1985 [NS 1105]. *Nepālay hānā sthaviravād wayeketa wa Nepāl Bhāṣā hwayeketa Dharmācārya* [The place of Dharmacharyya in returning "Sthaviravad" to Nepal and reviving Nepal Bhasha]. Kathmandu: Malati Lacoul.

———. 1995. "Manisharsha Jyoti gujāmha sajjana khah?" [What kind of good person was Maniharsha Jyoti? in NBh]. In P. R. Vajracharya, ed., *Maniharsa Jyota Smritigrantha*, 108–115.

———. 2001 [NS 1121]. "Jivanay nhāpā thaḥgu bhāsā buddha dharma patrikā khanā utsāh, umang danā wala" [The first time in my life that I saw a magazine on Buddhism in my own language I was enormously encouraged; in NBh] (interview). In D. R. Shakya, ed., *Dharmāditya Dharmācārya*, 15–17.

Laidlaw, J. 1995. *Riches and Renunciation: Religion, Economy, and Society among the Jains*. Oxford: Clarendon Press.

Lall, Kesar. 1986. *A Brief Biography of Ven. Bhikkhu Amritananda*. Kathmandu: Ananda Kuti Vihara Trust.

———. 2001. *The Newar Merchants in Lhasa*. Kathmandu: Ratna Pustak Bhandar.

Lecomte-Tilouine, M. 2003. "Sur le de-Sanskritisation des Magars: ethno-histoire d'une groupe sans histoire." *Purusartha* 23: 297–327.

Legge, J., trans. 1965 [1886]. *A Record of Buddhistic Kingdoms, Being an Account by the Chinese Monk Fa-hien of His Travels in India and Ceylon (A.D. 399–414) in Search of the Buddhist Books of Discipline*. New York: Dover.

Leslie, I. J. 1989. *The Perfect Wife: The Orthodox Hindu Woman according to the* Strjdharmapaddhati *of Tryambakayajvan*. Delhi: Oxford University Press.

Leve, L. 1999. "Contested Nationhood/Buddhist Innovation: Politics, Piety and Personhood in Theravada Buddhism in Nepal." Ph.D. diss., Princeton University.

———. 2002. "Subjects, Selves, and the Politics of Personhood in Theravada Buddhism in Nepal." *Journal of Asian Studies* 61(3): 833–860.

Lévi, S. 1937. "Les donations religieuses des rois de Valabhî." In *Mémorial Sylvain Lévi*, 218–234. Paris: P. Hartmann.

Lévi, S. and E. Charannes 1916. "Les seize arhats protecteurs de la loi." *Journal Asiatique* (July-August): 5–50.

LeVine, S. 2000. "At the Cutting Edge: Theravada Buddhist Nuns of Nepal." In *Innovative Buddhist Women* K. L. Tsomo, ed., 13–29.

———. 2001. "The Finances of a Twentieth-Century Buddhist Mission: Building Support for the Theravāda Nuns' Order of Nepal." *JIABS* 24(2): 217–240.

Lewis, T. 1984. "The Tuladhars of Kathmandu: A Study of Buddhist Tradition in a Newar Merchant Community." Ph.D. diss., Columbia University (UMI 8506008).

———. 1988. "Newars and Tibetans in the Kathmandu Valley: Three New Translations from Tibetan Sources." *Journal of Asian and African Studies* 36: 187–211.

———. 1989. "Newars and Tibetans in the Kathmandu Valley: Ethnic Boundaries and Religious History." *Journal of Asian and African Studies* 38: 31–57.

———. 1995. "Buddhist Merchants in Kathmandu: The Asan Tol Market and Uray Social Organization." In Gellner and Quigley, eds., *Contested Hierarchies*, 38–79.

———. 1996a. "Religious Belief in a Buddhist Merchant Community, Nepal" *Asian Folklore Studies* 55: 237–270.

———. 1996b. "A Chronology of Newar-Tibetan Relations in the Kathmandu Valley." In S. Lienhard, ed., *Change and Continuity*, 149–166.

———. 2000a. *Popular Buddhist Texts from Nepal: Narratives and Rituals of Newar Buddhism*, Albany: SUNY Press.

———. 2000b. "On the Revival of Newar Buddhism: One Scholar's Reflections." *Buddhist Himalaya* [Nepal] 9(1–2): 15–19.

Li, Y. 2000. "Ordination, Legitimacy, and Sisterhood: The International Full Ordination Ceremony at Bodhgaya." In K. L. Tsomo, ed., *Innovative Buddhist Women*, 168–200.

Li Rongxi 1995. *A Biography of the Tripitaka Master of the great Ci'en Monastery of the great Tang Dynasty*, Taisho vol. 50, no. 2053. Trans. Sramana Huili and Shi Yacong. Berkeley, Calif.: Numata Center for Buddhist Translation and Research.

Liechty, M. 1997. "Selective Exclusion: Foreigners, Foreign Goods, and Foreignness in Modern Nepali History" *Studies in Nepali History and Society* 2(1): 5–68.

———. 2003. *Suitably Modern: Making Middle-Class Culture in a New Consumer Society*. Princeton, N.J., and Oxford: Princeton University Press.

Lienhard, S. 1984. "Nepal: The Survival of Indian Buddhism in a Himalayan Kingdom." In *The World of Buddhism*, ed. H. Bechert & R. F. Gombrich, 108–114. London: Thames and Hudson.

Lienhard, S., ed. *Change and Continuity: Studies in the Nepalese Culture of the Kathmandu Valley*. Alessandria: Edizioni dell'Orso/CESMEO.

Ling, T. 1993. "Introduction: Towards an Account of 'Buddhisms' in Country-Specific Terms." In *Buddhist Trends in Southeast Asia*, ed. T. Ling, 1–5. Singapore: Institute of Southeast Asian Studies.

Lo Bue, E. 1999. "The Role of Newar Scholars in Transmitting the Indian Buddhist Heritage to Tibet (c. 750–c. 1200)." In S. Karmay and P. Sagant, eds., *Les habitants du foît du monde*, 629–658.

Locke, J. 1985. *Buddhist Monasteries of Nepal: A Survey of the Bahas and Bahis of the Kathmandu Valley*. Kathmandu: Sahayogi.

———. 1987. "The Upoṣadha Vrata of Amoghapāśa Lokeśvara in Nepal." *L'Ethnographie* 83(100–1): 159–189.

Lopez, D. ed. 1995. *Curators of the Buddha: The Study of Buddhism under Colonialism*. Chicago and London: University of Chicago Press.

———. 1998. *Prisoners of Shangri-La: Tibetan Buddhism and the West*. Chicago and London: University of Chicago Press.

Luce, G. H. 1970. *Old Burma—Early Pagan*. New York: J. J. Augustin.

Macdonald, A. W. 1991. Review of *High Religion*, by S. B. Ortner. *JIABS* 14: 341–344.

Macdonald, A. W., and A. Vergati Stahl. 1979. *Newar Art*. Warminster: Aris and Phillips.

Macdonald, A. W., and D.-P. Rin-po-che. 1981. "Un guide peu lu des lieux-saints du Népal." *Mélanges chinois et bouddhiques* 20: 237–273.

McHugh, E. 2001. *Love and Honor in the Himalayas: Coming to Know Another Culture*. Philadelphia: University of Pennsylvania Press.

MacKenzie, V. 1992 [1988]. *Reincarnation: The Boy Lama*. New Delhi: Time Books International.

McNamara, J. A. K. 1996. *Sisters in Arms: Catholic Nuns Through the Millennia*. Cambridge, Mass.: Harvard University Press.

Mahapragya, Bauddha Rishi. 1976. "Nepāli bauddha ra buddha dharma" [Nepali Buddhists and Buddhism; in N.]. *Ananda Bhoomi* 1(9): 2–3.

———. 1983. *Sāhityasutā karmasthānācārya wa bauddharsi Mahāprajñāyā ātmakathā* [An Autobiography of Mahaprajna, the First Theravadi Bhikshu of Modern Nepal; in NBh]. Trans. and Ed. D. Newami. 3 vols. Rishi Ashram: Sakalopasika.

Maharjan, K. L. forthcoming. "The Spread of Vihar Buddhism among Rural Newars in the Kathmandu Valley." In *Northern South Asia: Political and Social Transformations*, ed. H. Ishii, D. N. Gellner, and K. Nawa. Delhi: Manohar.

Malalgoda, K. 1976. *Buddhism in Sinhalese Society, 1750–1900: A Study of Religious Revival and Change*. Berkeley: University of California Press.

Malla, K. P. 1979. *Nepāl Bhāsāyā dhwānā saphuyā dhalah (Bibliography of Nepal Bhasha): N. S. 1020–1097* [in NBh]. Kathmandu: Layta Dabu.

Maniharsha 1995 (no author). "Maniharsha Jyoti." In P.R. Bajracharya, ed., *Maniharsha Jyoti Smṛtigrantha*, 764–770.

Mendelson, M. 1975. *Sangha and State in Burma: A Study of Monastic Sectar-*

ianism and Leadership. Ed. J. P. Ferguson. Ithaca, N.Y.: Cornell University Press.

Moran, P. 2004. *Buddhism Observed: Travelers, Exiles and Tibetan Dharma in Kathmandu*. London and New York: RoutledgeCurzon.

Mumford, S. R. 1989. *Himalayan Dialogue: Tibetan Lamas and Gurung Shamans in Nepal*. Madison: University of Wisconsin Press.

Nakarmi, I. K., and A. S. Tuladhar. 1999. "Dharmakirti Vihara: An Introduction." In *Dhamma and Dhammawati*, ed. S. R. Tuladhar and R. Tuladhar, 7–18. Kathmandu: Dharmakirti Buddhist Study Circle.

Narada 1948 (no author). "The Venerable Narada in Nepal." *The Maha-Bodhi* 56(8): 262–267.

Nissan, E. 1984. "Recovering Practice: Buddhist Nuns in Sri Lanka" *South Asia Research* 4(1): 32–49.

Nyanaponika, Thera. 1965. *The Heart of Buddhist Meditation*. York Beach, Maine: Samuel Weiser.

———. 1998. *Abhidhamma Studies: Buddhist Explorations of Consciousness and Time*. Boston: Wisdom.

Obeyesekere, G. 1970. "Religious Symbolism and Political Change in Ceylon." *Modern Ceylon Studies* 1(1). Reprinted 1972 in Bardwell Smith, ed., *Two Wheels of Dhamma: Essays in the Theravada Tradition in India and Ceylon*, 58–78. Chambersburg, Penn.: American Academy of Religion.

———. 1976. "Personal Identity and Cultural Crisis: The Case of Anagarika Dharmapala of Sri Lanka." In *The Biographical Process: Studies in the History and Psychology of Religion*, ed. F. Reynolds and D. Capps, 221–252. The Hague: Mouton.

———. 1995a. "On Buddhist Identity in Sri Lanka." In *Ethnic Identities: Cultural Continuities and Change*, ed. G. de Vos and L. Romanucci-Ross. Walnut Creek, Calif.: Alta Mira Press. (Originally published in 1975 by Mayfield Press.)

———. 1995b. "Buddhism, Nationhood, and Cultural Identity: A Question of Fundamentals." In *Fundamentalisms Comprehended*, ed. M. E. Marty and R. S. Appleby, 231–256. Chicago: University of Chicago Press.

Onta, P. 1996. "Ambivalence Denied: The Making of *Rastriya Itihas* in Panchayat Era Textbooks." *Contributions to Nepalese Studies* 23(1): 213–254.

———. 1999. "The Career of Bhanubhakta as a History of Nepali National Culture, 1940–1999." *Studies in Nepali History and Society* 4(1): 65–136.

Ortner, S. B. 1978. *Sherpas Through Their Rituals*. Cambridge: Cambridge University Press.

———. 1983. "The Founding of the First Sherpa Nunnery, and the Problem of 'Women' as an Analytic Category." In *Feminist Re-Visions: What Has Been and What Might Be,* ed. V. Patraka and L. Tilly. Ann Arbor: University of Michigan Women's Studies Program. Reissued as ch. 6 in Ortner, *Making Gender*, 1996.

———. 1989a. *High Religion: A Cultural and Political History of Sherpa Buddhism*. Princeton, N.J.: Princeton University Press.

———. 1989b. "Cultural Politics: Religious Activism and Ideological Transformation among 20th Century Sherpas." *Dialectical Anthropology* 14: 197–211.

———. 1995. "The Case of the Disappearing Shamans, or No Individualism, No Relationalism." *Ethos* 23(3): 355–90. Reissued 1998 in D. Skinner, A. I. Pach III, and D. Holland, eds., *Selves in Time and Place*, 239–268.

———. 1996. *Making Gender: The Politics and Erotics of Culture.* Boston: Beacon Press.

———. 1999. *Life and Death on Mt Everest: Sherpas and Himalayan Mountaineering.* Princeton, N.J.: Princeton University Press.

———. 2003. *New Jersey Dreaming: Capital, Culture, and the Class of '58.* Durham, N.C.: Duke University Press.

Pannapadipo, Phra Peter. 2002. *Little Angels: The Real-Life Stories of Twelve Thai Novice Monks.* Bangkok: Post Books.

Pao-chang. 1981. *Pi-chiu-ni-chan: Biographies of Buddhist Nuns.* Trans. Li Jung-hsi. Osaka: Tohokai.

Parajuli, P. 1996. "Life of Guru Urgyen Tulku Rimpoche (1920–1996)." *Buddhist Himalaya* 7(1–2): 1–5.

———. 1999. "Nepālā pracalit mahāyān buddhadharmako avadhāraṇā, vartamān sthiti ra sudhārko nimitta upāyaharu" [The concept of Mahayana Buddhism in Nepal: Its present state and ways to reform it; in N.]. In *Nepālmandalyā Bauddha Samskrti Sammelan—1998 (A Conference on the Buddhist Heritage of Nepal Mandal—1998)*, ed. B. Shakya, 269–78. Lalitpur: Lotus Research Center. (English version on LRC Web site. Available at *www.lrcnepal.org.*)

———. 2000 [VS 2057]. "Vyoma kusuma anuvād samitikā prayāsharu" [Projects of the Skyflower Translation Committee; in N.]. In *Gumbā vyavasthā tathā vikās samitiko smārikā—2057* [Yearbook of the Gompa establishment and development committee, 2000–2001; in N.], ed. A. Yonjan-Tamang. Kathmandu: Sampadā Bahu-udesīya Sahakārī Samsthā.

Paranavitana, S. 1970. *Inscriptions of Ceylon*, vol I. Colombo: Archaeology Department.

Patrul Rimpoche. 1994. *The Words of my Perfect Teacher.* Trans. Padmakara Translation Group. San Francisco and London: Harper Collins.

Perumal, S. 1998. "Revival of Tamil Buddhism: A Historical Survey." In *Buddhism in Tamil Nadu: Collected Papers*, ed. R. S. Murthy and M. S. Nagarajan, 529–542. Chennai: Institute of Asia Studies.

Pickett, M. 2003. "Caste and Kingship in the Newar City of Lalitpur." Ph.D. diss, Tribhuvan University, Kathmandu.

Pitzer-Reyl, R. 1984. *Die Frau im fruhen Buddhismus* (Marburger Studien Zur Afrika und Asienkunde, Serie B.Asien. Band 7). Berlin: Dietrich Reimer.

Pradhan, Bhuvan Lal. 1985. *The Shakyas of Nepal.* Kirtipur: Nagar Mandap Shrikirti Vihar.

———. 1997. "Jñānamālā Bhajan Khalah: A Movement for Building up the Newar Society." *Newāh Vijñāna* 1(1): 1–5. (First published in Gyanmala Smarika 1996.)

Prebish, C. S. 1999. *The Practice and Study of Buddhism in America*. Berkeley: University of California Press.

Prothero, S. 1996. *The White Buddhist: The Asian Odyssey of Henry Steel Olcott*. Bloomington, Ill., and Indianapolis: Indiana University Press.

Quigley, Declan. 1995. "Śreṣṭhas: Hindu Patrons." In Gellner and Quigley, eds., *Contested Hierarchies*, 80–108.

———. 1996. "Social Mobility and Social Fragmentation in the Newar Caste System." In S. Lienhard, ed., *Change and Continuity*, 69–84.

Ra We Thon. 1963. *Tamichet* (Dear Daughter, in Burmese). Trans. Bhikshu Gyanapurnik, as *Yamha Mhyāy* (N.Bh., 1980, Kathmandu: Dharmakirti Study Circle). Trans. Moti Kaji Sakya as *Snehī Chorī* (N., 1990, Kathmandu: Dharmakirti Study Circle).

Ratnatunga, S. 1991. *They Turned the Tide: The 100 Year History of the Maha Bodhi Society of Sri Lanka*. Colombo: Government Press.

Raychaudhuri, T. 1988. *Europe Reconsidered: Perceptions of the West in Nineteenth Century Bengal*. Delhi: Oxford University Press.

Rospatt, A. von. 2000. "The Periodic Renovations of the Thrice Blessed Svayambhūcaitya of Kathmandu." Habilitation diss., Hamburg University.

Rosser, C. 1966. "Social Mobility in the Newar Caste System." In *Caste and Kin in Nepal, India and Ceylon*, ed. C. von Fürer-Haimendorf, 68–139. New York: Asia Publishing House.

Roth, G. 1970. *Bhiksuni-Vinaya, Manual for the Discipline of Buddhist Nuns*. Patna: K. P. Jayaswal Research Institute.

Sakya, A. M. 2000. "Newar Marriage and Kinship in Kathmandu, Nepal." Ph.D. diss., Brunel University, London.

Salgado, N. 2000a. "Teaching Lineages and Land: Renunciation and Domestication Among Buddhist Nuns in Sri Lanka." In E. B. Findly, ed., *Women's Buddhism*, 175–200.

———. 2000b. "Unity and Diversity among Buddhist Nuns in Sri Lanka." In K. L. Tsomo, ed., *Innovative Buddhist Women*, 30–41.

Samuel, G. 1993. *Civilized Shamans: Buddhism in Tibetan Societies*. Washington, D.C.: Smithsonian Press.

Sangharakshita, Bhikshu. 1952. "Buddhism and the Youth of Nepal." *The Maha-Bodhi* 60(2): 63–71.

———. 1956. "Glimpses of Buddhist Nepal." *The Maha-Bodhi* 64(4): 130–140.

———. 1980. *Flame in Darkness: The Life and Sayings of Anagarika Dharmapala*. Pune: Triratna Grantha Mala.

———. 1996. *Great Buddhists of the Twentieth Century*. Birmingham: England Windhorse.

———. 1997. *The Rainbow Road: From Tooting Broadway to Kalimpong: Memoirs of an English Buddhist*. Birmingham: England Windhorse. (Originally published as *The Thousand-Petalled Lotus*, 1990, London: Heinemann.)

Schopen, G. 1997. *Bones, Stones, and Buddhist Monks: Collected Papers on the Archeology, Epigraphy, and Texts of Monastic Buddhism in India*. Honolulu: University of Hawaii Press.

Seager, R. H. 1995. *The World's Parliament of Religions*. Bloomington: Indiana University Press.

Seneviratne, H. L. 1989. "Identity and Conflation of Past and Present." In H. L. Seneviratne, ed., *Identity, Consciousness and the Past*, 3–22. Adelaide: University of Adelaide Press.

Sever, A. 1993. *Nepal Under the Ranas*. New Delhi: Oxford and IBH.

Shakya, Asha Ram. 1997. *Achheswor Maha Bihar Buddhist Monastery*. Lalitpur: Bauddha Vihara Sangh.

———. 1998. "Jī mhasyũmha śrāddheya Dharmāditya Dharmācārya (Kha. Jagatmān Vaidya)" [The respectworthy Dharmaditya I knew; in N.Bh.]. *Dharmāditya Dharmācārya Lumanti-Pau* 1119: 7–11.

Shakya, Biswa. 2004 [NS 1124]. "Buddha āū" [Buddha come; in N.]. In *Jñānmālā mye munā—tāsā 1* [Collected Gyanmala songs, vol. 1; in N. & N.Bh.], 12. Nag Bahal, Lalitpur: Taremam Sangha.

Shakya, Chatra Raj. 1997 [NS 1117]. "Buddhadharmako vikāsmā Tānsen, Palpāko den ra jñānmālāko mādhyam" [The contribution of Tansen, Palpa, and of the Gyanmala in the development of Buddhism]. Working paper for the second national Gyanmala conference, 12 pp.

Shakya ["Trishuli"], Dharma Ratna. 1999. "Nepāle sthaviravād buddha dharma punarutthāne anagārikā (gurumā) pīgu den" [The contribution of Anagarikas (Gurumas) in the reestablishment of Sthaviravad (Theravada) in Nepal; in N.Bh.]. *Dharmakirti* 17(7): 83–89.

———. 2001. "Tāremām Saṃghayā saṃkṣipta paricay" [A brief introduction to the Taremam Sangha]. In *Swarṇa-Smārikā (Golden Jubilee Issue 2001)*, ed. P. R. Shakya, 1–4. Lalitpur: 2545 Buddha Jayanti Committee.

Shakya, Dharma Ratna. ed. 2001. *Dharmāditya Dharmācārya Lumanti Pau* [Memorial magazine for Dharmaditya Dharmacharyya; in N.Bh.]. Lalitpur: Ma Bhay Puchah.

Shakya, Gyan Bahadur. 2001. "Buddha jayantiyā paramparā" [The tradition of Buddha Jayanti; in N.Bh.]. *Swāyā Punhi, Svarna-Smārikā*. Lalitpur: Hiranyavarna Mahabihar, Taremam Sangha.

Shakya, Hemraj. 1978 [NS 1098]. *Śri svayambhū mahācaitya* [The blessed great chaitya Swayambhu; in N.Bh.]. Kathmandu: Swayambhu Vikas Mandal.

———. 1995. *Akṣeśvara Mahāvihāra Puco: Chagu Adhyayan* [Aksheshwar Mahavihara, a study; in N.Bh.]. Lalitpur: Bauddha Vihara Sangh.

Shakya, Janak "Newa." 1996. "Dharmodaya sabhā: hijo ra āja" [The Dharmodaya Sabha yesterday and today; in N.]. *Dharmodaya Smarika* (5th National Conference). Kathmandu: Dharmodaya Sabha.

Shakya, Mahendra Ratna. 1996. *Śri Sumangal Vihār: Ek Adhyayan* [Sumangal Vihara, a study; in N.]. Lalitpur: Shri Sumangal Vihara Sangh.

Shakya, Min Bahadur. 1983. Introd. to *An Autobiography of a Buddhist Yogi: Mahāprajnā*. In Mahapragya, *Sāhityasutā Karmasthānācārya*, a–n.

———. 1997a. *The Life and Contribution of the Nepalese Princess Bhrikuti Devi to Tibetan History: From Tibetan Sources*. Delhi: Book Faith India.

———. 1997b [1978]. Introd. to *Lalitavistara Sūtra*, by Pt. N. Bajracharya Taipei: The Corporated Body of the Buddha Educational Foundation (1978 edition: Lalitpur: YMBA).

———. n.d. "Dharmachari Anagarika: A Short Biography." Unpublished ms.

Shakya, R. J. 2002. *Shree Punyodaya Padmavarna Mahayan Vihar and Its Role in Mahayan* [N. and English]. Lalitpur: Padmavarna Mahayan Pustakalaya.

Shakya, Ratna Sundar. 1992a. *Bābāsāheb Dā. Ambedkar* [in N.]. Bhaktapur: Bauddha Sangh.

———. 1992b. *Bauddha jagatkā smaraniya byaktiharu (prathama bhāg)* [Memorable personalities of the Buddhist world, part one; in N.]. Ananda Kuti Vihara: Bhikshu Mahanama.

———. 1993. *Bauddha-Ṛṣi Mahāprajñā* [in N.]. Bhaktapur: Sangha Ratna Shakya et al.

Shakya, Suren. 2003. "Kāryapatra: Jñānmālā ra yasko vikās evam nirantaratā" [Working paper: Gyanmala, its development and continuity; in N.]. Unpublished ms.

Shakyavamsha, Buddhiraj. 1990. *Kyānchyā lāmājū kanābijyāhgu Kunsāmlāmesyālū Dondu* [The teachings of the Kun bzang bla ma'i zhal lung as taught by Kyangtse Lama; in N.Bh.]. Ed. S. M. Joshi. Lalitpur: Bodhi Prakashan Kendra.

Sharf, R. H. 1995. "The Zen of Japanese Nationalism." In D. Lopez, ed., *Curators of the Buddha*, 107–160.

Shneiderman, S. 1999. "Appropriate Treasure? Reflections on Women, Buddhism and Cross-Cultural Exchange." In K. L. Tsomo, ed., *Buddhist Women Across Cultures*, 221–240.

Shrestha, Bal Gopal. 2002. *The Ritual Composition of Sankhu: The Socio-Religious Anthropology of a Newar Town in Nepal*. Leiden: B. G. Shrestha.

Singh, H. L. 1996. *Reflections on Buddhism of the Kathmandu Valley*. Kathmandu: Educational Enterprise.

Singh. R. P. S. 1988. *The Real History of the Tharus*. Patna.

Skilling, P. 1994. "A Note on the History of the Bhikkhuni-sangha (II): The Order of Nuns after the Parinirvana." *W. F. B. Review* 31(1): 29–49.

———. 1995. "Female Renunciants (nang chi) in Siam According to Travellers' Accounts." *Journal of the Siam Society* 83(1–2): 55–61.

———. 2001. "Nuns, Laywomen, Donors, Goddesses: Female Roles in Early Indian Buddhism." *JIABS* 24(2): 241–274.

Skinner, D., and D. Holland. 1996. "Schools and the Cultural Construction of the Educated Person in a Nepalese Hill Community." In *The Cultural Construction of the Educated Person: Critical Ethnographies of Schooling Practice*, ed. B. A. Levinson, D. E. Foley, and D. C. Holland, 273–299. Albany, N.Y.: SUNY Press.

Skinner, D., A. I. Pach III, and D. Holland, eds, 1998. *Selves in Time and Place: Identities, Experience and History in Nepal*. Lanham, Md.: Rowman and Littlefield.

Snellgrove, D., 1957. *Buddhist Himalaya*. Oxford: Bruno Cassirer.

———. 1987. *Indo-Tibetan Buddhism*. Boulder, Colo.: Shambala.

Soma Thera. 1941. *The Way of Mindfulness: The Satipatthana Sutta and Commentary*. Kandy: Buddhist Publication Society.

Spencer, J. 1995. "The Politics of Tolerance: Buddhists and Christians, Truth and Error in Sri Lanka." In *The Pursuit of Certainty: Religions and Cultural Formulations*, ed. W. L. James, 195–214. London and New York: Routledge.

Spiro, M. E. 1982 (1970). *Buddhism and Society: A Great Tradition and its Vicissitudes*. Berkeley: University of California Press.

Sponberg, A. 1992. "Attitudes Towards Women and the Feminine in Early Buddhism." In *Buddhism, Sexuality and Gender*, ed. J. I. Cabezón. New York: SUNY Press.

Stiller, L. F. 1968. *Prithinarayan Shah in Light of the Dibya Upadesh*. Kathmandu: Himalaya Book Center.

Sudarshan, Bhikshu. 1982. *Mahāparitrān (Nepāl Bhāsā artha sahit)* [Mahaparitrana (text), with Nepal Bhasha gloss; Pali and N.Bh.]. Gana Baha, Kathmandu: Sakala Shraddhālupì.

———. 1999. "Newāḥ buddhadharmayā samrakṣaṇay theravād paramparāyā bhūmikā" [The role of the Theravada tradition in the preservation of Newar Buddhism; in N.Bh.]. In *Nepālmaṇḍalyā bauddha saṃskṛti sammelana-1998 (A Conference on the Buddhist Heritage of Nepal Mandal, 1998)*, ed. B. Shakya, 391–402. Lalitpur: Lotus Research Center. (English version on LRC Web site. Available at www.lrcnepal.org./papers, accessed June 9th, 2005).

Takakusu, J. trans. 1966. *A Record of the Buddhist Religion as Practised in India and the Malay Archipelago (AD 671–695) by I-ching*. New Delhi: Munshiram Manoharlal.

Tambiah, S. 1984. *The Buddhist Saints of the Forest and the Cult of Amulets*. Cambridge: Cambridge University Press.

Tamblyn, B. 2002. "Ancient Dialogue amidst a Modern Cacophony: Gurung Religious Pluralism and the Founding of Tibetan Buddhist Monasteries in the Pokhara Valley." *European Bulletin of Himalayan Research* 22: 81–100.

Tartakov, G. 2003. "B. R. Ambedkar and the Navayana Diksha." In *Religious Conversion in India: Modes, Motivations, and Meanings*, ed. R. Robinson and S. Clarke, 192–215. Delhi: Oxford University Press.

Tewari, R. C. 1983. "Socio-Cultural Aspects of Theravada Buddhism in Nepal." *JIABS* 6: 67–93.

Thapa, Deepak and Bandita Sijapati. 2004. *Kingdom under Siege: Nepal's Maoist Insurgency, 1996 to 2004*. London: Zed.

Thapa, K. B., 1988. *Major Aspects of Social, Economic and Administrative History of Modern Nepal*. Kathmandu: Abhika Thapa.

Tiyavanich, K. 1997. *Forest Recollections: Wandering Monks in Twentieth-Century Thailand*. Honolulu: University of Hawaii.

Toffin, G. 1984. *Societé et réligion chez les Newar du Népal.* Paris: CNRS.

Trevithick, A. 1988. "A Jerusalem of the Buddhists in British Bodh Gaya: 1874–1949." Ph.D. diss., Harvard University.

———. 1999. "British Archaeologists, Hindu Abbots, and Burmese Buddhists: The Mahabodhi Temple at Bodh Gaya, 1811–1877." *Modern Asian Studies* 33(3): 635–656.

Tsai, K. A. 1981. "The Chinese Buddhist Monastic Order for Women: The First Two Centuries." *Historical Reflections* 8(3): 1–20.

Tsomo, K. L. 1988a. "The Bhikṣuṇi Issue." In K. L. Tsomo, ed., *Sakyadhita* 215–224.

———. 1988b. "Nuns of Japan: Part II." In K. L. Tsomo, ed., *Sakyadhita* 127–130.

———. 1988c. "Nuns of the Buddhist Traditions." In K. L. Tsomo, Sakyadhita ed., 103–108.

———. 1996. *Sisters in Solitude: Two Traditions of Buddhist Monastic Ethics for Women.* Albany, N.Y.: SUNY Press.

Tsomo, K. L. ed., 1988. *Sakyadhitā: Daughters of the Buddha.* Ithaca: Snow Lion. (Reissued 1998, Delhi: Sri Satguru Publications.)

———. ed. 1999. *Buddhist Women Across Cultures: Realizations.* Albany, N.Y.: SUNY Press.

———. ed. 2000. *Innovative Buddhist Women: Swimming Against the Stream.* Richmond: Curzon.

Tucci, G. 1971. "The Wives of Sroṅ btsan sgam po." In *Opera Minor*, part 2, ed. G. Bardi, 605–611. Rome: Scuola Orientale, University of Rome. (Originally published 1962 in *Oriens Extremis* 9: 121–126.)

Tuladhar, Kul Dharmaratna. 2001. "Bahu āyāmik vandya Dharmāditya Dharmācārya" [The multisided Shakya, Dharmaditya Dharmacharyya; in N.Bh.]. In D. R. Shakya, ed., *Dharmāditya Dharmācārya*, 52–67.

Tuladhar, Laxmi Prabha. 1995. "Kijā Maniharsha Jyotiyā bāre chatwāḥ khã" [One story about my younger brother Maniharsha Jyoti; in N.Bh.]. In P. R. Bajracharya, ed., *Maniharsa Jyoti Smṛtigrantha*, 102–107.

Tuladhar, P. 1999. "Dhammawati Gurumā wa Dharmakirti patrikā" [Dhammawati Guruma and Dharmakirti magazine; in N.Bh.]. *Dharmakirti* 17(7): 95–97.

Tuladhar, Prem Hira. 2002. "Nepālmā buddhadharmakā punaruddhārak Niṣṭhānanda Vajrācārya" [Nisthananda Vajracharya, the reviver of Buddhism in Nepal; in N.]. *Tri-Bodhi* 2: 43–44.

Tuladhar, Subarna Man. 1995. "Sāhu Maniharsha Jyotiju jigu mikhāy" [My view of Maniharsha Jyoti; in N.Bh.]. In P. R. Bajracharya, ed., *Maniharsa Jyoti Smṛtigrantha*, 122–125.

Tuladhar, Sumon Kamal. 1997. "Buddha dharmamā Nepālkā anāgārikāharuko dena" [The contribution of Nepal's anagarikas to Buddhism]. *Dharmakirti* 15(1): 51–63.

———. 1999. "Dhammawati Guruma the 'Yomha Mhyaaya' of Nepal." In *Dhamma and Dhammawati*, ed. S. R. Tuladhar & R. Tuladhar, 19–29. Kathmandu: Dharmakirti Buddhist Study Circle.

UNICEF. 2004. *The State of the World's Children, 2004*. New York: UNICEF.

Upasak, C. S. 1975. *Dictionary of Early Buddhist Monastic Terms*. Varanasi: Bharati Publications.

Vajracharya, Dhana Vajra. 1973 [VS 2030]. *Licchavikālkā Abhilekh* [Licchavi period inscriptions; in N]. Kathmandu: CNAS.

Vajracharya, Gautam. 1987. "An Interpretation of Two Similar Nepalese Paintings in the Light of Nepalese Cultural History." In *Heritage of the Kathmandu Valley* (Nepalica 4), ed. N. Gutschow and A. Michaels, 29–42. Sankt Augustin: VGH Wissenschaftsverlag.

Vargas-O'Brian, I. M. 2001. "The Life of dGe sLong Ma dPal Mo: The Experiences of a Leper, Founder of a Fasting Ritual and Transmitter of Buddhist Teachings on Suffering and Renunciation in Tibetan Religious History." *JIABS* 24(2):157–185.

Vipassi, Bhikkhu. 1999. *Bhagavān Sarana* [46 collected essays]. Kathmandu: Nagar Mandap Shri Kirti Vihara.

———. 2001. "Buddhism in Nepal." M. A. diss., Mahamakut Buddhist University, Bangkok.

Viswanathan, G. 1998. *Outside the Fold: Conversion, Modernity, and Belief*. Princeton, N.J.: Princeton University Press.

Wangmo, J. 2005. *The Lahudo Lama: Stories of Reincarnation from the Mount Everest Region*. Kathmandu: Vajra.

Webster, P. 1981. "To Plough or Not To Plough? A Newar Dilemma: Taboo and Technology in the Kathmandu Valley, Nepal." *Pacific Viewpoint* 22(2): 99–135.

Whelpton, J. 1991. *Kings, Soldiers and Priests: Nepalese Politics and the Rise of Jang Bahadur Rana, 1830–57*. New Delhi: Manohar.

———. 1997. "Political Identity in Nepal: State, Nation, and Community." In D. N. Gellner et al., eds., *Nationalism and Ethnicity*, 39–78.

Willis, J. D. 1984. "Tibetan Ani-s: The Nuns' Life in Tibet." *The Tibetan Journal* 9(4): 14–32.

———. 1992. "Female Patronage in Indian Buddhism." In *The Powers of Art: Patronage in Indian Culture*, ed. B. Stoler Miller, 46–53. Delhi: Oxford University Press.

Wilson, L. 1996. *Charming Cadavers: Horrific Figurations of the Feminine in Indian Buddhist Hagiographic Literature*. Chicago: University of Chicago Press.

Woodward, F. L., trans. 1932. *The Book of Gradual Sayings (Anguttara-Nikāya)*. London: OUP for PTS.

Wright, D. 1972 [1877]. *History of Nepal*. Kathmandu: Nepal Antiquated Book Publishers.

Wylie, T. 1970. *A Tibetan Religious Geography of Nepal* (Serie Orientale 42). Rome: ISMEO.

Young, R. F., and G. P. V. Somaratne. 1996. *Vain Debates: The Buddhist-Christian Controversies of Nineteenth-Century Ceylon*. Vienna: De Nobili Research Library.

Zelliott, E. 1996. *From Untouchable to Dalit: Essays on the Ambedkar Movement*, 2nd rev. ed. Delhi: Manohar.

Zürcher, E. 1972. *The Buddhist Conquest of China: The Spread and Adaptation of Buddhism in Early Medieval China*. Leiden: E. J. Brill.

Index

Harvard University Press is a member of Green Press Initiative
(greenpressinitiative.org), a nonprofit organization working to
help publishers and printers increase their use of recycled paper
and decrease their use of fiber derived from endangered forests.
This book was printed on 100% recycled paper containing
50% post-consumer waste and processed chlorine free.